Instructor's Manual
and
Solutions Manual

to accompany

Foundations of
Financial Management

Tenth Edition

Stanley B. Block
Texas Christian University

Geoffrey A. Hirt
DePaul University

McGraw-Hill
Irwin

Boston   Burr Ridge, IL   Dubuque, IA   Madison, WI   New York   San Francisco   St. Louis
Bangkok   Bogotá   Caracas   Kuala Lumpur   Lisbon   London   Madrid   Mexico City
Milan   Montreal   New Delhi   Santiago   Seoul   Singapore   Sydney   Taipei   Toronto

McGraw-Hill Higher Education

A Division of The McGraw-Hill Companies

Instructor's Manual and Solutions Manual to accompany
FOUNDATIONS OF FINANCIAL MANAGEMENT
Stanley B. Block and Geoffrey A. Hirt

3 4 5 6 7 8 9 0 BKM/BKM 0 9 8 7 6 5 4 3 2

ISBN 0-07-242266-1

www.mhhe.com

Preface

The Instructor's Manual contains answers to the discussion questions at the end of each chapter and detailed solutions to all the problems. These are presented jointly for each chapter. The first few problems at the back of each chapter are quite basic in nature, the next grouping is of moderate difficulty, and finally there are complex problems. The one or two comprehensive problems at the end of many chapters often require and hour or more to solve and obviously necessitate some direction on the professor's part before the student begins the problem. Every problem at the end of the chapters was custom designed by the authors for the text. Therefore, there is consistency in terminology used and each solution in the Instructor's Manual closely parallels the text. Also, there are more problems per chapter than in almost any other book in the field, and these problems should serve the instructor with fresh assignments over a number of semesters.

Each chapter starts with the Author's Overview followed by the Chapter Concepts. The authors provide teaching notes for each chapter, as well as a comprehensive outline of each chapter. Within these outlines we have placed the transparencies where appropriate and we have added author perspectives. These perspectives provide suggestions to aid classroom presentation and discussion of various topics. The perspectives in the Instructors Manual are often more complete than the abbreviated versions found in the Instructors edition of the text. In this edition, we have also included a short introduction to each **Finance in Action** box found in the text, including the title so that you have it for easy reference in class. This short introduction allows the professor to know whether or not he or she wants to highlight or expand on the material found in these boxes. Hopefully, this manual will point out key areas in each chapter, as well as stumbling blocks for students. It would be presumptuous of the authors to suggest their classroom methodology is better than that of other textbook users, but we do wish to key in on approaches that have been successful for us in the past.

All problem solutions in this instructor's manual are set in large type, which allows the instructor to make highly readable transparencies. Those users who do not have the capability to make transparencies from transparency masters should contact the publisher for assistance. The teaching support material accompanying the 10th edition of **Foundations of Financial Management** includes transparencies for all odd-numbered problem solutions and sequential problems that continue from odd to even numbered problems. This material will be provided by Irwin/McGraw-Hill to adopters of Block and Hirt's **Foundations of Financial Management**. At the end of each chapter's teaching notes the Instructor's Manual lists all transparencies available for use with this book.

The user of the text also should be aware of a separate Test Bank that has been tailored to the material in the book. Over 1,900 multiple-choice, true-false, and matching questions and problems are available in the booklet. The questions are both descriptive and numerical in nature.

A separate Study Guide also has been prepared by Professor Dwight C. Anderson and contains chapter outlines and solved questions and problems for various chapters. The Study Guide may be ordered by the classroom instructor for purchase by the student at the appropriate bookstore.

A **Self-Study CD-ROM** is included in the instructor's and student's version of the text. Included on this CD is the Self-Study software program that allows students to take practice objective exams. The program includes approximately 900 true-false and multiple-choice questions created to be similar but not exactly the same as those provided in the test bank. The student may make individual chapter quizzes or tests combining as many as 10 chapters. Self-Study allows the user to choose true-false questions, multiple-choice questions or a combination of both. The questions are selected randomly so that the student does not get patterned responses after many times through the questions. Additionally, Self-Study includes the complete glossary from Block and Hirt keyed to true-false and multiple-choice responses and also formatted to provide matching quizzes. This tutorial provides chapter concepts and an outline of each chapter. The authors feel that this tutorial is extremely interactive and greatly aids the student learning process.

The assumption of the authors throughout the development of this text is that a good course in managerial finance must be supplemented by a wide range of problems and avenues of teaching support. We believe we have been successful in this regard.

Lastly, the authors would like to thank Joe Thompson and Timothy Scheppa for their help in checking the accuracy of the problem solutions.

Stanley B. Block
Geoffrey A. Hirt

Contents

Part B: Solutions to End-of-Chapter Problems

Solutions for all of the chapters are contained in this section.

Table of Contents for Teaching/Solution Acetates

Table of Contents for
Transparency Solutions to Chapter Problems

Number Problem Title

Number Problem Title

Number Problem Title

Number Problem Title

Number Problem Title

Number Problem Title

Number Problem Title

Part A:

Lecture Outlines

The Goals and Functions of Financial Management

Author's Overview

The major thrust of this chapter is to establish the objectives of financial management and the importance of the financial manager to the organization. The instructor should highlight the importance of stockholder wealth maximization as a goal and briefly relate it to valuation concepts associated with risk and return. In addition, the role of functions of the financial markets in allocating capital should be emphasized as well as the pressures of institutional investors on financial managers. The student should also be directed to the shortfalls of profit maximization as the ultimate goal of the firm. A short discussion of social responsibility and its relationship to the financial objectives of the firm can engage students in a discussion of how wealth maximization and social responsibility can co-exist. The Finance in Action box on McDonald's is a good example. We end the chapter with a short discussion of the Internet and its impact on the capital markets.

Chapter Concepts

* The field of finance integrates concepts from economics, accounting, and a number of other areas.

* The relationship of risk to return is a central focus of finance.

* The primary goal of financial managers is to maximize the wealth of the shareholders.

* Financial managers attempt to achieve wealth maximization through daily activities such as credit and inventory management and through longer-term decisions related to raising funds.

* Financial managers must carefully consider domestic and international business conditions in carrying out their responsibilities.

* Daily price changes in the financial markets provide feedback about the company's performance and help investors allocate their capital between firms.

Annotated Outline and Strategy

I.   **The role of financial management has substantially increased in importance.**

   A.   The stresses of unpredictable economic turns, fluctuating interest rates, inflation and disinflation etc. have generated the need for top level management possessing financial skills.

   B.   The demand for financial management skills exists in many sectors of our society including corporate management, financial institutions, and consulting.

II. **Finance as a field of study has evolved over time in response to changing business management needs.**

   A.   The field of finance is closely tied to economics and accounting.

   B.   Finance achieved recognition as a separate field of study in response to the merger-acquisition growth of giant corporations at the turn of the century.

   C.   During the Great Depression, emphasis shifted from raising capital to preservation of capital and maintenance of liquidity. This period was marked by a strengthening of government intervention in the financial aspects of business.

   D.   The most significant step in the evolution of contemporary financial management began in the mid-fifties. Emphasis was placed on the analytically determined employment of resources within the firm. The decision-making nature of financial management was manifested in the enthusiasm for the study of:

   1.   Fixed asset management: capital budgeting.
   2.   Efficient utilization of current assets.
   3.   Capital structure composition.
   4.   Dividend policy.

   E.   For the past 30 years, emphasis has been placed on the risk-return relationship.

   F.   The question for the 21st century is how technology will impact financial decision making. The Internet has created a "new economy" which will have a major impact on financial management.

III. **Functions of Financial Management.** **A financial manager is responsible for financing an efficient level and composition of assets by obtaining financing through the most appropriate means.**

PPT 1-1	Functions of the Financial Manager (Figure 1-1)

A.   Daily financial management activities

     1.   Credit management
     2.   Inventory control
     3.   Receipt and disbursement of funds

B.   Less-routine activities

     1.   Sale of stocks and bonds
     2.   Capital budgeting
     3.   Dividend decisions

C.   Forms of organization: The finance function may be carried out within a number of different forms of organizations.

     1.   Sole proprietorship

         a.   Single ownership
         b.   Simplicity of decision making
         c.   Low organizational and operating costs
         d.   Unlimited liability
         e.   Earnings are taxed as personal earnings of the individual owner

2.   Partnership

   a.   Two or more partners
   b.   Usually formed by articles of partnership agreement
   c.   Unlimited liability for all partners unless a limited partnership is formed which provides limited liability for one or more partners. At least one partner must be a general partner.
   d.   Earnings are taxed as personal earnings of partners

3.   Corporation

   a.   Most important form of business in terms of revenue and profits
   b.   Legal entity
   c.   Formed by articles of incorporation
   d.   Stockholders (owners) have limited liability
   e.   Easy divisibility of ownership
   f.   Managed by the board of directors
   g.   Double taxation of earnings: Earnings of the corporation are subject to the corporate income tax; dividends (distributed net income) are subject to personal taxation. Small subchapter S corporations, however, avoid the double taxation disadvantage.

IV.   Goals of Financial Management.

A.   The integration of the external investor point of view with the internal management orientation is evidenced by the goal of financial management: To make those decisions and engage in those activities that will maximize the overall valuation of the firm for the benefit of the stockholders.

B.   During the last decade much attention has been devoted to the relationship between the owners of the firm and the managers of the firm.   In large corporations, the hired management acts as agents for owners.   The study of the relationship between owners and managers as well as other agent relationships is referred to as agency theory.

C.   Included in agency theory is a trend that developed in the 1990s for large institutional shareholders to exert pressure on management to be responsive to shareholder goals.

D.   The goal of maximizing profits is not the same as maximizing shareholder wealth.

E.   The valuation approach to wealth maximization focuses on how investors value the future earnings stream.

F.   Shareholder wealth maximization is a long-term goal and its attainment is influenced by changing investor expectations and emphasis.

G.   While not all managements focus on maximizing shareholder wealth, the consequence of this behavior for publicly traded firms can be hostile takeovers or institutional investor pressure on the board of directors.

H.   The goal of maximizing shareholder wealth cannot ignore corporate responsibility to social issues and cannot operate without ethical standards. Eventually, the company's value will be negatively impacted over the long-term by irresponsible behavior.

Perspective 1-2: The use of Figure 1-1 (covering functions of the financial manager and their relationship to stockholder wealth maximization) is a good way to tie a number of important concepts together. At the same time, the instructor may wish to discuss the role of social responsibility in finance. The mention of Ivan Boesky and Michael Milkin along with insider trading also seems to bring student comments and questions into the discussion.

Finance in Action: McDonald's Corporation – Good Corporate Citizen

Balancing wealth maximization and social responsibility is difficult. You may want to focus on the McDonald's Corporation as a way of showing that good management can accomplish both goals, of wealth maximization and social responsibility.

V.   **The Role of Financial Markets. Wealth maximization depends on the perception and expectations of the market. Through daily price changes in the common stock of each publicly traded company, the market provides managers with a performance report card.**

A.   Structure and Functions of the Financial Markets. Money markets (Chapter 7) and Capital markets (Chapter 14) are more fully presented in later chapters but the students may find that some current examples from the *Wall Street Journal* will create a sense of realism about this course.

B.   Allocation of Capital. Students need to understand how the market price reflects risk and return expectations and how a company's ability to raise funds is influenced by its financial performance and corporate behavior.

C.   Reemphasize the impact that institutional investors have on publicly owned companies. While this was touched on previously in the chapter in the area of agency theory, here we emphasize the power of these investors to force restructuring of public companies. Many examples are included.

D.   Internationalization of the Financial Markets. Emphasize the globalization of the capital markets and the worldwide pool of capital available to many companies. Use the international companies highlighted in the text to get across the point that the search for capital is global.

E.   The Internet and technology has dramatically changed the way the capital markets operate. Technology is responsible for the rise in on-line retail brokers such as E-Trade and electronic markets have put pressure on the exchanges to become more efficient. This has led to worldwide consolidations in restructuring of the world's stock, bond and futures exchanges. We think the next decade will continue this trend.

Summary Listing of Transparencies

PPT 1-1   Functions of the Financial Manager (Figure 1-1)
LT 1-1   Chapter 1 – Outline
LT 1-2   Finance is a Combination of Accounting and Economics
LT 1-3   Short-Term vs. Long-Term Financing
LT 1-4   The Risk-Return Tradeoff
LT 1-5   Financial Capital vs. Real Capital
LT 1-6   Stocks vs. Bonds
LT 1-7   Forms of Organization
LT 1-8   Goals of Financial Management

Review of Accounting

Author's Overview

This chapter, either used in whole or in part, can prove invaluable to the instructor and the student. Though it is assumed that every student taking the introductory course in managerial finance has had course work in accounting, many students are in need of a review. By explicitly covering this review material early in the course, the student is able to grasp later material more easily and the instructor does not have to continually close the "accounting gaps" during the course. The instructor must, of course, decide whether to lecture on this material or merely assign it as reading. Some may choose to forego it altogether.

Chapter Concepts

* The income statement measures profitability.

* The price-earnings ratio indicates the relative valuation of earnings.

* The balance sheet shows assets and the financing of those assets.

* The statement of cash flows indicates the change in the cash position of the firm.

* Depreciation provides a tax reduction benefit.

Annotated Outline and Strategy

I. Financial Statements

    A.   The Income Statement

PPT 2-1	Kramer Corporation-Income Statement (Table 2-1)

          1.   The income statement begins with the aggregate amount of sales (revenues) that are generated within a specific period of time.

          2.   The various expenses that occur in generating the sales are subtracted in stair-step fashion to arrive at the net income for the defined period.

          3.   The separation of the expense categories such as cost of goods sold, selling and administrative expenses, depreciation, interest and taxes enables the management to assess the relative importance and appropriateness of the expenditures in producing each level of sales.

          4.   The "bottom line" value, net income, is the aggregate amount available to the owners.

          5.   Net income is converted from an aggregate value to an earnings per share (EPS) value by dividing net income by the number of shares of outstanding stock.

          6.   The EPS is a measurement of the return available to providers of equity capital to the firm. The return to the providers of debt capital, interest, appears earlier in the income statement as a tax-deductible expense.

          7.   The earnings per share may be converted to a measure of current value through application of the price/earnings (P/E) ratio.

          8.   The P/E ratio is best used as a relative measure of value because the numerator, price, is based on the future and the denominator, earnings, is a current measure.

PPT 2-2	P/E Ratios for Selected U.S. Companies (Table 2-3)

9.   There are limitations associated with income statement. For example, the income statement reflects only income occurring to the individual or business firm from verifiable transactions as opposed to the economists' definition of income, which reflects changes in real worth.

B.   Balance Sheet

1.   Whereas the income statement provides a summary of financial transactions for a period of time, the balance sheet portrays the cumulative results of transactions at a point in time. The balance sheet may present the position of the firm as a result of transactions for six months, twenty-five years, or other periods.

2.   The balance sheet is divided into two broad categories. The assets employed in the operations of the firm compose one category while the other, liabilities and net worth, is composed of the sources of financing for the employed assets.

PPT 2-3	Kramer Corporation - Statement of Financial Position (Table 2-4)

3.   Within the asset category, the assets are listed in their order of liquidity.

    a.   Cash (including demand deposits)
    b.   Marketable securities: investments of temporarily excess cash in highly liquid securities
    c.   Accounts receivable
    d.   Inventory
    e.   Prepaid expenses: future expense items that have already been paid
    f.   Investments: investments in securities and other assets for longer than one operating cycle

9

g.   Plant and equipment adjusted for accumulated depreciation

4.   The various sources of financing of a firm are listed in their order of maturity. Those sources that mature earliest, current liabilities, are listed first. The more permanent debt and equity sources follow.

    a.   Accounts payable
    b.   Notes payable
    c.   Accrued expenses: an obligation to pay is incurred but payment has not been made
    d.   Long-term debt: all or a majority of the principal will be paid beyond the current period
    e.   Preferred stock
    f.   Common stock accounts:
        (1)   Common stock (par value)
        (2)   Capital paid in excess of par
        (3)   Retained earnings

5.   Confusing balance-sheet-related terms

    a.   Retained earnings: All of the assets of a firm are listed on the asset side of the balance sheet, yet many individuals envision a pile of money when the term retained earnings is used. Retained earnings is simply a cumulative total of the earnings of the firm since its beginning until the date of the balance sheet that have not been paid to the owners. Earnings that are retained are used to purchase assets, pay liabilities, throw a big party for the management, etc. Regardless, there is no money available from a "container" labeled retained earnings.
    b.   Net worth or book value of the firm is composed of the various common equity accounts and represents the net contributions of the owners to the business.
    c.   Book value is a historical value and does not necessarily coincide with the market value of the owner's equity.

6. Limitation of the balance sheet: Values are recorded at cost; replacement cost of some assets, particularly plant and equipment, may greatly exceed their recorded value. The Financial Accounting Standards Board (FASB) issued a ruling in October 1979 that required many large companies to disclose inflation adjusted accounting data in their annual reports. However, the standard is no longer in force and the inclusion of inflation adjusted accounting data in financial reports is purely a voluntary act.

Perspective 2-2: **This is a good point in the discussion to illustrate the substantial differences that may exist between market definitions of value and accounting definitions. Table 2-5 may be used to provide a strong illustration of this point.**

PPT 2-4	Comparison of Market Value to Book Value Per Share (Table 2-5)

C. Statement of Cash Flows

1. In November 1987, the accounting profession replaced that statement of changes in financial position (and the sources and uses of funds statement) with the Statement of Cash Flows as a required financial statement.
2. The new statement emphasizes the critical nature of cash flow to the operations of the firm.
3. The three primary sections of the statement of cash flows are:

    a. cash flows from operating activities.
    b. cash flows from investing activities.
    c. cash flows from financing activities.

PPT 2-5	Illustration of Concepts Behind Statement of Cash Flows (Figure 2-1)

4. Income from operations may be translated from an accrual basis to a cash basis in two ways to obtain cash flow from operations.

    a. Direct method -- each and every item on the income statement is adjusted from accrual accounting to cash accounting.
    b. Indirect method-a less tedious process than the direct method is

11

usually preferred. Net income is used as the starting point and adjustments are made to convert net income to cash flows from operations. Beginning with net income,

(1) Add depreciation for the current period, decreases in individual current asset accounts (other than cash) and increases in current liabilities;

(2) Subtract increases in current asset accounts (other than cash) and decreases in current liabilities.

Perspective 2-3: **To effectively illustrate the steps necessary for computing cash flow from operations, the instructor may wish to refer to Figure 2-2. Also, the actual numerical material can be found in Table 2-1 (an earlier referenced transparency related to the income statement) and Table 2-6 (Comparative Balance Sheets) and Table 2-7 (cash flows from operating activities).**

PPT 2-6   Steps in Computing Net Cash Flows from Operating Activities Using the Indirect Method (Figure 2-2)

PPT 2-7   Kramer Corporation-Comparative Balance Sheets (Table 2-6)

PPT 2-8   Cash Flows from Operating Activities (Table 2-7)

---

5. Cash flow from investing is found by summing the changes of investment in securities and plant and equipment. Increases are uses of funds and decreases are sources of funds.

6. Cash flow from financing activities is found by summing the sale or retirement of corporate securities and dividends. The sale of securities is a source of funds and the retirement of securities and payment of dividends are uses of funds.

7. Cash flows from operations, cash flows from investing, and cash flows from financing are combined to arrive at the statement of cash flows. The net increase or decrease shown in the statement of cash flows will be equal to the change in the cash balance on the balance sheet.

Perspective 2-4: *The three sections of the statements are brought together in Table 2-10. The instructor may wish to highlight in the example how cash flows from operating activities are funding investing and financing activities.*

PPT 2-9   Kramer Corporation -- Statement of Cash Flows (Table 2-10)

II.   Depreciation and Funds Flow

     A.   Depreciation is an attempt to allocate an initial asset cost over its life.

     B.   Depreciation is an accounting entry and does not involve the movement of funds.

     C.   As indicated in the statement of cash flows, depreciation is added back to net income to arrive at cash flow.

Perspective 2-5: *To illustrate how the initial purchase of an asset and the subsequent write-off affects cash flow, the instructor may wish to refer to Table 2-11.*

PPT 2-10   Comparison of Accounting and Cash Flows (Table 2-11)

Finance in Action:
Funny Money Accounting: The Impact of Pension Plan Gains on the Bottom Line

This box explains how pension fund gains can be misleading, and that most employees will receive a set amount upon retirement regardless of how a companies pension fund assets perform. Pension fund accounting then allows companies to place excess income into an account that will be amortized in future years, and cover a lot of potentially bad actual operating decisions.

III.   Another important term is free cash flow.

     A.   Free cash flow is equal to cash flow from operating activities:
            Minus: Capital expenditures required to maintain the productive capacity of the firm.

Minus: Dividends

    B.   The amount of free cash flow is often a determining factor as to whether a leveraged-out is possible.

IV.   Income Tax Considerations

    A.   Personal taxes at varying rates apply to the earnings of proprietors and partners.

    B.   Corporate earnings are subject to taxation at two levels -- at the corporate level and at the personal level when received as dividends. The corporate tax rates have been changed by Congress four times since 1980.

    C.   The aftertax cost of a tax-deductible business expense can be calculated by taking the (expense) × (1 - tax rate).

    D.   Although depreciation is a noncash expense, it does affect cash flow by reducing taxes. Tax reduction in cash outflow for taxes resulting from depreciation charges may be computed by multiplying the (depreciation expense) × (tax rate).

Finance in Action: Who's Auditing the Auditors?

This article discusses the Big Five accounting firms, and the dilemma they faced while competing for consulting contracts with the same companies they were auditing. As a result, four out of the five major accounting firms have split off their consulting activities from their primary accounting duties.

Summary Listing of Transparencies

Solution Transparencies to Chapter Problems

Financial Analysis

Author's Overview

The student should be directed to view the thirteen ratios as an overall package that can be used to evaluate any firm. The use of the Saxton Company analysis provides continuity to the discussion. Though the student must be familiar with the calculation and meaning of each individual ratio, the primary emphasis is on the inter-relationship between the ratios (such as that stressed by the Du Pont system of analysis). The discussion of inflation/disinflation and distortions in financial reporting represents an important lesson for the student: do not automatically accept the bottom line.

Chapter Concepts

*   Ratio analysis provides a meaningful comparison of a company to its industry.

*   Ratios can be used to measure profitability, asset utilization, liquidity and debt utilization.

*   The Du Pont system of analysis identifies the true sources of return on assets and return to stockholders.

*   Trend analysis shows company performance over time.

*   Reported income must be further evaluated to identify sources of distortion.

Annotated Outline and Strategy

I.   Ratio analysis

      A.   Uses of ratios:

            1.   Provide a basis for evaluating the operating performance of a firm.

            2.   Facilitate comparison with other firms, using data from firms such as Dun & Bradstreet, Standard & Poor's, Value Line Investment Survey, etc.

B.   Overall considerations in using ratios

      1.   There are 13 basic ratios presented in the text
      2.   We shall break them down into four categories
      3.   Ratio analysis is like solving a mystery - what you learn from one ratio, you apply to another

PPT 3-1	The Classification System for Ratios

C.   Classification and computation

      1.   Profitability: Measures of returns on sales, total assets and invested capital

         a.   Profit margin = Net income/Sales
         b.   Return on assets (investment) = Net income/Total assets
         c.   Return on equity = Net income/Stockholders' equity = Return on assets/(1 - Debt/assets)

PPT 3-2	Saxton Co. - Financial Statement for Ratio Analysis (Table 3-1)

PPT 3-3	Profitability Ratios for the Saxton Company

2. Asset utilization: Measures of the speed at which the firm is turning over accounts receivable, inventories, and longer term assets.

    a. Receivables turnover = Sales/Receivables
    b. Average collection period = Accounts receivable/Average daily credit sales
    c. Inventory turnover = Sales/Inventory or COGS/Inventory
    d. Fixed asset turnover = Sales/Fixed assets
    e. Total asset turnover = Sales/Total assets

Perspective 3-3: **The asset utilization ratios help explain the asset turnover component that is a critical part of profitability ratio. Referring to 2b on page 55 illustrates how asset utilization ratios relate to profitability ratios.**

3. Liquidity ratios: Measures of the firm's ability to pay off short-term obligations as they come due

    a. Current ratio = Current assets/Current liabilities

    b. Quick ratio = Current assets minus inventory/Current liabilities

4. Debt Utilization Ratios: Measures the prudence of the firm's debt management policies.

    a. Debt to total assets

           b.   Times interest earned
           c.   Fixed charge coverage

| PPT 3-8 | Debt Utilization Ratios |

       5.   Summary and evaluation of all ratios for the Saxton Company with conclusions

| PPT 3-9 | Ratio Analysis (Table 3-3) |

Perspective 3-4: *The instructor can use Figure 3-2 to illustrate the importance of trends to the Saxton Company. An even better illustration can be found in Table 3-4, which compares 18 years of profitability for IBM, Compaq and Apple Computer.*

       6.   Trend analysis is as important as industry comparisons

| PPT 3-10 | Trend Analysis for the Saxton Company (Figure 3-2) |

| PPT 3-11 | Trend Analysis for IBM, Compaq and Apple (Table 3-4) |

II.   Impact of Inflation and Disinflation on Financial Analysis

A.   Impact on profits

1. First-in, first-out (FIFO) inventory valuation during inflation periods "understates" cost of goods sold and causes "inventory profits."
2. The use of replacement cost accounting reduces income and interest coverage during inflationary periods.
3. A leveling off of prices referred to as disinflation, may cause a reduction in profits.

B.   Impact on Asset Value

1. Assets on the balance sheet are recorded at cost.
2. In inflationary periods, the replacement cost of long-term assets may greatly exceed the reported values.
3. Cash flows from the depreciation process may be insufficient to replace assets as they wear out.
4. The use of replacement cost accounting increases asset values during inflationary periods. This increase lowers the debt to asset ratio but does not necessarily enhance the firm's ability to service its debt.

PPT 3-12	Comparison of Replacement Cost and Historical Costs (Table 3-7)

C.   Raising capital

1. Investors generally require higher rates of return during periods of inflation.
2. Although earnings may drop because of disinflation, the declining rate of return demanded by investors may cause the value of a firm's securities to increase.
3. The movement away from financial assets (stocks and bonds) into tangible assets (gold, silver, etc.) by investors during periods of inflation makes it difficult and more expensive for firms to raise capital. Likewise the reverse trend during periods of disinflation enhances a firm's ability to issue securities.

20

III. Other Elements of Distortion in Reported Income

> PPT 3-13   Illustration of Conservative versus High Reported Income Firms
>   (Table 3-8)

A.   Recognition of revenue

1.   A conservative firm may recognize long-term installment sales revenues when payments are received, whereas other firms report the full amount of the sale as soon as possible.

2.   Firms may use different inventory write-off policies to influence profits.

Finance in Action:
Funny Money: When is a Sale Truly a Sale and Not Merely a Loan

This box focuses on accounting methods that can distract reported income and is a good follow up to the last section of the chapter.

B.   Extraordinary losses are reported in total as deductions from operating income by some firms but shown as deductions (net of taxes) from net income by others.

Summary Listing of Transparencies

Solution Transparencies to Chapter Problems

Other Chapter Supplements

Cases for Use with Foundations of Financial Management, Chem-Med Company (ratio analysis case)

Financial Forecasting

Author's Overview

Developing pro forma statements is a fairly involved process. However, the rewards to students are high in terms of understanding the interaction of accounting data and financial forecasting. The development of pro forma financial statements is an integrative exercise, so there is little reward for a halfway approach.

The percent-of-sales method, presented at the back of the chapter, is a second approach to financial forecasting. It has the virtue of being easily understood and quickly mastered, but does the full validity of developing pro forma statements. It is really a matter of instructor preference.

Chapter Concepts

* Financial forecasting is essential to the strategic growth of the firm.

* The three financial statements for forecasting are the pro forma income statement, the cash budget and the pro forma balance sheet.

* The percent-of-sales method may also be used for forecasting on a less precise basis.

* The various methods of forecasting enable the firm to determine the amount of new funds required in advance.

* The process of forecasting forces the firm to consider seasonal and other effects on cash flow.

Annotated Outline and Strategy

I.   Need for Financial Planning

    A.   Growth requires additions to assets; arrangements for financing such asset additions must be made in advance.

    B.   Financial planning is necessary not only for success but for survival as well.

C.   Lenders frequently require evidence of planning prior to making funds available.

II.   **The most comprehensive means for doing financial planning is through the development of pro forma financial statements; namely the pro forma income statement, the cash budget, and the pro forma balance sheet.**

Perspective 4-1: At a very early stage the instructor must indicate how the pro forma income and cash budget are used to develop the pro forma balance sheet. The road map is presented in Figure 4-1. Only after the overall plan for analysis is presented through Figure 4-1 should the instructor go into more detailed coverage of other tables and schedules.

PPT 4-1   Development of Pro Forma Statements (Figure 4-1)

A.   Pro Forma Income Statement: A projection of how much profit a firm will make over a specific time period

　　1.   Establish a sales projection

　　　　a.   Forecast economic conditions
　　　　b.   Survey sales personnel

PPT 4-2   Projected Wheel and Caster Sales (Table 4-1)

**Finance in Action: Sales Forecasting –
Where Marketing and Finance Come Together**

Students need to understand that many of the numbers financial managers work with are provided by other functional areas in the firm. Sales forecast are usually generated by the marketing function and projected sales for wheels and casters in Table 4-1 are derived outside of the finance area. Radio Shack stores are given as an example in this box.

Perspective 4-2: *A number of steps are necessary to convert the sales forecast into production requirements, cost of goods sold and gross profit. There are no shortcuts here. Tables 4-2, 4-3, 4-4, 4-5 and Table 4-6 are all brought together into one transparency, so the instructor can show all the relationships at once.*

2.   Determine production needs, cost of goods sold, and gross profits based on the sales forecast

     a.   Determine units to be produced

            Projected unit sales
            Desired ending inventory
        - <u>Beginning inventory</u>
            Production requirements

     b.   Determine the cost of producing the units
         (1)   Unit cost = materials + labor + overhead
         (2)   Total costs = number of units to be produced × unit cost
     c.   Compute cost of goods sold
         (1)   Estimate unit sales
         (2)   Cost of goods sold = unit sales X unit cost (FIFO or LIFO)

     d.   Compute gross profit

3.   Compute other expenses

     a.   General and administrative
     b.   Interest expense

4. Finally construct the pro forma income statement

        Sales revenue
       -<u>Cost of goods sold</u>
        Gross profit
       -<u>General and administrative expenses</u>
        Operating profit
       -<u>Interest expense</u>
        Earnings before taxes
       -<u>Taxes</u>
        <u>Earnings after taxes</u>
       -<u>Common stock dividends</u>
        <u>Increase in retained earnings</u>

B. Cash budget: A summary of expected cash receipts and disbursements for a specific period of time

PPT 4-4	Pro Forma Income Statement (Table 4-8)

1. Estimate cash sales and collection timing of credit sales

PPT 4-5	Summary of Monthly Sales Pattern (Table 4-9), Monthly Cash Receipts (Table 4-10) and Component Costs of Manufactured Goods (Table 4-11)

2. Forecast cash payments

    a. Payments for materials purchase according to credit terms
    b. Wages
    c. Capital expenditures
    d. Principal payments
    e. Interest payments
    f. Taxes
    g. Dividends

PPT 4-6	Summary of Average Monthly Manufacturing Costs (Table 4-12), and All Monthly Cash (Table 4-13)

3. Determine monthly cash flow (receipts minus payments)

4.   Construct cash budget

Total receipts (for each month, week, etc.)
- Total payments (for each month, week, etc.)
  Net cash flow (for the period)
+ Beginning cash balance
  Cumulative cash balance

Note: The beginning cash balance for each period of the cash budget is equal to the cumulative cash balance of the previous period in the absence of borrowing or investing of cash balances.

5.   Determine cash excess or need for borrowing

Cumulative cash balance (at end of period)
        Loan required or cash excess (desired cash balance
-       cumulative cash balance)
        Ending cash balance

C.   Pro Forma Balance Sheet: An integrated projection of the firm's financial position based on its existing position, forecasted profitability (from pro forma income statement), anticipated cash flows (cash budget), asset requirements and required financing

1.   Construction of pro forma balance sheet

a.   Assets (source of information)
       (1)   Cash - (cash budget)
       (2)   Marketable securities - (previous balance sheet and cash budget)
       (3)   Accounts receivable - (sales forecast, cash budget)
       (4)   Inventory - (COGS computation for pro forma income statement)
       (5)   Plant and equipment - (previous balance sheet + purchases - depreciation)

b.   Liabilities and Net Worth
       (1)   Accounts payable - (cash budget work sheet)
       (2)   Notes payable - (previous balance sheet and cash budget)

28

(3)   Long-term debt - (previous balance sheet plus new issues)

(4)   Common stock - (previous balance sheet plus new issues)

(5)   Retained earnings - (previous balance sheet plus projected addition from pro forma income statement)

Perspective 4-3: *The instructor may wish to use Figure 4-2 to reinforce the pattern used to arrive at the pro forma balance sheet.*

PPT 4-8   Balance Sheet (Table 4-16)

PPT 4-9   Development of a Pro Forma Balance Sheet (Figure 4-2)

PPT 4-10   Pro Forma Balance Sheet (Table 4-17)

Perspective 4-4: *Table 4-17 is the last piece in the puzzle in that it represents the actual pro forma balance sheet. The amounts in the 10 accounts in the table can be clarified by the explanations following the table in the text.*

III.   **Percent-of-Sales Method: Shortcut, less exact, alternative for determining financial needs**

     A.   Assume balance sheet accounts maintain a given relationship to sales

$$\frac{\text{Assets}}{\text{Current Sales}} = \% \text{ of sales}$$

PPT 4-11   Balance Sheet and Percentage-of-Sales Table (Table 4-18)

Perspective 4-5: *Table 4-18 can be tied in with formula 4-1 to demonstrate the percent-of-sales method.*

B.   Project asset levels on basis of forecasted sales (percent of sales of each asset × forecasted sales)

C.   Project spontaneous financing: Some financing is provided spontaneously when asset levels increase; for example, accounts payable increase when a firm buys additional inventory on credit.

D.   Project internal financing from profit = profit margin × forecasted sales

E.   Determine external financing = required new assets to support sales - spontaneous

$$\text{Required new funds} = \frac{A}{S}(\Delta S) - \frac{L}{S}(\Delta S) - PS_2(1-D)$$

financing - retained earnings.   The relationship is expressed as follows:
Where:
   A/S = percentage relationship of variable assets to sales
   ΔS = change in sales
   L/S = percentage relationships of variable liabilities to sales
   P = profit margin
   S_2 = new sales level
   D = payout ratio.

Summary Listing of Transparencies

PPT 4-1	Development of Pro Forma Statements (Figure 4-1)
PPT 4-2	Projected Wheel and Caster Sales (Table 4-1)
PPT 4-3	Stock of Beginning Inventory, Production Requirements, Unit Costs, Total Production Costs, Gross Profit and Value of Ending Inventory. Tables 4-2, 4-3, 4-4, 4-5, 4-6, & 4-7.
PPT 4-4	Pro Forma Income Statement (Table 4-8)
PPT 4-5	Summary of Monthly Sales Pattern (Table 4-9), Monthly Cash Receipts (Table 4-10), and Component Costs of Manufactured Goods (Table 4-11)
PPT 4-6	Summary of Average Monthly Manufacturing Costs (Table 4-12), and All Monthly Cash Payments (Table 4-13)
PPT 4-7	Monthly Cash Flow (Table 4-14) and Cash Budgeting with Borrowing and Repayment (Table 4-15)
PPT 4-8	Balance Sheet (Table 4-16)
PPT 4-9	Development of a Pro Forma Balance Sheet (Figure 4-2)
PPT 4-10	Pro Forma Balance Sheet (Table 4-17)
PPT 4-11	Balance Sheet and Percent-of-Sales Table (4-18)
LT 4-1	Chapter 4 Outline
LT 4-2	What is Financial Forecasting?
LT 4-3	2 Methods of Financial Forecasting
LT 4-4	3 Financial Statements for Forecasting
LT 4-5	Steps in a Pro Forma Income Statement (I/S)
LT 4-6	Determining Production Requirements
LT 4-7	Percent-of-Sales Method

Solution Transparencies to Chapter Problems

ST 4-1	ER Medical Supplies
ST 4-3	Ross Pro's Sports Equipment
ST 4-5	Hoover Electronics
ST 4-7	Lemon Auto Parts
ST 4-8	Convex Mechanical Supplies
ST 4-9	Convex Mechanical Supplies
ST 4-11	Monica's Flower Shops
ST 4-13	Pirate Video Company
ST 4-15	Wright Lighting Fixtures
ST 4-17	Graham Potato Company
ST 4-19	Hickman Avionics
ST 4-21	Jordan Aluminum Supplies
CP 4-1	Landis Corporation (Comprehensive Problem)
CP 4-2	Adams Corporation (Comprehensive Problem)

Operating and Financial Leverage

Author's Overview

Though the student has probably covered break-even analysis in other courses, the material in Chapter 5 offers an opportunity to more fully explore the financial effects of all forms of leverage on the firm. The contrast between aggressive and conservative approaches should be emphasized particularly through the useful technique of computing degrees of leverage. This chapter also serves as a good basis for much of the later discussion in the text on the cost of capital. The student begins to appreciate the positive benefits of debt, but also realizes that unlimited use of debt increases the financial risk of the firm and perhaps the cost of various other sources of financing.

Chapter Concepts

* Leverage represents the use of fixed cost items to magnify the firm's results.

* Operating leverage indicates the extent fixed assets (plant & equipment) are utilized by the firm.

* Financial leverage shows how much debt the firm employs in its capital structure.

* By increasing leverage, the firm increases its profit potential, but also its risk of failure.

Annotated Outline and Strategy

I. **Leverage: The use of fixed charge obligations with the intent of magnifying the potential return to the firm.**

    A. Fixed operating costs: Those operating costs that remain relatively constant regardless of the volume of operations such as rent, depreciation, property taxes, and executive salaries.

    B. Fixed financial costs: The interest costs arising from debt financing that must be paid regardless of the level of sales or profits.

II. Break-Even Analysis and Operating Leverage

A. Break-even analysis: A numerical and graphical technique used to determine at what point the firm will break even.

1. Break-even point: the unit sales where total revenue = total costs

2. Break-even point formula:

$$BE = \frac{FixedCosts}{Contribution\ Margin} = \frac{FixedCosts}{Price - VariableCost\ perUnit} = \frac{FC}{P - VC}$$

PPT 5-1	Break-Even Chart: Leveraged Firm (Figure 5-1)

Perspective 5-1: The instructor can best establish factors related to break-even analysis by illustrating the operations of a highly leveraged firm versus a conservative one. The material is presented in Figure 5-1, Table 5-2, Figure 5-2, and Table 5-3.

PPT 5-2	Volume-Cost-Profit Analysis: Leveraged Firm (Table 5-2)

PPT 5-3	Break-Even Chart: Conservative Firm (Figure 5-2)

PPT 5-4	Volume-Cost-Profit Analysis: Conservative Firm (Table 5-3)

B.   The risk factor in using financial leverage depends on the firm's operations relative to its breakeven point and it operating leverage. Management's willingness to take risk is also a function of its view of future economic conditions.

C.   Cash break-even analysis

    1.   Deducting non-cash fixed expenses such as depreciation in the break-even analysis enables one to determine the break-even point on a cash basis.

    2.   Cash break-even point formula:

$$\text{Cash BE} = \frac{\text{Fixed Costs} - (\text{Non-cash Fixed Costs})}{P - VC}$$

    3.   Although cash break-even analysis provides additional insight, the emphasis in the chapter is on the more traditional accounting-data related break-even analysis.

D.   Operating leverage: A reflection of the extent fixed assets and fixed costs are utilized in the business firm. The employment of operating leverage causes operating profit to be more sensitive to changes in sales.

    1.   The use of operating leverage increases the potential return but it also increases potential losses.

    2.   The amount of leverage employed depends on anticipated economic conditions, nature of the business (cyclical or noncyclical), and the risk aversion of management.

    3.   The sensitivity of a firm's operating profit to a change in sales as a result of the employment of operating leverage is reflected in its degree of operating leverage.

    4.   Degree of operating leverage (DOL) is defined as the ratio of percentage change in operating income in response to percentage change in volume.

$$DOL = \frac{\%\text{ change in operating income}}{\%\text{ change in volume}}$$

    5.   The DOL may also be computed using the formulation:

$$DOL = \frac{Q(P - VC)}{Q(P - VC) - FC}$$

where:

Q	=	quantity at which DOL is computed
P	=	price per unit
VC	=	variable cost per unit
FC	=	fixed costs

6. DOL and other measures of leverage always apply to the starting point for the range used in the computation.

PPT 5-5	Operating Income or Loss (Table 5-4)

Perspective 5-2: DOL can easily be computed from the summary data on the leveraged and conservative firm. The summary data is presented in Table 5-4 and is drawn from previously mentioned Tables 5-2 and Table 5-3.

---

7. The normal assumption in doing break-even analysis is that a linear function exists for revenue and costs as volume changes. This is probably reasonable over a reasonable range. However, for more extreme levels of operations, there may be revenue weakness and cost overruns. Some non-linearity may exist.

III. **Financial Leverage: A measure of the amount of debt used in the capital structure of the firm.**

PPT 5-6	Nonlinear Break-Even Analysis (Figure 5-3)

A. Two firms may have the same operating income but greatly different net incomes due to the magnification effect of financial leverage. The higher the financial leverage, the greater the profits or losses at high or low levels of operating profit, respectively.

B. While operating leverage primarily pertains to the left-hand side of the balance sheet (assets and associated costs), financial leverage deals with the right-hand side of the balance sheet (liabilities and net worth).

C. Financial leverage is beneficial only if the firm can employ the borrowed funds to earn a higher rate of return than the interest rate on the borrowed amount. The extent of a firm's use of financial leverage may be measured by computing its degree of financial leverage (DFL). The DFL is the ratio of the percentage change in net income (or earnings per share) in response to a percentage change in EBIT.

D. The DFL may also be computed utilizing the following formula:

$$DFL = \frac{\% \text{ change in EPS}}{\% \text{ change in EBIT}}$$

E. The DFL is associated with a specific level of EBIT and changes as EBIT changes.

F. The purpose of employing financial leverage is to increase return to the owners but its use also increases their risk.

Perspective 5-3: The financial information for computing these measures is found in Table 5-5. The impact of financial leverage can also be viewed in Figure 5-4.

PPT 5-7   Impact of Financial Plan on Earnings Per Share (Table 5-5)

PPT 5-8   Financing Plans and Earnings Per Share (Figure 5-4)

G. The use of financial leverage is not unlimited.

　　1. Interest rates that a firm must pay for debt-financing rise as it becomes more highly leveraged.
　　2. As the risk to the stockholders increases with leverage, their required rate of return increases and stock prices may decline.

IV. Combined Leverage

A. Combining operating and financial leverage provides maximum magnification of returns-it also magnifies the risk.

B. The combined leverage effect can be illustrated through the income statement.

PPT 5-9   Income Statement (Table 5-6)

Perspective 5-4: This is an excellent place to go directly to the income statement in Table 5-6 to illustrate what part of the income statement operating leverage controls and what part financial leverage controls and how the interaction provides combined leverage. The student should clearly see that operating income is the end result of operating leverage and the beginning factor for financial leverage (in the form of earnings before interest and taxes). These relationships are further enforced through Figure 5-5.

PPT 5-10   Combining Operating and Financial Leverage (Figure 5-5)

C. The degree of combined leverage (DCL) is a measure of the effect on net income as a result of a change in sales. The DCL is computed similar to DOL or DFL

$$DCL = \frac{\% \text{ change in EPS}}{\% \text{ change in sales}}$$

D.   The DCL may also be computed as follows:

$$DCL = \frac{Q(P - VC)}{Q(P - VC) - FC - I}$$

PPT 5-11	Operating and Financial Leverage (Table 5-7)

> ***Perspective 5-5:*** *In concluding the chapter, the instructor may wish to reenforce the interactive nature of the various forms of leverage. Firms in the Japanese economy normally not only use high operating leverage, but they also use high financial leverage. Because of their high combined leverage, they are very hesitant to lose volume and therefore are extremely in pricing and in other ways. Problem nine at the back of the chapter illustrates the high combined leverage of a Japanese company.*
>
> *After the problems in Chapter 5, there is a comprehensive review problem for Chapters 2 through 5. This problem covers ratio analysis, break-even analysis, operating and financial leverage, and an analysis of new funds required.*

Finance in Action: Why Japanese Firms Tend to be so Competitive

Perspective 5-5 highlights the impact of high combined leverage on the competitive behavior of Japanese firms presented in this Finance in Action box. The professor may wish to also focus on the difference between the U.S. and Japanese financial markets and how the Japanese markets make high financial leverage more attainable than that possible for U.S. firms.

Summary Listing of Transparencies

PPT 5-1   Break-Even Chart: Leveraged Firm (Figure 5-1)
PPT 5-2   Volume-Cost-Profit Analysis: Leveraged Firm (Table 5-2)
PPT 5-3   Break-Even Chart: Conservative Firm (Figure 5-2)
PPT 5-4   Volume-Cost-Profit Analysis: Conservative Firm (Table 5-3)
PPT 5-5   Operating Income or Loss (Table 5-4)
PPT 5-6   Nonlinear Break-Even Analysis (Figure 5-3)
PPT 5-7   Impact of Financial Plan on Earnings Per Share (Table 5-5)
PPT 5-8   Financing Plans and Earnings Per Share (Figure 5-4)
PPT 5-9   Income Statement (Table 5-6)
PPT 5-10   Combining Operating and Financial Leverage (Figure 5-5)
PPT 5-11   Operating and Financial Leverage (Table 5-7)
LT 5-1   Chapter 5 Outline
LT 5-2   What is Leverage?
LT 5-3   Break-Even (BE) Point
LT 5-4   Operating Leverage
LT 5-5   Financial Leverage
LT 5-6   Leverage Means Risk
LT 5-7   Combined or Total Leverage

Solution Transparencies to Chapter Problems

ST 5-1   The Hazardous Toys Company
ST 5-3   Shawn Penn & Pencil Sets, Inc.
ST 5-5   Labor-intensive and capital-intensive break-even graphs
ST 5-7   Harding Company
ST 5-9   Leno Drug Stores and Hall Pharmaceuticals
ST 5-11   Susaki Company
ST 5-13   Desoto Tools, Inc.
ST 5-15   Dickinson Company
ST 5-17   Katz-Doberman
CP 5-1   Aspen Ski Company
            (Comprehensive Problem Chapters 2-5)

Other Supplements to Chapter

Cases for Use with Foundations of Financial Management, Glen Mount Furniture Company (financial leverage)

Cases for Use with Foundations of Financial Management, Genuine Motor Products (combined leverage)

Working Capital and the Financing Decision

Author's Overview

The chapter introduces the student to the topic of working capital management. The emphasis is on the build-up of current assets and how they can best be financed. Examples of McGraw-Hill, Kmart, and J.C. Penny are used to show that seasonal earning and sales go hand in hand. Companies in cyclical or seasonal industries have a more challenging job of managing their current assets. Such key topics as the impact of production on financing needs and the differences between temporary and permanent assets are considered. Also, the relative costs and volatility of short and long-term financing are evaluated with an emphasis on the term structure of interest rates. The chapter provides the framework from which to move into the next two chapters, which cover the management of specific short-term assets and sources of short-term financing.

Chapter Concepts

* Working capital management involves financing and controlling the current assets of the firm.

* Management must distinguish between those current assets that are easily converted to cash and those that are more permanent in nature.

* The financing of an asset should be tied to how long the asset is likely to be on the balance sheet.

* Long-term financing is usually more expensive than short-term financing based on the theory of the term structure of interest rates.

* Risk as well as profitability determine the financing plan for current assets.

Annotated Outline and Strategy

I. **Working Capital Management**

    A. Management of working capital is the financial manager's most time-consuming function.

    B. Success in managing current assets in the short run is critical for the firm's long-run existence.

    C. Nature of asset growth

        1. Changes in current assets may be temporary (seasonal) or "permanent."

            a. Current assets by definition are those expected to become cash in one operating cycle, but the level of the current assets may be "permanent" or increasing.

            b. Businesses subject to cyclical sales may have temporary fluctuations in the level of current assets.

PPT 6-1	The Nature of Asset Growth (Figure 6-1)

---

        2. Matching sales and production

            a. Both accounts receivable and inventory rise when sales increase as production increases. When sales rise faster than production, inventory declines and receivables rise.

            b. Level production (matching production and sales over an entire cycle) may cause large buildups in current assets when sales are slack. These buildups drop rapidly during peak demand periods since sales exceed the level production output.

II. **Both seasonal and permanent increases in working capital must be financed.**

    A. Ideally, temporary increases in current assets are financed by short-term funds and permanent current assets are financed with long-term sources.

    B. Figure 6-2 demonstrates the seasonal nature of textbook sales for McGraw-Hill, while Figure 6-3 illustrates the same principle for Kmart and J.C. Penney. In both cases, as sales grow over time, these permanent increases in associated working capital have to be financed.

The following transparencies relate to the Yawakuzi example.

PPT 6-2	Yawakuzi Sales Forecast (Table 6-1)
PPT 6-3	Yawakuzi's Production Schedule and Inventory (Table 6-2)
PPT 6-4	Sales Forecast, Cash Receipts and Payments, and Cash Budget (Table 6-3)
PPT 6-5	Total Current Assets, First Year (Table 6-4)
PPT 6-6	The Nature of Asset Growth (Figure 6-4)
PPT 6-7	Cash Budget and Assets for Second Year with no Growth in Sales (Table 6-5)

PPT 6-8	Matching Long-Term and Short-Term Needs (Figure 6-5)

C. The patterns of financing are flexible based on management's willingness to accept risk.

   1. Point out that matching short-term funds with short-term assets allows the company to increase and decrease sources and uses of funds as the company's sales fluctuate.

   2. Many firms, however, choose or are forced to use plans that do not match up financing with asset needs.

PPT 6-9	Using Long-Term Financing for Part of Short-Term Needs (Figure 6-6) and Using Short-Term Financing for Part of Long-Term Needs (Figure 6-7)

3.   Financing a high percentage of short-term assets with long-term funds means the financial manager will have excess funds to invest at seasonal or cyclical troughs, in other words excess financing.

4.   Financing permanent current assets and some long-term assets with short-term funds is quite risky because short-term funds will be permanently needed and thus cost is highly volatile and sources of short-term funds are not always available in tight credit markets.

5.   Figure 6-8 presents the various sources of Financing that can be used by a corporation.

III.   The term structure of interest rates indicates the relative cost of short and long-term financing and is important to the financing decision.

A.   The relationship of interest rates at a specific point in time for securities of equal risk but different maturity dates is referred to as the term structure of interest rates.

B.   The term structure of interest rates is depicted by yield curves.

PPT 6-10   Long-Term and Short-Term Interest Rates (Figure 6-10)

C.   There are three theories describing the shape of the yield curve.
     1.   Liquidity premium theory: the theory states that long-term rates should be higher than short-term rates because long-term securities are less liquid and more price sensitive.

C.   Market segmentation theory: the yield curve is "shaped" by the relative demand for securities of various maturities. Some institutions such as commercial banks are primarily interested in short-term securities. Others such as insurance companies manifest a preference for much longer term securities.

D.   Expectations hypothesis: the expectations hypothesis says that long-term rates reflect the average of expected short-term rates over the time period that the long-term security is outstanding.

E.   Types of yield curves

F.   Normal: upward sloping; shorter maturities have lower required yields.

G.   Humped: intermediate interest rates are higher than both the short-term and long-term rates.

H.   Inverted, downward sloping: short-term rates are higher than intermediate or long-term rates.

I. Yield curves shift upward and downward in response to changes in anticipated inflation rates and other conditions of uncertainty.

J. **A Decision Process**

K. The composition of a firm's financing of working capital is made within the risk-return framework.

L. Short-term financing is generally less costly but more risky than long-term financing.
    2. During tight money periods, short-term financing may be unavailable or very

---

PPT 6-11   Alternative Financing Plans (Table 6-7) and Impact of Financing Plans on Earnings (Table 6-8)

---

expensive.

M. Applying probabilities of occurrence of various economic conditions, an expected value of alternative forms of financing may be computed and used as a decision basis.

PPT 6-12   Expected Returns Under Different Economic Conditions (Table 6-9) and Expected Returns for High-Risk Firm (Table 6-10)

N. **Shift in Asset Structure**

O. Risk versus return considerations also affect the composition of the left-hand side of the balance sheet.

P. A firm may compensate for high risk on the financing side with high liquidity on the asset side or vice versa.

44

Q. Since the early 1960's, business firms have reduced their liquidity as a result of:

R. Profit-oriented financial management.
S. Better utilization of cash balances, through electronic funds transfer.

T. **Toward an Optimum Policy**

U. An aggressive firm will borrow short term and carry high levels of inventory and longer term receivables. The firm's position is represented by panel 1 of Table 6-11.

V. The conservative firm (panel 4) will maintain high liquidity and utilize more long-term financing.

W. Moderate firms compensate for short-term financing with highly liquid assets (panel 2) or balance low liquidity with long-term financing (panel 3).

PPT 6-13	Asset Liquidity and Financing Needs (Table 6-11)

Finance in Action: Working Capital Problems in a Small Business

The solution to seasonal working capital problems that plague small businesses is sufficient flexible planning to ensure that profits produced during the peak season are available to cover losses during the off-season. This is true because small firms have trouble finding sources of funds for seasonal needs. This can be tied back into financial markets and the changing structure of banking.

Summary Listing of Transparencies

Solution Transparencies to Chapter Problems

Other Supplements to Chapter

Cases for Use with Foundations of Financial Management, Gale Force Surfing (working capital)

Current Asset Management

Author's Overview

The instructor should stress the profitability-liquidity trade-offs to be found in the current asset accounts. The student should think of the less liquid current assets as representing a competitive investment for capital. The four different topics for discussion in the chapter are all worthy of detailed coverage. The material on cash management has real contemporary importance and is usually of interest to the student who has struggled with his or her own cash management. The management of accounts receivable and inventories represents an excellent opportunity to cover decision making tools that are an important part of financial management.

Chapter Concepts

* Current asset management is an extension of concepts discussed in the previous chapter and involves the management of cash, marketable securities, accounts receivable and inventory.

* Cash management involves control over the receipt and payment of cash so as to minimize nonearning cash balances.

* The management of marketable securities involves selecting between various short-term investments.

* Accounts receivable and inventory management require credit and inventory level decisions to be made with an eye toward profitability.

* An overriding concept is that the less liquid an asset is, the higher the required return.

Annotated Outline and Strategy

I. **Cash Management**

    A.   Cash is a necessary but low earning asset.

    B.   Financial managers attempt to minimize cash balances and yet maintain sufficient amounts to meet obligations in a timely manner.

    C.   The three main reasons for holding cash are for:

        1.   Transactions
        2.   Compensating balances
        3.   Precautionary needs

    D.   Temporarily, excess cash balances are transferred into interest-earning marketable securities.

    E.   The cash flow cycle can be used to describe how funds move in and out of the firm.

Finance in Action: The Impact of the Internet on Working Capital Management

This article discusses the two major trends that will affect corporate practices and profitability. The first trend is the business-to-business (B2B) industry supply, and the second is online auction companies. These two trends will significantly reduce costs and raise industrialized countries' growth rates about .25 percent over the next decade.

PPT 7-1	Expanded Cash Flow Cycle (Figure 7-2)

II. **Collections and Disbursements**

    A.   The financial manager attempts to get maximum use of minimum balances by speeding up inflows and slowing outflows.

    B.   Playing the float: Using the difference in the cash balances shown on the bank's records and those shown on the firm's records.

C.   Improving collection

     1.   Decentralized collection centers speed collection of accounts receivable by reducing mailing time.

     2.   Wire transfer of funds-excess cash balances are transferred from collection points to a centralized location for use.

     3.   Lock-box system-customers mail payment to a post office box serviced by a local bank in their geographical area. Checks are cleared locally and balances transferred by wire to a central location.

D.   Extended disbursement to take advantage of slower clearing of checks. The primary benefits of speeding up inflows or slowing outflows is the earnings generated from the freed up balances. The benefits must be weighed against the cost.

E.   Cost Benefit Analysis

F.   Electronic Funds Transfer takes place through automated clearing houses and internationally, through SWIFT.

G.   International Cash Management

     1.   Multinational firms shift funds from country to country daily, maximizing returns and balancing foreign exchange risk.

     2.   Difference in time zones, banking systems, culture and other differences create a non uniform system in some cases.

     3.   Over 4000 banks use SWIFT for standardized interbank electronic funds transfer.

Perspective 7-1: The instructor may wish to use Figure 7-3 as an example of how funds are freed up. He or she can then apply a potential rate of return on these funds and relate that to the maximum cost that should be incurred.

III. Marketable Securities

A. Because marketable securities normally represent funds held in reserve, the maturity should be kept reasonably short to avoid interest rate risk.

> *Perspective 7-2: The instructor can use Table 7-3 to highlight the attributes of the various securities and instruments, stressing the ever-changing nature of the market and competition between financial institutions.*

B. There is a wide array of securities from which to choose.

1. Federal government securities
2. Federal agency securities
3. Nongovernment securities

> PPT 7-4   An Examination of Yield and Maturity Characteristics (Figure 7-5)

a. Certificates of deposit
b. Commercial paper
c. Banker's acceptances
d. Eurodollar deposits
e. Savings Accounts
f. Money market funds
g. Money market deposit accounts

> PPT 7-5   Types of Short-Term Investments (Table 7-3)

IV. Management of Accounts Receivable

A. Accounts receivable as a percentage of total assets almost doubled between 1960 and the early 2000s for the typical U.S. corporation. The primary reasons for the increases have been:
1. Increasing sales.
2. Inflation.
3. Extended credit terms during recessions.

B.   Accounts receivable are an investment.

    1.   Investment in accounts receivable should generate a return equal to or in excess of the return available on alternative investments.

Perspective 7-3: *Discuss a credit decision relating the sales function to the credit created by the new accounts. Stress that the emphasis should be on rate of return.*

C.   There are three primary variables for credit policy administration.

    1.   Credit standards

        a.   The firm screens credit applicants on the basis of prior record of payment, financial stability, current net worth, and other factors.

        b.   5 C's of Credit: character, capital, capacity, conditions, collateral.

        c.   Dun & Bradstreet Information Services (DBIS)
           (1)   Business Information Report
           (2)   Commercial Credit Scoring Report
           (3)   Industry Credit Score Report (See Table 7-4)

        d.   D-U-N-S Data Universal Number System is a unique nine digit code used globally and accepted by the United National and other international agencies as a global business identification number. See Figure 7-6.

PPT 7-6   Trucking Industry Credit Score Report (Table 7-4)

---

    2.   Terms of trade

    3.   Collection policy: Some measures used to assess collection efficiency are:

        a.   Average collection period.
        b.   Ratio of bad debts to sales.
        c.   Aging of accounts receivable.

IV.   Inventory Management

A.   Inventory is the least liquid of current assets.

B.   A firm's level of inventory is largely determined by the cyclicality of sales and whether it follows a seasonal or level production schedule. The production decision is based on the trade-off of cost savings of level production versus the additional inventory carrying costs.

C.   Rapid price movements complicate the inventory level decision.

D.   There are two basic costs associated with inventory:

      1.   Carrying costs:

            a.   Interest on funds tied up in inventory.
            b.   Warehouse space costs.
            c.   Insurance.
            d.   Material handling expenses.
            e.   Risk of obsolescence (implicit cost).

      2.   Ordering and processing costs

E.   Carrying costs vary directly with average inventory levels.

F.   Total carrying costs increase as the order size increases.

G.   Total ordering costs decrease as the order size increases.

H.   The first step toward achieving minimum inventory costs is determination of the optimal order quantity.   This quantity may be derived by use of the economic order quantity formula:

$$EOQ = \frac{\sqrt{2S0}}{C}$$

Perspective 7-4: Combine the EOQ formula with Figure 7-8 to clearly illustrate the impact of selecting the optimum order size.

I.   Assumptions of the basic EOQ model:
1.   Inventory usage is at a constant rate.
2.   Order costs per order are constant.
3.   Delivery time of orders is consistent and order arrives as inventory reaches zero.

J.   Minimum total inventory costs will result if the assumptions of the model are applicable and the firm's order size equals the economic ordering quantity.

K.   Just-in-Time Inventory Management (JIT)

1.   Began in Japan and now used in the U.S.
2.   Suppliers are located near manufactures who are able to make orders in small lot sizes because of short delivery time.
3.   Lower inventory means lower costs
4.   The downside of (JIT) is that any glitch in delivery can shut down the whole production process.

Finance in Action: NASA–The National Aeronautics and Space Administration Inventory Control System

This box illustrates how the use of technology can save time and reduce costs. NASA, with the help of their prime contractor United Space Alliance (USA), have installed a radio frequency data communications system which can pinpoint 98 percent of the 300,000 inventory items found among 100 buildings in a matter of seconds. This system saves almost $1 billion annually by reducing the time it takes to locate equipment.

Summary Listing of Transparencies

PPT 7-1	Expanded Cash Flow Cycle (Figure 7-2)
PPT 7-2	The Use of Float to Provide Funds (Table 7-1) and Playing the Float (Table 7-2)
PPT 7-3	Cash Management Network (Figure 7-3)
PPT 7-4	An Examination of Yield and Maturity Characteristics (Figure 7-5)
PPT 7-5	Types of Short-Term Investments (Table 7-3)
PPT 7-6	Trucking Industry Credit Score Report (Table 7-4)
PPT 7-7	Determining the Optimum Inventory Level (Figure 7-8)
LT 7-1	Chapter 7 Outline
LT 7-2	What is Current Asset Management?
LT 7-3	Cash Management
LT 7-4	Ways to Improve Collections
LT 7-5	Marketable Securities
LT 7-6	3 Primary Variables of Credit Policy
LT 7-7	Inventory Management
LT 7-8	Level vs. Seasonal Production
LT 7-9	Economic Ordering Quantity

Solution Transparencies to Chapter Problems

ST 7-1	Cats Copiers, Inc.
ST 7-3	City Farm Insurance
ST 7-5	Darla's Cosmetics
ST 7-6	Darla's Cosmetics (Continued)
ST 7-7	Hubbell Electronics Wiring Company
ST 7-9	Nowlin Pipe and Steel Company
ST 7-10	Howe Corp.
ST 7-11	Howe Corp. (Continued)
ST 7-13	Dimaggio Sports Equipment, Inc.
ST 7-15	Collins Office Supplies
ST 7-16	Curtis Toy Manufacturing Company
ST 7-17	Curtis Toy Manufacturing Company (Continued)
ST 7-18	Maddox Resources
ST 7-19	Maddox Resources (Continued)
ST 7-20	Maddox Resources (Continued)
ST 7-21	Maddox Resources (Continued)
CP 7-1	Bailey Distributing Company (Comprehensive Problem)

Other Supplements to Chapter

Cases for Use With Foundations of Financial Management, Fresh & Fruity Foods, Inc. (current asset management). This case can also be used after Chapter 8 in the text.

Sources of Short-Term Financing

Author's Overview

The instructor has the opportunity to cover the various sources of short-term financing with an eye toward the borrower's size and the relative cost of doing business. Since banking is such a rapidly changing area, the instructor may wish to highlight some of the changes that are taking place. The student should also get some exposure to the various considerations in computing interest costs. Throughout the chapter, there are ample opportunities to indicate the advantages and drawbacks of trade credit, bank credit, commercial paper, foreign borrowing and collateralized borrowing arrangements.

Chapter Concepts

*   Trade credit from suppliers is normally the most available form of short-term financing.

*   Bank loans are usually short-term in nature and should be paid off from the normal operations of the firm.

*   Commercial paper represents a short-term, unsecured promissory note issued by the firm.

*   Through borrowing in foreign markets, a firm may lower its borrowing costs.

*   By using accounts receivable and inventory as collateral for a loan, the firm may be able to borrow larger amounts.

Annotated Outline and Strategy

I. **Trade Credit**

    A.   Usually the largest source of short-term financing

    B.   A spontaneous source of financing that increases as sales expand or contract

    C.   Credit period is set by terms of credit but firms may be able to "stretch" the payment period.

    D.   Cash discount policy

        1.   Suppliers may provide a cash discount for early payment.

        2.   Foregoing discounts can be very expensive. The cost of failing to take a discount is computed as follows:

$$\frac{\text{Cost of failing}}{\text{to take discount}} = \frac{\text{Discount \%}}{100\% - \text{Discount \%}} \times \frac{360}{\text{Final due date} - \text{Discount period}}$$

        3.   Whether a firm should take a discount depends on the relative costs of alternative sources of financing.

    E.   Net Credit Position

        1.   The relationship between a firm's level of accounts receivable and its accounts payable determines its net credit position.

        2.   If the firm's average receivables exceed average payables, it is a net provider of credit. If payables exceed receivables, the firm is a net user of trade credit.

II. **Bank Credit**

    A.   Banks prefer short-term, self-liquidating loans

Perspective 8-1: Before going into the technical aspects of banking, the instructor may wish to enliven the discussion by talking about changes going on in the banking and savings and loan industry. Deregulation has caused increased competition between all financial institutions (and with some non-financial institutions as well).

B.   Bank loan terms and concepts

    1.   Prime rate: The interest rate charged the most credit-worthy borrowers

        a.   The prime rate serves as a base in determining the interest rate for various risk classes of borrowers.

        b.   The prime rate of New York banks receives much attention from government officials in managing the economy.

        c.   The prime rate has been more volatile in the last couple of decades than in previous decades.

PPT 8-1   Movement of the Prime Rate and the London Interbank Offer Rate (LIBOR) on US dollar deposits (Figure 8-1)

---

        d.   The London Interbank Offer Rate (LIBOR) on U.S. dollar deposits is being used worldwide as a base lending rate on dollar loans.

    2.   Compensating Balances

        a.   As a loan condition, a borrower may be required to maintain an average minimum account balance in the bank equal to a percentage of loans outstanding or a percentage of future commitments and/or pay a fee for services.

        b.   Compensating balances raise the cost of a loan and compensate the bank for its services.

        c.   If a compensating balance is required, the borrower must borrow more than the amount needed.

    3.   Maturity Provisions

        a.   Most bank loans are short-term and mature within a year.

        b.   In the last decade more banks have extended intermediate-term loans (one to seven years) that are paid in installments.

    4.   Costs of Commercial Bank Financing

        a.   The effective interest rate depends on the loan amount, interest paid, length of the loan, and method of repayment.

C.   Annual Percentage Rate

     1.   The Truth in Lending Act enacted by Congress in 1968 requires that the annual percentage rate (APR) be given to the borrower. The thrust of the legislation was to protect unwary individuals from paying more than the stated rate without his or her knowledge.

     2.   The APR requires the use of the actuarial method of compounded interest and corresponds to the effective rate used throughout the text.

D.   Bank Credit Availability Tends to Cycle

     1.   Credit crunches seem to appear every 3-5 years.

     2.   The pattern of the credit crunch has been as follows:

          a.   The Federal Reserve tightens the money supply to fight inflation.

          b.   Lendable funds shrink, interest rates rise.

          c.   Business loan demand increases due to price-inflated inventories and receivables.

          d.   Depositors withdraw savings from banks seeking higher return elsewhere, further reducing bank credit availability.

          e.   In the early 1990s, the U.S. saw a different kind of credit crunch from too many bad loans. The supply of funds dwindled and caused record bankruptcies for bank and savings and loans.

III.   Commercial Paper

A.   Short-term, unsecured promissory notes issued to the public in minimum units of $25,000.

B.   Issuers

     1.   Finance companies such as General Motors Acceptance Corporation (GMAC) that issue paper directly. Such issued are referred to as finance paper or direct paper.

     2.   Industrial or utility firms that issue paper indirectly through dealer. This type of issue is called dealer paper.

C. There has been very rapid growth in the commercial paper market in the last few decades.

PPT 8-2	Total Commercial Paper Outstanding (Figure 8-2)

D. Traditionally, commercial paper has been a paper certificate issued to the lender to signify the lender's claim to be repaid. There is a growing trend among companies that sell and buy commercial paper to handle the transaction electronically. Actual paper certificates are not created. Documentation of the transactions is provided by computerized book-entry transactions and transfers of money are accomplished by wiring cash between lenders and commercial paper issuers.

E. Advantages

    1. Commercial paper may be issued at below the prime rate at commercial banks.
    2. No compensating balances are required, though lines of credit are necessary.
    3. Prestige.

F. The primary limitation is the possibility that the commercial paper market might "dry up" unexpectedly as it does whenever an investment grade company has its credit rating lowered by Standard & Poor's, Moody's or Fitch.

PPT 8-3	Comparison of Commercial Paper Rate to Bank Prime Rate (Table 8-1)

IV. **Foreign Borrowing**

A. Loans from foreign banks are an increasing source of funds for U.S. firms.

B. Foreign loans denominated in U.S. dollars are called Euro-dollar loans. These loans are usually short to intermediate term in maturity.

C. A possibly cheaper alternative to borrowing Euro-dollars is the borrowing of foreign currencies which are converted to dollars and forwarded to the U.S. parent company.

V. The Use of Collateral in Short-Term Financing

A. The lending institution may require collateral to be pledged when granting a loan.

B. Lenders lend on the basis of the cash-flow capacity of the borrower. Collateral is an additional but secondary consideration.

Finance in Action: Liquid Assets as Collateral–Pubmaster Securitizes Liquid Assets

This article discusses how Pubmaster, a UK pub company, created an asset backed lending policy in which it buys and sells large pub companies to fit its portfolio.

C. Accounts Receivable Financing

    1. Pledging accounts receivable as collateral

        a. Convenient means of financing. Receivables levels are rising as the need for financing is increasing.

        b. May be relatively expensive and preclude use of alternative financing sources.

        c. Lender screens accounts and loans a percentage (60% - 80%) of the acceptable amount.

        d. Lender has full recourse against borrower.

        e. The interest rate, which is usually well in excess of the prime rate, is based on the frequently changing loan balance outstanding.

    2. Factoring Receivables

        a. Receivables are sold, usually without recourse, to a factoring firm.

        b. A factor provides a credit-screening function by accepting or rejecting accounts.

        c. Factoring costs.
            1) Commission of 1% - 3% of factored invoices
            2) Interest on advances

    3. Asset-backed public offerings

        a. Public offerings of securities backed by receivables as collateral is a recently employed means of short-term financing.

        b. Several problems must be resolved:
            1) Image: Historically, firms that sold receivables were

considered to be in financial trouble.
2) Computer upgrading to service securities.
3) Regulatory roadblocks limiting bank participation.

VI. Inventory Financing

A. The collateral value of inventory is based on several factors.

    1. Marketability

        a. Raw materials and finished goods are more marketable than goods-in-process inventories.

        b. Standardized products or widely traded commodities qualify for higher percentage loans.

    2. Price Stability
    3. Perishability
    4. Physical Control

        a. Blanket inventory liens: Lender has general claim against inventory of borrower. No physical control.

        b. Trust receipts: Also known as floor planning; the borrower holds specifically identified inventory and proceeds from sale in trust for the lender.

        c. Warehousing: Goods are physically identified, segregated, and stored under the director of an independent warehousing company. Inventory is released from warehouse openly upon presentation of warehouse receipt controlled by the lender.

            1) Public warehouse -- facility on the premises of the warehousing firm.

            2) Field warehouse -- independently controlled facility on the premises of borrower.

B. Inventory financing and the associated control methods are standard procedures in many industries.

VII. Hedging to Reduce Borrowing Risk

A. Firms that continually borrow to finance operations are exposed to the risk of interest rate changes.

B.   Hedging activities in the financial futures market reduces the risk of interest rate changes.

> *Perspective 8-3:* ***Hedging and the use of derivative products is one of the hottest topics in finance. Although at this point the student may lack the background to appreciate an in depth discussion, the general concept of hedging can be explained through the use of the example in the text.***

Finance in Action: Hedging Activities of British Petroleum

The mathematics and mechanics of hedging are beyond the scope of this book, yet this example illustrates how important derivative financial instruments are to international companies. While this box is more complex than some professors may wish, it can be skipped without concern. On the other hand, it allows those who choose so to discuss real life situations such as Barings Bank, Orange County, Bankers Trust and other examples of hedging gone wrong. The British Petroleum example is one that makes sense and works well.

Summary Listing of Transparencies

Solution Transparencies to Chapter Problems

Other Supplements to Chapter

Cases for Use with Foundations of Financial Management, Pierce Control System (bank financing)

Cases for Use with Foundations of Financial Management, Modern Kitchenware Co. (cash discount)

Time Value of Money

Author's Overview

This is one of the most important chapters in the book as far as student comprehension is concerned. The instructor should first determine how much prior knowledge of time value of money the students have acquired from accounting or lower mathematics. While most students are generally familiar with the concepts of future value and present value, they often lack the ability to identify and categorize the nature of the problem before them.

The material in this chapter will serve as a springboard to the remaining chapters in this section on valuation, cost of capital and capital budgeting related topics. A good background in time value of money will ease the transition. The authors suggest a liberal use of homework problems and a quiz to reinforce the importance of this material.

This chapter has in-text acetate overlays that should be particularly helpful to students in understanding concepts. We feel these overlays are very good at relating future value to present value, present value to the present value of annuities, and future value to future value of annuities.

Chapter Concepts

* Money has a time value associated with it and therefore a dollar received today is worth more than a dollar received in the future.

* The future value and present value of a dollar is based on the number of periods involved and the going interest rate.

* Tables for future value and present value can be applied to any problem to ease the analysis.

* Not only can future value and present value be computed, but other factors such as yield (rate of return) can be determined as well.

Annotated Outline and Strategy

I. **Money has a time value associated with it.**

    A.   The investor/lender demands that financial rent be paid on his or her funds.

    B.   Understanding the effective rate on a business loan, the return on an investment, etc., is dependent on using the time value of money.

II. **Future Value -- Single Amount**

    A.   In determining future value, we measure the value of an amount that is allowed to grow at a give interest rate over a period of time.

$$FV = PV(1+i)^n$$

    B.   The relationship may be expressed by the following formula:

$$FV = PV \times FV_{IF}$$

    C.   The formula may be restated as:

           The FV_{IF} term is found in Table 9-1 (Also Appendix A)

PPT 9-1	Future Value of $1 (Table 9-1)

> *Perspective 9-1: The instructor should direct the student to Table 9-1 (excerpted from Appendix A at the back of the text). One or two numerical examples of using the tables are helpful at this point. The instructor may also wish to make mention of the foldover time value card that is inserted in the text.*

III. **Present Value -- Single Amount**

    A.   The present value of a future sum is the amount invested today, at a given interest rate, that will equal the future sum at a specified point in time.

Perspective 9-2: The instructor may wish to use Figure 9-1 to demonstrate the relationship between present and future value.

B.   The relationship may be expressed in the following formula:

$$PV = FV \frac{1}{(1+i)^n}$$

C.   The formula may be restated as:

$$PV = FV \times PV_{IF}$$

The PV_{IF} term is found in Table 9-2 (Also Appendix B)

PPT 9-3   Present Value of $1 (Table 9-2)

IV.   **Future Value -- Annuity**

   A.   An annuity represents consecutive payments or receipts of equal amount.

   B.   The annuity value is normally assumed to take place at the end of the period.

   C.   The future value of an annuity represents the sum of the future value of the individual flows.

PPT 9-4   Compounding Process for Annuity (Figure 9-2)

   D.   The formula for the future value for an annuity is:

$$FV_A = A \times FV_{IFA} \quad \text{(Proof is in Footnote 1)}$$

The FV_{IFA} term is found in Table 9-3 (Also Appendix C)

PPT 9-5	Future Value of an Annuity of $1 (Table 9-3)

**Finance in Action: Starting Salaries 50 Years From Now –
Will $248,745 Be Enough?**

The rate of inflation will determine the acceptable levels of salary in the future. Although inflation did increase in the US to double digits, 3-4% is the historical average. This box demonstrates a real world example of how money compounds.

V.　　**Present Value -- Annuity**

　　A.　　The present value of an annuity represents the sum of the present value of the individual flows.

　　B.　　The formula for the present value of an annuity is:

$$PV_A = A \times PV_{IFA} \qquad \text{(Proof is in Footnote 2)}$$

　　　　The PV_{IFA} term is found in Table 9-4

PPT 9-6	Present Value of an Annuity of $1 (Table 9-4)

VI.　　**Graphical Presentation of Time Value Relationships**

　　A.　　Use Exhibits 9-1 and 9-2 to show that present value and future value are opposite sides of the page.

　　B.　　Use Exhibits 9-3 and 9-4 to demonstrate how annuities are the sums of single period values.

VII.　　**Annuity Equaling a Future Value**

68

A.   The process can be reversed to find an annuity value that will grow to equal a future sum.

B.   The terms in the formula for the future value of an annuity are transformed to find A.

$$FV_A = A \times FV_{IFA}$$

$$A = \frac{FV_A}{FV_{IFA}}$$

The FV_{IFA} term is found in Table 9-3

VIII.   Annuity Equality a Present Value

A.   The terms in the formula for the present value of an annuity are transformed to find A.

$$PV_A = A \times PV_{IFA}$$

$$A = \frac{PV_A}{PV_{IFA}}$$

The PV_{IFA} term is found in Table 9-4.

B.   The annuity value equal to a present value is often associated with withdrawal of funds from an initial deposit or the repayment of a loan.

PPT 9-7	Relationship of Present Value to Annuity (Table 9-5)

Perspective 9-3: This can be a good point to demonstrate how annuities work in everyday situations. The withdrawal example and payoff table are shown in Tables 9-5 and 9-6, respectively.

PPT 9-8	Payoff Table for Loan (amortization table) (Table 9-6)

69

IX. Determining the Yield on an Investment

PPT 9-9	Review of Formulas (1st six)

> **Perspective 9-4:** *Six different formulas have been presented so far. This is a good point in the discussion to review them. After this has been accomplished, the instructor can feel more comfortable in presenting additional material.*

A. The unknown value is now assumed to be the yield.

    1. Yield -- Present value of a single amount

        a. The rate equating FV to PV must be found.

$$PV_{IF} = \frac{PV}{PV_{IF}}$$

        b. The first step is to determine PV_{IF}.

        c. The next step is to find this value in Table 9-2 so the yield may be identified.

        d. Interpolation may be used to find a more exacting answer.

    2. Yield -- Present value of an annuity

        a. The rate equating A to PV must be found.

$$PV_{IFA} = \frac{PV_A}{A}$$

        b. The first step is to determine PV_{IFA}.

        c. The next step is to find this value in Table 9-4 so the yield may be identified.

        d. Interpolation may be used to find a more exacting answer.

X.   **Special considerations in Time Value Analysis**

    A.   Semi-annual, quarterly, monthly, etc compounding.

    B.   Present value of deferred annuity.

        1.   Two step solution process

PPT 9-10	Present Value of Deferred Annuity -- Two Step Process

        2.   Single step solution

$$PV_{IFA} \text{ for total period}$$
$$\underline{- \; PV_{IFA} \text{ for initial period}}$$
$$PV_{IFA} \text{ for deferred period} \times \text{annuity}$$

Summary Listing of Transparencies

PPT 9-1   Future Value of $1 (Table 9-1)

PPT 9-2   Relationship of Present Value and Future Value (Figure 9-1)

PPT 9-3   Present Value of $1 (Table 9-2)

PPT 9-4   Compounding Process for Annuity (Figure 9-2)

PPT 9-5   Future Value of an Annuity of $1 (Table 9-3)

PPT 9-6   None

PPT 9-7   Relationship of Present Value to Annuity (Table 9-5)

PPT 9-8   Payoff Table for Loan (amortization table) (Table 9-6)

PPT 9-9   Review of Formulas (1st six)

PPT 9-10   Present Value of Deferred Annuity

LT 9-1   Chapter 9 Outline

LT 9-2   Time Value of Money

LT 9-3   Future Value and Present Value

LT 9-4   Annuity

LT 9-5   2 Questions to Ask in Time Value of Money Problems

LT 9-6   Adjusting for Non-Annual Compounding

Solution Transparencies to Chapter Problems

ST 9-1   Present Value

ST 9-3   Present Value

ST 9-5   Future Value

ST 9-7   Present Value

ST 9-9   Present Value

ST 9-11   Future Value

ST 9-13   Present Value

ST 9-15   Compounding Quarterly

ST 9-17   Annuity Due

ST 9-19   Payments Required

ST 9-21   Yield with Interpolation

ST 9-23   Yield with Interpolation

ST 9-25   Solving for an Annuity

ST 9-27   Deferred Annuity

ST 9-29   Loan Repayment

ST 9-31   Annuity Consideration

ST 9-33   Annuity Consideration

ST 9-34   Special Considerations of Annuities and Time Periods

Other Supplements to Chapter

<u>Cases for Use With Foundations of Financial Management</u>, Allison Boone, M.D. (time value of money), and Billy Wilson, All American (time value of money)

Valuation and Rates of Return

Author's Overview

The student can clearly see that the material covered in the previous chapter on time value of money is now being applied. The recurring theme throughout the chapter is that valuation is based on the present value of benefits to be received in the future. The instructor should establish this point at the outset and then repeatedly demonstrate it in the evaluation of bonds, preferred stock, and common stock. The instructor should also emphasize the relationship of the discount rate in present value analysis to the required rate of return demanded by security holders. The authors suggest that the instructor go through the process of defining the investor's required return in terms of a real rate of return, an inflation premium, and a risk premium. The instructor can then vary one of these components and show the impact on overall required return and valuation.

Chapter Concepts

*   The valuation of a financial asset is based on the present value of future cash flows

*   The required rate of return in valuing an asset is based on the risk involved

*   Bond valuation is based on the process of determining the present value of interest payments plus the principal payment at maturity

*   Stock valuation is based on determining the present value of the future benefits of equity ownership

*   A price-earnings ratio may also be applied to a firm's earnings to determine value

Annotated Outline and Strategy

> PPT 10-1 Relationship between Time Value of Money, Required Return, Cost of Financing, and Investment Decisions (Figure 10-1)

I. Valuation Concepts

A. The value of an asset is the present value of the expected cash flows associated with the asset. In order to compute the present value of an asset, an investor must know or estimate the amount of expected cash flows, the timing of expected cash flows and the risk characteristics of the expected flows.

B. Actually, the price (present value) of an asset will be based on the collective assessment of the asset's cash flow characteristics by the many capital market participants.

II. Valuation of Bonds

A. The value of a bond is derived from cash flows composed of periodic interest payments and a principal payment at maturity.

$$P_b = \sum_{t=1}^{n} \frac{I_t}{(1+Y)^t} + \frac{P_n}{(1+Y)^n}$$

B. The present value (price) of a bond can be expressed as follows: where:

P_b	=	the market price of the bond
I_t	=	the periodic interest payments
P_n	=	the principal payment at maturity
t	=	the period from 1 to n
n	=	the total number of periods
Y	=	the yield to maturity (required rate of return)

C. The present value tables may be used to compute the price of a bond. The stream of periodic interest payments constitutes an annuity. The present value of the stream of interest payments may be computed by multiplying the periodic interest payment by the present value of an annuity interest factor.

$$PV_A = A \times PV_{IFA}$$

The present value of the principal payment may be computed by applying the present value of a $1 formula.

$$PV = FV \times PV_{IF}$$

The present value (price) of the bond will be the sum of the present value of the interest payments plus the present value of the principal.

D.   Yield to maturity

     1.   Three factors influence an investor's required rate of return on a bond.

          a.   The required real rate of return-the rate of return demanded for giving up current use of funds on a non-inflation adjusted basis.

          b.   An inflation premium-a premium to compensate the investor for the effect of inflation on the value of the dollar.

          c.   Risk premium-all financial decisions are made within a risk-return framework. An astute investor will require compensation for risk exposure. There are two types of risk of primary interest in determining the required rate of return (yield to maturity) on a bond:

               (1)   Business risk-the possibility of a firm not being able to sustain its competitive position and growth in earnings.

               (2)   Financial risk-the possibility that a firm will be unable to meet its debt obligations as they come due.

     2.   Bond prices are inversely related to required rates of return. A change in the required rate of return will cause a change in the bond price in the opposite direction. The impact of the change in required rate of return on the bond price is dependent upon the remaining time to maturity. The impact will be greater the longer the time to maturity.

PPT 10-2	Bond Price Table (Table 10-1)

Perspective 10-1: Table 10-1 illustrates the impact of differences between yield to maturity and coupon rates on bond prices. Bond prices go from as high as $2,308.10 to as low as $407.40. Table 10-2 shows the critical effect of time to maturity on bond price sensitivity, and is further supported by Figure 10-2.

Perspective 10-2: This table shows the critical effect of time to maturity on bond price sensitivity.

PPT 10-4   Relationship Between Time to Maturity and Bond Price (Figure 10-2)

Perspective 10-3: The critical effect of time to maturity on bond price sensitivity is further supported by this figure.

E.   Determining yield to maturity

     1.   If the bond price, coupon rate, and number of years to maturity are known, the yield to maturity (market determined required rate of return) can be computed.

        a.   Trial and error process. This process requires one to "guess" various yields until the yield to maturity that will cause the present value of the stream of interest payments plus the present value of principal payment to equal the bond price is determined. The initial "guess" is not completely blind, however, since the relationship between the coupon rate, yield to maturity (market rate), and the bond price is known.

        b.   Often, a less exact calculation of the yield to maturity is sufficient. Using the approximate yield to maturity approach:

$$\text{Approximate Yield to Maturity} = \frac{\text{Annual interst payment} + \dfrac{\text{Principal payment} - \text{Price of the bond}}{\text{Number of years to maturity}}}{.6\,(\text{Price of the bond}) + .4\,(\text{Principal payment})}$$

c.   An exact calculation of the yield to maturity can be made using a good calculator or computer software.

Perspective 10-4: Some instructors may choose to make specific references to Appendix E at the back of the text which covers the use of the Texas Instruments BA-35 and HP 12C calculators to compute yield to maturity and other values.

F.   Often interest payments are made more frequently than once a year. Semiannual interest payments are common. To compute the price of such a bond, we divide the annual amount of interest and yield to maturity by two and multiply the number of years to maturity by two.

Perspective 10-5: Although the initial presentation in the chapter is based on annual payments, the instructor should probably cover the section on semiannual payments as well. Students have the opportunity to use both approaches in working problems at the back of the chapter.

III. Valuation of Preferred Stock

A. Preferred stock is usually valued as a perpetual stream of fixed dividend payments.

$$P_p = \frac{D_p}{(1+K_p)^1} + \frac{D_p}{(1+K_p)^2} + \frac{D_p}{(1+K_p)^3} + ... + \frac{D_p}{(1+K)^n}$$

where:

P_p = the price of preferred stock
D_p = the annual dividend for preferred stock
K_p = the required rate of return (discount rate) applied to preferred stock dividends

B. Since the dividend stream is a perpetuity, the preferred stock valuation formula can be reduced to a more usable form

$$P_p = \frac{D_p}{K_p}$$

C. If K_p changes after preferred stock is issued, P_p will change in an inverse fashion.

1. Since preferred stock theoretically has a perpetual life, it is highly sensitive to changes in the required rate of return (K_p).

D. If the market price of preferred stock and the annual dividend are known, the market determined required rate of return may be computed by using the valuation equation and solving for K_p.

$$P_p = \frac{D_p}{K_p}$$

$$K_p = \frac{D_p}{P_p}$$

IV.   Valuation of Common Stock

A.   The value of a share of common stock is the present value of an expected stream of

$$P_0 = \frac{D_1}{(1+K_e)} + \frac{D_2}{(1+K_e)^2} + \frac{D_3}{(1+K_e)^3} + \ldots + \frac{D_n}{(1+K_e)^n}$$

dividends.

where:

P_0 = price of the stock at time zero (today)
D = dividend for each year
K_e = the required rate of return for common stock

B.   Unlike dividends on most preferred stock, common stock dividends may vary. The valuation formula may be applied, with modification, to three different circumstances: no growth in dividends, constant growth in dividends, and variable growth in dividends.

1.   No growth in dividends. Common stock with constant (no growth) dividends

$$P_0 = \frac{D_0}{K_e}$$

is valued in the same manner as preferred stock.

where:

P_0 = price of common stock
D_0 = current annual dividend on common stock = D_1
(expected to remain the same in the future)
K_e = required rate of return for common stock

2.   Constant growth in dividends. The price of common stock with constant growth in dividends is the present value of an infinite stream of growing dividends. Fortunately, in this circumstance the basic valuation equation can be reduced to the more usable form below if the discount rate (K_e) is assumed to be greater than the growth rate.

80

$$P_o = \frac{D_1}{(K_e - g)}$$

where:

D_1	=	dividend expected at the end of the first
year	=	$D_o (1+g)$
g	=	constant growth rate in dividends
P_o, K_e	=	same as previously defined

a. The above formula, which is labeled 10-9 in the text, can also be thought to represent the present value of dividends for a period of time (such as n = 3) plus the present value of the stock price after a period of time (such as P_3). Since P_3 represents the present value of dividends from D_4 through D , P_o will still represent the present value of all future dividends.

Perspective 10-6: *The authors use problem 27 at the back of the chapter to illustrate the equality described above. Of course, it is up to the instructor to decide if he or she wished to go into this much detail.*

---

b. The value of P_o is quite sensitive to any change in K_e (required rate of return) and g (the growth rate).

c. Rearrangement of the constant growth equation allows the calculation of the required rate of return, K_e, when P_o, D_1, and g are given. The first term represents the dividend yield that the stockholder expects to receive and the second term represents the anticipated growth in dividends, earnings and stock price.

3. Variable growth in dividends. The most likely variable growth case is one of

$$K_e = \frac{D_1}{P_o} + g$$

supernormal growth followed by constant growth.

a. Value can be found through taking the present value of the dividends during the supernormal growth period plus the price of the stock at end of the supernormal growth period. Since growth is then constant,

Formula 10-9 can be used.

b. Another type of variable growth is where the firm is assumed to pay no dividends for a period of time and then begins paying dividends. In this case, the present value of deferred dividends can be computed as a representation of value.

c. If no dividends are ever intended, then valuation may rest solely on the present value of future earnings and the present value of a future stock price.

4. Stock valuation may also be linked to the concept of price-earnings ratios discussed in Chapter 2. Although this is a less theoretical, more pragmatic approach than the dividend valuation models, the end results may be similar because of the common emphasis on risk and growth under either approach.

Perspective 10-7: *This table illustrates how P/E ratios are shown in the financial press. Nabisco can be used as an example, and dividend yield and price changes can also be mentioned to stimulate interest.*

Perspective 10-8: *The use of the appendix is optional.*

Finance in Action: Valuation of High Technology Companies–Throw Away the Book

This box discusses how newer measures of valuation are replacing more traditional measures when it comes to high technology, Internet-related companies.

**Finance in Action: An Important Question –
What's a Small Business Really Worth?**

This box presents some of the practical issues faced in valuing a small business and serves as a contrast to the formulas presented in the text.

PPT 10-5 Stock Valuation Under Supernormal Analysis

Summary Listing of Transparencies

PPT 10-1   Relationship between Time Value of Money, Required Return, Cost of Financing, and Investment Decisions (Figure 10-1)
PPT 10-2   Bond Price Table (Table 10-1)
PPT 10-3   Impact of Time to Maturity on Bond Prices (Table 10-2)
PPT 10-4   Relationship Between Time to Maturity and Bond Price (Figure 10-2)
PPT 10-5   Stock Valuation Under Supernormal Growth Analysis (Figure 10B-1)
LT 10-1   Chapter 10 Outline
LT 10-2   Valuation of Bonds
LT 10-3   3 Factors that Influence the Required Rate of Return
LT 10-4   Relationship Between Bond Prices and Yields
LT 10-5   Preferred Stock
LT 10-6   Valuation of Common Stock
LT 10-7   Valuation Using the Price-Earnings Ratio
LT 10-8   High vs. Low P/Es

Solution Transparencies to Chapter Problems

ST 10-1   Burns Fire and Casualty Company
ST 10-3   Kilgore Natural Gas
ST 10-4   Kilgore Natural Gas (Continued)
ST 10-5   Effect of Maturity on Bond Price
ST 10-7   Westlake Drilling Company
ST 10-8   Further Analysis of Problem
ST 10-9   Bo Boatler – Quantum Corp.
ST 10-11   West Motel Chain
ST 10-13   Robert Brown III – Southwest Technology
ST 10-14   Holtz Corporation
ST 10-15   Ultra Corp.
ST 10-17   Venus Sportswear Corporation
ST 10-19   BioScience Inc.
ST 10-21   Maxwell Communications
ST 10-23   Common Stock Required Rate of Return
ST 10-25   Cellular Systems
ST 10A-1   Medford Corporation
ST 10B-1   Surgical Supplies Corporation

Other Supplements to Chapter

Cases for use with Foundations of Financial Management, Gilbert Enterprises (stock valuation)

Cost of Capital

Author's Overview

Chapter 11 on "Cost of Capital" naturally follows Chapter 10 on "Valuation and Rates of Return." The instructor should emphasize, at the outset, that the investors' required rate of return translates into the cost of financing for the firm. There should be a dual emphasis on properly determining the aftertax cost for each type of financing and on determining the appropriate weights to be assigned to the various sources of financing.

The cost of debt and the cost of preferred stock are reasonably straightforward, but additional guidance is required in determining the cost of common equity. The instructor should indicate the firm's ability to acquire equity capital through retained earnings or through new common stock and the associated cost of each. The cost of retained earnings should be explained as an opportunity cost for the use of the stockholders' funds. For that reason, it is assumed the stockholders can earn as much on these funds, if distributed, as they are currently earning in the firm. Thus, the cost of retained earnings is also equal to K_e (the firm's return on common equity).

After the various costs are computed, the instructor can direct more attention to the weighing scheme given to the components in the capital structure. The instructor may wish to refer to the authors' example in which the increased use of debt initially decreases the cost of capital, but then ultimately increases it. The interdependent nature (of costs and weights) should be stressed in discussing the optimal capital structure. An extensive discussion of the historical and present nature of Capital Structure Theory and Modiglioni and Miller is presented in Appendix 11B.

The instructor has the option of introducing the student to the capital asset pricing model in the text and more fully in Appendix 11A. There the concepts of regression analysis, the beta coefficient, and the security market line are introduced and related to previously discussed material on the cost of capital. This chapter as well as subsequent chapters is fully comprehensible without the use of this material. The appendix is available, however, for those instructors who wish to go over the capital asset pricing model in detail.

Chapter Concepts

* The cost of capital represents the overall cost of financing to the firm.

* The cost of capital is normally the discount rate to use in analyzing an investment.

* The cost of capital is based on the valuation techniques from the previous chapter and is applied to bonds, preferred stock and common stock.

* A firm attempts to find a minimum cost of capital through varying the mix of its sources of financing.

* The cost of capital may eventually increase as larger amounts of financing are utilized.

Annotated Outline and Strategy

I. **The Overall Concept**

   A. A business firm must strive to earn at least as much as the cost of the funds that it uses.

   B. Usually a firm has several sources of funds and each source may have a different cost.

   C. The overall cost of the funds employed is a proportionate average of the various sources.

   D. The firm's required rate of return that will satisfy all suppliers of capital is called its cost of capital.

   E. There are several steps in measuring a firm's cost of capital.

      1. Compute the cost of each source of capital.
      2. Assign weights to each source.
      3. Compute the weighted average of the component costs.

II.   The Cost of Debt

A.   The basic cost of debt to the firm is the effective yield to maturity. The yield to maturity is a market determined rate and can be found by examining the relationships of security price, periodic interest payments, maturity value, and length of time to maturity. The yield to maturity for a corporate bond may be found by solving for Y' in

$$Y' = \frac{I_t + \dfrac{P_n - P_b}{n}}{0.6\,(P_b) + 0.4\,(P_n)}$$

the following equation:
Where:

Y'=   the approximate yield to maturity
P_b=   the market price of the bond
I_t =   the periodic interest payments
P_n=   the principal at maturity
t =   the period from 1 to n
n =   the total number of periods

B.   Since interest is tax deductible, the actual cost of debt to the firm is less than the yield to maturity.

$$K_d = .10\,(1 - .34) = .066$$

C.   The aftertax cost of debt is:
The aftertax cost to a firm of bonds issued at par paying $100 annually in interest would be 6.6 percent if the firm's marginal tax rate were 34 percent.

D.   The example of New Jersey Bell Telephone in Table 11-2 presents the opportunity for the professor to expose the students to the information found in the Standard & Poor's Bond Guide.

III. The Cost of Preferred Stock

A. Preferred stock is similar to debt in that the preferred dividend is fixed but dissimilar in that dividends are not tax deductible.

B. The cost of preferred stock to a firm may be determined by examining the relationship of its annual (usually fixed) dividend and its market determined price. Preferred stock, unlike debt, has no maturity and therefore the dividends are expected to be perpetual.

C. The cost of preferred stock K_p is computed by dividing the annual dividend payment by the net proceeds received by the firm in the sale of preferred stock.

$$K_p = \frac{D}{(P-F)}$$

where: K_p = cost of preferred stock
D = preferred stock dividend
F = flotation costs per share
P = market price of preferred stock

IV. The Cost of Common Equity

A. The basis of computation of the price of common stock is the Dividend Valuation Model.

$$P_o = \frac{D_1}{(K_e - g)}$$

B. Assuming constant growth, the Dividend Valuation Model can be reduced to:

$$K_e = \frac{D_1}{P_o} + g$$

and then solved for the required rate of return K_e,

87

Where:

K_e = required rate of return
D_1 = expected dividend in first year
P_0 = price per share of stock
g = constant growth rate in dividends

C.   The equation for common stock cost is composed of two parts, the dividend yield, D_1/P_0 plus the anticipated growth rate, g, of dividends.

D.   Alternative Calculation of the Required Return on Common Stock - using the Capital Asset Pricing Model (CAPM).

  1.   Under the CAPM, the required return for common stock can be described by

$$K_j = R_f + \beta (K_m - R_f)$$

  the following formula:

Where:

K_j =   Required Return on Common Stock
R_f =   Risk-free rate of return; usually the current rate on Treasury bill securities
β =   Beta coefficient. The beta measures the historical volatility of an individual stock's return relative to a stock market index. A beta greater than 1 indicates greater volatility (price movements) than the market, while the reverse would be true for a beta less than 1.
K_m =   Return in the market as measured by an appropriate index

  2.   Both K_j and K_e should be equal under the case of market equilibrium.
  3.   Appendix 11A presents the capital asset pricing model in more detail for those who wish to expand the textbook coverage on this concept.

E.   Common stock financing is available through the retention of earnings belonging to present stockholders or by issuing new common stock.

1. The cost of retained earnings is equivalent to the rate of return on the firm's common stock. This is the opportunity cost. Thus the cost of common equity in the form of retained earnings is:

$$K_e = \frac{D_1}{P_0} + g$$

2. The cost of new common stock is higher than the cost of retained earnings because the firm's proceeds from sale of the stock is less than the price paid by the stockholder due to flotation costs (F). The cost of new common stock, K_n is:

$$K_n = \frac{D_1}{(P_0 - F)} + g$$

V. Optimal Capital Structure - Weighing Costs

A. The firm should seek to minimize its cost of capital by employing the optimal mix of capital financing.

B. The Baker Corporation example on page 305 demonstrates the concept of weighted average cost of capital numerically while Figure 11-1 does so graphically.

PPT 11-2	Cost of Capital Curve (Figure 11-1)

C. Although debt is the cheapest source of capital, there are limits to the amount of debt capital that lenders will provide (recall the D/E relationships discussed in Chapter 3). The cost of both debt and equity financing rise as debt becomes a larger portion of the capital structure.

D. Traditional financial theory maintains that the weighted average cost of capital declines as lower costing debt is added to the capital structure. The optimum mix of debt and equity corresponds to the minimum point on the average cost of capital curve.

E.   The optimal debt-equity mix varies among industries. The more cyclical the business, the lower the D/E ratio is required to be.

PPT 11-3   Debt as a Percentage of Total Assets (Table 11-3)

F.   The weights applied in computing the weighted average cost should be market value weights.

VI.   **Capital Acquisition and Investment Decision Making**

A.   The discount rate used in evaluating capital projects should be the weighted average cost of capital.

B.   If the cost of capital is earned on all projects, the residual claimants of the earnings stream, the owners, will receive their required rate of return. If the overall return of the firm is less than the cost of capital, the owners will receive less than their desired rate of return because providers of debt capital must be paid.

C.   For most firms, the cost of capital is fairly constant within a reasonable range of debt-equity mixes (flat portion of curve in Figure 11-2). Changes in money and capital market conditions (supply and demand for money), however, cause the cost of capital for all firms to vary upward and downward over time.

Perspective 11-2: This is a good time to discuss the impact of economic cycles on the cost of capital. Often when interest rates are low, the economy is not expanding rapidly and capital needs are not crucial. Recognizing that costs of capital shift from time to time over the business cycle is important in pointing out that companies raise capital in an uneven fashion, often raising capital before it is all needed in anticipation of rising costs.

PPT 11-4   Cost of Capital Over Time (Figure 11-2)

D.   Cost of Capital in the Capital Budgeting Decision

1.   It is the current cost of each source of funds that is important.
2.   The cost of each source of capital will vary with the amount of capital derived from that source.
3.   The required rate of return or discount rate for capital budgeting decisions will be the weighted average cost of capital.

PPT 11-5	Investment Projects Available to the Baker Corporation (Table 11-4)

PPT 11-6	Cost of Capital and Investment Projects for the Baker Corporation (Figure 11-3)

Finance In Action: EVA Breathes New Life into the Concept of Cost of Capital: Just Ask Eli Lilly & Co.

Using EVA or economic value added as a measure of corporate performance contributes a real world dimension to this chapter. The Stern Stewart & Co. has been providing EVA analysis to companies like Eli Lilly for several decades. While the intricacies of this concept are more fully covered in advanced courses, a small introduction to EVA will add value to the students' knowledge of what goes on in the corporate world of finance.

VII. Marginal Cost of Capital

A. The marginal cost of debt (the cost of the last amount of debt financing) will rise as more debt financing is used. The marginal cost of equity also rises when the shift from retained earnings to external (common stock) equity financing is necessary.

PPT 11-7	Cost of Capital for Different Amounts of Financing (Table 11-5) and Cost of Capital for Increasing Amounts of Financing (Table 11-6)

Perspective 11-3: The following series of transparencies provide the major presentation of the marginal cost of capital and its shifting costs as the amount of capital required increases. Comparing Figure 11-4 with Figure 11-3 graphically shows how an increased marginal cost of capital eliminates project E from the acceptable range.

PPT 11-9	Cost of Components in the Capital Structure (Table 11-7)

VIII. Appendix 11A: Cost of Capital and the Capital Asset Pricing Model

A.   The Capital Asset Pricing Model (CAPM) relates the risk-return tradeoffs of individual assets to market returns.

B.   The CAPM encompasses all types of assets but is most often applied to common stock.

C.   The basic form of the CAPM is a linear relationship between returns on individual stocks and the market over time. Using least squares regression analysis, the return on

$$K_j = \alpha + \beta \, K_m + e$$

an individual stock K_j is:

where: $K_j =$ Return on individual common stock of company
$\alpha \; =$ Alpha, the intercept on the y-axis
$\beta \; =$ Beta, the coefficient
$K_m =$ Return on the stock market (an index of stock returns is used, usually the Standard & Poor's 500 Index)
$e \; =$ Error term of the regression equation

PPT 11-11   Performance of PAI and the Market (Table 11A-1)

PPT 11-12   Linear Regression of Returns Between PAI and the Market (Figure 11A-1)

D.   Using historical data, the beta coefficient is computed. The beta coefficient is a measurement of the return performance of a given stock relative to the return performance of the market.

E.   The CAPM is an expectational model. There is no guarantee that historical data will be repeated.

F.   The CAPM evolved into a risk premium model.

1.   Investors expect higher returns if higher risks are taken.
2.   The minimum return expected by investors will never be less than can be obtained from a riskless asset (usually considered to be U.S. Treasury bills). The relationship is expressed as follows:

$$K_j = R_f + \beta (K_m - R_f)$$

where: R_f =Risk-free rate of return
       β =Beta coefficient from Formula 11A-1
       K_m =Return on the market index
       $K_m - R_f$ = Premium or excess return of the market versus the risk-free rate (since the market is riskier than R_f, the assumption is that the expected K_m will be greater than R_f)
       $\beta(K_m - R_f)$ =Expected return above the risk-free rate for the stock of Company j, given the level of risk

3.   Beta measures the sensitivity of an individual security's return relative to the market.

a.   By definition, the market beta = 1.
b.   A security with a beta = 1, is expected to have returns equal to and as volatile as the market. One with a beta of 2 is twice as volatile (up or down).

4. Beta measures the impact of an asset on an individual's portfolio of assets.

G.   A risk-return graph can be derived from the risk premium model. The graphed relationship between risk (measured by beta) and required rates of return is called the Security Market Line (SML).

PPT 11-13   The security market line (SML) (Figure 11A-2)

H.   Cost of capital considerations

93

1. If required returns rise, prices of securities fall to adjust to the new equilibrium return level and as required returns fall, prices rise.
2. A change in required rates of return is represented by a shift in the SML.

PPT 11-14	The Security Market Line and Changing Interest Rates (Figure 11A-3)

a. The new SML will be parallel to the previous one if investors attempt to maintain the same risk premium over the risk-free rate.
b. If investors attempt to maintain purchasing power in an inflationary economy, the slope of the new SML may be greater than before due to an inflation premium.
c. An investor's required rate of return and thus a firm's cost of capital will also change if investors risk preferences change. The slope of the SML would change even if the risk-free rate remained the same.

PPT 11-15	The Security Market Line and Changing Investor Expectations (Figure 11A-4)

Summary Listing of Transparencies

Solution Transparencies to Chapter Problems

Other Supplements to Chapter

Cases for Use With Foundations of Financial Management, Berkshire Instruments, (Cost of Capital)

The Capital Budgeting Decision

Author's Overview

While early comments on administrative procedures and accounting considerations are helpful, the major thrust of Chapter 12 is on the various methods for ranking investment proposals.
The basic selection methods are established, mutually exclusive versus non-mutually exclusive events are compared, the reinvestment assumption, capital rationing and the net present value profile are presented.

The Chapter continues with a comprehensive discussion of procedures for depreciation write-off and integrates the resultant cash flow determination with the capital budgeting decision. There is also a presentation of a replacement decision which examines the process of selling an old piece of equipment and replacing it with a new version. The tax consequences of replacement are carefully examined and included in the example presented.

Chapter Concepts

* A capital budgeting decision represents a long-term investment decision.

* Cash flow rather than earnings is used in the capital budgeting decision.

* The three methods of ranking investments are the payback method, the internal rate of return, and the net present value.

* The discount or cut-off rate is normally the cost of capital.

* The two primary cash inflows analyzed in a capital budgeting decision are the aftertax operating benefits and the tax shield benefits of depreciation.

Annotated Outline and Strategy

I. **Characteristics of Capital Budgeting Decisions**

    A. Capital expenditures are outlays for projects with lives extending beyond one year and perhaps for many years.

    B. Intensive planning is required.

    C. Capital expenditures usually require initial cash flows, often large, with the expectation of future cash inflows. The differing time periods of inflows and outflows require present-value analysis.

    D. The longer the time horizon associated with a capital expenditure, the greater the uncertainty. Areas of uncertainty are:

        1. Annual costs and inflows.
        2. Product life.
        3. Interest rates.
        4. Economic conditions.
        5. Technological change.

II. **Administrative Considerations**

> PPT 12-1   Capital budgeting procedures (Figure 12-1)

    A. Search and discovery of investment opportunities

    B. Collection of data

    C. Evaluation and decision making

    D. Reevaluation and adjustment

III. **Accounting Flows versus Cash Flows**

    A. The capital budgeting process focuses on cash flows rather than income. Income figures do not reflect the cash available to a firm due to the deduction of noncash expenditures such as depreciation.

B. Accounting flows are not totally disregarded in the capital budgeting process.

1. Investors' emphasis on earnings per share may, under certain conditions, require use of income rather than cash as the decision criterion.
2. Top management may elect to glean the short-term personal benefits of an income effect rather than the long-run cash-flow effects which are more beneficial, from the owner's viewpoint.

Finance In Action: Ford Leads the Way in Reinventing the Auto Industry

Ford is moving at a faster pace than its competitors when it comes to innovation related to the Internet in the auto industry. However, this creates challenges for auto dealers, and they will have to figure out a way to connect to Ford's "information highway."

IV. Methods for Ranking Investment Proposals

A. Payback Method

1. The payback period is the length of time necessary for the sum of the expected annual cash inflows to equal the cash investment. A cutoff period is established for comparison. Capital proposals with a payback in excess of the cutoff are rejected.

2. Deficiencies of the method

a. Inflows after the cutoff period are ignored.
b. The pattern of cash flows is ignored, therefore, time value of money is not considered.

3. Though not conceptually sound, the payback method is frequently used.

       a.   Easy to use

       b.   Emphasizes liquidity

       c.   Quick return is important to firms in industries characterized by rapid technological development.

PPT 12-3   Investment alternatives (Table 12-3) and Capital Budgeting Results (Table 12-4)

Perspective 12-1: *We adequately point out in the text that the net present value method and internal rate of return methods are theoretically superior to the payback method for ranking proposals. Nevertheless, it is worth discussing why companies still use payback as a decision tool. During periods of high inflation, a low payback on a project indicates a rapid return of funds for reinvestment at perhaps even higher inflated returns and many companies preferred this method over the superior IRR and NPV methods.*

B.   Internal Rate of Return (IRR)

      1.   The IRR method requires calculation of the rate that equates the cash investment with the cash inflows.

      2.   The calculation procedure is the same as the yield computation presented in Chapter 9.

            a.   If the inflows constitute an annuity, the IRR may be computed directly.

$$\frac{\text{Investment}}{\text{Annuity}} = IF_{pva}$$

                The IF may then be found in the present value of an annuity table and its correspondent interest rate (IRR).

            b.   If the cash inflows do not constitute an annuity, determination of IRR is a trial-and error process.

C.   Net Present Value (NPV)

    1.   In this method, the cash inflows are discounted at the firm's cost of capital or some variation of that measure.

    2.   If the present value of the cash inflows equals or exceeds the present value of the cash investment, the capital proposal is acceptable.

V.   Selection Strategy

A.   All non-mutually exclusive projects having a NPV>= 0
(which also means IRR >= cost of capital should be accepted under normal conditions.)

B.   The NPV method and the IRR method always agree on the accept-reject decision on a capital proposal.

C.   A disagreement may arise between the NPV and IRR methods when a choice must be made from mutually exclusive proposals or all acceptable proposals cannot be taken due to capital rationing.

    1.   The primary cause of disagreement is the differing reinvestment assumptions. The NPV method inherently assumes reinvestment of cash inflows at the cost of capital. The IRR method assumes reinvestment of cash inflows at the internal rate of return.

    2.   The more conservative net present-value technique is usually the recommended approach when a conflict in ranking arises.

PPT 12-4   The reinvestment assumption-net present value ($10,000 investment)
(Table 12-6)

Perspective 12-2: The reinvestment assumption is quite important in reality and one way of getting the point across would be to use an example from investments in certificates of deposits. For example as high yield CD's come due they are reinvested at lower returns and thus, the investor cannot earn the original rate of return on a continuous basis. Using the term structure of interest rates from Chapter six provides demonstration of how difficult it is to predict future reinvestment returns.

VI. Capital Rationing

A.   Management may implement capital rationing by artificially constraining the amount of investment expenditures.

```
┌────────────────────────────────────────────────────────────────────┐
│ PPT 12-5      Capital Rationing (Table 12-7)                        │
└────────────────────────────────────────────────────────────────────┘
```

B.   Under capital rationing, some acceptable projects may be declined due to management's fear of growth or hesitancy to use external financing.

C.   Under capital rationing, projects are ranked by NPV and accepted until the rationed amount of capital is exhausted.

VII. Net Present Value Profile

A.   The characteristics of an investment may be summarized by the use of the net present value profile.

```
┌────────────────────────────────────────────────────────────────────┐
│ Perspective 12-3: The net present value profile is an excellent way │
│ to examine the rate of return characteristics of projects with      │
│ different lives under various rate of return assumptions. This is a  │
│ good opportunity to reinforce the inverse nature of required rates   │
│ of return and present value interest factors and the resultant      │
│ impact on discounted cash flow streams.                             │
└────────────────────────────────────────────────────────────────────┘
```

B.   The NPV profile provides a graphical representation of an investment at various discount rates.

C.   Three characteristics of an investment are needed to apply the net present value profile:

1.   The net present value at a zero discount rate.
2.   The net present value of the project at the normal discount rate (cost of capital).
3.   The internal rate of return for the investment.

```
┌────────────────────────────────────────────────────────────────────┐
│ PPT 12-6      Net present value profile (Figure 12-2)              │
└────────────────────────────────────────────────────────────────────┘
```

D.   The NPV profile is particularly useful in comparing projects when they are mutually exclusive or under conditions of capital rationing.

PPT 12-7	Net present value profile with crossover (Figure 12-3)

VIII. Combining Cash Flow Analysis and Selection Strategy

A.   The Rules for Depreciation: The Tax Reform Act of 1986 created classified eight different categories which determine the allowable rate of depreciation. Each class is referred to as an "MACRS category" or Modified Accelerated Cost Recovery Range.

PPT 12-8	Categories for Depreciation Write Off (Table 12-8)

PPT 12-9	Depreciation Percentage (Table 12-9)

PPT 12-10	Depreciation schedule (Table 12-10)

IX.   Actual Investment Decision

PPT 12-11	Cash Flow related to the purchase of machinery (Table 12-11)

PPT 12-12	Net present value analysis (Table 12-12)

X. The Replacement Decision

    A.   Sale of Old Asset

    B.   Incremental Depreciation

PPT 12-13	Analysis of incremental depreciation benefits (Table 12-15)

    C.   Cost Savings

PPT 12-14	Analysis of incremental cost savings benefits (Table 12-16)

PPT 12-15	Present value of the total incremental benefits (Table 12-17)

Finance in Action: Capital Budgeting Practices Utilized by Smaller, Privately Held Businesses
The payback method or some other unsophisticated approach dominates the decision making process at small firms. This may be due to lack of sophisticated financial skills and/or because lenders to small businesses are usually bankers worrying about being repaid on schedule.

Summary Listing of Transparencies

Solution Transparencies to Chapter Problems

Other Supplements to Chapter

Cases for Use With Foundations of Financial Management, Aerocomp, Inc. (Methods of investment evaluation)

Risk and Capital Budgeting

Author's Overview

Though risk is discussed throughout the text, Chapter 13 provides the most explicit portrayal of its impact on the decision-making process of the firm. The actual measurement of risk through the computation of the mean, standard deviation, and coefficient of variation is presented in detail. The introduction of the risk-adjusted discount rate brings together the key material in Chapter 12 and this chapter. Simulation analysis also is introduced to emphasize how complicated decision variables can be reduced to a more manageable scale through examining, in advance, outcomes and probabilities of outcomes. Finally, the portfolio effect of an investment is introduced. The coefficient of correlation is defined in a general sense that should prove quite workable to the student. An example of the efficient frontier is demonstrated in Figure 13-11.

Chapter Concepts

*   The concept of risk is based on uncertainty about future outcomes.

*   Most investors are risk averse, which means they dislike uncertainty.

*   Because investors dislike uncertainty, they will require higher rates of return from risky projects.

*   Simulation models and decision trees can be used to help assess the risk of an investment.

*   Not only the risk of an individual project must be considered, but also how the project affects the total risk of the firm.

Annotated Outline and Strategy

I.   Risk in Capital Budgeting

    A.   Management's ability to achieve the goal of owner's wealth maximization will largely depend on success in dealing with risk.

    B.   Definition: Variability of possible outcomes. The wider the distribution of possible outcomes for a particular investment, the greater its risk.

    C.   Risk aversion is a basic assumption of financial theory. Investors require a higher expected return the riskier an investment is perceived to be.

II.   The Concept of Risk Adverse

> *Perspective 13-1:* *Depending on the prerequisite statistics knowledge of the student, this chapter could be easy or difficult mathematically. We provide a brief statistical review of standard deviations, mean, variance, etc., but most students should not have to spend too much time on the statistics. Instead, focus on applying of these measures to financial decision making.*

> PPT 13-1   Variability and Risk (Figure 13-1)

    A.   The basic risk measurement is the standard deviation, which is a measure of dispersion around an expected value. A numerical example appears on page 378.

        1.   The expected value is a weighted average of the possible outcomes of an event times their probabilities.

$$D \text{ (expected value)} = \Sigma \, DP$$

        2.   The formula for computing the standard deviation is:

$$\sigma \text{ (standard deviation)} = \sqrt{\Sigma \, (D - \overline{D})^2 \, P}$$

    B.   The Coefficient of Variation

1. The standard deviation is limited as a risk measure for comparison purposes. Two projects A and B may both be characterized by a standard deviation of $10,000 but A may have an expected value of $50,000 and B $100,000.

2. The size problem is eliminated by employing the coefficient of variation, V, which is the ratio of the standard deviation of an investment to its expected

$$\text{Coefficient of variation}(V) = \frac{\sigma}{\overline{D}}$$

v
a
l
u

$$V_A = \frac{\$10,000}{\$50,000} = .20 \qquad V_B = \frac{\$10,000}{\$100,000} = .10$$

e. The higher the coefficient of variation, the higher the risk.

PPT 13-2	Probability distribution with differing degrees of risk (Figure 13-3)

C. Beta (β) is another measure of risk that is widely used in portfolio management. Beta measures the volatility of returns on an individual stock relative to a stock market index of returns. (See Appendix 11A for a thorough discussion.)

PPT 13-3	Betas for a five-year period (1994-1999) (Table 13-2)

Perspective 13-2: If the faculty like to use beta as a measure of risk, transparency 13-3 allows for a good discussion of industry/company factors that may cause risk. Table 13-2 moves from stable utilities to more volatile industries such as airlines, brokerage firms, and pharmaceuticals. Students generally like to explore what causes these differences.

III. **Risk and the Capital Budgeting Process**

  A. The expected inflows from capital projects usually are risky-they are not certain.

  B. Cash flows of projects bearing a normal amount of risk undertaken by the firm should be discounted at the cost of capital.

  C. The required rate of return of lenders and investors increases as the risk they are subjected to increases.

  D. The cost of capital is composed of two components: the risk-free rate (time value of money only) and a risk premium (risk associated with usual projects of a business).

  E. Adjustments must be made in the evaluation process for projects bearing risk levels (more or less) other than normal.

    1. Risk-adjusted discount rate approach: The discount rate is adjusted upward for a more risky project and downward for projects bearing less than normal risk. A firm may establish a risk-adjusted discount rate for each of various categories of investment such as new equipment, new market, etc.

    2. Risk adjusted discount rates may be based on several measures of risk such as: the standard deviation, coefficient of variation or beta.

| PPT 13-4 | Relationship of risk to discount rate (Figure 13-5) |

Perspective 13-3: Discuss foreign projects and how they are evaluated based on risk. International capital budgeting often has higher risks associated with emerging market systems or political instability.

  F. Increasing risk over time: Our ability to forecast diminishes as we forecast farther out in time.

  G. Qualitative measures may mean that management makes up various risk classes for projects having similar characteristics.

| PPT 13-5 | Risk Categories and Associated Discount Rates (Table 13-3) |

PPT 13-6	Capital Budgeting Analysis (Table 13-4)

Perspective 13-4: Tables 13-4 and 13-5 bring back Investments A and B from Chapter 12 and demonstrate how a different decision would be made if Investment B had been adjusted for risk.

PPT 13-7	Capital Budgeting Decision Adjusted for Risk (Table 13-5)

IV. Simulation Models

A. The uncertainty associated with a capital budgeting decision may be reduced by projecting and preparing for the various possible outcomes resulting from the decision. Simulation models and decision trees enhance management's initial capital budget decision efforts and also expedite intermediate decisions (Whether to continue, etc.) once the initial decision has been made.

B. Simulation models - various values for economic and financial variables affecting the capital budgeting decision are randomly selected and used as inputs in the simulation model. Although the process does not ensure that a manager's decision will be correct (in terms of actual events), decisions can be made with a greater understanding of possible outcomes.

Finance In Action: How Much Risk is in Your Genes?

The focus of the discussion should be on the risk assigned by biotech companies, and the uncertainty of successful research that will generate cash flow.

PPT 13-8	Simulation flow chart (Figure 13-7)

C.   Decision trees - the sequential pattern of decisions and resulting outcomes and associated probabilities (managerial estimates based on experience and statistical processes) are tracked along the branches of the decision tree. Tracing the sequence of possible events in this fashion is a valuable analytical tool in the decision making process.

PPT 13-9	Decision Trees (Figure 13-8)

V.   The Portfolio Effect

A.   A risky project may actually reduce the total risk of the firm through the portfolio effect.

B.   Projects that move in opposite directions in response to the same economic stimulus are said to be negatively correlated. Since the movement of negatively correlated projects are in opposite directions, the total deviation is less than the deviations of the projects individually.

C.   The relationship between project movements is expressed by the coefficient of correlation which varies from the extremes of -1 (perfectly negative) to +1 (perfectly positive) correlation. Non-correlated projects have a correlation coefficient of zero.

D.   Although projects with correlation coefficients of -1 are seldom found, some risk reduction will occur, however minor, when projects are negatively correlated or have low positive correlation.

PPT 13-10	Rates of return for Conglomerate, Inc., and two merger candidates (Table 13-7)

> *Perspective 13-5: Table 13-7 is a good example of how negatively correlated projects can reduce risk when combined. Since students often have difficulty understanding this concept, all three companies have the same standard deviation and the two merger candidates also have identical mean returns. After the merger, the two rates of return are the same but the risk levels are quite different.*

  E. The firm should strive to achieve two objectives in combining projects according to their risk-return characteristics.

    1. Achieve the highest possible return at a given risk level.
    2. Allow the lowest possible risk at a given return level.

  F. The various optimal combinations of projects are located along a risk-return line referred to as the "efficient frontier."

PPT 13-11   Risk-return trade-offs (Figure 13-11)

V. The Share Price Effect

  A. Higher earnings do not necessarily contribute to the firm's goal of owner's wealth maximization. The firm's earnings may be discounted at a higher rate because investors perceive that the firm is pursuing riskier projects to generate the earnings.

  B. The risk aversion of investors is verified in the capital market. Firms that are very sensitive to cyclical fluctuations tend to sell at lower P/E multiples.

Summary Listing of Transparencies

PPT 13-1   Variability and Risk (Figure 13-1)
PPT 13-2   Probability Distribution with Differing Degrees of Risk (Figure 13-3)
PPT 13-3   Betas for a Five-Year Period (1994-1999) (Table 13-2)
PPT 13-4   Relationship of Risk to Discount Rate (Figure 13-5)
PPT 13-5   Risk Categories and Associated Discount Rates (Table 13-3)
PPT 13-6   Capital Budgeting Analysis (Table 13-4)
PPT 13-7   Capital Budgeting Decision Adjusted for Risk (Table 13-5)
PPT 13-8   Simulation Flow Chart (Figure 13-7)
PPT 13-9   Decision Trees (Figure 13-8)
PPT 13-10   Rates of Return for Conglomerate, Inc., and Two Merger Candidates (Table 13-7)
PPT 13-11   Risk-return Trade-offs (Figure 13-11)
LT 13-1   Chapter Outline
LT 13-2   What is Risk?
LT 13-3   Statistical Measurement of Risk
LT 13-4   Beta
LT 13-5   Coefficient of Correlation
LT 13-6   The Efficient Frontier

Solution Transparencies to Chapter Problems

ST 13-1   Myers Business Systems
ST 13-3   Coefficient of Variation
ST 13-4   Coefficient of Variation
ST 13-5   Risk-Averse
ST 13-7   Bridget's Modeling Studios
ST 13-9   Larry's Athletic Lounge
ST 13-11   Mr. Monty Terry
ST 13-12   Mr. Monty Terry (Continued)
ST 13-13   Roper Fashions
ST 13-15   The Palo Alto Microchip Corp.
ST 13-17   Hooper Chemical Co.
CP 13-1   Tobacco Company of America (Comprehensive Problem)
CP 13-2   Ace Trucking Company (Comprehensive Problem)

Other Supplements to Chapter

Cases for Use With Foundations of Financial Management, Inca, Inc. (capital budgeting with risk)

Cases for Use With Foundations of Financial Management, Galaxy Systems, Inc. (Divisional cost of capital) This case is also related to risk analysis.

Capital Markets

Author's Overview

This chapter on capital markets is basic to the understanding of the flow of funds through the economy and the relationship of capital markets to corporate bonds, stocks, and preferred stock. Students often view bonds as uninteresting and unimportant securities, so special emphasis has been placed on them to show their dominant positions as a source of external capital. The instructor may wish to stress the point that corporations do not operate in a vacuum but in a competitive capital market with government units.

Although much of this chapter is descriptive, it reinforces the concepts of risk and return and wealth maximization by describing the markets that create wealth and either reward or penalize the investor for assuming risk. The allocation of capital in a capitalistic economy is crucial to the understanding of our economic system, and the instructor will wish to point out the role of the securities markets in this allocation process.

Also, the ever increasing role of international capital markets should be stressed. The events in Asia during 1997 and 1998 and the Russian government debt default are just recent examples of how the international markets are linked. NAFTA and the European Monetary Union also highlight trading blocks that help create competitive markets.

The changing nature of securities markets can be seen by the decimalization of our markets. Additionally, the traditional markets are meeting competition from electronic communication networks (ECNs). Changes in our market structure will continue to be motivated by competition and technology.

We have taken the opportunity to include a section on market efficiency. There is a discussion of efficiency in the more traditional sense of liquidity, stability, and continuity, and this is linked with the concept of the efficient markets hypothesis in the weak, semi-strong and strong forms. The important matter of securities market regulation is also covered in the chapter.

Chapter Concepts

* The capital markets are made up of securities that have a life of one year or longer (often much longer).

* The primary participants raising funds in the capital markets are the U.S. Treasury; other agencies of the federal, state, and local governments; and corporations.

* The United States is a three-sector economy in which households, corporations, and governmental units allocate funds between themselves.

* Securities markets consist of organized exchanges and over-the-counter markets.

* Security markets are considered to be efficient when prices adjust rapidly to new information.

* Security legislation is intended to protect investors against fraud, manipulation, and illegal insider trading.

Annotated Outline and Strategy

I.   Money and Capital Markets

   A.   Money market: Short-term market for securities maturing in a year or less.

   B.   Capital market: Long-term market for securities with maturities greater than one year.

   C.   More often, companies search all capital markets including world markets for capital at the lowest cost.

II.   International Capital Markets

   A.   Competition for low cost funding is worldwide.

   B.   Money flows between countries include U.S. investment abroad and foreign investments in the U.S.

III.   Competition for Funds in the U.S. Capital Market

PPT 14-1	Depreciation and retained earnings as a percentage of internal funds (Figure 14-1)

A.   Government Securities

1.   Long-term financing of the U.S. is no longer a major issue as the government reached a surplus in 1998 and is projected to continue in this situation for the next decade.

2.   Large amounts of long-term capital in the United States have been supplied by foreigners. Foreign investors have been attracted by the relatively high interest rates and political stability available in the United States.

3.   Federally sponsored credit agencies, charged with funding the large numbers of federal programs, issue securities in the capital markets. Agencies such as the Federal National Mortgage Association, the Federal Home Loan Banks, the Farm Credit Banks, has varied widely but has been rising in percentage terms as the U.S. Treasury has no need to finance large deficits by selling U.S. government securities.

4.   State and local municipalities are usually required by law to balance their budgets so their borrowing is often short-term or project related. The interest paid on these issues is exempt from federal income tax.

B.   Corporate Securities

    1.   New issues of corporate securities have been predominantly bonds in recent years. Bonds are more widely used to raise capital when interest rates are low.

    2.   Though very similar to debt, the lack of the tax deductibility of preferred stock dividends has constrained the popularity of preferred stock issues.

    3.   New issues of common stock mushroomed in the late 1990s as the dot.com craze swept the IPO market.

PPT 14-2	Suppliers of funds to credit markets (March, 2000) (Figure 14-3)

C.   The majority of internally generated funds are not included in reported earnings. Funds from operations but not included in reported earnings through the depreciation process provide the primary "source" of internal funding. Although the percentage between retained earnings and depreciation varies based on profits and capital spending patterns.

IV.   The Supply of Capital Funds

PPT 14-5	Flow of funds through the economy (Figure 14-6)

A.   Business and government have been net demanders of funds and the household sector the major supplier of funds in our three-sector economy.

B.   Household sector savings are usually channeled to the demanders of funds through financial institutions such as commercial banks, savings and loans, mutual savings banks, and credit unions. See Figure 14-3 on page 410 for the major suppliers of U.S. credit market funds.

C.   Other intermediaries in the flow-of-funds process include mutual funds, pension plans, and insurance firms.

D.   The Role of the Security Markets

   1.   Securities markets aid the allocation of capital between the sectors of the economy and the financial intermediaries.
   2.   Security markets enable the demanders of capital to issue securities by providing the necessary liquidity for investors in two ways:

      a.   Corporations are able to sell new issues of securities rapidly at fair competitive prices.
      b.   The markets allow the purchaser of securities to convert the securities to cash with relative ease.

V.   The Organization of the Security Markets

A.   Several national and regional exchanges provide a centrally located auction market for buyers and sellers of securities who use the services of brokers having representatives on the floor of the exchanges.

   1.   The primary exchanges are the New York Stock Exchange (NYSE) and the American Stock Exchange (AMEX) which merged with NASDAQ in 1998. By the time you read this, NASDAQ and the AMEX may very well be independent organizations once again.
   2.   Exchanges of lesser importance include the Midwest, Pacific, Detroit, Boston, Cincinnati, and PBW (Philadelphia, Baltimore, and Washington) exchanges. Ninety percent of the volume on these regional Exchanges is from dually traded stocks on the NYSE.

B.   New York Stock Exchange (NYSE)

   1.   The NYSE accounts for approximately 80 percent of the dollar volume of all listed stock traded in the U.S.
   2.   To be listed on the NYSE, firms must meet certain minimum requirements pertaining to earnings power, level of assets, market value and number of shares of publicly-held common stock, and the number of shareholders. See the web exercise at the end of the chapter.
   3.   Beginning in August 2000, U.S. security markets started trading in decimals rather than fractions. The impact of this move by the SEC is still being scrutinized.

C.   The global nature of capital markets is evidenced by the increasing volume and security listings on stock markets around the world. The Tokyo stock exchange is the largest in the world and companies such as Intel, IBM, and McDonald's trade there and on the Frankfurt stock exchange. Likewise, many foreign companies trade on the NYSE. As more companies trade on exchanges around the world in multiple time zones, the easier it will be for trading to be continuous for 24 hours per day.

PPT 14-6	Global Stock Markets (Table 14-3)

Perspective 14-3: **With the rising tide of capitalism in Eastern Europe, students might be interested in the emerging capital markets in Poland, Hungary, and other developing countries. It may also be worthwhile to discuss the advent of world-wide trading on a continuous, 24-hour basis in large, globally recognized firms like Sony, Coca Cola and Nestle.**

D.   Corporations that do not meet listing requirements or choose not to be listed on the exchanges are traded in the over-the-counter market (OTC).

1.   The OTC market is a national network of dealers linked by computer display terminals, telephones, and teletypes.

2.   OTC dealers own the securities they trade and seek to earn a profit from their buying and selling, whereas brokers receive a commission as an agent of the buyer or seller of securities.

3.   The National Association of Securities Dealers (NASD) which supervises the OTC market has divided the OTC market into groups:

a.   The National Market List is composed of the largest OTC companies.
b.   The National List includes smaller firms centered in one state or city.
c.   The Supplemental List includes very small developmental companies and closely held firms with very few shares available for trading.

4.   Due to the lower prices of OTC stocks, the dollar volume of exchange listed stocks is larger. Due to the great amount of debt securities traded OTC, however, the OTC market is the largest market for all security transactions in total dollars.

E.   Electronic Communications Networks (ECNs) are electronic trading systems that match, buy and sell orders at specified prices. ECNs lower the cost of trading by creating better execution, more price transparency and by allowing "after hours trading."

120

VI. Market Efficiency

A. Criteria of Efficiency

1. Rapid adjustment of prices to new information
2. Continuous market; successive prices are close
3. Market is capable of absorbing large dollar amounts of securities without destabilizing the price.

B. The more certain the income stream, the less volatile price movements will be and the more efficient the market will be.

C. Screen based trading systems versus floor trading is becoming a trend that most observers would agree increase market efficiency.

D. The efficiency of the stock market is stated in three forms.

1. Weak form: Past price information is unrelated to future prices, trends cannot be predicted and taken advantage of by investors.
2. Semi-strong form: Prices reflect all public information.
3. Strong form: Prices reflect all public and private information.

E. A fully efficient market, if it exists, precludes insiders and large institutions from making profits from security transactions in excess of the market in general.

F. The efficiency of the market is debatable but most would agree that the movement is toward greater efficiency.

VII. Regulation of the Security Markets

A. Organized securities markets are regulated by the Securities and Exchange Commission (SEC) and through self-regulation. The OTC market is regulated by the National Association of Securities Dealers (NASD).

B. Three major laws govern the sale and trading of securities.

1. Securities Act of 1933: This act was a response to abuses present in the securities markets during the Wall Street "Crash" era. Its purpose was to provide full disclosure of all pertinent investment information on new corporate security issues.

Finance In Action: Long Term Capital Management LP- The Collapse of a Hedge Fund
One of the most significant events in the capital markets during the 1990s was the near collapse of Long Term Capital when Russia defaulted on their sovereign debt. To make matters more intense for the academic community, two Nobel Laureates, Myron Scholes and Robert Merton, were involved with the firm. No matter how smart you are, you can make mistakes if you misjudge your risks or take too many risks. Markets are not always rational and when markets become perverse, even smart people can lose money.

2. The Securities Exchange Act of 1934 created the Securities and Exchange Commission (SEC) and empowered it to regulate the securities markets.

3. The Securities Acts Amendments of 1975 directed the SEC to supervise the development of a national securities market, prohibited fixed commissions on public transactions, and prohibited financial institutions and insurance companies from buying stock exchange memberships to save commission costs.

Summary Listing of Transparencies

PPT 14-1   Depreciation and Retained Earnings as a Percentage of Internal Funds (Figure 14-1)
PPT 14-2   Suppliers of Funds to Credit Markets (Figure 14-3)
PPT 14-3   None
PPT 14-4   None
PPT 14-5   Flow of Funds Through the Economy (Figure 14-2)
PPT 14-6   Global Stock Markets (Table 14-3)
LT 14-1   Chapter 14 Outline
LT 14-2   Capital Markets vs. Money Markets
LT 14-3   Government Securities
LT 14-4   Corporate Securities
LT 14-5   Organized Stock Exchanges
LT 14-6   Over-the-Counter Market
LT 14-7   Regulation of the Securities Markets

Investment Banking: Public and Private Placement

Author's Overview

This chapter presents a detailed account of the functions of the investment banker. By making maximum use of material covered under the "distribution process," the instructor can present a good picture of the marketing channels and pricing mechanisms that are frequently utilized in a public distribution. Such topics as the underwriter spread, pricing of the security, market stabilization, and after-market considerations are usually interesting to the student.

The advantages and disadvantages of going public is an area worthy of consideration. While it seems that the ultimate goal of every small firm is to grow large enough to one day be public, there are some very sound reasons to challenge this objective.

The continuing importance of private placement can be viewed from statistical data in the chapter and its impact on traditional investment banking can be considered. Also, the instructor should cover the phenomenon of the leveraged buy-out, a significant development of the 1980s that has left its impact on the 1990s and capital markets.

Chapter Concepts

*   Investment bankers are intermediaries between corporations in need of funds and the investing public.

*   Investment bankers, rather than corporations, normally take the risk of successfully distributing corporate securities.

*   Investment bankers also advise corporations on potential mergers and acquisitions and other important matters.

*   Corporations turn to investment bankers and others in making the critical decision about whether to go public (distribute their securities in the public markets) or stay private.

*   Leveraged buy-outs rely heavily on debt in the restructuring of a corporation.

Annotated Outline and Strategy

I. The late 1990s may well be called the dot.com era for investment banking, as record numbers of companies from Amazon.com to eBay went public. Emphasis on this phenomenon is a great way to make this chapter interesting from the start.

II. The role of investment banking has been to act as the middleman between investors with money and companies in need of capital.

   A. Investment bankers have been merging and the industry has consolidated to the point where the top 10 underwriters controlled almost 74 percent of the global market by July of 2000.

   B. In 1999 Congress passed the Gramm-Leach-Bliley Act which repealed the Glass-Stegal Act. The Glass-Stegal Act required that commercial banks and investment banks operate independently of each other. While the investment banking market was already competitive, Gramm-Leach-Bliley will allow combinations between investment banks and commercial banks much like Citibank and Travelers.

III. **Functions of the Investment Banker.**

   A. Underwriter: The risk-taking function. The underwriter bears the risk of fluctuations in the selling price of the security issue. The investment banker may handle the issues of unknown corporations on a nonrisk-bearing "best efforts" basis only.

   B. Market maker: The investment banker may engage in buying and selling of a security to ensure an available market.

   C. Advising: Corporations may seek an investment banker's advice on the size, timing, and marketability of security issues. Advice is also rendered pertaining to merger and acquisition decisions, leveraged buyouts, and corporate restructuring.

   D. Agency functions: As an agent, the investment banker assists in the private placement of security issues and in the negotiating process of merger and acquisition transactions.

IV. The Distribution Process.

A. The managing investment banker forms an underwriting syndicate of investment bankers to increase marketability of the issue and spread the risk.

B. Syndicate members, acting as wholesalers, sell the securities to brokers and dealers who eventually sell the securities to the public.

PPT 15-1   Distribution process in investment banking (Figure 15-1)

Finance In Action: The Investment Banker and the Roadshow

This box discusses the responsibilities a company's investment banker has developing a market and creating demand for its stock.

C. The spread is the difference in the price of a security to the public and the amount paid to the issuing firm and represents the compensation of those participating in the distribution.

1. The spread is divided among the distribution participants. The lower a party falls in the distribution hierarchy, the lower the portion of the spread received.
2. Usually, the larger the dollar value of an issue, the smaller the spread.
3. The spread on equity issues is greater than on debt issues because of the greater price uncertainty.

PPT 15-2   Allocation of underwriting spread (Figure 15-2)

IV. Pricing the Security

A.   Several factors must be considered by the managing investment banker when negotiating the issue price of a security of a first-time issuer.

        1.   Experience of the firm in the market.
        2.   Financial position of the issuing firm.
        3.   Expected earnings and dividends.
        4.   P/E multiples of firms in the same industry.
        5.   Anticipated public demand.

Perspective 15-2: Some time can be spent discussing the pricing of new stock issues and their relation to the valuation material in Chapter 10. Investment bankers get paid to take price risk but they are motivated to price issues low so that they sell out the issue without being stuck with unsold issues. Corporations have the objective of getting the highest price possible and thereby selling fewer shares. This would create less dilution of earnings. The conflict between the investment banker and client may create interesting situations and is worthy of discussions.

B.   The issue price of securities of firms with existing securities outstanding are usually determined by "underpricing."

        1.   Price is set slightly below current market value.
        2.   Underpricing is partially a result of the dilutive effect of spreading earnings over a greater number of shares of stock.

C.   Dilution: When new common stock is sold, the new shares issued immediately cause earnings per share to decline until the earnings can be increased from the investment of new funds.

128

D. Market Stabilization. The managing investment banker seeks to stabilize the market (keep the sales price up) by repurchasing securities while at the same time selling them.

E. Aftermarket: Research has indicated that initial public offering often do well in the immediate aftermarket.

F. Shelf Registration

    1. Large companies are permitted to file one comprehensive registration statement and then wait (hold securities on shelf) until market conditions are favorable before issuing securities without further SEC approval. Previously, a registration statement had to be filed for each security issue. Shelf registration has been used primarily for debt issues.

    2. A greater concentration of business among the stronger firms in the investment banking industry has resulted from the shelf registration process.

VI. Public versus Private Financing

A. Advantages of being public

    1. Greater availability of funds
    2. Prestige
    3. Higher liquidity for stockholders
    4. Established price of public issues aids a stockholder's estate planning
    5. Enables a firm to engage in merger activities more readily

B. Disadvantages of being public

    1. Company information must be made public through SEC and state filings
    2. Accumulating and disclosing information is expensive in terms of dollars and time
    3. Short-term pressure from security analysts and investors
    4. Embarrassment from public failure
    5. High cost of going public

VII. Public Offerings

A. A classic example of instant wealth. EDS goes public

    1. The example of Ross Perot's initial public offering is very educational about

shopping around for the right investment banker.

2. Following this example through to today may illustrate how small companies become large and provide the founder with resources for political or social activities.

B. Internet Capital is a company students may know. They may not however be familiar with its initial public offering. The Internet Capital IPO demonstrates the change in the investment banking arena, with both a domestic and international division of shares and fewer bankers participating in the syndicate.

VIII. Private Placement. Private placement refers to selling securities directly to insurance companies, pension funds, and others rather than going through security markets. Private placement is used more for debt than equity issues

1. Advantages of private placement

  a. Eliminates the lengthy, expensive registration process with the SEC
  b. Greater flexibility in negotiating terms of issue
  c. Costs of issue are less

2. The usually higher interest cost on a privately placed debt instrument is a disadvantage.

Perspective 15-3: Discuss the consequences for public markets if the trend to utilize private placement and placement in foreign markets increases.

PPT 15-3 Public versus private placement of bonds; Corporate bonds 1976-99
(Figure 15-4)

B. Going Private and Leveraged Buyouts

1. Firms that elect to go private are usually small companies that are seeking to avoid large auditing and reporting expenses. In the 1980's, however, large firms have been going private to avoid the pressure of pleasing analysts in the short term. There are two basic ways to go private. The public firm can be purchased by a private firm or the company can repurchase all publicly traded shares from the stockholders.

130

2. Many firms have gone private through leveraged buyouts. Management or some external group borrows the needed cash to repurchase all the shares of the company. Frequently the management of the private firm must sell off assets in order to reduce the heavy debt load.

3. Several firms that have gone private during the 1980s have restructured and returned to the public market at an increased market value. In some cases the firm was divided and the divisions were sold separately. The "breakup value" of some firms such as Beatrice and Uniroyal was substantially higher than the market value of the unified entity.

IX. International Investment Banking Deals

A. Privatization: The 1990s have been the decade of many state owned companies around the world issuing ownership securities to private individuals.

B. Table 15-4 lists the biggest international privatization deals country by country.

Summary Listing of Transparencies

PPT 15-1   Distribution Process in Investment Banking (Figure 15-1)
PPT 15-2   Allocation of Underwriting Spread (Figure 15-2)
PPT 15-3   Public Versus Private Placement of Bonds; Corporate Bonds 1976-94 (Figure 15-4)
LT 15-1   Chapter 15 Outline
LT 15-2   What is Investment Banking?
LT 15-3   Functions of the Investment Banker
LT 15-4   Underwriting Spread
LT 15-5   Public vs. Private Companies
LT 15-6   Advantages and Disadvantages of a Public Company
LT 15-7   Initial Public Offering and Leveraged Buyout

Solution Transparencies to Chapter Problems

ST 15-1   Louisiana Timber Company
ST 15-2   Louisiana Timber Company (Continued)
ST 15-3   Blaine and Company
ST 15-5   Womenpower Temporaries, Inc.
ST 15-7   Skyway Airlines
ST 15-9   Richmond Rent-A-Car
ST 15-11   The Alston Corporation
ST 15-13   The Presley Corporation
ST 15-15   Rowe Boat Company
CP 15-1   Anton Corporation (Comprehensive Problem)

Other Supplements to Chapter

Cases for Use With Foundations of Financial Management, Robert Boyle & Associates, Inc. (Going public and investment banking)

Long-Term Debt and Lease Financing 16

Author's Overview

After establishing the facts related to the astronomical growth in corporate debt since World War instructor can cover secured versus unsecured debt, sinking fund provisions, bond prices, yields, and rating, and conversion and call features. The student gets a good indoctrination into the various influences on bond prices, which can be strongly reinforced by problems at the back of the chapter. Table 16-4 summarizes various points about bond pricing such as coupon rate versus market rate and the influence of bond ratings.

The bond refunding decision is covered from the approach of a capital budgeting problem and leasing is examined as a special form of debt, rather than as a separate type of financing. Studies and pronouncements by the accounting profession have taken the authors in this direction. However, the reasons for a lease arrangement are clearly enumerated. Additional material on the lease versus purchase decision is also covered in Appendix 16-B.

Financial alternatives for distressed times are covered in Appendix 16A, with a discussion of out-of-court and in-court settlements. Disposal of assets under liquidation are also examined in this appendix.

Chapter Concepts

* Analyzing long-term debt requires consideration of the collateral pledged, method of repayment, and other key factors.

* Bond yields and prices are influenced by how bonds are rated by major bond rating agencies.

* An important corporate decision is whether to call in and reissue debt (refund the obligation) when interest rates decline.

* Innovative bond forms are represented by zero-coupon rate bonds and floating rate bonds.

* Long-term lease obligations have many similar characteristics to debt and are recognized as a form of indirect debt by the accounting profession.

Annotated Outline and Strategy

I.   The Expanding Role of Debt

> *Perspective 16-1: The expanding role of debt is not just an issue for corporations but also for federal and state governments and consumers.*

A.   Corporate debt has expanded dramatically since World War II.

B.   The rapid expansion of corporate debt is the result of:

    1.   Rapid business expansion.
    2.   Inflation.
    3.   At times, inadequate funds generated from the internal operations of business firms.

C.   Corporations have suffered a decline in interest coverage in the last two decades.

> PPT 16-1   Times Interest Earned for Standard & Poor's Industrials (Figure 16-1)

II.   Debt Contract Terminology and Provisions

A.   Par Value-the face value of a bond

B.   Coupon Rate-the actual interest rate on a bond; annual interest/par value

C.   Maturity Date-the final date on which repayment of the debt principal is due

D.   Indenture-lengthy, legal agreement detailing the issuer's obligations pertaining to a bond issue. The indenture is administered by an independent trustee.

E.   Security provisions
    1.   Secured claim-specific assets are pledged to bondholders in the event of default.
    2.   Mortgage agreement-real property is pledged as security for loan.
    3.   Senior claims require satisfaction in liquidation proceedings prior to junior claims.
    4.   New property may become subject to a security provision by an "after acquired property clause."

F. Unsecured debt

    1. Debenture-an unsecured, long-term corporate bond
    2. Subordinated debenture-an unsecured bond in which payment will be made to the bondholder only after the holders of designated senior debt issues have been satisfied.

G. Methods of Repayment of Principal

    1. Lump-sum payment at maturity
    2. Serial payments-bonds are paid off in installments over the life of the issue; each bond has a predetermined maturity date.
    3. Sinking fund-the issuer is required to make regular contributions to fund under the trustee's control. The trustee purchases (retires) bonds in the market with the contributions.
    4. Conversion-retirement by converting bonds into common stock; this is the option of the holder but it may be forced. (See Chapter 19.)
    5. Call Feature-an option of the issuing corporation allowing it to retire the debt issue prior to maturity. Requires payment of a call premium over par value of 5 percent to 10 percent to the bondholder. The call is usually exercised by the firm when interest rates have fallen.

PPT 16-2	Priority of Claims (Figure 16-2)

H. An Example: Mead Corporation's 8.125 percent bond. Also see table 16-1 and 16-2.

III. Bond Prices, Yields, and Ratings

A. Bond prices are largely determined by the relationship of their coupon rate to the going market rate and the number of years until maturity.

    1. If the market rate for the bond exceeds the coupon rate, the bond will sell below par value. If the market rate is less than the coupon rate, the bond will sell above par value.

135

2.   The more distant the maturity date of a bond, the farther below or above par value the price will be given the coupon rate and market rate relationship.

PPT 16-3   Bond Price Table (Table 16-3)

B.   Bond yields are quoted on three different bases. Assume a $ 1,000 par value bond pays $ 100 per year interest for 10 years. The bond is currently selling at $900 in the market.

> **Perspective 16-2:** *It is important for students to understand the difference between the various bond yields. The most important yield is the yield to maturity which is a function of price change as well as annual cash flow.*

1.   Coupon rate (nominal yield) -- Stated interest payment divided by par value $100/$1,000 = 10%
2.   Current yield -- Stated interest payment divided by the current price of the bond, $100/$900 = 11.11%
3.   Yield to Maturity -- The interest rate that will equate future interest payments and payment at maturity to current market price (the internal rate of return). The yield to maturity may be computed approximately by the following formula.

$$\text{Approximate Yield to Maturity} = \frac{\text{Annual interest payment} + \dfrac{\text{Principal payment} - \text{Price of the bond}}{\text{Number of years to maturity}}}{.6\,(\text{Price of the bond}) + .4\,(\text{Principal payment})}$$

C.   Bond ratings

1.   There are two major bond rating agencies-Moody's Investor Service and Standard and Poor's Corporation.
2.   The higher the rating, the lower the interest rate that must be paid.
3.   The ratings are based on:

    a.   the firm's ability to make interest payments.

b.   its consistency of performance.

c.   its size.

d.   its debt/equity ratio.

e.   its working capital position.

f.   and other factors.

D.   Examining actual bond ratings: See Table 16-4 and discussion.

IV.   The Refunding Decision

A.   The process of calling outstanding bonds and replacing them with new ones is termed refunding. This action is most likely to be pursued by businesses during periods of declining interest rates.

B.   Interest savings from refunding can be substantial over the life of a bond but the costs of refunding can also be very large.

Perspective 16-3: *Compare the refunding decision with paying off a high-cost mortgage early and refinancing it at a lower rate with all the resultant costs of financing, points, closing fees, lawyers, etc.*

C.   A refunding decision is a capital budgeting problem. The refunding costs constitute the investment and the net reduction in annual cash expenditures are the inflows.

PPT 16-4   Restatement of Facts

D.   A major difference in evaluating a capital expenditure for refunding is that the discount rate applied is the aftertax cost of debt rather than the cost of capital because the annual savings are known with greater certainty.

PPT 16-5   Net Present Value

V.   Other Forms of Bond Financing

A.   Zero-Coupon Rate Bonds

1. Do not pay interest; sold at deep discounts from face value.
2. These bonds provide immediate cash inflow to the corporation (sell bonds) without any outflow (interest payments) until the bonds mature.
3. Since the difference between the selling price and the maturity value is amortized for tax purposes over the life of the bond, a tax reduction benefit occurs without a current cash outflow.
4. Allows investor to "lock-in" a multiplier of the initial investment.
5. Most investors in these bonds are tax exempt because the annual increase in bond value is taxed as ordinary income even though no payment is received.
6. Brokerage houses are marketing future interests in government securities which is a variation of the zero-coupon rate bond.

PPT 16-6	Zero-Coupon and Floating Rate Bonds (Table 16-5)

B. Floating Rate Bonds

1. The interest rate varies with market conditions.

2. Unless market rates move beyond floating rate limits, the price of the floating rate bond should not change, therefore, the investor is assured (within limits) of the market value of his investment.

VI. Advantages and Disadvantages of Debt

A. Benefits of Debt

1. Tax deductibility of interest.
2. The financial obligation is specific and fixed (with the exception of floating rate bonds).
3. In an inflationary economy, debt may be repaid with "cheaper dollars."
4. Prudent use of debt may lower the cost of capital.

B. Drawbacks of Debt

1. Interest and principal payments must be met when due regardless of the firm's financial position.
2. Burdensome bond indenture restrictions.

138

3. Imprudent use of debt may depress stock prices.

C. Eurobond Market

1. Usually denominated is dollars but not always.
2. Disclosure less stringent then U.S. Securities and Exchange Commission.
3. Not able to rely on rating agencies.
4. See examples in Table 16-6.

| PPT 16-7 | Examples of Eurobonds (Table 16-6) |

Finance In Action: For Companies with Financial Problems, Thank Heaven for Chapter 11

Even with the outstanding business conditions, there has been a 75 percent increase in the number of companies seeking Chapter 11 protection between 1997 and 1999. This seems to be a result of companies using Chapter 11 as a strategic tool in everything from litigation defense to merger negotiations.

VII. Leasing as a Form of Debt

A. A long-term, noncancellable lease has all the characteristics of a debt obligation.

B. The position of the accounting profession that companies should fully divulge all information about leasing obligations was made official for financial reporting purposes in November, 1976. The Financial Accounting Standards Board (FASB) issued Statement No. 13.

1. Prior to FASB Statement No. 13, lease obligations could be divulged in footnotes to financial statements.
2. FASB No. 13 requires that certain types of leases be shown as long-term obligations on a firm's financial statements.

C. Leases that substantially transfer all the benefits and risks of ownership from the owner to the lessee must be capitalized. A capital lease is required whenever any one of the following conditions exists.

1. Ownership of the property is transferred to the lessee by the end of the lease term.
2. The lease contains a bargain purchase price (sure to be purchased) at the end of the lease.
3. The lease term is equal to 75 percent or more of the estimated life of the leased property.
4. The present value of the minimum lease payments equals or exceeds 90 percent of the fair value of the leased property at the beginning of the lease.

D. A lease that does not meet any of the four criteria is an operating lease.

1. Usually short-term.
2. Often cancelable at the option of the lessee.
3. The lessor frequently provides maintenance.
4. Capitalization and presentation on the balance sheet is not required.

E. Impact of capital lease on the income statement

1. The intangible leased property under capital lease (asset) amount is amortized and written off over the life of the lease.

2. The obligation under capital lease (liability) is written off through amortization with an "implied" interest expense on the remaining balance.

F.   Advantages of leasing

    1.   Lessee may not have sufficient funds to purchase or borrowing capability.
    2.   Provisions of lease may be less restrictive.
    3.   May be no down payment.
    4.   Expert advice of leasing (lessor) company.
    5.   Creditor claims on certain types of leases are restricted in bankruptcy and reorganization procedures.
    6.   Tax considerations

        a.   Obtain maximum benefit of tax advantages.
        b.   Tax deductibility of lease payments for land.

    7.   Infusion of capital through a sale-leaseback.

VIII. **Appendix 16A: Financial Alternatives for Distressed Firms**

A.   Financial Distress

    1.   Technical Insolvency-firm has positive net worth but is unable to pay its bills as they come due.
    2.   Bankruptcy-a firm's liabilities exceed the value of its assets-negative net worth.

B.   Out-of-court Settlements

    1.   Extension-creditors allow the firm more time to meet its financial obligations.
    2.   Composition-creditors agree to accept a fractional settlement on their original claim.
    3.   Creditor committee-a creditor committee is established to run the business in place of the existing management.
    4.   Assignment-a liquidation of the firm's assets without going through formal court action.

C. In-court Settlements-Formal Bankruptcy

1. Bankruptcy proceedings may be initiated voluntarily by the firm or forced by the creditors-involuntary bankruptcy.
2. The decisions of a court appointed referee who arbitrates the bankruptcy proceedings are final subject to court review.
3. Reorganization-a fair and feasible plan to reorganize the bankrupt firm.

   a. Internal reorganization-necessitates an evaluation of existing management and policies. An assessment and possible redesign of the firm's capital structure is also required.
   b. External reorganization-a financially strong and managerially competent merger partner is found for the bankrupt firm.

4. Liquidation-if reorganization of the firm is determined to be infeasible, the assets of the firm will be sold to satisfy creditors. The priority of claims is:

   a. Bankruptcy administrative costs (legal fees)
   b. Wages of workers earned within 3 months of bankruptcy declaration
   c. Federal, state and local taxes
   d. Secured creditors-designated assets
   e. General creditors-there is a priority within this category also
   f. Preferred stockholders
   g. Common stockholders

IX. **Appendix 16B: Lease versus Purchase Decision**

A. Leasing as a means of financing is often compared to borrow-purchase arrangements when assets are to be acquired. This procedure is particularly appropriate for comparing an operating lease to purchasing.

B. The present value of all after-tax cash outflows associated with each form of financing is computed. The procedure requires consideration of all tax shields for each method. Since all outflows are fixed by contract, the discount rate employed in computing the present value of the outflows is the after-tax cost of debt.

142

C.   Although qualitative factors must be considered, the usual decision criterion **is** to accept the financing method, leasing or borrow-purchase, that has the lowest present value of cash outflows. The cash inflows should be the same whether the asset is leased or purchased.

Summary Listing of Transparencies

PPT 16-1   Times Interest Earned (Figure 16-1)
PPT 16-2   Priority of Claims (Figure 16-2)
PPT 16-3   Bond Price Table (Table 16-3)
PPT 16-4   Restatement of Facts
PPT 16-5   Net Present Value
PPT 16-6   Zero-Coupon and Floating Rate Bonds (Table 16-5)
PPT 16-7   Examples of Eurobonds (Table 16-6)
LT 16-1   Chapter 16 Outline
LT 16-2   Bond Terminology
LT 16-3   More Bond Terminology
LT 16-4   Priority of Claims
LT 16-5   Methods of Repayment
LT 16-6   3 Types of Bond Yields
LT 16-7   Other Forms of Bond Financing
LT 16-8   Advantages and Disadvantages of Debt
LT 16-9   2 Types of Leases
LT 16-10   Advantages of Leasing

Solution Transparencies to Chapter Problems

ST 16-1   The Pioneer Petroleum Company
ST 16-3   The Southeast Investment Fund
ST 16-5   Evans Corporation
ST 16-7   Interest Rates and Bond Ratings
ST 16-9   Zero-coupon Bond Yield
ST 16-11   U.S. Aluminum Corporation
ST 16-13   The Delta Corporation
ST 16-14   The Sunbelt Corporation
ST 16-15   The Sunbelt Corporation (Continued)
ST 16-17   The Bradley Corp.
ST 16A-1   Immobile Corporation (Appendix)
ST 16B-1   Edison Electronics (Appendix)

Other Supplements to Chapter

Cases for Use with Foundations of Financial Management, Leland Industries (Debt Financing) and Atlantel Co. (Bond Refunding)

Cases for Use With Foundations of Financial Management, Warner Motor Oil Co. (Bond refunding)

Common and Preferred Stock Financing

Author's Overview

The first part of the chapter gives the student a clear view of the changing nature of stock ownership through increasing institutional participation and the declining importance of individual stock ownership. The residual nature of common stock as compared to other securities is examined as well as cumulative voting and rights offerings. We also stress the various classes of common stock that exist.

Preferred stock should be introduced as a hybrid form of security. The unusual tax features of preferred stock are compared to debt by highlighting the non-tax deductibility of preferred dividends to the paying corporation and the partial tax-exempt nature of preferred dividends to corporate owners. The cumulative nature of preferred stock is also important to the discussion, with lesser recognition given to the conversion, call, and participating features (some of these topics have been covered under the discussion of debt).

Chapter Concepts

*   Common stockholders are the owners of the corporation and therefore have a claim to undistributed income, the right to elect the board of directors, and other privileges.

*   Cumulative voting provides minority stockholders with the potential for some representation on the board of directors.

*   A rights offering gives current stockholders a first option to purchase new shares.

*   Poison pills and other similar provisions may make it difficult for outsiders to take over a corporation against management's wishes.

*   Preferred stock is an intermediate type of security that falls somewhere between debt and common stock.

Annotated Outline and Strategy

I. **Common Stock and Common Stockholders**

    A.   Although management controls the corporation on a daily basis, ultimate control of the firm resides in the hands of the stockholders.

    B.   Management has become increasingly sensitive to the growing institutional ownership of common stock. Mutual funds, pension funds, insurance companies and bank trust accounts are examples of financial institutions that in combination own a large percentage of many leading corporations.

II. **Common stockholders' claim to income**

    A.   Common stockholders have a residual claim on the income stream; the amount remaining after creditors and preferred stockholders have been satisfied belongs to the owners (common stockholders) whether paid in dividends or retained.

    B.   A corporation may have several classes of common stock that differ in regard to voting rights and claim on the earnings stream (e.g. Dow Jones Co and General Motors).

> PPT 17-1   Institutional Ownership of U.S. Companies (Table 17-1)

III. **The Voting Right**

    A.   Owners of common stock have the right to vote on all major issues including election of the board of directors.

> *Perspective 17-1:* **The voting right is a very important issue and the Ford family provides an interesting example for students.**

    B.   Majority voting-holders of majority of stock can elect all directors.

    C.   In some firms such as Ford Motor Company, different classes of stock are entitled to elect a specified percentage of the board of directors.

D. Cumulative voting-possible for minority stockholders (own less than 50 percent of stock) to elect some of the directors.

    1. The stockholder can cast one vote for each share of stock owned times the number of directors to be elected.

    2. The following formula may be employed to determine the number of shares needed to elect a given number of directors under cumulative voting.

$$\text{Shares Required} = \frac{\text{Number of directors desired} \times \text{Total number of shares outstanding}}{\text{Total number of directors to be elected}} + 1$$

IV. The Right to Purchase New Shares

A. The stockholder may have the right to maintain his percentage of ownership, voting power, and claim to earnings through the preemptive right provision which requires that existing stockholders be given the first option to purchase new shares.

> **Perspective 17-2:** *The Ericsson offering in 1995 is an example of a major rights offering. See the box later in the chapter for a discussion of both the rights and ADRs that were involved.*

B. Financing through rights offerings.

    1. Even if the preemptive right provision is not required, the corporation may finance through a rights offering.

    2. Each stockholder receives one right for each share of stock owned, and is allowed to buy new shares of stock at a reduced price (below market value) plus the required number of rights/share.

    3. The number of rights required to purchase a new share equals the ratio of shares outstanding to the new shares issued.

$$\frac{\text{Number of rights required}}{\text{to purchase one new share}} = \frac{\text{Number of shares outstanding}}{\text{Number of shares to be issued}}$$

4.   Rights have market value since they entitle the holder to purchase shares of stock at less than market price.

   a.   Initially, after the rights offering announcement, stock trades "rights-on." The formula for the value of a right during the rights-on

$$R = \frac{(M_0 - S)}{(N + 1)}$$

   period is:
   M_0 =   Market value of stock, rights-on
   S   =   Subscription price
   N   =   Number of rights required to purchase a new share of stock

   b.   After a certain period, the right no longer trades with the stock but may be bought and sold separately. On the "ex-rights" date the stock price falls by the theoretical value of a right. The ex-rights value of a

$$R = \frac{(M_e - S)}{N}$$

   right is:
   M_e =   Market value of stock, ex-rights

5.   Existing stockholders usually do not have a monetary gain from a rights offering. The gain from purchasing shares at less than market price is eliminated by dilution of previously owned shares.

6.   A stockholder has three options when presented with a rights offering.
   a.   Exercise the rights; no net gain or loss
   b.   Sell the rights; no net gain or loss
   c.   Allow the rights to lapse; a loss will be incurred due to the dilution of existing shares that is not offset by value of unsold or unexercised rights.

C.   Desirable features of rights offerings

    1.   Protects stockholders' voting position and claim on earnings
    2.   Existing stockholders provide a built-in market for new issues; distribution costs are lower
    3.   May create more interest in stock than a straight offering
    4.   Lower margin requirements

D.   Poison Pills

    1.   A "poison pill" is a rights offering made to existing shareholders of a company with the sole purpose of thwarting an acquisition attempt by another company. The increased number of shares may dilute the ownership percentage of the firm pursuing the takeover.
    2.   Some investors feel that a poison pill strategy is contrary to the goal of maximizing the wealth of the owners.

V.   American Depository Receipts (ADRs)

A.   ADRs are shares of foreign stock held in trust by U.S. Banks that issues a claim on these trust receipts.

B.   ADRs allow foreign companies to raise funds in U.S. markets and provide investors with english annual reports using U.S. GAAP accounting.

C.   The example of ADRs gives the professor yet another chance to emphasize how important international markets are to both U.S. and foreign firms.

Finance in Action: Telephon A.B. Ericsson Rights Offering
This box appears after the sections on rights offerings and ADRs. Ericsson is a foreign company with ADRs that were affected by their rights offering and the students need to understand both rights and ADRs before reading to box. It can be pointed out that rights offerings are more common in Europe than the U.S.

VI. Preferred Stock Financing

A. Characteristics of preferred stock

    1. Stipulated dividends must be paid before dividends on common stock but are not guaranteed or required.

    2. Dividends are not tax-deductible.

PPT 17-2	Before Tax Yields on Corporate Bonds and High-grade Preferred Stock (Table 17-2)

B. Preferred stock contributes to capital structure balance by expanding the capital base without diluting common stock or incurring contractual obligations.

C. Primary purchasers of preferred stock are corporate investors, insurance companies and pension funds primarily because 70 percent of dividend income received by corporations is exempt from taxation whereas interest received is fully taxable.

D. Provisions associated with preferred stock

    1. Cumulative dividends

    2. Conversion feature

    3. Call feature

    4. Participation provision

    5. Floating rate

    6. Dutch Auction Preferred Stock

    7. Par value

VII. Comparing Features of Common and Preferred Stock and Debt

PPT 17-3	Features of Alternative Security Issues (Table 17-3)

PPT 17-4	Risk and Expected Return for Various Security Classes (Figure 17-1)

Summary Listing of Transparencies

Solution Transparencies to Chapter Problems

Other Supplements for Chapter

Cases for Use with Foundations of Financial Management, Alpha Biogenetics (poison pill)

Cases for Use with Foundations of Financial Management, Midsouth Exploration Company (preferred stock)

Dividend Policy and Retained Earnings $\boxed{18}$

Author's Overview

The key initial question to be asked is: How does a corporation determine the amount of dividends to be paid? The discussion should move to the marginal principle of retained earnings with the associated emphasis on dividends as a passive variable in the decision-making process. The corporate life-cycle curve is included to relate growth to dividend policy. Because few students would accept the theory that a corporation sets its dividend payment entirely on the basis of whether the corporation or stockholder can make a higher return on the funds, the passive approach to dividends is seen as a good but incomplete theory that must be supplemented with further considerations. The instructor can then cover other relevant functions of dividends such as resolution of uncertainty and information content (Gordon, Solomon, etc.), and integrate the marginal principle of retained earnings with considerations of investor preferences. Other influences on dividend policy such as legal requirements, cash position of the firm, access to capital markets, and the like are presented.

Additional material is also provided on dividend payment procedures and dividend reinvestment plans. Cash dividends are now a more attractive alternative then they once were. The equal treatment of cash dividends and long-term capital gains under the Tax Reform Act of 1986 is still an important issue since the return of a preferential capital-gains tax is still a possibility.

Stock repurchase as an alternative to the cash dividend has received increasing attention in the literature and in the popular press and makes a good ending discussion point.

Chapter Concepts

*   Corporate management must decide what to do with retained earnings: pay them out as dividends or reinvest them in future projects.

*   Dividends may have positive or negative information content for shareholders. Dividend policy can also provide information about where the firm is on its life cycle curve.

*   Many other factors also influence dividend policy such as legal rules, the cash position of the firm, the tax position of shareholders, and so on.

*   Stock dividends and stock splits provide common stockholders with new shares, but their value must be carefully assessed.

*   Some firms make a decision to repurchase their shares in the market rather than increase dividends.

Annotated Outline and Strategy

I.   **The Marginal Principle of Retained Earnings**

II.   **Life cycle growth and dividends**

    A.   The corporate growth rate in sales is a major influence on dividends.

    B.   A firm's dividend policy will usually reflect the firm's stage of development.

        1.   Stage I -- small firm, initial stage of development -- no dividends.

        2.   Stage II -- successful firm, growing demand for products and increasing sales, earnings and assets -- stock dividends followed later by cash dividends.

        3.   Stage III -- cash dividends rise as asset expansion slows and external funds are more readily available -- stock dividends and stock splits also common.

        4.   Stage IV -- the firm reaches maturity and maintains a stable sales growth rate and cash dividends tend to be 40-60 percent of earnings.

PPT 18-1   Life Cycle Growth and Dividend Policy (Figure 18-1)

Perspective 18-1: The life cycle curve is a very important concept and the impact of growth on cash flow can be tied back into cash forecasting in Chapter 4, and external and internal funds in Chapter 14. The particular life cycle curve we use is different than the one used in marketing classes in that it divides the growth phase into two parts: growth (accelerating growth) and expansion (decelerating growth). This is an important distinction for corporate dividend policy.

    C.   According to the passive residual theory of dividends, earnings should be retained as long as the rate earned is expected to exceed a stockholder's rate of return on the distributed dividend.

    D.   The residual dividend theory assumes a lack of preference for dividends by investors.

        1.   Much disagreement exists as to investors' preference for dividends or retention of earnings.

        2.   Relevance of dividends arguments

            a.   Resolves uncertainty

            b.   Information content

III. Corporate Dividend Policy - Dividend Stability

A. Growth firms with high rates of return usually pay relatively low dividends.

B. Mature firms follow a relatively high payout policy.

C. The average payout of U.S. corporations since WW II has been 40 to 50 percent of aftertax earnings.

D. The stable dividend policy followed by U.S. corporations indicates that corporate

PPT 18-2	Corporate Dividend Policy (Table 18-1)

management feels that stockholders have a preference for dividends.

> ***Perspective 18-2:*** *Figure 18-2 highlights the residual nature of retained earnings for the economy as a whole as companies preserve dividend payouts. This macro data may not support the theory as applied to individual firms.*

IV. Other Factors Influencing Dividend Policy

PPT 18-3	Corporate Profits and Dividends for manufacturing corporations (Figure 18-2)

A. Legal rules -- most states have enacted laws protecting corporate creditors by forbidding distribution of the firm's capital in the form of dividends.

B. Cash position-the firm must have cash available regardless of the level of past or current earnings in order to pay dividends.

C. Access to capital markets- the easier the access to capital markets, the more able the firm is to pay dividends rather than retain earnings.

D. Desire for control

1.   Small, closely-held firms may limit dividends to avoid restrictive borrowing provisions or the need to sell new stock.
2.   Established firms may feel pressure to pay dividends to avoid stockholders' demand for change of management.

E.   Tax position of shareholders

    1.   High tax-bracket stockholders may prefer retention of earnings.
    2.   Lower tax-bracket individuals, institutional investors, and corporations receiving dividends prefer higher dividend payout.

V.   Dividend Payment Procedures

A.   Dividends are usually paid quarterly.

B.   Three key dividend dates:

    1.   Holder of record date-the date the corporation examines its books to determine who is entitled to a cash dividend.
    2.   Ex-dividend date-two business days prior to the holder of record date. If an investor buys a share of stock after the third day prior to the holder of record date, the investor's name would not appear on the firm's books.
    3.   Payment date-approximate date of mailing of dividend checks.

VI.   Stock Dividends and Stock Splits

A.   Stock dividends -- an additional distribution of stock shares, typically about 10 percent of outstanding amount.

PPT 18-4	XYZ Corporation's Financial Position Before Stock Dividend (Table 18-3)
	XYZ Corporation's Financial Position After Stock Dividend (Table 18-4)

    1.   An accounting transfer is required at fair market from retained earnings. The par value of the stock dividend is transferred to the common stock account and the remainder (if any) is added to the capital in excess of par account.
    2.   Unless total cash dividends increase, the stockholder does not benefit from a stock dividend.
    3.   Use of stock dividends

a. Informational content-retention of earnings for reinvestment

b. Camouflage inability to pay cash dividends

B. Stock split -- a distribution of stock that increases the total shares outstanding by 20-25 percent or more.

PPT 18-5 XYZ Corporation Before and After Stock Split (Table 18-5)

1. Accounting transfer from retained earnings is not required. Par value of stock is reduced and the number of shares increases proportionately.
2. Benefits to stockholders, if any, are difficult to identify.
3. Primary purpose is to lower stock price into a more popular trading range.

VII. Repurchase of Stock

A. Alternative to payment of dividends

1. Most often used when firm has excess cash and inadequate investment opportunities.
2. With the exception of a lower capital gains tax (preferential tax treatment of capital gains was eliminated by the tax Reform Act of 1986) the stockholder would be as well off with a cash dividend.

Finance In Action: Is Oracle a Miracle?

By electing to retain all its earnings for subsequent reinvestment in the firm, Oracle has engaged in numerous stock splits in order to keep its stock highly visible. Not paying cash dividends has worked well for Oracle, but the same dividend policy might be disastrous for a more mature company that has stockholders who want cash dividends.

B. Other reasons for repurchase

1. Management may deem that stock is selling at a very low price and is the best investment available.
2. Use for stock options or as part of a tender offer in a merger or acquisition.

3.   To reduce the possibility of being "taken over."

PPT 18-6   Stock Repurchases (Table 18-7)

VII.   **Dividend Reinvestment Plans**

A.   Begun during the 1970s, plans provide investors with an opportunity to buy additional shares of stock with the cash dividend paid by the company.

B.   Types of plans

1.   The company sells treasury stock or authorized but unissued shares. The stock is often sold at a discount since no investment banking or underwriting fees have to be paid. This plan provides a cash flow to the company.

2.   The company's transfer agent buys shares of stock in the market for the stockholder. This plan does not provide a cash flow to the firm but is a service to the stockholder.

C.   Plans usually allow stockholders to supplement dividends with cash payments   up to $1,000 per month in order to increase purchase of stock.

Summary Listing of Transparencies

PPT 18-1	Life Cycle Growth and Dividend Policy (Figure 18-1)
PPT 18-2	None
PPT 18-3	Corporate Profits and Dividends (manufacturing corporations) (Figure 18-2)
PPT 18-4	XYZ Corporation's Financial Position Before Stock Dividend (Table 18-3)
	XYZ Corporation's Financial Position After Stock Dividend (Table 18-4)
PPT 18-5	XYZ Corporation Before and After Stock Split (Table 18-5)
PPT 18-6	Stock Repurchases (Table 18-7)
LT 18-1	Chapter 18 Outline
LT 18-2	Dividends vs. Retained Earnings
LT 18-3	Life Cycle Growth and Dividend Policy
LT 18-4	Other Factors Influencing Dividend Policy
LT 18-5	Cash and Stock Dividends
LT 18-6	Stock Splits
LT 18-7	Repurchase of Stock

Solution Transparencies to Chapter Problems

ST 18-1	Moon and Sons, Inc.
ST 18-3	Growth and Dividend Policy
ST 18-5	Squash Delight, Inc.
ST 18-7	Pills Berry Corporation
ST 18-9	Goren Bridge Contribution Company
ST 18-11	Peabody Mining Company
ST 18-13	Rolex Discount Jewelers
ST 18-15	Eastern Telecom
ST 18-17	Vegas Products
ST 18-19	Majestic Corporation

Other Supplements to Chapter

Cases for Use with Foundations of Financial Management, Montgomery Corporation (Dividend policy)

Cases for Use With Foundations of Financial Management, Orbit Chemical Co. (Dividend policy). This case also considers stock repurchases and stock options.

Convertibles, Warrants, and Derivatives

Author's Overview

Because the material in the chapter can be viewed from both a corporate finance and investments perspective, the student's interest in the chapter is usually quite high. The student is given an in depth exposure to convertibles, with primary attention devoted to valuation procedures. There is also material on the usefulness, advantages, and disadvantages of convertibles to the corporation. Many real world examples are included in the text and can be woven into the lecture. Accounting considerations related to APB #15 are covered using step-by-step procedures for computing primary and fully diluted earnings per share.

The discussion of warrants parallels many of the points considered under convertibles. The topic of leverage, as it applies to warrants, also is appropriately introduced at this point and provide valuable background material for the student who progresses to subsequent courses in investments.

We provide a brief introduction to options and future in a corporate finance context. We discuss put and call options and focus on employee stock options which may be of interest to those students entering the job market. Futures are presented in combination with corporate hedging activities using oil and currency futures.

Chapter Concepts

* Convertible securities can be converted to common stock at the option of the owner.

* Because these securities can be converted to common stock, they may move with the value of common stock.

* Interest rates on convertibles are lower.

* Warrants are similar to convertibles in that they give the warrant holder the right to acquire common stock.

* Accountants require that the potential effect of convertibles and warrants on earnings per share be reported on the income statement.

*   Derivative securities such as options and futures can be used by corporate financial managers for hedging activities.

Annotated Outline and Strategy

I.   **Convertible Securities**

    A.   A convertible is a fixed income security, bond, or preferred stock that can be converted at the option of the holder into common stock. (The chapter focuses on convertible bonds.)

    B.   Convertible terminology

        1.   Conversion ratio-number of shares of common stock into which the security may be converted

        2.   Conversion price-face value of bond divided by the conversion ratio

        3.   Conversion value-conversion ratio times the market price per share of common stock

        4.   Conversion premium-market value of convertible bond minus the conversion value

        5.   Pure bond value-the value of the convertible bond as a straight bond; the present value of the annual interest payment and maturity payment discounted at the market rate of interest

    C.   Value of a convertible bond

        1.   At issue, investors pay a conversion premium and the price of the convertible exceeds both the pure bond value and the conversion value.

        2.   If the market price of the common stock exceeds the conversion price, the market value of the bond will rise above its par value to the conversion value or higher.

        3.   The convertible bond's value is limited on the downside by its pure bond value, which is considered the "floor value."

PPT 19-1	Price Movement Pattern for a Convertible Bond (Figure 19-1)

PPT 19-2   Pricing Pattern for Convertible Bonds Outstanding, November 6, 2000 (Table 19-1)

D.   Is this Fool's Gold? Disadvantages to the Investor

     1.   All downside risk is not eliminated. When the conversion value is very high, the investor is subject to much downward price movement.

     2.   The pure bond value will fall if interest rates rise.

     3.   Interest rates on convertibles are less than on nonconvertible straight bonds of the same risk.

     4.   Convertibles are usually subject to the call provision.

E.   Advantages to the Corporation

     1.   Lower interest rate than a straight bond

     2.   May be only means of gaining access to the capital market

     3.   Enables the sale of stock at higher than market price

F.   Forcing conversion

PPT 19-3   Successful Convertible Bonds Not Yet Called-Table 19-3

     1.   Conversion may be forced if the company calls the convertible when the conversion value exceeds the call price.

     2.   Conversion is encouraged by a "step-up" provision in the conversion price.

II. **Accounting considerations with Convertibles**

    A.   Prior to 1969 the possible dilution effect of convertible securities on earnings per share was not required to be reflected in financial reports.

    B.   Currently earnings per share must be reported in two ways.

$$Basic earnings per share = \frac{earnings\ aftertaxes}{Shares\ of CommonStock}$$

$$Diluted\ earnings = \frac{Adjusted\ earnings\ after\ taxes}{Shares\ outstanding + AllConvertibleSecurities}$$

    where convertible securities include warrants, other options and any convertible securities that create common stock.

PPT 19-4   Selected Issues of Convertible Eurobonds, November 6, 2000 (Table 19-5)

III. Warrants

    A.   A warrant is an option to buy a stated number of shares of stock at a specified price over a given period.

        1.   Sweetens a debt issue
        2.   Usually detachable
        3.   Speculative; value dependent on market movement of stock

B.   Value of a warrant

$$I = (M - E) \times N$$

1.   Applying this formula, the minimum value of a warrant may be found:
where:

I =   intrinsic value of a warrant
M =   market value of a common stock
E =   exercise price of a warrant
N =   number of shares each share entitles the holder to purchase

2.   The actual price of the warrant may substantially exceed the formula value due to the speculative nature of warrants.

C.   Use of warrants for corporate financing

1.   Enhances a debt issue
2.   Add-on in a merger or acquisition
3.   Cannot be forced with a call, but option price is sometimes "stepped-up."
4.   Equity base expands when warrants are exercised but the underlying debt remains.

D.   Potential dilution of earnings per share upon exercise of warrants must be disclosed in financial reports.

PPT 19-6   Market Price Relationships for a Warrant (Figure 19-2)

E.   Accounting Considerations with warrants

IV.   **Derivatives**

A.   Call options are similar to employer stock options in that it is an option to buy securities at a set price for a specified period of time.

164

B.   A put option is the opposite of a call option. A put allows the put holder to sell shares to the put writer at a set price for a specified period of time.

C.   Futures contracts give the owner the right but not the obligation to buy or sell the underlying security or commodity at a future date.

D.   Derivatives can be used for speculation as well as hedging. Corporations generally use derivatives to hedge risk.

Summary Listing of Transparencies

PPT 19-1   Price Movement Pattern for a Convertible Bond (Figure 19-1)
PPT 19-2   Pricing Pattern for Convertible Bonds Outstanding, November 6, 2000 (Table 19-1)
PPT 19-3   Successful Convertible Bonds Not Yet Called (Table 19-3)
PPT 19-4   Diluted Earnings Per Share
PPT 19-5   Relationships Determining Warrant Prices (Table 19-5)
PPT 19-6   Market Price Relationships for a Warrant (Figure 19-2)
PPT 19-7   Review of Formulas
LT 19-1   Chapter 19 Outline
LT 19-2   Convertible Security
LT 19-3   Convertible Terminology
LT 19-4   Advantages and Disadvantages of Convertible Securities
LT 19-5   Warrant
LT 19-6   Use of Warrants in Corporate Finance
LT 19-7   Options

Solution Transparencies to Chapter Problems

ST 19-1   Preston Toy Company
ST 19-3   Goldman Sack Company
ST 19-5   Iowa Meat Packers
ST 19-6   D. Hilgers Technology
ST 19-7   D. Hilgers Technology (Continued)
ST 19-9   Eastern Digital Corporation
ST 19-11   Laser Electronics Company
ST 19-13   The Redford Investment Company
ST 19-15   Julie Aird
ST 19-17   Myers Business Systems
CP 19-1   Furgeson Corporation (Comprehensive Problem)
CP 19-2   I.M. Stern, Inc. (Comprehensive Problem)

Other Supplements to Chapter

Cases for Use with Foundations of Financial Management, Hamilton Products (convertible bonds)

External Growth Through Mergers

Author's Overview

The discussion of mergers and acquisitions brings together a number of topics discussed earlier in the text. The instructor is able to take a second look at earnings per share growth, price-earnings ratios, stockholder wealth maximization, and portfolio considerations. These topics are considered in the present existing merger environment. Most students enjoy hearing about unfriendly takeovers, proxy battles, White Knights and various defensive strategics.

A central consideration in the chapter is the effect of differential P/E ratios on postmerger earnings per share. Once this concept is understood, the student should be encouraged to consider why P/E ratios may differ for the acquiring firm and the merger candidate. At least one major variable affecting P/E ratios is the possibility of differential future growth rates. Through numerical analysis, the student begins to see that the short-term impact on earnings per share can be very different from the long-term effect. Of greater importance, the student is forced to consider what the impact of these short and long-term effects will be on the postmerger valuation. Another important consideration is the portfolio effect associated with the merger.

The price movement pattern associated with mergers is also worthy of consideration. Not only is the material of interest to students who relate well to investment oriented subjects, but it is also an important consideration to corporate financial management. The premium offered and the associated price movement may determine management's strategy is regard to accepting or fighting a proposal. This is particularly relevant in the latest merger movement in which unfriendly offers for undervalued assets are commonplace.

Chapter Concepts

* Firms engage in mergers for financial motives and to increase operating efficiency.

* Companies may be acquired through cash purchases or by one company exchanging its shares for another company's shares.

*   The potential impact of the merger on earnings per share and stock value must be carefully assessed.

*   The diversification benefits of a merger should be evaluated.

*   Some buyouts are of an unfriendly nature and are strongly opposed by the potential candidate.

Annotated Outline and Strategy

I.   **Motives and Characteristics of Recent Merger Movements**

    A.   The major theme of the merger movement in the latter part of the 1970s and 1980s was that it was cheaper to acquire other companies than it was to expand through new product development or the purchase of new plant and equipment.

    B.   In the 1990s, merger activity picked up because of low interest rates, changing regulations, intense competition, and evolving technology.

PPT 20-1	Ten Largest Acquisitions Ever (Table 20-1)

    C.   The biggest mergers occurred in 1998, 1999 and 2000 and were concentrated in the communications, oil, financial service and pharmaceutical industry..

II. **Motives for Business Combinations**

    A.   Business combinations may be either mergers or consolidations.

        1.   Merger: A combination of two or more companies in which the resulting firm maintains the identity of the acquiring company.

        2.   Consolidation: Two or more companies are combined to form an entirely new entity.

    B.   Financial motives

1. Risk reduction as a result of the portfolio effect

   a. Lower required rate of return by investors.
   b. Higher value of the firm.

2. Improved financing posture

   a. Greater access to financial markets to raise debt and equity capital.
   b. Attract more prestigious investment bankers to handle financing.
   c. Strengthen cash position and/or improve debt/equity ratio.

3. Obtain a tax loss carry forward, although the tax Reform Act of 1986 placed limitations on this process.

C. Non-financial motives

   1. Expand management and marketing capabilities.
   2. Acquire new products.
   3. Synergism: $2 + 2 = 5$.

D. Motives of selling stockholders

   1. Desire to receive acquiring firm's stock which may have greater acceptability in the market.
   2. Provides opportunity to diversify their holdings.
   3. Gain on sale of stock at an attractive price.
   4. Avoid the bias against smaller businesses.

III. Terms of Exchange

    A.   Cash purchases

        1.   Capital budgeting decision: Net present value of purchasing a going concern equals the present value of cash inflows including anticipated synergistic benefits minus cash outlays including adjustment for tax shield benefit from any tax loss carryforward.

        2.   Many firms were purchased for cash in the 1970s and 1980s at a price below the replacement costs of their assets, but the rising stock market of the 1990s has made this difficult to duplicate. Even after the stock market retreat in 2000 and early 2001, companies are still selling well above replacement costs.

    B.   Stock for stock exchange

        1.   Emphasizes the impact of the merger on earnings per share.

        2.   If the P/E ratio of the acquiring firm is greater than the P/E ratio of the acquired firm, there will be an immediate increase in earnings per share.

        3.   Stockholders of the acquired firm are usually more concerned with market value exchanged than earnings, dividends, or book value exchanged.

PPT 20-2	Financial Data on Potential Merging Firms (Table 20-2)

    C.   In addition to the immediate impact on earnings per share, the acquiring firm must be concerned with the long-run impact of the merger on market value.

        1.   An acquired firm may have a low P/E ratio because its future rate of growth is expected to be low. In the long run, the acquisition may reduce the acquiring firm's earnings per share and its market value.

2.   The acquisition of a firm with a higher P/E ratio causes an immediate reduction in earnings per share. In the long run, however, the higher growth rate of the acquired firm may cause earnings per share and the market value of the acquiring company to be greater than if the merger did not take place.

D.   Determinants of earnings per share impact of a merger

    1.   Exchange ratio
    2.   Relative growth rates
    3.   Relative sizes of the firms

PPT 20-3	Postmerger Earnings Per Share (Table 20-3), and Risk-Reduction Portfolio Benefits (Figure 20-1)

> ***Perspective 20-2****: The portfolio effect pertaining to mergers reinforces concepts in Chapter 13. Issue of earnings correlation and synergy can be discussed and, if possible, present a current merger situation with potential benefits.*

E.   Portfolio effect

    1.   If the risk assessment of the acquiring firm is decreased by a merger, its market value will rise even if the earnings per share remain constant.

    2.   Two types of risk reduction may be accomplished by a merger.

        a.   Business risk reduction may result from acquiring a firm that is influenced by an opposite set of factors in the business cycle.
        b.   Financial risk reduction may result from a lower use of debt in the post-merger financial structure of the acquiring firm.

IV.   Accounting Considerations in Mergers and Acquisitions

A.   Prior to December 2000, a merger was treated as either a pooling of interests or a purchase of assets on the books of the acquiring firm. After December 6, 2000 pooling of interests was no longer allowed.

171

B.   Criteria for pooling of interests treatment before December, 2000.

1.   The acquiring firm issues only common stock, with rights identical to its old outstanding voting stock in exchange for substantially all the voting stock of the acquired company.

2.   The acquired firm's stockholders maintain an ownership position in the surviving firm.

3.   The merged firm does not intend to dispose of a significant portion of the assets of the combined companies within two years.

4.   The combination is effected in a single transaction.

C.   Purchase of assets

1.   Necessary when the tender offer is in cash, bonds, preferred stock, or common stock with restricted rights.

2.   Any excess of purchase price over book value is recorded as goodwill and written off over a maximum period of 40 years (with some exceptions).

3.   Before the accounting change goodwill had to be written off over a maximum of 40 years. This caused a negative effect on postmerger earnings. Under the new rules, goodwill does not have to be written off unless there is a verifiable decrease in the value of the acquired firm.

V.   Negotiated versus Tender Offers

A.   Friendly versus unfriendly mergers

1.   Most mergers are friendly and the terms are negotiated by the officers and directors of the involved companies.

2.   Goodwill. During the 1970s and 1980s, takeover tender offers have occurred frequently and many proposed mergers have been opposed by the management of candidate firms.

B.   Unfriendly takeover attempts have resulted in additions to the Wall Street vocabulary.

1.   Saturday Night Special - a surprise offer made right before the market closes for the weekend.

2.   White Knight - a third firm that management of the target firm calls upon to help avoid the initial, unwanted tender offer.

172

3. Leveraged takeover - the acquiring firm negotiates a loan based on the target company's assets (particularly a target company with large cash balances).

C. Actions by target companies to avoid unwanted takeovers.

1. White Knight arrangements.
2. Moving corporate offices to states with protective provisions against takeovers.
3. Buying up company's own stock to reduce amount available for takeover.
4. Encouraging employees to buy stock under corporate pension plan.
5. Increasing dividends to keep stockholders happy.
6. Staggering election of members of the board of directors.
7. Buying other firms to increase size.
8. Avoiding large cash balances which encourage leveraged takeover attempts.

VI. Premium Offers and Stock Price Movements

A. The average premium paid over market value in mergers or acquisitions has been in the 40-60 percent range.

VII. Two step buyout

A. The acquiring firm attempts to gain control by offering a very high cash price for 51 percent of the outstanding shares of the target firm. Simultaneously, a second lower price is announced that will be paid, either in cash, stock, or bonds at a subsequent point in time.

B. One problem with merger premiums is they usually disappear if the merger is called off.

C. The procedure provides a strong incentive for stockholders of the target firm to quickly react to the offer. Also, the two step buyout enables the acquiring firm to pay a lower total price than if a single offer is made.

D. The SEC is keeping a close watch on the two step buyout because of fears that the less sophisticated stockholders may be at a disadvantage when competing against arbitragers and institutional investors.

Summary Listing of Transparencies

PPT 20-1	Ten Largest Acquisitions Ever (Table 20-1)
PPT 20-2	Financial Data on Potential Merging Firms (Table 20-2)
PPT 20-3	Risk-Reduction Portfolio Benefits (Figure 20-1) and Postmerger Earnings Per Share (Table 20-3)
LT 20-1	Chapter 20 Outline
LT 20-2	Mergers vs. Consolidations
LT 20-3	Why Merge?
LT 20-4	3 Types of Mergers
LT 20-5	Motives of Selling Stockholders
LT 20-6	Terms of Exchange
LT 20-7	Negotiated vs. Tender Offers
LT 20-8	Wall Street Takeover Terminology

Solution Transparencies to Chapter Problems

ST 20-1	The Clark Corporation
ST 20-3	Texas Investments, Inc.
ST 20-5	The Mantle Corporation
ST 20-7	Surgical Inc.
ST 20-9	Meneeley Construction Company

Other Supplements to Chapter

Cases for Use with Foundations of Financial Management, National Brands versus A-1 Holdings (Merger Analysis).

Cases for Use with Foundations of Financial Management, KFC and the Colonel (General Business Considerations)

International Financial Management

Author's Overview

The instructor should stress the importance of international financial management (and international trade) to the class. The students can easily appreciate the everyday events that bring the world closer together. An important point is that international finance has the same elements as domestic financial management only the issues tend to be more involved. The firm must not only make a profit on a transaction, but convert that profit into the appropriate currency in a satisfactory manner. With the U.S. becoming a mature economy, it is increasingly important that students understand how to conduct business across international borders.

While we have attempted to integrate international material throughout the book, this chapter concentrates only on international issues and is a good introduction to the complexities of international financial decision making for those instructors wanting more depth in this area.

Chapter Concepts

* The multinational corporation is one that crosses international borders to gain expanded markets.

* A company operating in many foreign countries must consider the effect of exchange rates on its profitability and cash flow.

* Foreign exchange risk can be hedged or reduced.

* Political risk must carefully assessed in making a foreign investment decision.

* The potential means for financing international operations are much greater than for domestic operations and should be carefully considered.

Annotated Outline and Strategy

I. Introduction

    A. Many factors have contributed to greater economic interaction among the world's nations.

        1. Advances in communication and transportation.
        2. Adaptation of political systems.

            a. Post World War II rebuilding programs
            b. European Common Market
            c. NAFTA

        3. International flows of capital and technology.
        4. International currency: U.S. Dollar.
        5. Interdependence for scarce resources.

    B. International business operations are complex and risky and require special understanding.

PPT 21-1	International Activities of Selected U.S. Corporations (Table 21-1)

II. The Multinational Corporation (MNC)

    A. Basic forms of MNC.

        1. Exporter -- exportation to foreign markets of domestically produced products.
        2. Licensing Agreement -- granting of a license to an independent local (in the foreign country) firm to use the "exporting" firm's technology.
        3. Joint Venture -- cooperative business operation with a firm (or firms) in the foreign country.
        4. Fully Owned Foreign Subsidiary.

    B. International Environment Versus Domestic Environment.

1. More risky -- in addition to normal business risks, the MNC is faced with foreign exchange risk and political risk. The portfolio risk of the parent company, however, may be reduced if foreign and domestic operations are not correlated.
2. Potentially more profitable.
3. More complex -- the laws, customs, and economic environment of the host country may vary in many respects:

   a. Rates of inflation
   b. Tax rules
   c. Structure and operation of financial institutions
   d. Financial policies and practices
   e. Work habits and wages of laborers

III. Foreign Exchange Rates

A. To facilitate international trade, currencies must be exchanges. For example, and exporter will usually desire payment in the currency of his home country. The importer must swap his domestic currency for the currency desired by the exporter in order to pay his bill.

Finance In Action: The Debut of the Euro

Eleven European countries have a new currency and a new monetary authority, which will more closely link their economies and currencies together. The new currency is called the EURO and it will make international hedging more simple by reducing a large number of currency and it may help create more competitive markets in the Euro-Zone.

Perspective 21-1: The instructor may wish to use Table 21-2 to illustrate foreign exchange rates and how they change over time. He or she may wish to comment on the declining value of the dollar and give an update on the current value of the dollar.

B.   Factors affecting exchange rates

1.   Supply of and demand for the currencies of the various countries.
2.   The degree of central bank intervention.
3.   Inflation rate differentials (Purchasing Power Parity Theory).
4.   Interest rate differentials (Interest Rate Parity Theory).
5.   Balance of payments
6.   Government policies
7.   Other factors

a.   Capital market movements
b.   Changes in supply of and demand for the products and services of individual countries
c.   Labor disputes

C.   Many variables affect currency exchange rates. The importance of each variable or set of variables will change as economics and political conditions change throughout the world.

D.   Spot Rates, Forward Rates, and Cross Rates

Perspective 21-2: *There are a number of easily understood examples in the text on spot and forward rates as well as cross rates. The instructor can use these with students who have little or no international background.*

1.   Spot rate -- the exchange rate between currencies with immediate delivery
2.   Forward rate -- the rate of exchange between currencies when delivery will occur in the future.
3.   Cross rates -- the exchange rate between currencies such as Danish Krone and British Pounds based on their exchange rate with another currency such as U.S. Dollars.

IV. Managing Foreign Exchange Risk -- the possibility of experiencing a drop in revenue or an increase in cost in an international transaction due to a change in foreign exchange rates.

A. Three types of foreign exchange risk exposure

   1. Accounting or translation exposure -- depends upon accounting rules established by the parent company's government. Under FASB #52, all foreign currency denominated assets and liabilities are converted at the rate of exchange in effect on the date of balance sheet preparation.
   2. Transaction exposure -- in the U.S., foreign exchange gains and losses are reflected in the income statement for the current period -- this increases the volatility of earnings per share.
   3. Economic Exposure to different county GDP performance.

B. There are three strategies used to minimize transaction exposure:

   1. Hedging in the forward exchange market -- the recipient (seller) of foreign currency in an international transaction sells a forward contract to assure the amount that will be received in domestic currency.
   2. Hedging in the money market -- the recipient borrows foreign currency in the amount to be received and then immediately converts to domestic currency. When the receivable is collected, the loan is paid off.
   3. Hedging in the currency futures market -- futures contracts in foreign currencies began trading in the International Monetary Market (IMM) of the Chicago Mercantile Exchange on May 16, 1972 and on the London International Financial Futures Exchange (LIFFE) in September, 1982

V. **Foreign Investment Decisions**

A. Reasons for U.S. firms to invest in foreign countries

   1. Fear of import tariffs (in foreign countries).
   2. Lower production costs particularly with regard to labor costs.
   3. Ease of entry because of advanced American technology.
   4. Tax advantages.
   5. Strategic considerations -- competition.
   6. International diversification.

B.   Foreign firms are expanding their investment in the United States

    1.   Foreign investments in the United States provide employment for millions of people.

    2.   Reasons for foreign expansion in the U.S.

        a.   International diversification
        b.   Strategic considerations
        c.   Increasing labor costs
        d.   Saturated markets
        e.   Shortage of land for development
        f.   Large market in U.S.
        g.   Labor restrictions overseas
        h.   Access to advanced technology
        i.   Political stability

PPT 21-3   Risk Reduction from International Diversification (Figure 21-1)

C.   Analysis of Political Risk

    1.   The structure of the foreign government and/or those in control may change many times during the lengthy period necessary to recover an investment. "Unfriendly" changes may result in:

        a.   Foreign exchange restriction
        b.   Foreign ownership limitations
        c.   Blockage of repatriation of earnings
        d.   Expropriation of foreign subsidiary's assets

    2.   Safeguards against political risk

        a.   A thorough investigation of the country's political stability prior to investment.
        b.   Joint ventures with local (foreign) companies
        c.   Joint ventures with multiple companies representing multiple countries.

d.   Insurance through the federal government agency, Overseas Private Investment Corporation (OPIC).

V.   Financing International Business Operations

Finance in Action: High Stakes Espionage in International Travel

Corporate espionage is on the rise globally due to technological advances and the large number of corporate executives who now travel around the world with labtop computers full of critical company secrets. This box demonstrates the intensity of international competition. This is a good place to discuss ethics of business and the lack of consistent international ethical systems.

A.   Letters of credit -- in order to reduce the risk of non-payment, an exporter may require an importer to furnish a letter of credit. The letter of credit is normally issued by the importer's bank and guarantees payment to the exporter upon delivery of the merchandise if the specified conditions are met.

B.   Export credit insurance -- a private association of 60 U.S. insurance firms, the Foreign Credit Insurance Association (FCIA), may provide insurance against non-payment by foreign customers.

C.   Funding of transactions

       1.   Export-Import Bank (Eximbank) -- facilitates the financing of U.S. exports through several programs.

       2.   Loans from the parent company or sister affiliate.

            a.   Parallel loans -- an arrangement where two parent firms in different countries each make a loan to the affiliate of the other parent, The procedure eliminates foreign exchange risk.

            b.   Fronting loans -- loans from a parent firm to a foreign subsidiary via a bank located in the foreign country.

       3.   Eurodollar loans -- loans from foreign banks that are denominated in dollars.

            a.   There are many participants in the Eurodollar market from throughout the world particularly the U.S., Canada, Western Europe and Japan.

            b.   Lower borrowing costs and the absence of compensating balance requirements are significant incentives for U.S. firms.

c.   The lending rate is based on the London Interbank Offered Rate (LIBOR).

d.   Lending in the Eurodollar market is almost exclusively done by commercial banks. Large Euro-currency loans are frequently syndicated and managed by a lead bank.

4.   Eurobond market -- long-term funds may be secured by issuing Eurobonds. These bonds are sold throughout the world but are denominated primarily in U.S. dollars and duetsche marks.

     a.   Disclosure requirements are less stringent.

     b.   Registration costs are lower than in U.S.

     c.   Some tax advantages exist.

     d.   Caution must be exercised because of the exposure to foreign exchange risk.

5.   International equity markets -- selling common stock to residents of a foreign country provides financing and also reduces political risk.

     a.   Multinational firms list their shares on major stock exchanges around the world. Half the stocks listed on the Amsterdam stock exchange are foreign.

     b.   Marketing securities internationally requires firms to adjust their procedures. For example, commercial banks have a dominant role in the securities business throughout Europe.

     c.   Over 200 Foreign companies are listed on the NYSE.

     d.   American Depository Receipts (ADRs) are a common way for foreign firms to list shares in the U.S.

6.   International Finance Corporation (IFC) -- the IFC was established in 1956 and is unit of the World Bank. Its objective is to promote economic development in the 119 member countries of the World Bank.

     a.   A multinational firm may be able to raise equity capital by selling partial ownership to the IFC.

     b.   The IFC decides to participate in the venture on the basis of profitability and the potential benefit to the host country.

     c.   Once the venture is well established, the IFC frees up its capital by selling its ownership interest.

VII.   Unsettled Issues in International Finance

A.   The complexity of the multinational business environment generates questions for which there are no easy answers.

1.   Should a foreign affiliate design a capital structure similar to that of the parent firm or one that fits the acceptable pattern of the host country?
2.   Who should determine the dividend policy of a foreign affiliate -- the affiliate management or the parent management?

B.   Successful participation in the international business environment requires cohesive, coordinated financial management.

VII.   Appendix 21A: Cash Flow Analysis and the Foreign Investment Decision

A.   Cash Flow Analysis

B.   Tax Factors

C.   Foreign Exchange Considerations

D.   Present Value Analysis

E.   The Risk Factor

Perspective 21-3: **The appendix represents a reasonably complicated consideration of a foreign investment decision by a corporation. Because adequate coverage requires 30-45 minutes, it is relegated to the appendix.**

PPT 21-4   Cash Flow Analysis of a Foreign Investment (Table 21A-1)

Summary Listing of Transparencies

PPT 21-1   Data on International Activities of Selected U.S. Corporations (Table 21-1)

PPT 21-2   Selected Currencies and Exchange Rates. Dollar (fractions of dollar) that one can exchange for each unit of foreign currency ($/currency) (Table 21-2)

PPT 21-3   Risk Reduction from International Diversification (Figure 21-1)

PPT 21-4   Cash Flow Analysis of a Foreign Investment (Table 21A-1)

LT 21-1   Chapter 21 Outline

LT 21-2   Multinational Corporations

LT 21-3   Exchange Rates

LT 21-4   Spot Rates and Forward Rates

LT 21-5   Managing Foreign Exchange Risk

LT 21-6   Financing International Business Operations

Solution Transparencies to Chapter Problems

ST 21-1   Exchange Rates

ST 21-3   Spot and Forward Rates

ST 21-5   Cross Rates

ST 21-6   Purchasing Power Theory

ST 21-7   Continuation of Purchasing Power Theory

ST 21-9   Adjusting Returns for Exchange Rates

ST 21A-1   The Office Automation Corporation (Appendix)

Part B:

Solutions to
End-of-Chapter Problems

Chapter 1

Discussion Questions

1-1.   What advantages does a sole proprietorship offer? What is a major drawback of this type of organization?

A sole proprietor ship offers the advances of simplicity of decision making and low organizational and operating costs. A major drawback is that there is unlimited liability to the owner.

1-2.   What form of partnership allows some of the investors to limit their liability? Explain briefly.

A limited partnership allows some of the partners to limit their liability. Under this arrangement, one or more partners are designated general partners and have unlimited liability for the debts of the firm; other partners are designated limited partners and are liable only for their initial contribution. The limited partners are normally prohibited from being active in the management of the firm.

1-3.   In a corporation, what group has the ultimate responsibility for protecting and managing the stockholders' interests?

The board of directors.

1-4.   While a corporation has many advantages over other forms of organizations, it has one key disadvantage. What is that?

One of the key disadvantages of a corporation is double taxation of earnings; first at the corporate level and then at the stockholder level if dividends are paid.

1-5.   What issue does agency theory examine? Why is it important in a public corporation rather than in a private corporation?

Agency theory examines the relationship between the owners of the firm and the managers of the firm. In privately owned firms, management and the owners are usually the same people. Management operates the firm to satisfy its own goals, needs, financial requirements and the like. As a company moves from private to public ownership, management now represents all owners. This places management in the agency position of making decisions in the best interest of all shareholders.

1-6.   Why are institutional investors important in today's business world?

Because institutional investors such as pension funds and mutual funds own a large percentage of major U.S. companies, they are having more to say about the way publicly owned companies are managed. As a group, they have the ability to vote large blocks of shares for the election of a board of directors, which is suppose to run the company in an efficient, competitive manner. The threat of being able to replace poor performing boards of directors makes institutional investors quite influential. Since these institutions, like pension funds and mutual funds, represent individual workers and investors, they have a responsibility to see that the firm is managed in an efficient and ethical way.

1-7.   Why is profit maximization, by itself, an inappropriate goal? What is meant by the goal of maximization of shareholder wealth?

The problem with a profit maximization goal is that it fails to take account of risk, the timing of the benefits is not considered, and profit measurement is a very inexact process. The goal of shareholders wealth maximization implies that the firm will attempt to achieve the highest possible total valuation in the marketplace. It is the one overriding objective of the firm and should influence every decision.

1-8.   When does insider trading occur? What government agency is responsible for protecting against the unethical practice of insider trading?

Insider trading occurs when someone has information that is not available to the public and then users the information to profit from trading in a company's common stock.

1-9.   In the terms of the life of the securities offered, what is the difference between money and capital markets?

Money markets refer to those markets dealing with short-term securities that have a life of one year or less. Capital markets refer to securities with a life of more than one year.

1-10.   What is the difference between a primary and a secondary market?

A primary market refers to the use of the financial markets to raise new funds. After the securities are sold to the public (institutions and individuals), they trade in the secondary market between investors. It is in the secondary market that prices are continually changing as investors buy and sell securities based on the expectations of corporate prospects.

1-11.   Assume you are looking at many companies with equal risk, which ones will have the highest stock prices?

Given companies with equal risk, those companies with expectations of high return will have higher common stock prices relative to those companies with poor expectations.

1-12.   What changes can take place under restructuring? In recent times, what group of investors has often forced restructuring to take place?

Restructuring can result in changes in the capital structure (liabilities and equity on the balance sheet). It can also result in the selling of low-profit-margin divisions with the proceeds reinvested in better investment opportunities, and sometimes restructuring results in the removal of the current management team or large reductions in the work force. Restructuring has also included mergers and acquisitions.

Institutional investors have been very influential in forcing restructuring to take place in recent years.

1-13.   What impact has the Internet had on competition for full service brokers such as Merrill Lynch and Salomon Smith Barney?

Firms like Charles Schwabb, E-Trade, and Ameritrade allow customers to trade using the Internet. Full service brokers have had to follow suit, even though it is not as profitable to them for their customers to trade on the Internet rather than through the normal broker arrangement.

The shift to Internet trading has enabled a change in price quotes from fractions to more precise decimals. This also puts a squeeze on brokers' profits.

Chapter 2

Discussion Questions

2-1.   Discuss some financial variables that affect the price-earnings, ratio.

The price-earnings ratio will be influenced by the earnings and sales growth of the firm, the risk or volatility in performance, the debt-equity structure of the firm, the dividend payment policy, the quality of management, and a number of other factors. The ratio tends to be future-oriented, and the more positive the outlook, the higher it will be.

2-2.   What is the difference between book value per share of common stock and market value per share? Why does this disparity occur?

Book value per share is arrived at by taking the cost of the assts and subtracting out liabilities and preferred stock and dividing by the number of common shares outstanding. It is based on the historical costs of the assets. Market value per share is based on current assessed value of the firm in the marketplace and may bear little relationship to original cost. Besides the disparity between book and market value caused by the historical cost approach, other contributing factors are the growth prospects for the firm, the quality of management, and the industry outlook. To the extent these are quite negative or positive, market value may differ widely from book value.

2-3.   Explain how depreciation generates actual cash flows for the company.

The only way depreciation generates cash flows for the company is by serving as a tax shield against reported income. This non-cash deduction may provide cash flow equal to the tax rate times the depreciation charged. This much in taxes will be saved, while no cash payments occur.

2-4.   What is the difference between accumulated depreciation and depreciation expense? How are they related?

Accumulated depreciation is the sum of all past and present depreciation charges, while depreciation expense is the current year's charge. They are related in that the sum of all prior depreciation expense should be equal to accumulated depreciation (subject to some differential related to asset write-offs).

2-5.   How is the income statement related to the balance sheet?

The earnings (less dividends) reported in the income statement is transferred to the ownership section of the balance sheet as retained earnings. Thus, what we earn in the income statement becomes part of the ownership interest in the balance sheet.

2-6.   Comment on why inflation may restrict the usefulness of the balance sheet as normally presented.

The balance sheet is based on historical costs. When prices are rising rapidly, historical cost data may lose much of their meaning–particularly for plant and equipment and inventory.

2-7.   Explain why the statement of cash flows provides useful information that goes beyond income statement and balance sheet data.

The income statement and balance sheet are based on the accrual method of accounting, which attempts to match revenues and expenses in the period in which they occur. However, accrual accounting does not attempt to properly assess the cash flow position of the firm. The statement of cash flows fulfills this need.

2-8.   What are the three primary sections of the statement of cash flows? In what section would the payment of a cash dividend be shown?

The sections of the statement of cash flows are:

Cash flows from operating activities
Cash flows from investing activities
Cash flows from financing activities

The payment of cash dividends falls into the financing activities category.

2-9.   What is free cash flow? Why is it important to leveraged buyouts?

Free cash flow is equal to cash flow from operating activities:

| Minus: | Capital expenditures required to maintain the productive capacity of the firm. |

| Minus: | Dividends (required to maintain the payout on common stock and to cover any preferred stock obligation). |

The analyst or banker normally looks at free cash flow to determine whether there are insufficient excess funds to pay back the loan associated with the leveraged buy-out.

2-10.   Why is interest expense said to cost the firm substantially less than the actual expense, while dividends cost it 100 percent of the outlay?

Interest expense is a tax deductible item to the corporation, while dividend payments are not. The net cost to the corporation of interest expense is the amount paid multiplied by the difference of (one minus the applicable tax rate).

Problems

2-1.   Frantic Fast Foods had earnings after taxes of $390,000 in the year 2000 with 300,000 shares outstanding. On January 1, 2001, the firm issued 25,000 new shares. Because of the proceeds from these new shares and other operating improvements, earnings after taxes increased by 20 percent.

        a. Compute earnings per share for the year 2000.
        b. Compute earnings per share for the year 2001.

Solution:
Frantic Fast Foods

a. Year 2000

$$\text{Earnings per share} = \frac{\text{Earnings after taxes}}{\text{Shares outstanding}}$$

$$= \frac{\$390,000}{300,000} = \$1.30$$

b. Year 2001

$$\text{Earnings after taxes} = \$390,000 \times 1.20 = \$468,000$$

$$\text{Shares outstanding} = 300,000 + 25,000 = 325,000$$

$$\text{Earnings per share} = \frac{\$468,000}{325,000} = \$1.44$$

2-2.   Given the following information, prepare, in good form, an income statement for the Dental Drilling Company.

Selling and administrative expense	$ 60,000
Depreciation expense	70,000
Sales	470,000
Interest expense	40,000
Cost of goods sold	140,000
Taxes	45,000

Solution:

Dental Drilling Company
Income Statement

Sales	$ 470,000
Cost of goods sold	$ 140,000
Gross Profit	$ 330,000
Selling and administrative expense	$ 60,000
Depreciation expense	$ 70,000
Operating profit	$ 200,000
Interest expense	$ 40,000
Earnings before taxes	$ 160,000
Taxes	$ 45,000
Earnings after taxes	$ 115,000

2-3.   Prepare in good form an income statement for ATM Cards, Inc. Take your calculations all the way to computing earnings per share.

Sales	$800,000
Shares outstanding	100,000
Cost of goods sold	300,000
Interest expense	20,000
Selling and administrative expense	40,000
Depreciation expense	30,000
Preferred stock dividends	80,000
Taxes	110,000

Solution:

ATM Cards, Inc.
Income Statement

Sales	$ 800,000
Cost of goods sold	300,000
Gross profit	$ 500,000
Selling and administrative expense	40,000
Depreciation expense	30,000
Operating profit	$ 430,000
Interest expense	20,000
Earnings before taxes	$ 410,000
Taxes	110,000
Earnings after taxes	$ 300,000
Preferred stock dividends	80,000
Earnings available to common stockholders	220,000
Shares outstanding	100,000
Earnings per share	$2.20

2-4.   Censored Books, Inc. sold 1,400 textbooks for $100 each to High Tuition University in 2001. These books cost $71 to produce. Censored Books spent $5,000 (selling expense) to convince the University to buy its books. In addition, Censored Books borrowed $46,000 on January 1, 2001, on which the company paid 10 percent interest. Both interest and principal were paid on December 31, 2001. The publishing firm's tax rate is 30 percent. Depreciation expense for the year was $8,000.

Did Censored Book Company make a profit in 2001? Please verify with an income statement presented in good form.

Solution:

Censored Books, Inc.
Income Statement
For the Year Ending December 31, 2001

Sales (1,400 books at $100 each)	$ 140,000
Cost of goods sold (1,400 books at $71 each)	99,400
Gross profit	$ 40,600
Selling expense	5,000
Depreciation expense	8,000
Operating profit	$ 27,600
Interest expense	4,600
Earnings before taxes	$ 23,000
Taxes @ 30%	6,900
Earnings after taxes	$ 16,100

2-5.   Lemon Auto Wholesalers had sales of $700,000 in 2001 and cost of goods sold represented 70 percent of sales. Selling and administrative expenses were 12 percent of sales. Depreciation expense was $10,000 and interest expense for the year was $8,000. The firm's tax rate is 30 percent.

a. Compute earnings after taxes.
b. Assume the firm hires Ms. Carr, an efficiency expert, as a consultant. She suggests that by increasing selling and administrative expenses to 14 percent of sales, sales can be expanded to $750,000. The extra sales effort will also reduce cost of goods sold to 66 percent of sales (there will be a larger makeup in prices as a result of more aggressive selling). Depreciation expense will remain at $10,000. However, more automobiles will have to be carried in

inventory to satisfy customers, and interest expense will go up to $15,000. The firm's tax rate will remain at 30 percent. Compute revised earnings after taxes based on Ms. Carr's suggestions for Lemon Auto Wholesalers. Will her ideas increase or decrease profitability?

Solution:

Lemon Auto Wholesales
Income Statement

a. Sales	$700,000
Cost of goods sold (70% of sales)	$490,000
Gross Profit	$ 210,000
Selling and administrative expense (12% of sales)	$ 84,000
Depreciation	$ 10,000
Operating profit	$ 116,000
Interest expense	$ 8,000
Earnings before taxes	$ 108,000
Taxes @ 30%	$ 32,400
Earnings after taxes	$ 75,600
b. Sales	$ 750,000
Cost of goods sold (66% of sales)	$ 495,000
Gross Profit	$ 255,000
Selling and administrative expense (14% of sales)	$ 105,000
Depreciation	$ 10,000
Operating profit	$ 140,000
Interest expense	$ 15,000
Earnings before taxes	$ 125,000
Taxes @ 30%	$ 37,500
Earnings after taxes	$ 87,500

Ms. Carr's idea will increase profitability.

2-6.   Classify the following balance sheet items as current or noncurrent.

Retained earnings   Bonds payable
Accounts payable   Accrued wages payable
Prepaid expenses   Accounts receivable
Plant and equipment   Capital in excess of par
Inventory   Preferred stock
Common stock   Marketable securities

Solution:

Retained earnings – noncurrent
Accounts payable – current
Prepaid expense – current
Plant and equipment – noncurrent
Inventory – current
Common stock – noncurrent
Bonds payable – noncurrent
Accrued wages payable – current
Accounts receivable – current
Capital in excess of par – noncurrent
Preferred stock – noncurrent
Marketable securities – current

2-7. Arrange the following income statement items so they are in the proper order of an income statement:

Taxes
Gross profit shares outstanding
Interest expense
Depreciation expense
Preferred stock dividends
Operating profit
Sales
Gross profit

Earnings per share
Earnings before taxes
Cost of goods sold
Earnings after taxes
Earnings available to common
  stockholders
Selling and administrative expenses

Solution:

Sales
Cost of goods sold
   Gross profit
Selling and administrative expense
Depreciation expense
   Operating profit
Interest expense
   Earnings before taxes
Taxes
   Earnings after taxes
Preferred stock dividends
Earnings Available to Common Stockholders
Shares Outstanding
Earnings per share

2-8.   Identify whether each of the following items increases or decreases cash flow:

Increase in accounts receivable   Decrease in prepaid expenses
Increase in notes payable   Increase in inventory
Depreciation expense   Dividend payment
Increase in investments   Increase in accrued expenses
Decrease in accounts payable

Solution:

Increase in accounts receivable – decreases cash flow (use)
Increase in notes payable – increases cash flow (source)
Depreciation expense – increases cash flow (source)
Increase in investments – decreases cash flow (use)
Decrease in accounts payable – decreases cash flow (use)
Decrease in prepaid expense – increases cash flow (source)
Increase in inventory – decreases cash flow (use)
Dividend payment – decreases cash flow (use)
Increase in accrued expenses – increases cash flow (source)

2-9.   Okra Snack Delights, Inc. has an operating profit of $210,000. Interest expense for the year was $30,000; preferred dividends paid were $24,700; and common dividends paid were $36,000. Taxes were $59,300. The firm has 16,000 shares of common stock outstanding.

    a.   Calculate the earnings per share and the common dividends per share.
    b.   What was the increase in retained earnings for the year?

Solution:

Okra Snack Delights, Inc.

a.

Operating profit (EBIT)	$ 210,000
Interest expense	30,000
Earnings before taxes (EBT)	$ 180,000
Taxes	59,300
Earnings after taxes (EAT)	$ 120,700
Preferred dividends	24,700
Available to common stockholders	$ 96,000
Common dividends	36,000
Increase in retained earnings	$ 60,000

$$\text{Earnings per Share} = \frac{\text{Earnings Available to Common Stockholders}}{\text{Number of Shares of Com. Stock Outstanding}}$$

$$= \$96,000 / 16,000 \text{ shares}$$

$$= \$6.00 \text{ per share}$$

$$\text{Dividends per Share} = \$36,000 / 16,000 \text{ shares}$$

$$= \$2.25 \text{ per share}$$

b. Increase in retained earnings = $60,000

2-10.   Quantum Technology had $640,000 of retained earnings on December 31, 2001.
        The company paid common dividends of $30,000 in 2001 and had retained
        earnings of $500,000 on December 31, 2000. How much did Quantum
        Technology earn during 2001, and what would its earnings per share be if 40,000
        shares of common stock were outstanding?

Solution:
Quantum Technology

Retained earnings, December 31, 2002............$ 640,000
Less: Retained earnings, December 31, 1999.. 500,000
      Change in retained earnings ....$ 140,000
Add: Common stock dividends........................ 30,000
Earnings available to common stockholders....$ 170,000

Earnings per share

$$= \frac{\$170,000}{40,000 \text{ shares}} = \$4.25 \text{ per share}$$

2-11.   Coastal Pipeline, Inc. anticipated cash flow from operating activities of $8 million
        in 2002. It will need to spend $1.5 million on capital investments in order to
        remain competitive within its industry. Common stock dividends are projected at
        $.6 million and preferred stock dividends at $.25 million.

        a. What is the firm's projected free cash flow for the year 2002?
        b. What does the concept of free cash flow represent?

Solution:
Coastal Pipeline, Inc.

a. Cash flow from operations activities $8.00   million
   - Capital Expenditures   1.50
   - Common stock dividends   .60
   - Preferred stock dividends   .25
     Free cash flow $5.65   million

b. Free cash flow represents the funds that are available for
   special financial activities, such as a leveraged buyout.

2-12.   Fill in the blank spaces with categories 1 through 7 below:

1. Balance sheet (BS).
2. Income statement (IS).
3. Current assets (CA).
4. Fixed assets (FA).

5. Current liabilities (CL).
6. Long-term liabilities (LL).
7. Stockholders' equity (SE).

Indicate Whether Item is on Balance Sheet (BS) or Income Statement (IS)	If on Balance Sheet, Designate Which Category	Item
_____	_____	Retained earnings
_____	_____	Income tax expense
_____	_____	Accounts receivable
_____	_____	Common stock
_____	_____	Capital in excess of par value
_____	_____	Bonds payable, maturity 2005
_____	_____	Notes payable (six months)
_____	_____	Net income
_____	_____	Selling and administrative expenses
_____	_____	Inventories
_____	_____	Accrued expenses
_____	_____	Cash
_____	_____	Plant and equipment
_____	_____	Sales
_____	_____	Operating expenses
_____	_____	Marketable securities
_____	_____	Accounts payable
_____	_____	Interest expense
_____	_____	Income tax payable

Solution:

1. Balance Sheet (BS)
2. Income Statement (IS)
3. Current Assets (CA)
4. Fixed Assets (FA)
5. Current Liabilities (CL)
6. Long-Term Liabilities (LL)
7. Stockholders Equity (SE)

Indicate Whether the item is on Income Statement or Balance Sheet	If the Item is on Balance Sheet, Designate Which Category	Item
BS	SE	Retained Earnings
IS		Income Tax Expense
BS	CA	Accounts Receivable
BS	SE	Common Stock
BS	SE	Capital in excess of par value
BS	LL	Bonds payable maturity 2005
BS	CL	Notes Payable (6 months)
IS		Net income (Earnings after taxes)
IS		Selling and Adm. Exp.
BS	CA	Inventories
BS	CL	Accrued expenses
BS	CA	Cash
BS	FA	Plant & equipment
IS		Sales
IS		Operating expenses
BS	CA	Marketable securities
BS	CL	Accounts payable
IS		Interest expense
BS	CL	Income tax payable

2-13.   The Jupiter Corporation has a gross profit of $700,000 and $240,000 in depreciation expense. The Saturn Corporation also has $700,000 in gross profit, with $40,000 in depreciation expense. Selling and administrative expense is $160,000 for each company.

Given that the tax rate is 40 percent, compute the cash flow for both companies. Explain the difference in cash flow between the two firms.

Solution:

Jupiter Corporation – Saturn Corporation

	Jupiter	Saturn
Gross profit	$700,000	$700,000
Selling and adm. expense	160,000	160,000
Depreciation	240,000	40,000
Operating profit	$300,000	$500,000
Taxes (40%)	120,000	200,000
Earnings after taxes	$180,000	$300,000
Plus depreciation expense	$240,000	$40,000
Cash Flow	$420,000	$340,000

Jupiter had $200,000 more in depreciation which provided $80,000 (0.40 × $200,000) more in cash flow.

2-14.   Arrange the following items in proper balance sheet presentation.

Accumulated depreciation	$300,000
Retained earnings	96,000
Cash	10,000
Bonds payable	136,000
Accounts receivable	48,000
Plant and equipment—original cost	680,000
Accounts payable	35,000
Allowance for bad debts	6,000
Common stock $1 par, 100,000 shares outstanding	100,000
Inventory	66,000
Preferred stock, $50 par, 1,000 shares outstanding	50,000
Marketable securities	20,000
Investments	20,000
Notes payable	33,000
Capital paid in excess of par (common stock)	88,000

Solution:

Assets

Current Assets:

Cash		$ 10,000
Marketable securities		20,000
Accounts receivable	$ 48,000	
Less: Allowance for bad debts ..	6,000	42,000
Inventory		66,000
Total Current Assets		$138,000

Other Assets:

Investments		20,000

Fixed Assts:

Plant and equipment	$680,000	
Less: Accumulated depreciation	300,000	
Net plant and equipment		380,000
Total Assets		$538,000

Liabilities and Stockholders' Equity

Current Liabilities:

Accounts payable...	$ 35,000
Notes payable..	33,000
Total current liabilities.................................	$ 68,000
Long-term Liabilities..	
Bonds payable...	136,000
Total Liabilities...	$204,000

Stockholders' Equity:

Preferred stock, $50 par, 1,000 shares outstanding	50,000
Common stock, $1 par, 100,000 shares outstanding	100,000
Capital paid in excess of par (common stock)	88,000
Retained earnings...	96,000
Total Stockholders' Equity	$334,000
Total Liabilities and Stockholders' Equity	$538,000

2-15.   Landers Nursery and Garden Stores has current assets of $220,000 and fixed assets of $170,000. Current liabilities are $80,000 and long-term liabilities are $140,000. There is $40,000 in preferred stock outstanding and the firm has issued 25,000 shares of common stock. Compute book value (net worth) per share.

Solution:

Landers Nursery and Garden Stores

Current assets	$220,000
Fixed assets	170,000
Total assets	$390,000
−Current liabilities	80,000
−Long-term liabilities	140,000
Stockholders' equity	170,000
−Preferred stock obligation	40,000
Net worth assigned to common	$130,000
Common shares outstanding	25,000
Book value (net worth) per share	$5.20

2-16.   Amigo Software, Inc. has total assets of $800,000, current liabilities of $150,000, and long-term liabilities of $120,000. There is $65,000 in preferred stock outstanding. Thirty-thousand shares of common stock has been issued.

a. Compute book values (net worth) per share.
b. If there is $48,000 in earnings available to common stockholders and the firm's stock has a P/E of 20 times earnings per share, what is the current price of the stock?
c. What is the ratio of market value per share to book value per share? (Round to two places to the right of the decimal point.)

Solution:
Amigo Software, Inc.

a. Total assets...	$800,000
−Current liabilities	150,000
−Long-term liabilities	120,000
Stockholders' equity...............................	$530,000
−Preferred stock	65,000
Net worth assigned to common............	$465,000
Common shares outstanding.................	30,000
Book values (net worth) per share.......	$15.50
b. Earnings available to common	$48,000
Shares outstanding...............................	30,000
Earnings per share...............................	$1.60

P/E ratio	×	earnings per share	=	price
20	×	$1.60	=	$32.00

c. Market value per share (price) to book value per share
   $32.00/$15.50 = 2.06

2-17.   In problem 16, if the firm sells at 2.5 times book value per share, what will the P/E ratio be? (Round to the nearest whole number.)

Solution:

Amigo Software, Inc. (continued)

$$2.5 \times \text{book value per share} = \text{price}$$

$$2.5 \times \$15.5 = \$38.75$$

$$\frac{\text{Price}}{\text{Earnings per share}} = \text{P/E}$$

$$\frac{\$38.75}{\$1.60} = 24.22 \quad \text{P/E ratio} \quad \text{round to 24x}$$

2-18.   For December 31, 2001, the balance sheet of Baxter Corporation is as follows:

Current Assets		Liabilities	
Cash	$ 10,000	Accounts payable	$ 12,000
Accounts receivable	15,000	Notes payable	20,000
Inventory	25,000	Bonds payable	50,000
Prepaid expenses	12,000		

Fixed Assets		Stockholders' Equity	
Plant and equipment (gross)	$250,000	Common stock	$ 75,000
Less: Accumulated		Paid-in-capital	25,000
Depreciation	50,000	Retained earnings	80,000
Net plant and equipment	200,000		
		Total liabilities and	
Total assets	$262,000	Stockholders' equity	$262,000

Sales for 2001 were $220,000, and the cost of goods sold was 60 percent of sales. Selling and administrative expense was $22,000. Depreciation expense was 8 percent of plant and equipment (gross) at the beginning of the year. Interest expense for the notes payable was 10 percent, and interest expense on the bonds payable was 12 percent. These interest expenses are based on December 31, 2000, balances. The tax rate averaged 20 percent.

Two thousand dollars in preferred stock dividend were paid and $8,400 in dividends were paid to common stockholders. There were 10,000 shares of common stock outstanding.

During 2001, the cash balance and prepaid expenses balance were unchanged. Accounts receivable and inventory increased by 10 percent. A new machine was purchased on December 31, 2001, at a cost of $35,000. Accounts payable increased by 25 percent. Notes payable increased by $6,000 and bonds payable decreased by $10,000, both at the end of the year. The common stock and paid-in capital in excess of par accounts did not change.

a. Prepare an income statement for 2001.
b. Prepare a statement of retained earnings for 2001.
c. Prepare a balance sheet as of December 31, 2001.

Solution:

Baxter Corporation
2001 Income Statement

a. Sales	$220,000
Cost of good sold (60%)	132,000
Gross profit	$ 88,000
Selling and administrative expense	22,000
Depreciation expense (8%)	20,000[1]
Operating profit (EBIT)	$ 46,000
Interest expense	8,000[2]
Earnings before taxes	$ 38,000
Taxes (20%)	7,600
Earnings after taxes (EAT)	$ 30,400
Preferred stock dividends	2,000
Earnings available to common stockholder.	$ 28,400
Shares outstanding	10,000
Earnings per share	$ 2.84

---

[1] 8% × $250,000 = $20,000

[2] (10% × $20,000) + (12% × $50,000) = $8,000

b. 2001 Statement of Retained Earnings

Retained earnings balance, January 1, 2001	$ 80,000
Add: Earnings available to common stockholders, 2001	28,400
Deduct: Cash dividend declared in 2001	8,400
Retained earnings balance, December 31, 2001	$100,000

2001 Balance Sheet

Current Assets		Liabilities	
Cash	$10,000	Accounts payable	$15,000
Accounts receivable........	16,500	Notes payable	26,000
Inventory...........	27,500	Bonds payable	40,000
Prepaid expenses	12,000		
	$66,000		$81,000

Fixed Assets		Stockholders' Equity	
Gross plant........	$285,000	Common stock....	$ 75,000
Accumulated depr	(70,000)[3]	Paid in capital in excess of par	25,000
Net plant...........	215,000	Retained earnings	100,000
Total assets........	$281,000	Total Liability & Equity	$281,000

---

[3] $50,000 + $20,000 = $70,000

2-19.   Prepare a statement of cash flows for the Jeter Corporation. Follow the general procedures indicated in Table 2-10 of the chapter.

Jeter Corporation
Income Statement
For the Year Ended December 31, 2001

Sales...	$3,300,000
Cost of goods sold	1,950,000
Gross profits	1,350,000
Selling and administrative expense	650,000
Depreciation expense...	230,000
Operating income	470,000
Interest expense	80,000
Earnings before taxes	390,000
Taxes...	140,000
Earnings after taxes	250,000
Preferred stock dividends	10,000
Earnings available to common stockholders........................	$ 240,000
Shares outstanding..	150,000
Earnings per share	$1.60

Statement of Retained Earnings
For the Year Ended December 31, 2001

Retained earnings, balance, January 1, 2001.........................	$800,000
Add: Earnings available to common stockholders, 2001	240,000
Deduct: Cash dividends declared and paid in 2001.........	140,000
Retained earnings, balance, December 31, 2001...................	$900,000

Comparative Balance Sheets
For 2000 and 2001

	Year-End 2000	Year-End 2001
Assets		
Current assets:		
Cash	$ 100,000	$ 120,000
Accounts receivable (net)	500,000	510,000
Inventory..	610,000	640,000
Prepaid expenses..	60,000	30,000
Total current assets	1,270,000	1,300,000
Investments (long-term securities)	90,000	80,000
Plant and equipment	2,000,000	2,600,000
Less: Accumulated depreciation...............	1,000,000	1,230,000
Net plant and equipment.............................	1,000,000	1,370,000
Total assets	$2,360,000	$2,750,000

Liabilities and Stockholders' Equity

Current liabilities:

Accounts payable	$ 300,000	$ 550,000
Notes payable	500,000	500,000
Accrued expenses	70,000	50,000
Total current liabilities	870,000	1,100,000
Long-term liabilities:		
Bonds payable, 2004	100,000	160,000
Total liabilities	970,000	1,126,000
Stockholders' equity:		
Preferred stock, $100 par value	90,000	90,000
Common stock, $1 par value	150,000	150,000
Capital paid in excess of par	350,000	350,000
Retained earnings	800,000	900,000
Total stockholders' equity	1,390,000	1,490,000
Total liabilities and stockholders' equity	$2,360,000	$2,750,000

(The following questions apply to the Jeter Corporation, as presented in Problem 19.)

Solution:

Jeter Corporation
Statement of Cash Flows
For the Year Ended December 31, 2001

Cash flows from operating activities:

Net income (earnings after taxes)	$250,000
Adjustments to determine cash flow from operating activities:	
Add back depreciation	$230,000
Increase in accounts receivable	(10,000)
Increase in inventory	(30,000)
Decrease in prepaid expenses	30,000
Increase in accounts payable	250,000
Decrease in accrued expenses	(20,000)
Total adjustments	$450,000
Net cash flows from operating activities	$700,000

Cash flows from investing activities:

Decrease in investments...................	10,000	
Increase in plant and equipment.......	(600,000)	
Net Cash flows from investing activities...		(590,000)

Cash flows from financing activities:

Increase in bonds payable	60,000	
Preferred stock dividends paid.........	(10,000)	
Common stock dividends paid.........	(140,000)	(90,000)
Net cash flows from financing.........		
Net increase (decrease) in cash flows		**$ 20,000**

The student should observe that the increase in cash flows of $20,000 equals the $20,000 change in the cash account on the balance sheet. This indicates the statement is correct.

2-20.   Describe the general relationship between net income and net cash flows from operating activities for the firm.

Solution:

Cash flows from operating activities far exceeds net income. This occurs primarily because we add back depreciation of $230,000 and accounts payable increase by $250,000. Thus, the reader of the cash flow statement gets important insights as to how much cash flow was developed from daily operations.

2-21.   Has the buildup in plant and equipment been financed in a satisfactory manner? Briefly discuss.

Solution:

The buildup in plant and equipment of $600,000 (gross) and $370,000 (net) has been financed, in part, by the large increase in accounts payable (250,000). This is not a very satisfactory situation. Short-term sources of funds can always dry up, while fixed asset needs are permanent in nature. This firm may wish to consider more long-term financing, such as a mortgage, to go along with profits, the increase in bonds payable, and the add-back of depreciation.

2-22.   Compute the book value per common share for both 2000 and 2001 for the Jeter Corporation.

Solution:

$$\frac{\text{Book value}}{\text{Per share}} = \frac{\text{Stockholders' equity} - \text{Preferred stock}}{\text{Common shares outstanding}}$$

$$\frac{\text{Book value}}{\text{Per share (2000)}} = \frac{(\$1,390,000 - \$90,000)}{150,000} = \frac{\$1,300,000}{150,000} = \$8.67$$

$$\frac{\text{Book value}}{\text{Per share (2001)}} = \frac{(\$1,490,000 - \$90,000)}{150,000} = \frac{\$1,400,000}{150,000} = \$9.33$$

2-23.   If the market value of a share of common stock is 3.1 times book value for 2001, what is the firm's P/E ratio for 2001? (Round to the nearest whole number.)

Solution:

Market value $= 3.1 \times \$9.33 = \$28.92$

P/E ratio $= \$28.92 / \$1.60 = 18.07$ or $18 \times$

Chapter 3

Discussion Questions

3-1.   If we divide users of ratios into short-term lenders, long-term lenders, and stockholders, which ratios would each group be *most* interested in, and for what reasons?

       Short-term lenders–liquidity because their concern is with the firm's ability to pay short-term obligations as they come due.

       Long-term lenders–leverage because they are concerned with the relationship of debt to total assets. They also will examine profitability to insure that interest payments can be made.

       Stockholders–profitability, with secondary consideration given to debt utilization, liquidity, and other ratios. Since stockholders are the ultimate owners of the firm, they are primarily concerned with profits or the return on their investment.

3-2.   Explain how the Du Pont system of analysis breaks down return on assets. Also explain how it breaks down return on stockholders' equity.

       The Du Pont system of analysis breaks out the return on assets between the profit margin and asset turnover.

$$\underbrace{\frac{\text{Net income}}{\text{Total assets}}}_{} = \underbrace{\frac{\text{Net income}}{\text{Sales}}}_{\textit{Profit Margin}} \times \underbrace{\frac{\text{Sales}}{\text{Total assets}}}_{\textit{Asset Turnover}}$$

       In this fashion, we can assess the joint impact of profitability and asset turnover on the overall return on assets. This is a particularly useful analysis because we can determine the source of strength and weakness for a given firm. For example, a company in the capital goods industry may have a high profit margin and a low asset turnover, while a foodprocessing firm may suffer from low profit margins, but enjoy a rapid turnover of assets.

       The modified form of the Du Pont formula shows:

$$\text{Return on equity} = \frac{\text{Return on assets (investment)}}{(1 - \text{Debt/Assets})}$$

This indicates that return on stockholders' equity may be influenced by return on assets, the debt-to-assets ratio or a combination of both. Analysts or investors should be particularly sensitive to a high return on stockholders' equity that is influenced by large amounts of debt.

3-3.   If the accounts receivable turnover ratio is decreasing, what will be happening to the average collection period?

If the accounts receivable turnover ratio is decreasing, accounts receivable will be on the books for a longer period of time. This means the average collection period will be increasing.

3-4.   What advantage does the fixed charge coverage ratio offer over simply using times interest earned?

The fixed charge coverage ratio measures the firm's ability to meet all fixed obligations rather than interest payments alone, on the assumption that failure to meet any financial obligation will endanger the position of the firm.

3-5.   Is there any validity in rule-of-thumb ratios for all corporations, for example, a current ratio of 2 to 1 or debt to assets of 50 percent?

No rule-of-thumb ratio is valid for all corporations. There is simply too much difference between industries or time periods in which ratios are computed. Nevertheless, rules-of-thumb ratios do offer some initial insight into the operations of the firm, and when used with caution by the analyst can provide information.

3-6.   Why is trend analysis helpful in analyzing ratios?

Trend analysis allows us to compare the present with the past and evaluate our progress through time. A profit margin of 5 percent may be particularly impressive if it has been running only 3 percent in the last ten years. Trend analysis must also be compared to industry patterns of change.

3-7.   Inflation can have significant effects on income statements and balance sheets, and therefore on the calculation of ratios. Discuss the possible impact of inflation on the following ratios, and explain the direction of the impact based on your assumptions.

a. Return on investment.
b. Inventory turnover.
c. Fixed asset turnover.
d. Debt-to-assets ratio.

a.   Return on investment $= \dfrac{\text{Net income}}{\text{Total assets}}$

Inflation may cause net income to be overstated and total assets to be understated. Too high a ratio could be reported.

b.   Inventory turnover $= \dfrac{\text{Sales}}{\text{Inventory}}$

Inflation may cause sales to be overstated. If the firm uses FIFO accounting, inventory will also reflect "inflation-influenced" dollars and the net effect will be nil.

If the firm uses LIFO accounting, inventory will be stated in old dollars and too high a ratio could be reported.

c.   Fixed asset turnover $= \dfrac{\text{Sales}}{\text{Fixed assets}}$

Fixed assets will be understated relative to sales and too high a ratio could be reported.

d.   Debt to total assets $= \dfrac{\text{Total debt}}{\text{Total assets}}$

Since both are based on historical costs, no major inflationary impact will take place in the ratio.

3-8.   What effect will disinflation following a highly inflationary period have on the reported income of the firm?

Disinflation tends to lower reported earnings as inflation-induced income is squeezed out of the firm's income statement. This is particularly true for firms in highly cyclical industries where prices tend to rise and fall quickly.

3-9.   Why might disinflation prove to be favorable to financial assets?

Because it is possible that prior inflationary pressures will no longer seriously impair the purchasing power of the dollar, lessening inflation also means that the required return that investors demand on financial assets will be going down, and with this lower demanded return, future earnings or interest should receive a higher current evaluation.

3-10.   Comparisons of income can be very difficult for two companies even though they sell the same products in equal volume. Why?

There are many different methods of financial reporting accepted by the accounting profession as promulgated by the Financial Accounting Standards Board. Though the industry has continually tried to provide uniform guidelines and procedures, many options remain open to the reporting firm. Every item on the income statement and balance sheet must be given careful attention. Two apparently similar firms may show different values for sales, research and development, extraordinary losses, and many other items.

Problems

3-1.   Database Systems is considering expansion into a new product line. Assets to support expansion will cost $500,000. It is estimated that Database can generate $1,200,000 in annual sales, with a 6 percent profit margin.

What would net income and return on assets (investment) be for the year?

Solution:

Database Systems

Net income $= \text{Sales} \times \text{profit margin}$

$$= \$1,200,000 \times 0.06$$

$$= \$72,000$$

Return on assets (investment) $= \dfrac{\text{Net income}}{\text{Total assets}}$

$$= \dfrac{\$72,000}{\$500,000}$$

$$= 14.4\%$$

3-2.   Polly Esther Dress Shops, Inc., can open a new store that will do an annual sales volume of $960,000. It will turn over its assets 2.4 times per year. The profit margin on sales will be 7 percent. What would net income and return on assets (investment) be for the year?

Solution:

Polly Esther Dress Shops, Inc.

$$\text{Assets} = \frac{\text{Sales}}{\text{Total asset turnover}}$$

$$= \frac{\$960,000}{2.4} = \$400,000$$

$$\text{Net income} = \text{Sales} \times \text{Profit Margin}$$

$$= \$960,000 \times 0.07 = \$67,200$$

$$\text{Return on assets (investment)} = \frac{\text{Net income}}{\text{Total assets}}$$

$$= \frac{\$67,200}{\$400,000} = 16.8\%$$

3-3. Billy's Chrystal Stores, Inc., has assets of $5,000,000 and turns over its assets 1.2 times per year. Return on assets is 8 percent. What is its profit margin (return on sales)?

Solution:

Billy Crystal Stores, Inc.

$$Sales = Assets \times total\ asset\ turnover$$

$$\$6,000,000 = \$5,000,000 \times 1.2$$

$$Net\ income = Assets \times Return\ on\ assets$$

$$\$400,000 = \$5,000,000 \times 8\%$$

$$\frac{Net\ income}{Sales} = \$400,000 / \$6,000,000 = 6.67\%$$

3-4. Neon Light Company has $1,000,000 in assets and $600,000 of debt. It reports net income of $100,000.

a. What is the return on assets?
b. What is the return on stockholders' equity?
c. If the firm has an asset turnover ration of 3 times, what is the profit margin (return on sales)?

Solution:

Neon Light Company

a.

$$Return\ on\ assets\ (investment) = \frac{Net\ income}{Total\ assets}$$

$$\frac{\$100,000}{\$1,000,000} = 10\%$$

b.

$$\text{Return on equity} = \frac{\text{Net income}}{\text{Stockholders' equity}}$$

$$\begin{aligned}\text{Stockholders' equity} &= \text{total assets} - \text{total debt}\\ &= \$1,000,000 - \$600,000 = \$400,000\end{aligned}$$

$$\frac{\text{Net income}}{\text{Stockholder's equity}} = \frac{\$100,000}{\$400,000} = 25\%$$

OR

$$\text{Return on equity} = \frac{\text{Return on assets (investment)}}{(1 - \text{Debt/Assets})}$$

$$\text{Debt/Assets} = \frac{\$600,000}{\$1,000,000} = 60\%$$

$$\text{Return on equity} = \frac{10\%}{(1-.60)} \qquad \frac{10\%}{.40} = 25\%$$

c.

$$\text{Sales} = \text{total assets} \times \text{total assets turnover}$$

$$= \$1,000,000 \times 3 = \$3,000,000$$

$$\text{Profit margin} = \frac{\text{Net income}}{\text{Sales}} = \frac{\$100,000}{\$3,000,000} = 3.3\%$$

3-5.   Network Communications has total assets of $1,400,000 and current assets of $600,000. It turns over its fixed assets 4 times a year. It has $300,000 of debt. Its return on sale is 5 percent. What is its return on stockholders' equity?

Solution:

Network Communications

total assets	$1,400,000
– current assets	600,000
Fixed assets	$ 800,000

Sales = Fixed assets × Fixed asset turnover =

$800,000 × 4 = $3,200,000

total assets	$1,400,000
– debt	300,000
Stockholders' equity	$1,100,000

Net income = Sales × profit margin =

$3,200,000 × 5% = $160,000

$$\text{Return on stockholders' equity} = \frac{\text{Net income}}{\text{Stockholders' equity}}$$

$$= \frac{\$160,000}{\$1,100,000} = 14.55\%$$

3-6.   a. Alpha Industries had an asset turnover of 1.4 times per year. If the return on total assets (investment) was 8.4 percent, what was Alpha's profit margin?

b. The following year, on the same level of assets, Alpha's asset turnover declined to 1.2 times and its profit margin was 7 percent.

How did the return on total assets change from that of the previous year?

Solution:
Alpha Industries

a.

$$\text{Total asset turnover} \times \text{Profit Margin} = \text{Return on Total assets}$$

$$1.4 \quad \times \quad ? \quad = 8.4\%$$

$$\text{Profit margin} = \frac{8.4\%}{1.4} = 6.0\%$$

b. $$\qquad\qquad 1.2 \quad \times \quad 7\% \quad = 8.4\%$$

It did not change at all because the increase in profit margin made up for the decrease in the asset turnover.

3-7.   The King Card Company has a return-on-assets (investment) ratio of 12 percent.

   a. If the debt-to-total-assets ratio is 40 percent, what is the return on equity?
   b. If the firm had no debt, what would the return-on-equity ratio be?

   Solution:

   # King Card Company

   a.

   $$\text{Return on equity} = \frac{\text{Return on assets (investment)}}{(1 - \text{Debt/Assets})}$$

   $$= \frac{12\%}{(1 - 0.40)}$$

   $$= \frac{12\%}{0.60}$$

   $$= 20\%$$

   b. The same as return on assets (12%).

3-8.   Using the Du Pont method, evaluate the effects of the following relationships for the Lollar Corporation.

a. Lollar Corporation has a profit margin of 5 percent and its return on assets (investment) is 13.5 percent. What is its asset turnover ratio?

b. If the Lollar Corporation has a debt-to-total-assets ratio of 60 percent, what will the firm's return on equity be?

c. What would happen to return on equity if the debt-to-total-assets ratio decreased to 40 percent?

Solution:

Lollar Corporation

a.   Profit margin $\times$ Total asset turnover = Return on asset investment

$$5\% \quad \times \quad ? \quad = 13.5\%$$

$$\text{Total asset turnover} = \frac{13.5\%}{5\%}$$

$$= 2.7x$$

b.

$$\text{Return on equity} = \frac{\text{Return on assets (investment)}}{(1 - \text{Debt/Assets})}$$

$$\text{Existing return on equity} = \frac{13.5\%}{(1 - 0.60)}$$

$$= \frac{13.5\%}{0.40}$$

$$= 33.75\%$$

c. $\text{Return on equity} = \dfrac{\text{Return on assets (investment)}}{(1 - \text{Debt/Assets})}$

$$= \dfrac{13.5\%}{(1 - .40)}$$

$$= \dfrac{13.5\%}{0.60}$$

$$= 22.50\%$$

3-9.   Jerry Rice and Grain Stores has $4,000,000 in yearly sales. The firm earns 3.5 percent on each dollar of sales and turns over its assets 2.5 times per year. It has $100,000 in current liabilities and $300,000 in long-term liabilities.

a. What is its return on stockholders' equity?
b. If the asset base remains the same as computed in part a, but total asset turnover goes up to 3, what will be the new return on stockholders' equity? Assume that the profit margin stays the same as do current and long-term liabilities.

Solution:
Jerry Rice and Grain Stores

a. Net income $= \text{Sales} \times \text{profit margin}$

$= \$4,000,000 \times 3.5\%$

$= \$140,000$

Stockholders equity $= \text{Total assets} - \text{Total liabilities}$

Total assets $= \text{Sales/Total asset turnover}$

$= \$4,000,000 / 2.5$

$= \$1,600,000$

$$\text{Total liabilities} = \text{Current liabilities} + \text{Long} - \text{term liabilities}$$

$$= \$100,000 + \$300,000$$

$$= \$400,000$$

$$\text{Stockholders' equity} = \$1,600,000 - \$400,000 = \$1,200,000$$

$$\text{Return on stockholders' equity} = \frac{\text{Net income}}{\text{Stockholders' equity}}$$

$$= \frac{\$140,000}{\$1,200,000} = 11.67\%$$

b. The Value for sales will be:

$$\text{Sales} = \text{Total assets} \times \text{Total asset turnover}$$

$$= \$1,600,000 \times 3$$

$$= \$4,800,000$$

$$\text{Net income} = \text{Sales} \times \text{Profit margin}$$

$$= \$4,800,000 \times 3.5\%$$

$$= \$168,000$$

$$\text{Return on stockholders' equity} = \frac{\text{Net income}}{\text{Stockholders' equity}}$$

$$= \frac{\$168,000}{\$1,200,000} = 14\%$$

3-10.   Assume the following data for Cable Corporation and Multi-Media, Inc.:

	Cable Corporation	Multi-Media, Inc.
Net income	$ 30,000	$ 100,000
Sales	300,000	2,000,000
Total assets	400,000	900,000
Total debt	150,000	450,000
Stockholders' equity	250,000	450,000

a. Compute return on stockholders' equity for both firms using ratio 3a. Which firm has the higher return?

b. Compute the following additional ratios for both firms.
    Net income/Sales
    Net income/Total assets
    Sales/Total assets
    Debt/Total assets

c. Discuss the factors from part b that added or detracted from one firm having a higher return on stockholders' equity than the other firm as computed in part a.

Solution:

Cable Corporation and Multi-Media, Inc.

a.   **Cable Corporation**   **Multi-Media, Inc.**

$$\frac{\text{Net income}}{\text{Stockholders' equity}} = \frac{\$30,000}{\$250,000} = 12\% \qquad \frac{\$100,000}{\$450,000} = 22.2\%$$

Multi-Media Inc. has a much higher return on stockholders' equity than Cable Corporation.

b.

	Cable Corporation	Multi-Media, Inc.
$\dfrac{\text{Net income}}{\text{Sales}}$	$= \dfrac{\$30,000}{\$300,000} = 10\%$	$\dfrac{\$100,000}{\$2,000,000} = 5\%$
$\dfrac{\text{Net income}}{\text{Total assets}}$	$= \dfrac{\$30,000}{\$400,000} = 7.5\%$	$\dfrac{\$100,000}{\$900,000} = 11.1\%$
$\dfrac{\text{Sales}}{\text{Total assets}}$	$= \dfrac{\$300,000}{\$400,000} = .75\text{x}$	$\dfrac{\$2,000,000}{\$900,000} = 2.2\text{x}$
$\dfrac{\text{Debt}}{\text{Total assets}}$	$= \dfrac{\$150,000}{\$400,000} = 37.5\%$	$\dfrac{\$450,000}{\$900,000} = 50\%$

As previously indicated, Multi-Media, Inc. has a substantially higher return on stockholder's equity than Cable Corporation (22.2% versus 12%). The reason is certainly not to be found on return on the sales dollar where Cable Corporation has a higher return than Multi-Media, Inc. (10% vs. 5%).

However, Multi-Media, Inc. has a higher return than Cable Corporation on total assets (11.1% vs. 7.5%). The reason is clearly to be found in total asset turnover, which strongly favors Multi-Media, Inc. over Cable Corporation (2.2x versus .75x). This factor alone leads to the higher return on total assets.

Multi-Media, Inc.'s superior return on stockholders' equity is further enhanced by a higher debt ratio than Cable Corporation (50% vs. 37.5%). This means that a smaller percentage of Multi-Media, Inc.'s total assets are being financed by stockholders' equity and thus the potentially higher return on stockholders' equity.

Although not requested in the question, one could show the following:

$$\frac{\text{Net income}}{\text{Stockholders' equity}} = \frac{\text{Net income/Total asssets}}{(1 - \text{debt/assets})}$$

$$\text{Multi - Media, Inc.} = 11.1\%(1-.50) = 11.17\%/.50 = 22.2\%$$

$$\text{Cable Corporation} = 7.5\%(1-.375) = 7.5\%/.625 = 12\%$$

3-11.   A firm has sales of $1.2 million, and 10 percent of the sales are for cash. The year-end accounts receivable balance is $180,000.

What is the average collection period? (Use a 360-day year.)

Solution:

$$\text{Average collection period} = \frac{\text{Accounts receivable}}{\text{Average daily credit sales}}$$

$$= \$180,000 \div \frac{(\$1,200,000 \times 90\%)}{360 \text{ days}}$$

$$= \frac{\$180,000}{\$3,000 \text{ per day}}$$

$$= 60 \text{ days}$$

3-12.   The Chamberlain Corporation has accounts receivable turnover equal to 12 times. If accounts receivable are equal to $90,000, what is the value for average daily credit sales?

Solution:

Chamberlain Corporation

$$\text{Average daily credit sales} = \frac{\text{Credit sales}}{360}$$

To determine credit sales, multiply accounts receivable by accounts receivable turnover.

$$\$90,000 \times 12 = \$1,080,000$$

$$\text{Average daily credit sales} = \frac{\$1,080,000}{360} = \$3,000$$

3-13.   Kamin Corporation has the following financial data for the years 2000 and 2001:

	2000	**2001**
Sales	$4,000,000	$5,000,000
Cost of good sold	3,000,000	4,500,000
Inventory	400,000	500,000

a. Compute inventory turnover based on ratio number 6, sales/inventory, for each year.
b. Compute inventory turnover based on an alternative calculation that is used by many financial analysts, cost of goods sold/inventory, for each year.
c. What conclusions can you draw from part *a* and part *b*?

Solution:

Kamin Corporation

a.   **2000**   **2001**

$$\frac{\text{Sales}}{\text{Inventory}} = \frac{\$4,000,000}{400,000} = 10x \qquad \frac{\$5,000,000}{500,000} = 10x$$

b.

$$\frac{\text{Cost of goods sold}}{\text{Inventory}} = \frac{\$3,000,000}{400,000} = 7.5x \qquad \frac{\$4,500,000}{500,000} = 9x$$

c. Based on the sales to inventory ratio, the turnover has remained constant at 10x. However, based on the cost of goods sold to inventory ratio, it has improved from 7.5x to 9x.

The latter ratio may be providing a false picture of improvement in this example simply because cost of goods sold has gone up as percentage of sales (from 75 percent to 90 percent). Inventory is not really turning over any faster.

Nevertheless, cost of goods sold used by many analysis in the numerator of the inventory turnover ratio because it is stated on a "cost" basis as is inventory. This is an important theoretical consideration.

Nevertheless, the authors prefer to use sales in the numerator of the inventory turnover ratio because that is the procedure used by Dun & Bradstreet, the most widely quoted sources for ratio analysis. Furthermore, for privately traded companies there may be only information available on sales and net cost of goods sold.

3-14.   The balance sheet for the Bryan Corporation is shown below. Sales for the year were $3,040,000, with 75 percent of the sales on credit.

Bryan Corporation
Balance Sheet 200X

Assets		Liabilities and Stockholders' Equity	
Cash	$ 50,000	Accounts payable	$220,000
Accounts receivable	280,000	Accrued taxes	80,000
Inventory	240,000	Bonds payable (long term)	118,000
Plant and equipment	380,000	Common stock	100,000
		Paid-in-capital	150,000
		Retained earnings	282,000
		Total liabilities and	
Total assets	$950,000	Stockholders' equity	$950,000

Compute the following ratios:

a. Current ratio.
b. Quick ratio.
c. Debt-to-total-assets ratio.
d. Asset turnover.
e. Average collection period.

Solution:

Bryan Corporation

a. Current ratio $\quad=\dfrac{\text{Current assets}}{\text{Current liabilities}}$

$\quad=\dfrac{\$570,000}{\$300,000}$

1.9x

b. Quick ratio $\quad=\dfrac{(\text{Current assets} - \text{inventory})}{\text{Current liabilities}}$

$\quad=\dfrac{\$330,000}{\$300,000}$

$=1.1\text{x}$

c. Debt to total assets $\quad=\dfrac{\text{Total debt}}{\text{Total assets}}$

$\quad=\dfrac{\$418,000}{\$950,000}$

$=44\%$

d. Asset turnover $\quad=\dfrac{\text{Sales}}{\text{Total assets}}$

$\quad=\dfrac{\$3,040,000}{\$950,000}$

$=3.2\text{x}$

e. $\begin{aligned}\text{Average collection} \\ \text{period}\end{aligned}$ $= \dfrac{\text{Accounts receivable}}{\text{Average daily credit sales}}$

$$= \$280,000 \div \dfrac{\left(\$3,040,000 \times 0.75\right)}{360 \text{ days}}$$

$$= \dfrac{\$280,000}{\$6,333 \text{ per day}}$$

$$= 44.21 \text{ days}$$

3-15. The Lancaster Corporation's income statement is given below.

a. What is the times-interest-earned ratio?
b. What would be the fixed-charge-coverage ratio?

Lancaster Corporation

Sales..	$200,000
Cost of goods sold	116,000
Gross profit.......................................	84,000
Fixed charges (other than interest)	24,000
Income before interest and taxes	60,000
Interest	12,000
Income before taxes...........................	48,000
Taxes (35%).......................................	16,800
Income after taxes..............................	$ 31,200

Solution:

Lancaster Corporation

a. Times interest earned $= \dfrac{\text{Income before interest and taxes}}{\text{Interest}}$

$$= \dfrac{\$60,000}{12,000}$$

$$= 5\text{x}$$

b. Fixed charge coverage $= \dfrac{\text{Income before fixed charges and taxes}}{\text{Fixed charges}}$

$$= \dfrac{\$60,000 + 24,000}{\$12,000 + 24,000}$$

$$= \dfrac{\$84,000}{\$36,000}$$

$$= 2.33\text{x}$$

3-16.   Using the income statement for Jason Kid's Furniture, compute the following ratios:

a. Times interest earned.
b. Fixed charge coverage.
    The total assets for this company equal $160,000. Set up the equation for the Du Pont system of ratio analysis, and compute the answer to part *c* below using ratio 2*b*.
c. Return on assets (investment).

Jason Kid's Furniture
Income Statement

Sales..	$200,000
Less: Cost of goods sold.............................	90,000
Gross profit...	$110,000
Less: Selling and administrative expense......	40,000
Less: Lease expense....................................	10,000
Operating profit*	$ 60,000
Less: Interest expense..................................	5,000
Earnings before taxes...................................	$ 55,000
Less: Taxes (40%)	22,000
Earnings after taxes......................................	$ 33,000

*Equals income before interest and taxes

Solution:
Jason Kid's Furniture

a. $\text{Times interest earned} = \dfrac{\text{Income before intest and taxes}}{\text{Interest}}$

$$= \dfrac{\$60,000}{5,000}$$

$$= 12x$$

b.　Fixed charge coverage $= \dfrac{\text{Income before fixed charges and taxes}}{\text{Fixed charges}}$

$$= \frac{\$60,000 + 10,000}{\$5,000 + 10,000}$$

$$= \frac{\$70,000}{\$15,000}$$

$$= 4.67\text{x}$$

c.　Return on assets
(Investment)　$= \dfrac{\text{Net income}}{\text{Sales}} \times \dfrac{\text{Sales}}{\text{Total assets}}$

$$= \frac{\$33,000}{\$200,000} \times \frac{\$200,000}{\$160,000}$$

$$= 16.5\% \times 1.25\text{x}$$

$$= 20.625\%$$

3-17.   A firm has net income before interest and taxes of $96,000 and interest expense of $24,000.

     a.   What is the times-interest-earned ratio?
     b.   If the firm's lease payments are $40,000, what is the fixed charge coverage?

Solution:

a. $\text{Times interest earned} = \dfrac{\text{Income before interest and taxes}}{\text{Interest}}$

$$= \dfrac{\$96,000}{\$24,000}$$

$$= 4\text{x}$$

b. $\text{Fixed charge coverage} = \dfrac{\text{IBIT} + \text{Before tax fixed charges}}{\text{Interest} - \text{Fixed charges}}$

$$= \dfrac{\$96,000 + \$40,000}{\$24,000 + \$40,000}$$

$$= \dfrac{\$136,000}{\$64,000}$$

$$= 2.13\text{x}$$

3-18.   In January 1992, the Status Quo Company was formed. Total assets were $500,000, of which $300,000 consisted of depreciable fixed assets. Status Quo uses straight-line depreciation, and in 1992 it estimated its fixed assets to have useful lives of 10 years. Aftertax income has been $26,000 per year each of the last 10 years. Other assets have not changed since 1992.

     a.   Compute return on assets at year-end for 1992, 1994, 1997, 1999 and 2001. (Use $26,000 in the numerator for each year.)
     b.   To what do you attribute the phenomenon shown in part *a*?
     c.   Now assume income increased by 10 percent each year. What effect would this have on your above answers? (A comment is all that is necessary.)

Solution:

Status Quo Company

a. Return on assets (investment) $= \dfrac{\text{Income after taxes}}{\text{Total assets}}$

The return on assets for Status Quo will increase over time as the assets depreciate and the denominator gets smaller. Fixed assets at the beginning of 1991 equal $300,000 with a ten-year life which means the depreciation expense will be $30,000 per year. Book values at year-end are as follows:

$$1992 = \$270,000;$$
$$1994 = \$210,000;$$
$$1997 = \$120,000;$$
$$1999 = \$60,000;$$
$$2001 = \text{-0-}$$

Return on assets (investment) $= \dfrac{\text{Income after taxes}}{\text{Current assets} + \text{Fixed assets}}$

$$1992 = \$26,000/\$470,000 = 5.53\%$$
$$1994 = \$26,000/\$410,000 = 6.34\%$$
$$1997 = \$26,000/\$320,000 = 8.13\%$$
$$1999 = \$26,000/\$260,000 = 10.00\%$$
$$2001 = \$26,000/200,000 = 13.00\%$$

b. The increasing return on assets over time is due solely to the fact that annual depreciation charges reduce the amount of investment. The increasing return is in no way due to operations.

Financial analysts should be aware of the effect of overall asset age on the return-on-investment ratio and be able to search elsewhere for indications of operating efficiency when ROI is very high or very low.

c. As income rises, return on assets will be higher than in part (b) and would indicate an increase in return partially from more profitable operations.

3-19.   Jodie Foster Care Homes, Inc. shows the following data:

Year	Net income	Total Assets	Stockholders' Equity	Total Debt
1998	$118,000	$1,900,000	$ 700,000	$1,200,000
1999	131,000	1,950,000	950,000	1,000,000
2000	148,000	2,010,000	1,100,000	910,000
2001	175,700	2,050,000	1,420,000	630,000

a. Compute the ratio of net income to total assets for each year and comment on the trend.
b. Compute the ratio of net income to stockholders' equity and comment on the trend. Explain why there may be a difference in the trends between parts *a* and *b*.

Solution:
Jodie Foster Care Homes, Inc.

a. $\dfrac{\text{Net income}}{\text{Total assets}}$

1998	6.21%
1999	6.72
2000	7.36
2001	8.57

Comment: There is a strong upward movement in return on assets over the four year period.

b. $$\frac{\text{Net income}}{\text{Stockholders' equity}}$$

1998	16.86%
1999	13.79
2000	13.45
2001	12.37

Comment: The return on stockholders' equity ratio is going down each year. The difference in trends between a and b is due to the larger portion of assets that are financed by stockholders' equity as opposed to debt.

Optional: This can be confirmed by computing total debt to total assets for each year.

$$\frac{\text{Total debt}}{\text{Total assets}}$$

1998	63.2%
1999	51.3
2000	45.3
2001	30.7

3-20. Quantum Moving Company has the following data. Industry information also is shown.

	Company Data		Industry Data on Net
Year	Net Income	Total Assets	Income/Total Assets
1999	$350,000	$2,800,000	11.5%
2000	375,000	3,200,000	8.4%
2001	375,000	3,750,000	5.5%

			Industry Data on
Year	Debt	Total Assets	Debt/Total Assets
1999	$1,624,000	$2,800,000	54.1%
2000	1,730,000	3,200,000	42.0%
2001	1,900,000	3,750,000	33.4%

As an industry analyst comparing the firm to the industry, are you more likely to praise or criticize the firm in inters of:

a. Net income/total assets?
b. Debt/total assets?

Solution:
Quantum Moving Company

a. Net income/total assets

Year	Quantum Ratio	Industry Ratio
1999	12.5%	11.5%
2000	11.7%	8.4%
2001	10.0%	5.5%

Although the company has shown a declining return on assets since 1999, it has performed much better than the industry. Praise may be more appropriate than criticism.

b. Debt/total assets

Year	Quantum Ratio	Industry Ratio
1999	58.0%	54.1%
2000	54.1%	42.0%
2001	50.7%	33.4%

While the company's debt ratio is improving, it is not improving nearly as rapidly as the industry ratio. Criticism may be more appropriate than praise.

3-21. The Global Products Corporation has three subsidiaries.

	Medical Supplies	Heavy Machinery	Electronics
Sales..................................	$20,000,000	$5,000,000	$4,000,000
Net income (after taxes)..	1,200,000	190,000	320,000
Assets...............................	8,000,000	8,000,000	3,000,000

a. Which division has the lowest return on sales?
b. Which division has the highest return on assets?
c. Compute the return on assets for the entire corporation.
d. If the $8,000,000 investment in the heavy machinery division is sold off and redeployed in the medical supplies subsidiary at the same rate of return on assets currently achieved in the medical supplies division, what will be the new return on assets for the entire corporation?

Solution:
Global Products Corporation

a.

	Medical Supplies	Heavy Machinery	Electronics
Net income/sales	6.0%	3.8%	8.0%

The heavy machinery division has the lowest return on sales.

b.

	Medical Supplies	Heavy Machinery	Electronics
Net income/ total assets	15.0%	2.375%	10.67%

The medical supplies division has the highest return on assets.

c. $\dfrac{\text{Corporate net income}}{\text{Corporate total assets}} = \dfrac{\$1,200,000 + \$190,000 + \$320,000}{\$8,000,000 + \$8,000,000 + \$3,000,000}$

$$= \frac{\$1,710,000}{\$19,000,000}$$

$$= 9.0\%$$

d. Return on redeployed assets in heavy machinery.

$15\% \times \$8,000,000 = \$1,200,000$

Return on assets for the entire corporation:

$$\frac{\text{Corporate net income}}{\text{Corporate total asset}} = \frac{\$1,200,000 + \$1,200,000 + \$320,000}{\$19,000,000}$$

$$= \frac{\$2,720,000}{\$19,000,000}$$

$$= 14.32\%$$

3-22.   The Canton Corporation shows the following income statement. The firm uses FIFO inventory accounting.

Canton Corporation
Income Statement for 2000

Sales...	$100,000	(10,000 units at $10)
Cost of goods sold	50,000	(10,000 units at $5)
Gross profit......................................	50,000	
Selling and administrative expense ..	5,000	
Depreciation.....................................	10,000	
Operating profit	35,000	
Taxes (30%)......................................	10,500	
Aftertax income	$ 24,500	

a. Assume in 2001 the same 10,000-unit volume is maintained, but that the sales price increases by 10 percent. Because of FIFO inventory policy, old inventory will still be charged off at $5 per unit. Also assume that selling and administrative expense will be 5 percent of sales and depreciation will be unchanged. The tax rate is 30 percent. Compute aftertax income for 2001.

b. In part *a*, by what percent did aftertax income increase as a result of a 10 percent increase in the sales price? Explain why this impact took place.

c. Now assume that in 2002 the volume remains constant at 10,000 units, but the sales price decreases by 15 percent from its 2001 level. Also, because of FIFO inventory policy, cost of goods sold reflects that inflationary conditions of the prior year and is $5.50 per unit. Further, assume that selling and administrative expense will be 5 percent of sales and depreciation will be unchanged. The tax rate is 30 percent. Compute the aftertax income.

Solution:

Canton Corporation

a. 2000

Sales............................	$110,000	(10,000 units at $11)
Cost of goods sold	50,000	(10,000 units at $5)
Gross profit................	$ 60,000	
Selling and adm.		
expense	5,500	(5% of sales)
Depreciation	10,000	
Operating profit.........	$ 44,500	
Taxes (30%).................	$ 13,350	
After tax income........	$31,150	

b. Gain in aftertax income

2001	$31,150
2000	24,500
Increase	$ 6,650

$$\frac{\text{Increase}}{\text{Base value}(2000)} = \frac{\$6,650}{\$24,500} = 27.14\%$$

Aftertax income increased much more than sales because of FIFO inventory policy (in this case, the cost of old inventory did not go up at all), and because of historical cost depreciation (which did not change).

c. 2002

Sales	$ 93,500	(10,000 units at $9.35*)
Cost of goods sold	55,000	(10,000 units at $5.50)
Gross profit	$ 38,500	
Selling and adm. expense	4,675	(5% of sales)
Depreciation	10,000	
Operating profit	$ 23,825	
Taxes (30%)	$ 7,148	
After tax income	$ 16,677	

*$11×0.85 = $9.35

The low profits indicate the effect of inflation followed by disinflation.

3-23.   Construct the current assets section of the balance sheet from the following data.

Yearly sales (credit)	$420,000
Inventory turnover	7 times
Current liabilities	$ 80,000
Current ratio	2
Average collection period	36 days

Current assets:
Cash	$_____
Accounts receivable	_____
Inventory	_____
Total current assets	_____

Solution:

Inventory	= $420,000/7
	= $ 60,000
Current assets	= 2×$80,000
	= $160,000
Account rec.	= ($420,000/360)×36
	= $42,000
Cash	= $160,000 − $60,000 − $42,000
	= $58,000

Cash	$ 58,000
Accounts receivable....	42,000
Inventory.....................	60,000
Total current assets	$160,000

3-24. The Shannon Corporation has credit sales of $750,000. Given the following ratios, fill in the balance sheet.

Total assets turnover......................................	2.5 times
Cash to total assets..	2.0 percent
Accounts receivable turnover	10.0 times
Inventory turnover	15.0 times
Current ratio...	2.0 times
Debt to total assets	45.0 percent

Shannon Corporation
Balance Sheet 200X

Assets		Liabilities and Stockholders' Equity	
Cash	_____	Current debt	_____
Accounts receivable........	_____	Long-term debt..............	_____
Inventory.........................	_____	Total debt	_____
Total current assets	_____	Net worth	_____
Fixed assets.....................	_____	Total debt and	
Total assets......................	_____	Stockholders' equity....	_____

Solution:

Shannon Corporation

Sales/total assets	= 2.5 times
Total assets	= $750,000/2.5
Total assets	= $300,000

Cash	= 2% of total assets
Cash	= 2% × $300,000
Cash	= $6,000

Sales/accounts receivable	= 10 times
Accounts receivable	= $750,000/10
Accounts receivable	= $75,000

Sales/inventory	= 15 times
Inventory	= $750,000/15
Inventory	= $50,000

Fixed assets	= Total assets − current assets
Current asset	= $6,000 + $75,000 + $50,000
	= $131,000
Fixed assets	= $300,000 − $131,000
	= $169,000

Current assets/current debt	= 2
Current debt	= Current assets/2
Current debt	= $131,000/2
Current debt	= $65,500

Total debt/total assets	= 45%
Total debt	= .45 × $300,000
Total debt	= $135,000

Long-term debt		= Total debt – current debt	
Long-term debt		= $135,000 – 65,500	
Long-term debt		= $69,500	
Net worth		= Total assets – total debt	
Net worth		= $300,000 – $135,000	
Net worth		= $165,000	

Shannon Corporation
Balance Sheet 200X

Cash	$ 6,000	Current debt........	$ 65,500
A/R.....................	$ 75,000	Long-term debt...	$ 69,500
Inventory............	$ 50,000	Total debt..........	$135,000
Total current assets	$131,000		
Fixed assets........	$169,000	Net worth............	$165,000
Total assets.........	$300,000	Total debt and stockholders' equity	$300,000

3-25.   We are given the following information for the Pettit Corporation.

Sales (credit)	$3,000,000
Cash	150,000
Inventory..	850,000
Current liabilities	700,000
Asset turnover...	1.25 times
Current ratio..	2.50 times
Debt-to-assets ratio	40%
Receivables turnover	6 times

Current assets are composed of cash, marketable securities, accounts receivable, and inventory. Calculate the following balance sheet items.

a. Accounts receivable.
b. Marketable securities.
c. Fixed assets.
d. Long-term debt.

Solution:

Pettit Corporation

a. Accounts receivable
$$= \text{Sales/Receivable turnover}$$
$$= \$3,000,000/6x$$
$$= \$500,000$$

b. Marketable securities
$$= \text{Current assets} - (\text{cash} + \text{accounts rec.} + \text{inventory})$$

Current Assets
$$= \text{Current ratio} \times \text{Current liabilities}$$
$$= 2.5 \times \$700,000$$
$$= \$1,750,000$$

Marketable securities
$$= \$1,750,000 - (\$150,000 + \$500,000 + \$850,000)$$
$$= \$1,750,000 - \$1,500,000$$
$$= \$250,000$$

c. Fixed assets
$$= \text{Total assets} - \text{Current assets}$$

Total assets
$$= \text{Sales/Asset turnover}$$
$$= \$3,000,000/1.2x$$
$$= \$2,500,000$$

Fixed assets
$$= \$2,5000,000 - \$1,750,000$$
$$= \$750,000$$

d. Long-term debt   = Total debt − current liabilities

   Total debt   = Debt to assets × total assets

                         = 40% × \$2,500,000

                         = \$1,000,000

   Long-term debt   = \$1,000,000 − \$700,000
                         = \$300,000

3-26.   The following information is from Harrelson Inc.'s financial statements. Sales (all credit) were \$20 million for 2000.

Sales to total assets .... 2 times
Total debt to assets.. 30%
Current ratio... 3.0 times
Inventory turnover .... 5.0 times
Average collection period............................ 18 days
Fixed asset turnover....................................... 5.0 times

Fill in the balance sheet:

Cash .... _____   Current debt .... _____
Accounts receivable........ _____   Long-term debt............. _____
Inventory........................ _____   Total debt .... _____
  Total current assets .... _____   Equity........................... _____
Fixed assets.................... _____   Total debt and equity .... _____
Total assets..................... _____

Solution:

Harrelson Inc.

Sales/total assets   = 2
Total assets   = \$20 million/2
Total assets   = \$10 million

Total debt/total assets = 30%

Total debt = $10 million × .3

Total debt = $3 million

Sales/inventory = 5.0x

Inventory = $20 million/5x

Inventory = $4 million

Average daily sales = $20 million/360 days

= $55,555.55 per day

Accounts receivable = 18 days × $55,555.56

= $1 million (or)

Accounts receivable $= \dfrac{\$20\ \text{million}}{\dfrac{360}{18}} = \$1,000,000$

Fixed assets = $20 million/5x

= $4 million

Current assets = Total assets – Fixed assets

= $10 million – $4 million

= $6 million

Cash = Current assets – Accounts
  receivable – inventory

= $6 million – $1 million – $4 million

= $1 million

Current liabilities = Current assets/3x

= $6 millio/3

= $2 million

Long-term debt   = Total debt – current debt
= \$3 million – \$2 million
= \$1 million

Equity   = Total assets – total debt
= \$10 million – \$3 million
= \$7 million

Cash	\$ 1.0 million	Current debt	\$ 2 million
Accounts receivable	\$ 1.0	Long-term debt.	\$ 1.0
Inventory	\$ 4.0	Total debt	\$ 3.0
Total current assets	\$ 6.0	Equity	\$ 7.0
Fixed assets	\$ 4.0		
Total assets	\$10.0 million	Total debt and equity	\$10.0 million

3-27.   Using the financial statements for the Snider Corporation, calculate the 13 basic ratios found in the chapter.

Snider Corporation
Balance Sheet
December 31, 2001

Assets

Current assets:

Cash	\$ 50,000
Marketable securities	20,000
Accounts receivable (net)	160,000
Inventory	200,000
Total current assets	\$ 430,000
Investments	60,000
Plant and equipment	600,000
Less: Accumulated depreciation	(190,000)
Net plant and equipment	410,000
Total assets	\$ 900,000

Liabilities and Stockholders' Equity

Current liabilities:

Accounts payable	$ 90,000
Notes payable	70,000
Accrued taxes	10,000
Total current liabilities	$ 170,000

Long-term liabilities:

Bonds payable	150,000
Total liabilities	$ 320,000

Stockholders' equity:

Preferred stock, $50 par value	100,000
Common stock, $1 par value	80,000
Capital paid in excess of par	190,000
Retained earnings	210,000
Total stockholders' equity	$ 580,000
Total liabilities and stockholders' equity	$ 900,000

Snider Corporation
Income Statement
For the Year Ending December 31, 2001

Sales (on credit)	$1,980,000
Less: Cost of goods sold	1,280,000
Gross profit	700,000
Less: Selling and administrative expenses	475,000*
Operating profit (EBIT)	225,000
Less: Interest expense	25,000
Earnings before taxes (EBT)	200,000
Less: Taxes	80,000
Earnings after taxes (EAT)	$ 120,000

*Includes $35,000 in lease payments.

Solution:

Snider Corporation

Profitability ratios
Profit margin = $120,000/$1,980,000 = 6.06%
Return on assets (investment) = $120,000/$900,000 = 13.3%
Return on equity = $120,000/$580,000 = 20.69%

Assets utilization ratios
Receivable turnover = $1,980,000/$160,000 = 12.38x
Average collection period = $160,000/$5,500 = 29.09 days
Inventory turnover = $1,980,000/$200,000 = 9.9x
Fixed asset turnover = $1,980,000/$410,000 = 4.83x
Total asset turnover = $1,980,000/$900,000 − 2.2x

Liquidity ratio

Current ratio = $430,000/$170,000 = 2.53x
Quick ratio = $230,000/$170,000 = 1.35x

Debt utilization ratios
Debt to total assets = $320,000/$900,000 = 35.56%
Times interest earned = $225,000/$25,000 = 9x
Fixed charge coverage = $260,000/$60,000 = 4.33x

3-28.   Given the financial statements for Jones Corporation and Smith Corporation shown here:

a. To which company would you, as credit manager for a supplier, approve the extension of (short-term) trade credit? Why? Compute all ratios before answering.

b. In which one would you buy stock? Why?

Jones Corporation

Current Assets		Liabilities	
Cash	$ 20,000	Accounts payable	$100,000
Accounts receivable	80,000	Bonds payable (long-term)	80,000
Inventory	50,000		

Long-Term Assets		Stockholders' Equity	
Fixed assets	$ 500,000	Common stock	$150,000
Less: Accum. Dep.	(150,000)	Paid-in capital	70,000
*Net fixed assets	350,000	Retained earnings	100,000
Total assets	$ 500,000	Total liab. and equity	$500,000

Sales (on credit)	$1,250,000
Cost of goods sold	750,000
Gross profit	500,000
†Selling and administrative expense	257,000
Less: Depreciation expense	50,000
Operating profit	193,000
Interest expense	8,000
Earnings before taxes	185,000
Tax expense	92,500
Net income	92,500

*Use net fixed assets in computing fixed asset turnover.
†Includes $7,000 in lease payments.

Smith Corporation

Current Assets			Liabilities		
Cash	$	35,000	Accounts payable	$	75,000
Marketable securities		7,500	Bonds payable (long-term)		210,000
Accounts receivable		70,000			
Inventory		75,000			

Long-Term Assets			Stockholders' Equity		
Fixed assets	$	500,000	Common stock	$	75,000
Less: Accum. Dep.		(250,000)	Paid-in capital		30,000
*Net fixed assets		250,000	Retained earnings		47,500
Total assets	$	437,500	Total liab. and equity	$	437,500

Sales (on credit)	$1,000,000
Cost of goods sold	600,000
Gross profit	400,000
†Selling and administrative expense	224,000
Less: Depreciation expense	50,000
Operating profit	126,000
Interest expense	21,000
Earnings before taxes	105,000
Tax expense	52,500
Net income	52,500

*Use net fixed assets in computing fixed asset turnover.
†Includes $7,000 in lease payments.

Solution:

Jones and Smith Comparison

One way of analyzing the situation for each company is to compare the respective ratios for each on, examining those ratios which would be most important to a supplier or short-term lender and a stockholder.

	Jones Corp.	Smith Corp.
Profit margin	7.4%	5.25%
Return on assets (investments)	18.5%	12.00%
Return on equity	28.9%	34.4%
Receivable turnover	15.63x	14.29x
Average collection period	23.04 days	25.2 days
Inventory turnover	25x	13.3x
Fixed asset turnover	3.57x	4x
Total asset turnover	2.5x	2.29x
Current ratio	1.5x	2.5x
Quick ratio	1.0x	1.5x
Debt to total assets	36%	65.1%
Times interest earned	24.13x	6x
Fixed charge coverage	13.33x	4.75x
Fixed charge coverage calculation	(200/15)	(133/28)

a. Since suppliers and short-term lenders are most concerned with liquidity ratios, Smith Corporation would get the nod as having the best ratios in this category. One could argue, however, that Smith had benefited from having its debt primarily long term rather than short term. Nevertheless, it appears to have better liquidity ratios.

b. Stockholders are most concerned with profitability. In this category, Jones has much better ratios than Smith. Smith does have a higher return on equity than Jones, but this is due to its much larger use of debt. Its return on equity is higher than Jones' because it has taken more financial risk. In terms of other ratios, Jones has its interest and fixed charges well covered and in general its long-term ratios and outlook are better than Smith's. Jones has asset utilization ratios equal to or better than Smith and its lower liquidity ratios could reflect better short-term asset management, and that point was covered in part a.

Note: Remember that to make actual financial decisions more than one year's comparative data is usually required. Industry comparisons should also be made.

Comprehensive Problems

CP 3-1.   Bob Adkins has recently been approached by his first cousin, Ed Lamar, with a proposal to buy a 15 percent interest in Lamar Swimwear. The firm manufactures stylish bathing suits and sunscreen products.

Mr. Lamar is quick to point out the increase in sales that has taken place over the last three years as indicated in the income statement, Exhibit 1. The annual growth rate is 25 percent. A balance sheet for a similar time period is shown in Exhibit 2, and selected industry ratios are presented in Exhibit 3. Note the industry growth rate in sales is only 10 to 12 percent per year.

There was a steady real growth of 3 to 4 percent in gross domestic product during the period under study.

The stock in the corporation has become available due to the ill health of a current stockholder, who is in need of cash. The issue here is not to determine the exact price for the stock, but rather whether Lamar Swimwear represents an attractive investment situation. Although Mr. Adkins has a primary interest in the profitability ratios, he will take a close look at all the ratios. He has no fast and firm rules about required return on investment, but rather wishes to analyze the overall condition of the firm. The firm does not currently pay a cash dividend, and return to the investor must come from selling the stock in the future. After doing a thorough analysis (including ratios for each year an comparisons to the industry), what comments and recommendations do you offer to Mr. Adkins?

Exhibit 1

Lamar Swimwear
Income Statement

	199X	199Y	199Z
Sales (all on credit)	$1,200,000	$1,500,000	$1,875,000
Cost of goods sold	800,000	1,040,000	1,310,000
Gross profit	$ 400,000	$ 460,000	$ 565,000
Selling and administrative expense*	239,900	274,000	304,700
Operating profit (EBIT)	$ 160,100	$ 186,000	$ 260,300
Interest expense	35,000	45,000	85,000
Net income before taxes	$ 125,100	$ 141,000	$ 175,300
Taxes	36,900	49,200	55,600
Net income	$ 88,200	$ 91,800	$ 119,700
Shares	30,000	30,000	38,000
Earnings per share	$2.94	$3.06	$3.15

*Includes $15,000 in lease payments for each year.

Exhibit 2

Lamar Swimwear
Balance Sheet

Assets	199X	199Y	199Z
Cash	$ 30,000	$ 40,000	$ 30,000
Marketable securities	20,000	25,000	30,000
Accounts receivable	170,000	259,000	360,000
Inventory	230,000	261,000	290,000
Total current assets	$ 450,000	$ 585,000	$ 710,000
Net plant and equipment	650,000	765,000	1,390,000
Total assets	$1,100,000	$1,350,000	$2,100,000

Liabilities and Stockholders' Equity	199X	199Y	199Z
Accounts payable	$ 200,000	$ 310,000	$ 505,000
Accrued expenses	20,400	30,000	35,000
Total current liabilities	$ 220,400	$ 340,000	$ 540,000
Long-term liabilities	325,000	363,600	703,900
Total liabilities	$ 545,400	$ 703,600	$1,243,900
Common stock ($2 par)	60,000	60,000	76,000
Capital paid in excess of par	190,000	190,000	264,000
Retained earnings	304,600	396,400	516,100
Total stockholders' equity	$ 554,600	$ 646,400	$ 856,100
Total liabilities and stockholders' equity	$1,100,000	$1,350,000	$2,100,000

Exhibit 3

Selected Industry Ratios

	199X	199Y	199Z
Growth in sales	-----	10.00%	12.00%
Profit margin	7.71%	7.82%	7.96%
Return on assets (investment)	7.94$	8.68%	8.95%
Return on equity	14.31%	15.26%	16.01%
Receivables turnover	9.02x	8.86x	9.31x
Average collection period	39.9 days	40.6 days	38.7 days
Inventory turnover	4.24x	5.10x	5.11x
Fixed asset turnover	1.60x	1.64x	1.75x
Total asset turnover	1.05x	1.10x	1.12x
Current ratio	1.96x	2.25x	2.40x
Quick ratio	1.37x	1.41x	1.38x
Debt to total assets	43.47%	43.11%	44.10%
Times interest earned	6.50x	5.99x	6.61x
Fixed charge coverage	4.70x	4.69x	4.73x
Growth in earnings per share	-----	10.10%	13.30%

CP 3-1

Solution: **Lamar Swimwear**

		199X	**199Y**	**199Z**
Growth in sales	(Company)		25%	25%
	(Industry)		10%	12%
Profit margin	(Company)	7.35%	6.12%	6.38%
	(Industry)	7.71%	7.82%	7.96%
Return on assets	(Company)	8.02%	6.80%	5.70%
	(Industry)	7.94%	8.68%	8.95%
Return on equity	(Company)	15.90%	14.20%	13.98%
	(Industry)	14.31%	15.26%	16.01%
Receivable turnover	(Company)	7.06x	5.79x	5.21x
	(Industry)	9.02x	8.86x	9.31x
Average collection period	(Company)	51.0 days	62.2 days	69.1 days
	(Industry)	39.9 days	40.6 days	38.7 days
Inventory turnover	(Company)	5.22x	5.75x	6.47x
	(Industry)	4.24x	5.10x	5.11x
Fixed asset turnover	(Company)	1.85x	1.96x	1.35x
	(Industry)	1.60x	1.64x	1.75x
Total asset turnover	(Company)	1.09x	1.11x	0.89x
	(Industry)	1.05x	1.10x	1.12x
Current ratio	(Company)	2.04x	1.72x	1.31x
	(Industry)	1.96x	2.25x	2.40x
Quick ratio	(Company)	1.00x	.95x	0.78x
	(Industry)	1.37x	1.41x	1.38x
Debt to total assets	(Company)	49.58%	52.12%	59.23%
	(Industry)	43.47%	43.11%	44.10%
Times interest earned	(Company)	4.57x	4.13x	3.06x
	(Industry)	6.50x	5.99x	6.61x
Fixed charge coverage	(Company)	3.50x	3.35x	2.75x
	(Industry)	4.70x	4.69x	4.73x
Growth in E.P.S.	(Company)	----	4.1%	2.9%
	(Industry)	----	10.1%	13.3%

Discussion of Ratios

While Lamar Swimwear is expanding its sales much more rapidly than others in the industry, there are some clear deficiencies in their performance. These can be seen in terms of a trend analysis over time as well as a comparative analysis with industry data.

In terms of profitability, the profit margin is declining over time. This is surprising in light of the 56.25 percent increase in sales over two years (25 percent per year). There obviously are no economies of scale for this firm. Higher costs of goods sold and interest expense appear to be causing the problem. The return on asset ratio starts out in 199X above the industry average (8.02 percent versus 7.94 percent) and ends up well below it (5.70 percent versus 8.95 percent) in 199Z. The decline of 2.32 percent for return on assets is serious, and can be attributed to the previously mentioned declining profit margin as well as a slowing total asset turnover (going from 1.09X to 0.89X).

Return on equity is higher than the industry average the first year, and then also falls far below it. This decline is particularly significant in light of the progressively larger debt that the firm is using. High debt utilization tends to contribute to high return on equity, but not in this case. There is simply too much deterioration in return on assets translating into low return on equity.

The previously mentioned slower turnover of assets can be analyzed through the turnover ratios. A problem can be found in accounts receivable where turnover has gone from 7.06X to 5.21X. This can also be stated in terms of an average collection period that has increased from 51 days to

69.1 days. While inventory turnover has been and remains superior to the industry, the same cannot be said for fixed asset turnover. A decline from 1.85X to 1.35X was caused by an increase in 113.8 percent in fixed assets (representing $740,000). We can summarize the discussion of the turnover ratios by saying that despite a 56.25 percent increase in sales, assets grew even more rapidly causing a decline in total asset turnover from 1.09X to 0.89X.

The liquidity ratios also are not encouraging. Both the current and quick ratios are falling against a stable industry norm of approximately two to one and one to one respectively.

The debt to total assets ratio is particularly noticeable in regard to industry comparisons. Lamar Swimwear has gone from being only 6.11 percent over the industry average to 15.13 percent above the norm (59.23 percent versus 44.10 percent). Their heavy debt position is clearly out of line with their competitors. Their downtrend in times interest earned and fixed charge coverage confirms the heavy debt burden on the company.

Finally, we see that the firm has a slower growth rate in earnings per share than the industry. This is a function of less rapid growth in earnings as well as an increase in shares outstanding (with the sale of 8,000 shares in 199Z). Once again, we see that the rapid growth in sales is not being translated down into significant earnings gains. This is true in spite of the fact that there is a very stable economic environment.

Investment Comments:

He would probably have difficultly justifying such an investment based on the performance of the firm. There are no dividend payout, so return to the investor would have to come in the form of capital appreciation if and when he was able to resell the shares. The prospects, at this point, would not appear to justify the purchase. This is particularly true when one considers that Mr. Adkins would be buying a minority interest (15%) and would not have control of the firm.

CP 3-2.

Amgen is the leading company in the biotechnology industry. It has the largest market capitalization, sales, and earnings of any of its biotech competitors. Amgen's current earnings are driven by its two blockbuster products, Epogen and Neupogen. In fact, there are only two $1 billion drugs in the biotech industry and both belong to Amgen. Epogen, an anti-anemia drug, and Neupogen, an immune system stimulator, account for 90% of sales while a third drug, Infergen, has been commercialized as a possible treatment for hepatitis C.

The income statement, balance sheet, and statement of cash flows for Amgen are shown in Exhibit 1, 2, and 3, respectively.

Consolidated Statements of Operations
(In millions, except per share data)

Exhibit 1	Year ended December 31,	1998	1997	1996
	Revenues:			
	Product sales	$2,514.4	$2,219.8	$2,088.2
	Corporate partner revenues	127.9	125.9	109.9
	Royalty income	75.9	55.3	41.7
	Total revenues	2,718.2	2,401.0	2,239.8
	Operating expenses:			
	Cost of sales	345.2	300.8	283.2
	Research and development	663.3	630.8	528.3
	Selling, general and administrative	515.4	483.8	470.6
	Loss of affiliates, net	28.6	36.1	52.8
	Legal (award) assessment	(23.0)	157.0	---
	Total operating expenses	1,529.5	1,608.5	1,334.9
	Operating income	1,188.7	792.5	904.9
	Other income (expense):			
	Interest and other income, net	45.7	72.6	63.6
	Interest expense, net	(10.0)	(3.7)	(6.2)
	Total other income (expense)	35.7	68.9	57.4
	Income before income taxes	1,224.4	861.4	962.3
	Provision for income taxes	361.2	217.1	282.5
	Net income	$ 863.2	$ 644.3	$ 679.8
	Earnings per share:			
	Basic	$ 1.69	$ 1.22	$ 1.28
	Diluted	$ 1.63	$ 1.17	$ 1.21
	Shares used in calculation of earnings per share:			
	Basic	510.1	528.3	529.7
	Diluted	528.7	549.3	561.4

Consolidated Balance Sheets
(In millions, except per share data)

Exhibit 2 December 31,	1998	1997
Assets		
Current assets:		
Cash and cash equivalents	$ **201.1**	$ 239.1
Marketable securities	**1,074.9**	787.4
Trade receivables, net of allowance for doubtful accounts of $17.1 in 1998 and $14.2 in 1997	**319.9**	269.0
Inventories	**110.8**	109.2
Other current assets	**156.6**	138.8
Total current assets	**1,863.3**	1,543.5
Property, plant and equipment at cost, net	**1,450.2**	1,186.2
Investments in affiliated companies	**120.9**	116.9
Other assets	**237.8**	263.6
	$3,672.2	$3,110.2
Liabilities and Stockholders' Equity		
Current liabilities:		
Accounts payable	$ **121.6**	$ 103.9
Commercial paper	**99.7**	----
Accrued liabilities	**659.7**	608.0
Current portion of long-term debt	**6.0**	30.0
Total current liabilities	**887.0**	741.9
Long-term debt	**223.0**	229.0
Contingencies		
Stockholders' equity:		
Preferred stock; $.0001 par value; 5 shares authorized; none issued or outstanding	----	----
Common stock and additional paid-in capital; $.0001 par value; 750 shares authorized; outstanding—509.2 shares in 1998 and 516.6 shares in 1997	**1,671.9**	1,218.2
Retained earnings	**894.3**	943.2
Accumulated other comprehensive loss	**(4.0)**	(22.1)
Total stockholders' equity	**2,562.2**	2,139.3
	$3,672.2	$3,110.2

Consolidated Statements of Cash Flows
(In millions)

Exhibit 3 Year ended December 31,	1998	1997	1996
Cash flows from operating activities:			
Net income	$ 863.2	$ 644.3	$ 679.8
Depreciation and amortization	143.8	117.1	100.3
Other non-cash expenses	33.1	----	----
Gain on sale of investments	(17.3)	----	----
Deferred income taxes	(5.6)	(31.4)	25.6
Loss of affiliates, net	28.6	36.1	52.8
Cash provided by (used in):			
Trade receivables, net	(50.9)	(43.6)	(26.1)
Inventories	(1.6)	(11.8)	(8.6)
Other current assets	(21.2)	5.0	(11.8)
Accounts payable	17.7	28.9	20.6
Accrued liabilities	51.7	158.3	(10.0)
Net cash provided by operating activities	1,041.5	902.9	822.6
Cash flows from investing activities:			
Purchases of property, plant and equipment	(407.8)	(387.8)	(266.9)
Proceeds from maturities of marketable securities	20.1	244.3	168.3
Proceeds from sales of marketable securities	466.2	647.1	762.4
Purchases of marketable securities	(766.3)	(767.5)	(854.8)
Increase in investments in affiliated companies	(6.5)	(3.3)	(14.6)
Decrease (increase) in other assets	20.6	(35.0)	(104.6)
Net cash used in investing activities	(673.7)	(302.2)	(310.2)
Cash flows from financing activities:			
Increase (decrease) in commercial paper	$ 99.7	$ ----	$ (69.7)
Repayment of long-term debt	(30.0)	(118.2)	----
Proceeds from issuance of long-term debt	---	200.0	----
Net proceeds from issuance of common stock upon the exercise of stock options and in connection with an employee stock purchase plan	345.5	134.3	112.6
Tax benefits related to stock options	108.2	54.7	48.6
Repurchases of common stock	(912.1)	(737.9)	(450.0)
Other	(17.1)	(63.8)	(51.3)
Net cash used in financing activities	(405.8)	(530.9)	(409.8)

(Decrease) increase in cash and cash equivalents	**(38.0)**	69.8	102.6
Cash and cash equivalents at beginning of period	**239.1**	169.3	66.7
Cash and cash equivalents at end of period	**$ 201.1**	$ 239.1	$ 169.3

CP Questions

1. Referring to Exhibit 1, compute the change (negative or positive) in diluted earnings per share between 1996-1997 and between 1997-1998.

2. Examine Exhibit 1 closely and see if you can come up with a reason for the relatively poor earnings per share figure for 1997. You do not actually have to compute ratios at this point, but see if you can find one expense account that impairs earnings the most in 1997.

3. Based on your answer to question 2, do you see the problem you identified as being continuing in nature?

4. Other firms in the industry, such as Biogen and Eli Lilly (which are in other industries as well) show the following returns on stockholders' equity for 1997 and 1998:

	1997	1998
Biogen	15.67%	19.37%
Eli Lilly	26.27%	34.07%

Compute net income to stockholders' equity for Amgen for 1997 and 1998, using Exhibit 1 and Exhibit 2, and compare the results to its two competitors.

5. Breakdown return on stockholders' equity for 1998 for Amgen by using formulas 2.*b*. and 3.*b*. in the chapter. You should refer to Exhibit 1 and Exhibit 2 to get your data to use in the formulas.

6. Describe the relative importance of the profit margin, total asset turnover, and the total debt to total assets ratios in producing the return on stockholders' equity value you computed in question 5.

7. In the statement of cash flows (exhibit 3), under the "Cash flows from financing activities" section, does the increase in commercial paper represent a source or use of funds?

8. The price of Amgen common stock was $20 at the beginning of 1997. What is the current stock price? (The company is listed on the NASDAQ). Has the company performed well in the stock market?

CP Solution:

1. Change in diluted earnings per share

1997	$1.17		1998	$1.63
1996	1.21		1997	1.17
	$(.04)			$ .46

2. The expense item that impairs earnings the most for 1997 is the $157 (million) charge for legal (award) assessment. Although not spelled out in the financial statements, this was a result of legal action between Amgen and Johnson and Johnson over funds they both have claimed the rights to.

3. It is not likely to be continuing in nature as a normal operating expense would be. For example in 1998, Amgen actually came out $23 (million) ahead of this account as indicated by the negative expense item (which is the equivalent of income).

4. Amgen = net income/stockholders' equity (all in millions)

   1997 $644.3/$2,139.3 = 30.12%

   1998 $863.2/$2,562.2 = 33.69%

Amgen was superior to Biogen in both years, and better than Eli Lilly in 1997, but slightly below Eli Lilly in 1998.

	1997	**1998**
Amgen	30.12%	33.69%
Biogen	15.67%	19.37%
Eli Lilly	26.27%	34.07%

5. Formula 2.b. (in millions)

$$\frac{\text{Net income}}{\text{Total assets}} = \frac{\text{Net income}}{\text{Sales}} \times \frac{\text{Sales}}{\text{Total assets}}$$

$$= \frac{\$863.2}{2,718.2} \times \frac{\$2,718.2}{3,672.2} =$$

$$= 31.76\% \times .74x = 23.51\%$$

Formula 3.b. (in millions)

$$\frac{\text{Net income}}{\text{Stockholders' equity}} = \frac{\text{Return on assets}}{(1 - \text{Debt/assets})}$$

$$= \frac{23.5\%}{(1 - \$1,100/\$3,672.2)}$$

$$= \frac{23.50\%}{(1 - .30)}$$

$$= \frac{23.51\%}{.70}$$

$$= 33.59\%$$

Note the answer of 33.57% for 1998 is very close to the answer of 33.69% for Amgen in 1998, which was computed for question 4. The difference is due to rounding procedures.

6. It would appear that Amgen's high return on stockholders' equity (33.57%) is related to the high profit margin (31.76%) and not to the low total assets ratio of .740x. The high profit margin contributes to a high return on total assets (23.50%). The high return on total assets ratio is further enhanced by the debt ratio of 30% to provide a return on stockholders' equity of 33.57%.

7. It is a source of funds in that more financing is being brought into the company. Commercial paper is a security that is sold to the public.

8. The answer to this question will depend on the time period under study. In March of 2000, the stock was selling at $60, which indicates a 200 percent increase over a time period slightly over three years. By any standard, that is an excellent performance.

Chapter 4

Discussion Questions

4-1.   What are the basic benefits and purposes of developing pro forma statements and a cash budget?

The pro-forma financial statements and cash budget enable the firm to determine its future level of asset needs and the associated financing that will be required. Furthermore, one can track actual events against the projections. Bankers and other lenders also use these financial statements as a guide in credit decisions.

4-2.   Explain how the collections and purchases schedules are related to the borrowing needs of the corporation.

The collections and purchase schedules measure the speed at which receivables are collected and purchases are paid. To the extent collections do not cover purchasing costs and other financial requirements, the firm must look to borrowing to cover the deficit.

4-3.   With inflation, what are the implications of using LIFO and FIFO inventory methods? How do they affect the cost of goods sold?

LIFO inventory valuation assumes the latest purchased inventory becomes part of the cost of goods sold, while the FIFO method assigns inventory items that were purchased first to the cost of goods sold. In an inflationary environment, the LIFO method will result in a higher cost of goods sold figure and one that more accurately matches the sales dollars recorded at current dollars.

4-4.   Explain the relationship between inventory turnover and purchasing needs.

The more rapid the turnover of inventory, the greater the need for purchase and replacement. Rapidly turning inventory makes for somewhat greater ease in foreseeing future requirements and reduces the cost of carrying inventory.

4-5.   Rapid corporate growth in sales and profits can cause financing problems.
        Elaborate on this statement.

        Rapid growth in sales and profits is often associated with rapid growth in asset
        commitment. A $100,000 increase in sales may occasion a $50,000 increase in
        assets, with perhaps only $10,000 of the new financing coming from profits. It is
        very seldom that incremental profits from sales expansion can meet new
        financing needs.

4-6.   Discuss the advantage and disadvantage of level production schedules in firms
        with cyclical sales.

        Level production in a cyclical industry has the advantage of allowing for the
        maintenance of a stable work force and reducing inefficiencies caused by
        shutting down production during slow periods and accelerating work during
        crash production periods. A major drawback is that a large stock of inventory
        may be accumulated during the slow sales period. This inventory may be
        expensive to finance, with an associated danger of obsolescence.

4-7.   What conditions would help make a percent-of-sales forecast almost as accurate
        as pro forma financial statements and cash budgets?

        The percent-of-sales forecast is only as good as the functional relationship of
        assets and liabilities to sales. To the extent that past relationships accurately
        depict the future, the percent-of-sales method will give values that reasonably
        represent the values derived through the pro-forma statements and the cash
        budget.

Problems

4-1.   Philip Morris is very excited because sales for his clothing company was expected to double from $500,000 to $1,000,000 next year. Philip notes that net assets (assets – liabilities) will remain at 50 percent of sales. His clothing firm will enjoy a 9 percent return on total sales. He will start the year with $100,000 in the bank and is bragging about the two Mercedes he will buy and the European vacation he will take. Does his optimistic outlook for his cash position appear to be correct? Compute his likely cash balance or deficit for the end of the year. Start with beginning cash and subtract the asset buildup (equal to 50 percent of the sales increase) and add in profit.

Solution:

Philip Morris

Beginning cash	$100,000	
– Asset buildup	(250,000)	(1/2 × $500,000)
Profit	90,000	(9% × $1,000,000)
Ending cash	($60,000)	Deficit

4-2.   In problem 1 if there had been no increase in sales and all other facts were the same, what would his ending cash balance be? What lesson do the examples in problems one and two illustrate?

Solution:

Philip Morris (continued)

Beginning cash	$100,000	
No asset buildup	-----	
Profit	45,000	(9% × $500,000)
Ending cash	$145,000	

The lesson to be learned is that increased sales can increase the financing requirements and reduce cash even for a profitable firm.

4-3. The Alliance Corp. expects to sell the following number of units of copper cables at the prices indicated under three difference scenarios in the economy. The probability of each outcome is indicated. What is the expected value of the total sales projection?

Outcome	Probability	Units	Price
A	0.30	200	$15
B	0.50	320	$30
C	0.20	410	$40

Solution:

Alliance Corporation

(1)	(2)	(3)	(4)	(5)	(6)
				Total	Expected Value
Outcome	Probability	Units	Price	Value	(2 × 5)
A	.30	200	$15	3,000	900
B	.50	320	$30	9,600	4,800
C	.20	410	$40	16,400	3,280
			Total expected values		$8,980

4-4. Sales for Western Boot Stores are expected to be 40,000 units for October. The company likes to maintain 15 percent of units sales for each month in ending inventory (i.e., the end of October). Beginning inventory for October is 8,500 units. How many units should Western Boot produce for the coming month?

Solution:

Western Boot Stores

+ Projected sales	40,000	units
+ Desired ending inventory ...	6,000	(15% × 40,000)
− Beginning inventory	8,500	
Units to be produced	37,500	

4-5.   Vitale Hair Spray had sales of 8,000 units in March. A 50 percent increase is expected in April. The company will maintain five percent of expected unit sales for April in ending inventory. Beginning inventory for April was 400 units. How many units should the company produce in April?

Solution:
Vitale Hair Spray

+	Projected sales.............	12,000	units (8,000 × 1.50)
+	Desired ending inventory	600	(5% × 12,000)
−	Beginning inventory....	400	
	Units to be produced ...	12,200	

4-6.   Delsing Plumbing Company has beginning inventory of 14,000 units, will sell 50,000 units for the month, and desires to reduce ending inventory to 40 percent of beginning inventory. How many units should Delsing produce?

Solution:
Delsing Plumbing Company

+	Projected sales....................	50,000	units
+	Desired ending inventory ...	5,600	(40% × 14,000)
−	Beginning inventory...........	14,000	
	Units to be produced	41,600	

4-7.   On December 31 of last year, Wolfson Corporation had in inventory 400 units of its product, which cost $21 per unit to produce. During January, the company produced 800 units at a cost of $24 per unit. Assuming that Wolfson Corporation sold 700 units in January, what was the cost of goods sold (assume FIFO inventory accounting)?

Solution:

Wolfson Corporation

Cost of goods sold on 700 units

Old inventory:

Quantity (Units).....................................	400
Cost per unit	$ 21
Total...	$ 8,400

New inventory:

Quantity (Units).....................................	300
Cost per unit	$ 24
Total	$ 7,200
Total Cost of Goods Sold........................	$15,600

4-8.　　　At the end of January, Higgins Data Systems had an inventory of 600 units which cost $16 per unit to produce. During February the company produced 850 units at a cost of $19 per unit. If the firm sold 1,100 units in February, what was its cost of goods sold? (Assume LIFO inventory accounting.)

Solution:
Higgins Data System

Cost of goods sold on 1,100 units

New inventory:

Quantity (Units).....................................	850
Cost per unit	$ 19
Total..	$16,150

Old inventory:

Quantity (Units).....................................	250
Cost per unit	$ 16
Total	$ 4,000
Total Cost of Goods Sold........................	$20,150

4-9.　　　The Bradley Corporation produces a product with the following costs as of July 1, 2001:

Material .... $2 per unit
Labor .... 4 per unit
Overhead .... 2 per unit

Beginning inventory at these costs on July 1 was 3,000 units. From July 1 to December 31, 2001, Bradley produced 12,000 units. These units had a material cost of $3, labor of $5, and overhead of $3 per unit. Bradley uses FIFO inventory accounting.

Assuming that Bradley sold 13,000 units during the last six months of the year at $16 each, what is their gross profit? What is the value of ending inventory?

Solution:

Bradley Corporation

Sales (13,000 @ $16)			$208,000
Cost of goods sold:			
Old inventory:			
Quantity (units)	3,000		
Cost per unit	$ 8		
Total.........................		$24,000	
New inventory:			
Quantity (units)	10,000		
Cost per unit	$ 11		
Total.........................		$110,000	
Total cost of goods sold			$134,000
Gross profit...............			$ 74,000

Value of ending inventory:	
Beginning inventory (3,000 × $8).............	$24,000
+ Total production (12,000 × $11).........	$132,000
Total inventory available for sale.....	$156,000
− Cost of good sold......	$134,000
Ending inventory	$ 22,000

or

2,000 units × $11 = $22,000

4-10.   Assume in problem 9 that the Bradley Corporation used LIFO accounting instead of FIFO, what would gross profit be? What would be the value of ending inventory?

Solution:

Bradley Corporation (Continued)

Sales (13,000 @ $16)		$208,000
Cost of goods sold:		
New inventory:		
Quantity (units)	12,000	
Cost per unit	$ 11	
Total..........................		$132,000
Old inventory:		
Quantity (units)	1,000	
Cost per unit	$ 8	
Total..........................		$ 8,000
Total cost of goods sold		$140,000
Gross profit..............		$ 68,000

Value of ending inventory:	
Beginning inventory (3,000 × $8).............	$ 24,000
+ Total production (12,000 × $11)........	$132,000
Total inventory available for sale.....	$156,000
− Cost of good sold......	$140,000
Ending inventory	$ 16,000

or

2,000 units × $8 = $16,000

4-11.   Sprint Shoes, Inc., had a beginning inventory of 9,000 units on January 1, 2001.

The costs associated with the inventory were:

Material . . . . $13.00 per unit
Labor . . . .   8.00 per unit
Overhead . . . .   6.10 per unit

During 2001, they produced 42,500 units with the following costs:

Material . . . . $15.50 per unit
Labor . . . .   7.80 per unit
Overhead . . . .   8.30 per unit

Sales for the year were 47,250 units at $39.60 each. Sprint Shoes uses LIFO accounting. What was the gross profit? What was the value of ending inventory?

Solution:

Sprint Shoes, Inc.

Sales (47,250 @ $39.60)		$1,871,100
Cost of goods sold:		
New inventory:		
Quantity (units)	42,500	
Cost per unit	$ 31.60	
Total..........................		$1,343,000
Old inventory:		
Quantity (units)	4,750	
Cost per unit	$ 27.10	
Total..........................		$ 128,725
Total cost of goods sold		$1,471,725
Gross profit..............		$ 399,375
Value of ending inventory:		
Beginning inventory (9,000 × $27.10).....	$ 243,900	

+ Total production	$1,343,000	
(42,500 × $31.60)...		
Total inventory available for sale.....	$1,586,900	
− Cost of good sold......	$1,471,725	
Ending inventory......	$ 115,175	

or

42,500 units × $27.10 = $115,175

4-12. Victoria's Apparel has forecast credit sales for the fourth quarter of the year as:

September (actual) $50,000

Fourth Quarter

October....................................... $40,000
November.................................... 35,000
December 60,000

Experience has shown that 20 percent of sales are collected in the month of sale, 70 percent in the following month, and 10 percent are never collected.

Prepare a schedule of cash receipts for Victoria's Apparel covering the fourth quarter (October through December).

Solution:

Victoria's Apparel

	September	*October*	*November*	*December*
Credit sales	$50,000	$40,000	$35,000	$60,000
20% Collected in month of sales		8,000	7,000	12,000
70% Collected in month after sales		35,000	28,000	24,500
Total cash receipts		$43,000	$35,000	$36,500

4-13. Watt's Lighting Stores made the following sales projections for the next six months. All sales are credit sales.

March	$30,000	June	$34,000
April	36,000	July	42,000
May	25,000	August	44,000

Sales in January and February were $33,000 and $32,000, respectively.

Experience has shown that of total sales, 10 percent are uncollectible, 30 percent are collected in the month of sale, 40 percent are collected in the following month, and 20 percent are collected two months after sale.

Prepare a monthly cash receipts schedule for the firm for March through August.

Of the sales expected to be made during the six months from March through August, how much will still be uncollected at the end of August? How much of this is expected to be collected later?

Solution:

Watt's Lighting Stores
Cash Receipts Schedule

	January	February	March	April	May	June	July	August
Sales	$33,000	$32,000	$30,000	$36,000	$25,000	$34,000	$42,000	$44,000
Collections (30% of current sales)			9,000	10,800	7,500	10,200	12,600	13,200
Collections (40% of prior month's sales)			12,800	12,000	14,400	10,000	13,600	16,800
Collections (20% of sales 2 months earlier)			6,600	6,400	6,000	7,200	5,000	6,800
Total cash receipts			$28,400	$29,200	$27,900	$27,400	$31,200	$36,800

Still due (uncollected) in August:

Bad debts: ($30,000 + $36,000 + $25,000 + $34,000 + $42,000 + $44,000) × .1 = (211,000) × .1 = $21,100

To be collected from July sales: ($42,000 × .20) = $8,400

To be collected from August sales: ($44,000 × .60) = $26,400

$21,100 + $8,400 + $26,400 = $55,900 due

Expected to be collected:

$55,900 due – $21,100 bad debts = $34,800

4-14.   Ultravision, Inc. anticipates sales of $240,000 from January through April. Materials will represent 50 percent of sales and because of level production, material purchases will be equal for each month over the four months of January, February, March, and April.

Materials are paid for after the month purchased. Materials purchased in December of last year were $20,000 (half of $40,000 in sales), labor costs for each of the four months are slightly different due to a provision in a labor contract in which bonuses are paid in February and April. The labor figures are:

January	$10,000
February	$13,000
March	$10,000
April	$15,000

Fixed overhead is $6,000 per month. Prepare a schedule of cash payments for January through April.

Solution:

Ultravision, Inc.
Cash Payment Schedule

	Dec.	Jan.	Feb.	March	April
* Purchases	$20,000	$30,000	$30,000	$30,000	$30,000
** Payment to material purchases		20,000	30,000	30,000	30,000
Labor		10,000	13,000	10,000	15,000
Fixed overhead		6,000	6,000	6,000	6,000
Total Cash Payments		$36,000	$49,000	$46,000	$51,000

For January through April

* Monthly purchases equal ($240,000 × 50%)/4 or $120,000/4 = $30,000

** Payment is equal to prior month's purchases.

4-15.   The Denver Corporation has forecast the following sales for the first seven months of the year:

January	$10,000	May	$10,000
February	12,000	June	16,000
March	14,000	July	18,000
April	20,000		

Monthly material purchases are set equal to 30 percent of forecasted sales for the next month. Of the total material costs, 40 percent are paid in the month of purchase and 60 percent in the following month. Labor costs will run $4,000 per month, and fixed overhead is $2,000 per month. Interest payments on the debt will be $3,000 for both March and June. Finally, the Denver salesforce will receive a 1.5 percent commission on total sales for the first six months of the year, to be paid on June 30.

Prepare a monthly summary of cash payments for the six-month period from January through June. (Note: Compute prior December purchases to help get total material payments for January.)

Solution

Denver Corporation
Cash Payments Schedule

	Dec.	Jan.	Feb.	March	April	May	June	July
Sales		$10,000	$12,000	$14,000	$20,000	$10,000	$16,000	$18,000
Purchases (30% of next month's sales)	3,000	3,600	4,200	6,000	3,000	4,800	5,400	
Payment (40% of current purchases)		1,440	1,680	2,400	1,200	1,920	2,160	
Material payment (60% of previous month's purchases)		1,800	2,160	2,520	3,600	1,800	2,880	
Total payment for materials		3,240	3,840	4,920	4,800	3,720	5,040	
Labor costs		4,000	4,000	4,000	4,000	4,000	4,000	
Fixed overhead		2,000	2,000	2,000	2,000	2,000	2,000	
Interest payments				3,000			3,000	
Sales commission (1.5% of $82,000)							1,230	
Total payments		$9,240	$9,840	$13,920	$10,800	$9,720	$15,270	

4-16. The Boswell Corporation forecasts its sale in units for the next four months as follows:

March	$6,000
April	8,000
May	5,500
June	4,000

Boswell maintains an ending inventory for each month in the amount of one and one half times the expected sales in the following month. The ending inventory for February (March's beginning inventory) reflects this policy Materials cost $5 per unit and are paid for in the month after production. Labor cost is $10 per unit and is paid for in the month incurred. Fixed overhead is $12,000 per month. Dividends of $20,000 are to be paid in May. Five thousand units were produced in February.

Compute a production schedule and a summary of cash payments for March, April, and May. Remember that production in any one month is equal to sales plus desired ending inventory minus beginning inventory.

Solution:

Boswell Corporation
Production Schedule

	March	April	May	June
Forecasted unit sales	6,000	8,000	5,500	4,000
+Desired ending inventory	12,000	8,250	6,000	
−Beginning inventory	9,000	12,000	8,250	
Units to be produced	9,000	4,250	3,250	

Cash Payments

	Feb	March	April	May
Units produced	5,000	9,000	4,250	3,250
Materials ($5/unit) month after production		$25,000	$45,000	$21,250
Labor ($10/unit) month of production		90,000	42,500	32,500
Fixed overhead		12,000	12,000	12,000
Dividends				20,000
Total Cash Payments		$127,000	$99,500	$85,750

4-17.   The Volt Battery Company has forecast its sales in units as follows:

January	800	May	1,350
February	650	June	1,500
March	600	July	1,200
April	1,100		

Volt Battery always keeps an ending inventory equal to 120 percent of the next month's expected sales. The ending inventory for December (January's beginning inventory) is 960 units, which is consistent with this policy.

Materials cost $12 per unit and are paid for the month after purchase. Labor cost is $5 per unit and is paid in the month the cost is incurred. Overhead costs are $6,000 per month. Interest of $8,000 is scheduled to be paid in March, and employee bonuses of $13,200 will be paid in June.

Prepare a monthly production schedule and a monthly summary of cash payments for January through June. Volt produced 600 units in December.

Solution:

Volt Battery Company
Production Schedule

	Jan.	Feb.	March	April	May	June	July
Forecasted unit sales	800	650	600	1,100	1,350	1,500	1,200
+ Desired ending inventory	780	720	1,320	1,620	1,800	1,440	
− Beginning inventory	960	780	720	1,320	1,620	1,800	
= Units to be produced	620	590	1,200	1,400	1,530	1,140	

Summary of Cash Payments

	Dec.	Jan.	Feb.	March	April	May	June
Units produced	600	620	590	1,200	1,400	1,530	1,140
Material cost ($12/unit) month after purchase		$7,200	$7,440	$7,080	$14,400	$16,800	$18,360
Labor cost ($5/unit) month incurred		3,100	2,950	6,000	7,000	7,650	5,700
Overhead cost		6,000	6,000	6,000	6,000	6,000	6,000
Interest				8,000			
Employee bonuses							13,200
Total Cash Payments		$16,300	$16,390	$27,080	$27,400	$30,450	$43,260

4-18.　　Lansing Auto Parts, Inc., has projected sales of $25,000 in October, $35,000 in November, and $30,000 in December. Of the company's sales, 20 percent are paid for by cash and 80 percent are sold on credit. The credit sales are collected one month after sale. Determine collections for November and December.

Also assume that the company's cash payments for November and December are $30,400 and $29,800, respectively. The beginning cash balance in November is $6,000, which is the desired minimum balance.

Prepare a cash budget with borrowing needed or repayments for November and December. (You will need to prepare a cash receipts schedule first.)

Solution:

Lansing Auto Parts, Inc.
Cash Receipts Schedule

		October	November	December
	Sales	$25,000	$35,000	$30,000
	Cash sales (20%)		7,000	6,000
	Collections (80% of previous month's sales)		20,000	28,000
	Total cash receipts		$27,000	$34,000

Cash Budget

	November	December
Cash receipts	$27,000	$34,000
Cash payments	30,400	29,800
Net Cash Flow	(3,400)	4,200
Beginning Cash Balance	6,000	6,000
Cumulative Cash Balance	2,600	10,200
Monthly Loan or (Repayment)	3,400	(3,400)
Cumulative Loan Balance	3,400	-0-
Ending Cash Balance	$ 6,000	$ 6,800

4-19.   Harry's Carryout Stores has eight locations. The firm wishes to expand by two more stores and needs a bank long to do this. Mr. Wilson, the banker, will finance construction if the firm can present an acceptable three-month financial plan for January through March. The following are actual and forecasted sales figures:

Actual	**Forecast**	**Additional Information**
November...$200,000	January.....$280,000	April forecast...$330,000
December ... 220,000	February... 320,000	
	March....... 340,000	

Of the firm's sales, 40 percent are for cash and the remaining 60 percent are on credit. Of credit sales, 30 percent are paid in the month after sale and 70 percent are paid in the second month after the sale. Materials cost 30 percent of sales and are purchased and received each month in an amount sufficient to cover the following month's expected sales. Materials are paid for in the month after they are received. Labor expense is 40 percent of sales and is paid in the month of sales. Selling and administrative expense is 5 percent of sales and is also paid in the month of sale. Overhead expense is $28,000 in cash per month. Depreciation expense is $10,000 per month. Taxes of $8,000 will be paid in January, and dividends of $2,000 will be paid in March. Cash at the beginning of January is $80,000 and the minimum desired cash balance is $75,000.

For January, February, and March, prepare a schedule of monthly cash receipts, monthly cash payments, and a complete monthly cash budget with borrowings and repayments.

Solution:

Harry's Carry-Out Stores
Cash Receipts Schedule

	November	December	January	February	March	April
Sales	$200,000	$220,000	$280,000	$320,000	$340,000	$330,000
Cash sales (40%)	80,000	88,000	112,000	128,000	136,000	132,000
Credit sales (60%)	120,000	132,000	168,000	192,000	204,000	198,000
Collections (month after credit sales) 30%		36,000	39,600	50,400	57,600	61,200
Collections (two months after credit sales) 70%			84,000	92,400	117,600	134,400
Total Cash Receipts			$235,600	$270,800	$311,200	

Harry's Carry-Out Stores (continued)
Cash Payments Schedule

	January	February	March
Payments for Purchases (30% of next month's sales paid in month after purchases—equivalent to 30% of current sales)...............	$ 84,000	$ 96,000	$102,000
Labor Expense (40% of sales)................	112,000	128,000	136,000
Selling and Admin. Exp. (5% of sales)........	14,000	16,000	17,000
Overhead............................	28,000	28,000	28,000
Taxes..................................	8,000		
Dividends.............................			2,000
Total Cash Payments*..................	$246,000	$268,000	$285,000

*The $10,000 of depreciation is excluded because it is not a cash expense.

Harry's Carry-Out Stores (continued)
Cash Budget

	January	February	March
Total Cash Receipts...........	$235,600	$270,800	$311,200
Total Cash Payments.........	246,000	268,000	285,000
Net Cash Flow	(10,400)	2,800	26,200
Beginning Cash Balance	80,000	75,000	75,000
Cumulative Cash Balance ...	69,600	77,800	101,200
Monthly Loan or (repayment)...	5,400	(2,800)	(2,600)
Cumulative Loan Balance ...	5,400	2,600	-0-
Ending Cash Balance.........	$ 75,000	$ 75,000	$ 98,600

4-20.   Archer Electronics Company's actual sales and purchases for April and May are shown here along with forecasted sales and purchases for June through September.

	Sales	Purchases
April (actual)..	$320,000	$130,000
May (actual)..	300,000	120,000
June (forecast).....................................	275,000	120,000
July (forecast)	275,000	180,000
August (forecast)	290,000	200,000
September (forecast)	330,000	170,000

The company makes 10 percent of its sales for cash and 90 percent on credit. Of the credit sales, 20 percent are collected in the month after the sale and 80 percent are collected two months after. Archer pays for 40 percent of its purchases in the month after purchase and 60 percent two months after.

Labor expense equals 10 percent of the current month's sales. Overhead expense equals $12,000 per month. Interest payments of $30,000 are due in June and September. A cash dividend of $50,000 is scheduled to be paid in June. Tax payments of $25,000 are due in June and September. There is a scheduled capital outlay of $300,000 in September.

Archer Electronics' ending cash balance in May is $20,000. The minimum desired cash balance is $10,000. Prepare a schedule of monthly cash receipts, monthly cash payments, and a complete monthly cash budget with borrowing and repayments for June through September. The maximum desired cash balance is $50,000. Excess cash (above $50,000) is used to buy marketable securities. Marketable securities are sold before borrowing funds in case of a cash shortfall (less than $10,000).

Solution:

Archer Electronics
Cash Receipts Schedule

	April	May	June	July	Aug.	Sept.
Sales	$320,000	$300,000	$275,000	$275,000	$290,000	$330,000
+ Cash Sales (10%)	32,000	30,000	27,500	27,500	29,000	33,000
+ Credit Sales (90%)	288,000	270,000	247,500	247,500	261,000	297,000
+ Collections (month after sale) 20%		57,600	54,000	49,500	49,500	52,200
+ Collections (second month after sale) 80%			230,400	216,000	198,000	198,000
Total Cash Receipts			$311,900	$293,000	$276,500	$283,200

Archer Electronics (continued)
Cash Payments Schedule

	April	May	June	July	Aug.	Sept.
Purchases	$130,000	$120,000	$120,000	$180,000	$200,000	$170,000
Payments (month after purchase—40%)		52,000	48,000	48,000	72,000	80,000
Payments (second month after purchase—60%)			78,000	72,000	72,000	108,000
Labor Expense (10% of sales)			27,500	27,500	29,000	33,000
Overhead			12,000	12,000	12,000	12,000
Interest Payments			30,000			30,000
Cash Dividend			50,000			
Taxes			25,000			25,000
Capital Outlay						30,000
Total Cash Payments			$270,500	$159,500	$185,000	$588,000

Archer Electronics (continued)
Cash Budget

	June	July	August	September
Cash Receipts	$311,900	$293,000	$276,500	$283,200
Cash Payments.........	270,500	159,500	185,000	588,000
Net Cash Flow	41,400	133,500	91,500	(304,800)
Beginning Cash Balance	20,000	50,000	50,000	50,000
Cumulative Cash Balance	61,400	183,500	141,500	(254,800)
Monthly Borrowing or (Repayment)	--	--	--	*28,400
Cumulative Loan Balance	--	--	--	28,400
Marketable Securities Purchased	11,400	133,500	91,500	--
(Sold)		--	--	(236,400)
Cumulative Marketable Securities	11,400	144,900	236,400	--
Ending Cash Balance.........	50,000	50,000	50,000	10,000

*Cumulative Marketable Sec. (Aug) $236,400
Cumulative Cash Balance (Sept)   –254,800
Required (ending) Cash Balance   <u>–10,000</u>
Monthly Borrowing   –$28,400

4-21.   Owen's Electronics has 90 operating plants in seven southwestern states. Sales for last year were $100 million, and the balance sheet at year-end is similar in percentage of sales to that of previous years (and this will continue in the future). All assets (including fixed assets) and current liabilities will vary directly with sales.

Balance Sheet
(in $ millions)

Assets		**Liabilities and Stockholders' Equity**	
Cash..............................	$ 2	Accounts payable.................	$15
Accounts receivable.....	20	Accrued wages.....................	2
Inventory......................	23	Accrued taxes......................	8
Current assets.............	$45	Current liabilities................	$25
Fixed assets.................	40	Notes payable......................	10
		Common stock	15
		Retained earnings.................	35
		Total liabilities and	
Total assets..................	$85	stockholders' equity............	$85

Owen's has an aftertax profit margin of 7 percent and a dividend payout ratio of 40 percent.

If sales grow by 10 percent next year, determine how many dollars of new funds are needed to finance the growth.

Solution:

Owens Electronics

$$\text{Required New Funds} = \frac{A}{S}(\Delta S) - \frac{L}{S}(\Delta S) - PS_2(1-D)$$

$$\Delta S = (10\%)(\$100 \text{ mil.})$$

$$\Delta S = \$10,000,000$$

$$\text{RNF (millions)} = \frac{85}{100}(\$10,000,000) - \frac{25}{100}(\$10,000,000) - .07$$

$$(\$110,000,000)(1-.40)$$

$$= .85(\$10,000,000) - .25(\$10,000,000) - .07(\$110,000,000)(.60)$$

$$= \$8,500,000 - \$2,500,000 - \$4,620,000$$

$$\text{RNF} = \$1,380,000$$

4-22.　The Manning Company has the following financial statements, which are representative of the company's historical average.

Income Statement

Sales	$200,000
Expenses	158,000
Earnings before interest and taxes	$ 42,000
Interest	7,000
Earnings before taxes	$ 35,000
Taxes	15,000
Earnings after taxes	20,000
Dividends	$ 6,000

Balance Sheet

Assets		Liabilities and Stockholders' Equity	
Cash..........................	$ 5,000	Accounts payable	$ 25,000
Accounts receivable..	40,000	Accrued wages	1,000
Inventory....................	75,000	Accrued taxes....................	2,000
Current assets..........	$120,000	Current liabilities.............	$ 28,000
Fixed assets	80,000	Notes payable....................	7,000
		Long-term debt..................	15,000
		Common stock	120,000
		Retained earnings..............	30,000
		Total liabilities and	
Total assets................	$200,000	stockholders' equity.........	$200,000

The firm is expecting a 20 percent increase in sales next year, and management is concerned about the company's need for external funds. The increase in sales is expected to be carried out without any expansion of fixed assets, but rather through more efficient asset utilization in the existing store. Among liabilities, only current liabilities vary directly with sales.

Using the percent-of-sales method, determine whether the company has external financing needs, or a surplus of funds. (Hint: A profit margin and payout ratio must be found from the income statement.)

Solution:

Manning Company

$$\text{Profit margin} = \frac{\text{Earnings after taxes}}{\text{Sales}} = \frac{\$20,000}{\$200,000} = 10\%$$

$$\text{Payout ratio} = \frac{\text{Dividends}}{\text{Earnings}} = \frac{\$6,000}{20,000} = 30\%$$

Change in Sales $= 20\% \times \$200,000 = \$40,000$

Spontaneous Assets = Current Assets = Cash + Acc. Rec. + Inventory

Spontaneous Liabilities = Acc. Payable + Accr. Wages + Accr. Taxes

$$RNF = \frac{A}{S}(\Delta S) - \frac{L}{S}(\Delta S) - PS_2(1-D)$$

$$= \frac{\$120,000}{\$200,000}(\$40,000) - \frac{\$28,000}{\$200,000}(\$40,000) - .10(\$240,000)(1-.30)$$

$$= .60(\$40,000) - .14(\$40,000) - .10(\$240,000)(.70)$$

$$= \$24,000 - \$5,600 - \$16,800$$

$$RNF = \$1,600$$

The firm needs $1,600 in external funds.

4-23. Conn Man's Shops, Inc., a national clothing chain, had sales of $300 million last year. The business has a steady net profit margin of 8 percent and a dividend payout ratio of 25 percent. The balance sheet for the end of last year is shown below.

Balance Sheet
End of Year
($ millions)

Assets		Liabilities and Stockholders' Equity	
Cash.............................	$ 20	Accounts payable	$ 70
Accounts receivable	25	Accrued expenses.................	20
Inventory	75	Other payables......................	30
Plant and equipment.....	120	Common stock	40
		Retained earnings.................	80
		Total liabilities and	
Total assets...................	$240	stockholders' equity............	$240

The firm's marketing staff has told the president that in the coming year there will be a large increase in the demand for overcoats and wool slacks. A sales increase of 15 percent is forecast for the company.

All balance sheet items are expected to maintain the same percent-of-sales relationships as last year, except for common stock and retained earnings. No change is scheduled in the number of common stock shares outstanding, and retained earnings will change as dictated by the profits and dividend policy of the firm. (Remember the net profit margin is 8 percent.)

a. Will external financing be required for the company during the coming year?
b. What would be the need for external financing if the net profit margin went up to 9.5 percent and the dividend payout ratio was increased to 50 percent? Explain.

Solution:

Conn Man's Shops, Inc.

a. Required New Funds $= \dfrac{A}{S}(\Delta S) - \dfrac{L}{S}(\Delta S) - PS_2(1-D)$

$$\Delta S = 15\% \times \$300{,}000{,}000 = \$45{,}000{,}000$$

$$RNF = \dfrac{240}{300}(\$45{,}000{,}000) - \dfrac{120}{300}(\$45{,}000{,}000) - .08$$

$$(\$345{,}000{,}000)(1-.25)$$

$$= .80(\$45{,}000{,}000) - .40(\$45{,}000{,}000) - .08$$

$$(\$345{,}000{,}000)(.75)$$

$$= \$36{,}000{,}000 - \$18{,}000{,}000 - \$20{,}700{,}000$$

$$RNF = (\$2{,}700{,}000)$$

A negative figure for required new funds indicates that an excess of funds ($2.7 mil.) is available for new investment. No external funds are needed.

b. $RNF = \$36{,}000{,}000 - \$18{,}000{,}000 - .095(\$345{,}000{,}000)$
$\times (1-.5)$

$$= \$36{,}000{,}000 - \$18{,}000{,}000 - \$16{,}387{,}500$$

$$= \$1{,}612{,}500 \text{ external funds required}$$

The net profit margin increased slightly, from 8% to 9.5%, which decreases the need for external funding. The dividend payout ratio increased tremendously, however, from 25% to 50%, necessitating more external financing. The effect of the dividend policy change overpowered the effect of the net profit margin change.

Comprehensive Problems

CP 4-1. Mansfield Corporation had 2001 sales of $100 million. The balance sheet items that vary directly with sales and the profit margin are as follows:

	Percent
Cash	5%
Accounts receivable	15
Inventory	20
Net fixed assets	40
Accounts payable	15
Accruals	10
Profit margin after taxes	10%

The dividend payout rate is 50 percent of earnings, and the balance in retained earnings at the end of 2001 was $33 million. Notes payable are currently $7 million. Long-term bonds and common stock are constant at $5 million and $10 million, respectively.

a. How much additional external capital will be required for next year if sales increase 15 percent? (Assume that the company is already operating at full capacity.)

b. What will happen to external fund requirements if Mansfield Corporation reduces the payout ratio, grows at a slower rate, or suffers a decline in its profit margin? Discuss each of these separately.

c. Prepare a pro forma balance sheet for 2002 assuming that any external funds being acquired will be in the form of notes payable. Disregard the information in part *b* in answering this question (that is, use the original information and part *a* in constructing your pro forma balance sheet).

CP Solution:

Mansfield Corporation

$$\Delta Sales = .15 \times \$100 \text{ million} = 15 \text{ million}$$

$$\text{Spontaneous assets} = 5\% + 15\% + 20\% + 40\% = 80\%$$

$$\text{Spontaneous liabilities} = 15\% + 10\% = 25\%$$

a. $\text{RNF} = \dfrac{A}{S}(\Delta S) - \dfrac{L}{S}(\Delta S) - PS_2(1-D)$

$\qquad = .8(\$15\text{ million}) - .25(\$15\text{ million}) - .10(\$115)(1-.5)$

$\qquad = \$12\text{ million} - \$3.75\text{ million} - \$5.75\text{ million}$

$\qquad = \$2.5\text{ million}$

b. If Mansfield reduces the payout ratio, the company will retain more earnings and need less external funds. A slower growth rate means that less assets will have to be financed and in this case, less external funds would be needed. A declining profit margin will lower retained earnings and force Mansfield Corporation to seek more external funds.

c.

Mansfield Corporation (continued)
Balance Sheet—December 31, 2002
(Dollars in Millions)

Cash	$ 5.75	Accounts Payable.......	$17.25
Accounts Receivable ...	17.25	Accruals	11.50
Inventory.....................	23.00	Notes Payable	17.50[1]
Net Fixed Assets	46.00	Long-Term Bonds......	5.00
		Common Stock	10.00
		Retained Earnings......	38.75[2]
	$92.00		$92.00

[1]Original notes payable plus required new funds. This is the plug figure.
[2]2002 retained earnings (beginning of 2001) + $PS_2(1-D)$

CP 4-2.   The difficult part of solving a problem of this nature is to know what to do with the information contained within a story problem. Therefore, this problem will be easier to complete if you rely on Chapter 4 for the format of all required schedules.

The Adams Corporation makes standard-size 2-inch fasteners, which it sells for $155 per thousand. Mr. Adams is the majority owner and manages the inventory and finances of the company. He estimates sales for the following months to be:

January.........................	$263,500 (1,700,000 fasteners)
February......................	$186,000 (1,200,000 fasteners)
March..........................	$217,000 (1,400,000 fasteners)
April...........................	$310,000 (2,000,000 fasteners)
May.............................	$387,500 (2,500,000 fasteners)

Last year Adams Corporation's sales were $175,000 in November and $232,500 in December (1,500,000 fasteners).

Mr. Adams is preparing for a meeting with his banker to arrange the financing for the first quarter. Based on his sales forecast and the following information he has provided, your job as his new financial analyst is to prepare a monthly cash budget, a monthly and quarterly pro forma income statement, a pro forma quarterly balance sheet, and all necessary supporting schedules for the first quarter.

Past history shows that Adams Corporation collects 50 percent of its accounts receivable in the normal 30-day credit period (the month after the sale) and the other 50 percent in 60 days (two months after the sale). It pays for its materials 30 days after receipt. In general, Mr. Adams likes to keep a two-month supply of inventory in anticipation of sales. Inventory at the beginning of December was 2,600,000 units. (This was not equal to his desired two-month supply.)

The major cost of production is the purchase of raw materials in the form of steel rods, which are cut, threaded, and finished. Last year raw material costs were $52 per 1,000 fasteners, but Mr. Adams has just been notified that material costs have risen, effective January 1, to $60 per 1,000 fasteners. The Adams Corporation uses FIFO inventory accounting. Labor costs are relatively constant at $20 per thousand fasteners, since workers are paid on a piecework basis. Overhead is allocated at $10 per thousand units, and selling and administrative expense is 20 percent of sales. Labor expense and overhead are direct cash outflows paid in the month incurred, while interest and taxes are paid quarterly.

The corporation usually maintains a minimum cash balance of $25,000, and it puts its excess cash into marketable securities. The average tax rate is 40 percent, and Mr. Adams usually pays out 50 percent of net income in dividends to stockholders. Marketable securities are sold before funds are borrowed when a cash shortage is faced. Ignore the interest on any short-term borrowings. Interest on the long-term debt is paid in March, as are taxes and dividends.

Adams Corporation
Balance Sheet
December 31, 200X

Assets

Current assets:		
Cash	$ 30,000	
Accounts receivable	320,000	
Inventory	237,800	
Total current assets		$ 587,800
Fixed assets:		
Plant and equipment	1,000,000	
Less: Accumulated depreciation	200,000	800,000
Total assets		$1,387,800

Liabilities and Stockholders' Equity

Accounts payable	$ 93,600
Notes payable	0
Long-term debt, 8 percent	400,000
Common stock	504,200
Retained earnings	390,000
Total liabilities and stockholders' equity	$1,387,800

CP Solution:

Adams Corporation
Forecasting with Seasonal Production

	Dec.	Jan.	Feb.	Mar.
Projected Unit Sales	1,500,000	1,700,000	1,200,000	1,400,000
+Desired Ending Inventory (2 months supply)	2,900,000	2,600,000	3,400,000	4,500,000
−Beginning Inventory	2,600,000	2,900,000	2,600,000	3,400,000
Units to be Produced	1,800,000	1,400,000	2,000,000	2,500,000

Monthly Cash Payments

	Dec.	Jan.	Feb.	Mar.
Units to be produced	1,800,000	1,400,000	2,000,000	2,500,000
Materials (from previous month)		$93,600	$84,000	$120,000
Labor ($20 per thousand units)		$28,000	$40,000	$50,000
Overhead ($10 per thousand units)		$14,000	$20,000	$25,000
Selling & adm. expense (20% of sales)		$52,700	$37,200	$43,400
Interest				$8,000
Taxes (40% tax rate)				$64,560*
Dividends				$48,420*
Total Payments		$188,300	$181,200	$359,380

*See the pro forma income statement, which follows this material later on, for the development of these values.

Monthly Cash Receipts (Adams Corporation)

	Nov.	Dec.	Jan.	Feb.	Mar.
Sales	$175,000	$232,500	$263,500	$186,000	$217,000
Collections (50% of Previous month)		87,500	$116,250	131,750	93,000
Collections (50% of 2 months earlier)			87,500	116,250	131,750
Total Collections			$203,750	$248,000	$224,750

Monthly Cash Flow

	January	February	March
Cash Receipts	$203,750	$248,000	$224,750
Cash Payments	188,300	181,200	359,380
Net Cash Flow	15,450	66,800	(134,630)

Adams Corporation (Continued)
Cash Budget

	January	February	March
Net Cash Flow	$15,450	$66,800	$(134,630)
Beginning Cash Balance	30,000	25,000	25,000
Cumulative Cash Balance	$45,450	$91,800	($109,630)
Loans and (Repayments)	-0-	-0-	47,380
Cumulative Loans	-0-	-0-	47,380
Marketable Securities	20,450	66,800	(87,250)
Cumulative Marketable Securities	20,450	87,250	-0-
Ending Cash Balance	$25,000	$25,000	$25,000

Adams Corporation (continued)
Pro Forma Income Statement

	Jan.	Feb.	Mar.	Total
Sales	$263,500	$186,000	$217,000	$666,500
Cost of Goods Sold	139,400	98,400	126,000	363,800
Gross Profit	124,100	87,600	91,000	302,700
Selling and Admin. Expense	52,700	37,200	43,400	133,300
Interest Expense	2,667	2,667	2,666	8,000
Net Profit Before Tax	$ 68,733	$ 47,733	$ 44,934	$161,400
Taxes	27,493	19,093	17,974	64,560
Net Profit After Tax	$ 41,240	$ 28,640	$ 26,960	$ 96,840
Less: Common Dividends				48,420
Increase in Retained Earnings				$ 48,420

Cost of Goods Sold

	Unit Cost per thousand before January 1st	Unit cost per thousand after January 1st
Material...........	$52	$60
Labor..............	20	20
Overhead.........	10	10
	$82	$90

Ending inventory as of December 31 was 2,900,000, therefore, sales for January and February had a cost of goods sold per thousand units of $82, and March sales reflect the increased cost of $90 per thousand units using FIFO inventory methods.

Pro Forma Balance Sheet (March)

Assets		Liabilities & Stockholders' Equity	
Current Assets:		Current Liabilities:	
Cash	$ 25,000	Accounts Payable	$ 150,000
Accounts Receivable	310,000	Notes Payable	47,380
Inventory...............	405,000	Long-Term Debt	400,000
Plant & Equip: Net Plan	800,000	Stockholders' Equity: Common Stock	504,200
Total Assets	$1,540,000	Retained Earnings, Total Liabilities & Stockholders' Equity	438,420 $1,540,000

Explanation of Changes in the Balance Sheet:		
Cash = ending cash balance from cash budget in March		
Accounts receivable		$217,000
= all of March sales		93,000
plus 50% of Feb.		$310,000
sales		

Inventory = ending inventory in March of 4,500,000 units at $90 per thousand

Plant and equipment did not change since we did not include depreciation.

$$RE = Old\ RE + (NI - dividends)$$
$$= \$390,000 + (\$96,840 - \$48,240) = \$438,420$$

Chapter 5

Discussion Questions

5-1.   Discuss the various uses for break-even analysis.

Such analysis allows the firm to determine at what level of operations it will break even and to explore the relationship between volume, costs, and profits.

5-2.   What factors would cause a difference in the use of financial leverage for a utility company and an automobile company?

A utility is in a stable, predictable industry and therefore can afford to use more financial leverage than an automobile company, which is generally subject to the influences of the business cycle. An automobile manufacturer may not be able to service a large amount of debt when there is a downturn in the economy.

5-3.   Explain how the break-even point and operating leverage are affected by the choice of manufacturing facilities (labor intensive versus capital intensive).

A labor-intensive company will have low fixed costs and a correspondingly low break-even point. However, the impact of operating leverage on the firm is small and there will be little magnification of profits as volume increases. A capital-intensive firm, on the other hand, will have a higher break-even point and enjoy the positive influences of operating leverage as volume increases.

5-4.   What role does depreciation play in break-even analysis based on accounting flows? Based on cash flows? Which perspective is longer term in nature?

For break-even analysis based on accounting flows, depreciation is considered part of fixed costs. For cash flow purposes, it is eliminated from fixed costs.

The accounting flows perspective is longer-term in nature because we must consider the problems of equipment replacement.

5-5.   What does risk taking have to do with the use of operating and financial leverage?

Both operating and financial leverage imply that the firm will employ a heavy component of fixed cost resources. This is inherently risky because the obligation to make payments remains regardless of the condition of the company or the economy.

5-6.   Discuss the limitations of financial leverage.

Debt can only be used up to a point. Beyond that, financial leverage tends to increase the overall costs of financing to the firm as well as encourage creditors to place restrictions on the firm. The limitations of using financial leverage tend to be greatest in industries that are highly cyclical in nature.

5-7.   How does the interest rate on new debt influence the use of financial leverage?

The higher the interest rate on new debt, the less attractive financial leverage is to the firm.

5-8.   Explain how combined leverage brings together operating income and earnings per share.

Operating leverage primarily affects the operating income of the firm. At this point, financial leverage takes over and determines the overall impact on earnings per share. A delineation of the combined effect of operating and financial leverage is presented in Table 5-6 and Figure 5-5.

5-9.   Explain why operating leverage decreases as a company increases sales and shifts away from the break-even point.

At progressively higher levels of operation than the break-even point, the percentage change in operating income as a result of a percentage change in unit volume diminishes. The reason is primarily mathematical — as we move to increasingly higher levels of operating income, the percentage change from the higher base is likely to be less.

5-10.   When you are considering two different financing plans, does being at the level where earnings per share are equal between the two plans always mean you are indifferent as to which plan is selected?

The point of equality only measures indifference based on earnings per share. Since our ultimate goal is market value maximization, we must also be concerned with how these earnings are valued. Two plans that have the same earnings per share may call for different price-earnings ratios, particularly when there is a differential risk component involved because of debt.

Problems

5-1.   Shock Electronics sells portable heaters for $25 per unit and the variable cost to produce them is $17. Mr. Amps estimates that the fixed costs are $96,000.

    a. Compute the break-even point in units.

    b. Fill in the table below (in dollars) to illustrate that the break-even point has been achieved.

Sales   _____

–Fixed costs   _____

–total variable costs   _____

Net profit (loss)   _____

Solution:

Shock Electronics

a. $$BE = \frac{\text{Fixed costs}}{\text{Price - variable cost per unit}}$$

$$= \frac{\$96,000}{\$25 - \$17} = \frac{\$96,000}{\$8} = 12,000 \text{ units}$$

b.

Sales	$300,000 (12,000 units × $25)
–Fixed costs	96,000
–Total variable costs	204,000 (12,000 units × $17)
Net profit (loss)	$ 0

5-2. The Hartnett Corporation manufactures baseball bats with Sammy Sosa's autograph stamped on. Each bat sells for $13 and has a variable cost of $8. There is $20,000 in fixed costs involved in the production process.

a. Compute the break-even point in units.
b. Find the sales (in units) needed to earn a profit of $15,000.

Solution:

Hartnett Corporation

a. $BE = \dfrac{\$20,000}{\$13 - \$8} = 4,000 \text{ units}$

b. $Q = \dfrac{\text{Profit} + FC}{(P - VC)} = \dfrac{\$15,000 + \$20,000}{\$13 - \$8}$

$= \dfrac{\$35,000}{\$5} = 7,000 \text{ units}$

5-3.   Therapeutic Systems sells its products for $8 per unit. It has the following costs:

Rent	$120,000
Factory labor	$1.50 per unit
Executive salaries	$112,000
Raw material	$ .70 per unit

Separate the expenses between fixed and variable cost per unit. Using this information and the sales price per unit of $6, compute the break-even point.

Solution:

Therapeutic Systems

	Fixed Costs	Variable Costs (per unit)
Rent	$120,000	
Factory labor		$1.50
Executive salaries	$112,000	
Raw materials		.70
	$232,000	$2.20

$$BE = \frac{FC}{P - VC} = \frac{\$232,000}{\$8.00 - \$2.20} = \frac{\$232,000}{\$5.80} = 40,000 \text{ units}$$

5-4. Draw two break-even graphs—one for a conservative firm using labor-intensive production and another for a capital-intensive firm. Assuming these companies compete within the same industry and have identical sales, explain the impact of changes in sales volume on both firms' profits.

Solution:

Labor-Intensive and capital-intensive break-even graphs

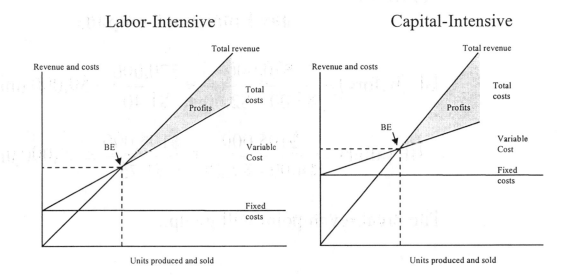

The company having the high fixed costs will have lower variable costs than its competitor since it has substituted capital for labor. With a lower variable cost, the high fixed cost company will have a larger contribution margin. Therefore, when sales rise, its profits will increase faster than the low fixed cost firm and when the sales decline, the reverse will be true.

5-5.   Jay Linoleum Company has fixed costs of $70,000. Its product currently sells for $4 per unit and has variable costs per unit of $2.60. Mr. Thomas, the head of manufacturing, proposes to buy new equipment that will cost $300,000 and drive up fixed costs to $105,000. Although the price will remain at $4 per unit, the increased automation will reduce variable costs per unit to $2.25.

As a result of Thomas's suggestion, will the break-even point go up or down? Compute the necessary numbers.

Solution:
Jay Linoleum Company

$$BE\ (before) = \frac{\$70,000}{\$4.00 - \$2.60} = \frac{\$70,000}{\$1.40} = 50,000\ units$$

$$BE\ (after) = \frac{\$105,000}{\$4.00 - \$2.25} = \frac{\$105,000}{\$1.75} = 60,000\ units$$

The break-even point will go up.

5-6.   Calloway Cab Company determines its break-even strictly on the basis of cash expenditures related to fixed costs. Its total fixed costs are $400,000, but 20 percent of this value is represented by depreciation. Its contribution margin (price minus variable cost) for each unit is $3.60. How many units does the firm need to sell to reach the cash break-even point?

Solution:
Calloway Cab Company

$$Cash\ related\ fixed\ costs = Total\ Fixed\ Costs - Depreciation$$
$$= \$400,000 - 20\%\ (\$400,000)$$
$$= \$400,000 - \$80,000$$
$$= \$320,000$$

$$Cash\ BE = \frac{\$320,000}{\$3.60} = 88,889$$

5-7.   The Sterling Tire Company income statement for 2001 is as follows:

Sterling Tire Company
Income Statement
For the Year Ended December 31, 2001

Sales (20,000 tires at $60 each)......................	$1,200,000
Less: Variable costs (20,000 tires at $30)...	600,000
Fixed costs...	400,000
Earnings before interest and taxes (EBIT)....	200,000
Interest expense....................................	50,000
Earnings before taxes (EBT)........................	150,000
Income tax expense (30%)..........................	45,000
Earnings after taxes (EAT).........................	$ 105,000

Given this income statement, compute the following:

a. Degree of operating leverage.
b. Degree of financial leverage.
c. Degree of combined leverage.
d. Break-even point in units.

Solution:
Sterling Tire Company

$Q = 20,000$, $P = \$60$, $VC = \$30$, $FC = \$400,000$, $I = \$50,000$

a. $\quad DOL = \dfrac{Q(P - VC)}{Q(P - VC) - FC}$

$$= \frac{20,000\,(\$60 - \$30)}{20,000\,(\$60 - \$30) - \$400,000}$$

$$= \frac{20,000\,(\$30)}{20,000\,(\$30) - \$400,000}$$

$$= \frac{\$600,000}{\$600,000 - \$400,000} = \frac{\$600,000}{\$200,000} = 3.00x$$

b. $DFL = \dfrac{EBIT}{EBIT - I} = \dfrac{\$200,000}{\$200,000 - \$50,000}$

$= \dfrac{\$200,000}{\$150,000} = 1.33x$

c. $DCL = \dfrac{Q(P - VC)}{Q(P - VC) - FC - I}$

$= \dfrac{20,000(\$60 - \$30)}{20,000(\$60 - \$30) - \$400,000 - \$50,000}$

$= \dfrac{\$600,000}{\$600,000 - \$400,000 - \$50,000} = \dfrac{\$600,000}{\$150,000} = 4x$

d. $BE = \dfrac{\$400,000}{\$60 - \$30} = \dfrac{\$400,000}{\$30} = 13,333 \text{ units}$

5-8.   The Harding Company manufactures skates. The company's income statement for 2001 is as follows:

Harding Company
Income Statement
For the Year Ended December 31, 2001

Sales (10,000 skates @ $50 each)............................	$500,000
Less: Variable costs (10,000 skates at $20)..........	200,000
Fixed costs	150,000
Earnings before interest and taxes (EBIT)..............	150,000
Interest expense...	60,000
Earnings before taxes (EBT).................................	90,000
Income tax expense (40%)....................................	36,000
Earnings after taxes (EAT)	$ 54,000

Given this income statement, compute the following:

a. Degree of operating leverage.
b. Degree of financial leverage.
c. Degree of combined leverage.
d. Break-even point in units (number of skates).

Solution:

Harding Company

$Q = 10{,}000$, $P = \$50$, $VC = \$20$, $FC = \$150{,}000$, $I = \$60{,}000$

a. $\quad DOL = \dfrac{Q(P - VC)}{Q(P - VC) - FC}$

$$= \dfrac{10{,}000\,(\$50 - \$20)}{10{,}000\,(\$50 - \$20) - \$150{,}000}$$

$$= \dfrac{10{,}000\,(\$30)}{10{,}000\,(\$30) - \$150{,}000}$$

$$= \dfrac{\$300{,}000}{\$300{,}000 - \$150{,}000} = \dfrac{\$300{,}000}{\$150{,}000} = 2.00\text{x}$$

b. $\quad DFL = \dfrac{EBIT}{EBIT - I} = \dfrac{\$150{,}000}{\$150{,}000 - \$60{,}000}$

$$= \dfrac{\$150{,}000}{\$90{,}000} = 1.67\text{x}$$

c. $\quad DCL = \dfrac{Q(P - VC)}{Q(P - VC) - FC - I}$

$$= \dfrac{10{,}000\,(\$50 - \$20)}{10{,}000\,(\$50 - \$20) - \$150{,}000 - \$60{,}000}$$

$$= \dfrac{\$10{,}000\,(\$30)}{\$10{,}000\,(\$30) - \$210{,}000} = \dfrac{\$300{,}000}{\$90{,}000} = 3.33\text{x}$$

d. $\quad BE = \dfrac{\$150{,}000}{\$50 - \$20} = \dfrac{\$150{,}000}{\$30} = 5{,}000 \text{ skates}$

5-9.   Moe & Chris' Delicious Burgers, Inc., sells food to University Cafeterias for $15 a box. The fixed costs of this operation are $80,000, while the variable cost per box is $10.

a. What is the break-even point in boxes?
b. Calculate the profit or loss on 15,000 boxes and on 30,000 boxes.
c. What is the degree of operating leverage at 20,000 boxes and at 30,000 boxes? Why does the degree of operating leverage change as the quantity sold increases?
d. If the firm has an annual interest expense of $10,000, calculate the degree of financial leverage at both 20,000 and 30,000 boxes.
e. What is the degree of combined leverage at both sales levels?

Solution:
Moe & Chris' Delicious Burgers, Inc.

a. $\quad BE = \dfrac{\$80{,}000}{\$15 - \$10} = \dfrac{\$80{,}000}{\$5} = 16{,}000 \text{ boxes}$

b.

	15,000 boxes	30,000 boxes
Sales @ $15 per box	$225,000	$450,000
Less: Variables Costs ($10)	($150,000)	($300,000)
Fixed Costs	($ 80,000)	($ 80,000)
Profit or Loss	($ 5,000)	$ 70,000

c. $$\text{DOL} = \frac{Q(P - VC)}{Q(P - VC) - FC}$$

$$\text{DOL at } 20{,}000 = \frac{20{,}000\,(\$15 - \$10)}{20{,}000\,(\$15 - \$10) - \$80{,}000}$$

$$= \frac{\$100{,}000}{\$20{,}000} = 5.0x$$

$$\text{DOL at } 30{,}000 = \frac{30{,}000\,(\$15 - \$10)}{30{,}000\,(\$15 - \$10) - \$80{,}000}$$

$$= \frac{\$150{,}000}{\$70{,}000} = 2.14x$$

Leverage goes down because we are further away from the break-even point, thus the firm is operating on a larger profit base and leverage is reduced.

d. $$\text{DFL} = \frac{\text{EBIT}}{\text{EBIT} - I}$$

First determine the profit or loss (EBIT) at 20,000 boxes. As indicated in part b, the profit (EBIT) at 30,000 boxes is $70,000:

	20,000 boxes
Sales @ $15 per box	$300,000
Less: Variable Costs ($10)	(200,000)
Fixed Costs	(80,000)
Profit or Loss	$ 20,000

$$DFL \text{ at } 20,000 = \frac{\$20,000}{\$20,000 - \$10,000}$$

$$= \frac{\$20,000}{\$10,000} = 2.0x$$

$$DFL \text{ at } 30,000 = \frac{\$70,000}{\$70,000 - \$10,000}$$

$$= \frac{\$70,000}{\$60,000} = 1.17x$$

e. $$DCL = \frac{Q(P - VC)}{Q(P - VC) - FC - I}$$

$$DCL \text{ at } 20,000 = \frac{20,000(\$15 - \$10)}{20,000(\$15 - \$10) - \$80,000 - \$10,000}$$

$$= \frac{\$100,000}{\$10,000} = 10.0x$$

$$DCL \text{ at } 30,000 = \frac{30,000(\$15 - \$10)}{30,000(\$15 - \$10) - \$80,000 - \$10,000}$$

$$= \frac{\$150,000}{\$60,000} = 2.50x$$

5-10.   Cain Auto Supplies and Able Auto Parts are competitors in the aftermarket for auto supplies. The separate capital structures for Cain and Able are presented below.

Cain		Able	
Debt @ 10%..........................	$ 50,000	Debt @ 10%..........................	$100,000
Common stock, $10 par	100,000	Common stock, $10 par	50,000
Total	$150,000	Total	$150,000
Common shares..................	10,000	Common shares..................	5,000

a. Compute earnings per share if earnings before interest and taxes are $10,000, $15,000, and $50,000 (assume a 30 percent tax rate).
b. Explain the relationship between earnings per share and the level of EBIT.
c. If the cost of debt went up to 12 percent and all other factors remained equal, what would be the break-even level for EBIT?

Solution:

Cain Auto Supplies and Able Auto Parts

a.

	Cain	Able
EBIT	$10,000	$10,000
Less: Interest	5,000	10,000
EBT	5,000	0
Less: Taxes @ 30%	1,500	0
EAT	3,500	0
Shares	10,000	5,000
EPS	$.35	0
EBIT	$15,000	$15,000
Less: Interest	5,000	10,000
EBT	10,000	5,000
Less: Taxes @ 30%	3,000	1,500
EAT	7,000	3,500
Shares	10,000	5,000
EPS	$.70	$.70
EBIT	$50,000	$50,000
Less: Interest	5,000	10,000
EBT	45,000	40,000
Less: Taxes @ 30%	13,500	12,000
EAT	31,500	28,000
Shares	10,000	5,000
EPS	$3.15	$5.60

b. Before-tax return on assets = 6.67%, 10% and 33% at the respective levels of EBIT. When the before-tax return on assets (EBIT/Total Assets) is less than the cost of debt (10%), Cain does better with less debt than Able. When before-tax return on assets is equal to the cost of debt, both firms have equal EPS. This would be where the method of financing has a neutral effect on EPS. As return on assets becomes greater than the interest rate, financial leverage becomes more favorable for Able.

c. 12% × $150,000 = $18,000 break-even level.

5-11. In Problem 10, compute the stock price for Cain if it sells at 18 times earnings per share and EBIT is $40,000.

Solution:

Cain Supplies and Able Auto Parts (Continued)

	Cain
EBIT	$40,000
Less: Interest	5,000
EBT	$35,000
Less: Taxes @ 30%	10,500
EAT	$24,500
Shares	10,000
EPS	$ 2.45
P/E	18x
Stock Price	$ 44.10

5-12.   Sterling Optical and Royal Optical both make glass frames and each is able to generate earnings before interest and taxes of $120,000.

The separate capital structures for Sterling and Royal are shown below:

Sterling		Royal	
Debt @ 12%	$ 600,000	Debt @ 12%	$ 200,000
Common stock, $5 par	400,000	Common stock, $5 par	800,000
Total	$1,000,000	Total	$1,000,000
Common shares	80,000	Common shares	160,000

a. Compute earnings per share for both firms. Assume a 25 percent tax rate.

b. In part *a*, you should have gotten the same answer for both companies' earnings per share. Assume a P/E ratio of 20 for each company, what would its stock price be?

c. Now as part of your analysis, assume the P/E ratio would be 16 for the riskier company in terms of heavy debt utilization in the capital structure and 25 for the less risky company. What would the stock prices for the two firms be under these assumptions? (Note: Although interest rates also would likely be different based on risk, we hold them constant for ease of analysis).

d. Based on the evidence in part *c*, should management only be concerned about the impact of financing plans on earnings per share or should stockholders' wealth maximization (stock price) be considered as well?

Solution:
Sterling Optical and Royal Optical

a.

	Sterling	Royal
EBIT	$120,000	$120,000
Less: Interest	72,000	24,000
EBT	48,000	96,000
Less: Taxes @ 25%	12,000	24,000
EAT	36,000	72,000
Shares	80,000	160,000
EPS	$.45	$.45

b. Stock price   = P/E × EPS

$$20 \times \$.45 = \$9.00$$

c.

Sterling	**Royal**
$16 \times \$.45 = \$7.20$	$25 \times \$.45 = \$11.25$

d. Clearly, the ultimate objective should be to maximize the stock price. While management would be indifferent between the two plans based on earnings per share, Royal Optical, with the less risky plan, has a higher stock price.

5-13. Firms in Japan often employ both high operating and financial leverage because of the use of modern technology and close borrower-lender relationships. Assume the Mitaka Company has a sales volume of 125,000 units at a price of $25 per unit; variable costs are $5 per unit and fixed costs are $1,800,000. Interest expense is $400,000. What is the degree of combined leverage for this Japanese firm?

Solution:

Mitaka Company

$$DCL = \frac{Q(P - VC)}{Q(P - VC) - FC - I}$$

$$= \frac{125,000\,(\$25 - \$5)}{125,000\,(\$25 - \$5) - \$1,800,000 - \$400,000}$$

$$= \frac{125,000\,(\$20)}{125,000\,(\$20) - \$2,200,000}$$

$$= \frac{\$2,500,000}{\$2,500,000 - \$2,200,000}$$

$$= 8.33x$$

5-14.   Sinclair Manufacturing and Boswell Brothers Inc. are both involved in the production of brick for the homebuilding industry. Their financial information is as follows:

Capital Structure

	Sinclair	Boswell
Debt @ 12%..	$ 600,000	0
Common stock, $10 per share......................	400,000	$1,000,000
Total	$1,000,000	$1,000,000
Common shares..	40,000	100,000

Operating Plan

	Sinclair	Boswell
Sales (50,000 units at $20 each)....................	$1,000,000	$1,000,000
Less: Variable costs......................................	800,000	500,000
	($16 per unit)	($10 per unit)
Fixed costs..	0	300,000
Earnings before interest and taxes (EBIT)....	$ 200,000	$ 200,000

a. If you combine Sinclair's capital structure with Boswell's operating plan, what is the degree of combined leverage? (Round to two places to the right of the decimal point.)

b. If you combine Boswell's capital structure with Sinclair's operating plan, what is the degree of combined leverage?

c. Explain why you got the results you did in part b.

d. In part b, if sales double, by what percent will EPS increase?

Solution:

Sinclair Manufacturing and Boswell Brothers

a. $$DCL = \frac{Q(P-VC)}{Q(P-VC)-FC-I}$$

$$= \frac{50,000\,(\$20-\$10)}{50,000\,(\$20-\$10)-\$300,000-\$72,000}$$

$$= \frac{500,000}{500,000-\$300,000-\$72,000}$$

$$= \frac{\$500,000}{\$128,000}$$

$$= 3.91x$$

b. $$DCL = \frac{Q(P-VC)}{Q(P-VC)-FC-I}$$

$$= \frac{50,000\,(\$20-\$16)}{50,000\,(\$20-\$16)-0-0}$$

$$= \frac{500,000\,(\$4)}{50,000\,(\$4)}$$

$$= \frac{\$200,000}{\$200,000}$$

$$= 1x$$

c. The leverage factor is only 1x because Boswell has no financial leverage and Sinclair has no operating leverage.

d. EPS will increase by 100 percent. However, there is no leverage involved. EPS merely grows at the same rate as sales.

5-15. The Norman Automatic Mailer Machine Company is planning to expand production because of the increased volume of mailouts. The increased mailout capacity will cost $2,000,000. The expansion can be financed either by bonds at an interest rate of 12 percent or by selling 40,000 shares of common stock at $50 per share. The current income statement (before expansion) is as follows:

Norman Automatic Mailer
Income Statement
200X

Sales		$3,000,000
Less: Variable costs (40%)	$1,200,000	
Fixed costs..	800,000	
Earnings before interest and taxes................		1,000,000
Less: Interest expense		400,000
Earnings before taxes		600,000
Less: Taxes (@ 35%)		210,000
Earnings after taxes		390,000
Shares...		100,000
Earnings per share		$3.90

Assume that after expansion, sales are expected to increase by $1,500,000. Variable costs will remain at 40 percent of sales, and fixed costs will increase by $550,000. The tax rate is 35 percent.

a. Calculate the degree of operating leverage, the degree of financial leverage, and the degree of combined leverage before expansion. (For the degree of operating leverage, use the formula developed in footnote 2; for the degree of combined leverage, use the formula developed in footnote 3. These instructions apply throughout this problem.)

b. Construct the income statement for the two financial plans.

c. Calculate the degree of operating leverage, the degree of financial leverage, and the degree of combined leverage, after expansion, for the two financing plans.

d. Explain which financing plan you favor and the risks involved.

Normal Automatic Mailer Machine

a. $$DOL = \frac{S - TVC}{S - TVC - FC}$$

$$= \frac{\$3,000,000 - \$1,200,000}{\$3,000,000 - \$1,200,000 - \$800,000}$$

$$= \frac{\$1,800,000}{\$1,000,000} = 1.8x$$

$$DFL = \frac{EBIT}{EBIT - I}$$

$$= \frac{\$1,000,000}{\$1,000,000 - \$400,000}$$

$$= \frac{\$1,000,000}{\$600,000} = 1.67x$$

$$DCL = \frac{S - TVC}{S - TVC - FC - I}$$

$$= \frac{\$3,000,000 - \$1,200,000}{\$3,000,000 - \$1,200,000 - \$800,000 - \$400,000}$$

$$= \frac{\$1,800,000}{\$600,000} = 3x$$

b. Income Statement After Expansion

	Debt	Equity
Sales	$4,500,000	$4,500,000
Less: Variable Costs (40%)	1,800,000	1,800,000
Fixed Costs	1,350,000	1,350,000
EBIT	1,350,000	1,350,000
Less: Interest	640,000[1]	400,000
EBT	710,000	950,000
Less: Taxes @ 35%	248,500	332,500
EAT (Net Income)	461,500	617,500
Common Shares	100,000	140,000[2]
EPS	$ 4.62	$ 4.41

(1) New interest expense level if expansion is financed with debt.
$400,000 + 12\% (\$2,000,000) = \$400,000 + \$240,000 = \$640,000$

(2) Number of common shares outstanding if expansion is financed with equity.
$100,000 + 40,000 = 140,000$

c. $DOL = \dfrac{S - TVC}{S - TVC - FC}$ (Same under either plan)

$$DOL\,(Debt/Equity) = \dfrac{\$4,500,000 - \$1,800,000}{\$4,500,000 - \$1,800,000 - \$1,350,000}$$

$$= \dfrac{\$2,700,000}{\$1,350,000} = 2x$$

$$DFL = \frac{EBIT}{EBIT - I}$$

$$DFL\,(Debt) = \frac{\$1,350,000}{\$1,350,000 - \$640,000} = \frac{\$1,350,000}{\$710,000} = 1.90x$$

$$DFL\,(Equity) = \frac{\$1,350,000}{\$1,350,000 - \$400,000} = \frac{\$1,350,000}{\$950,000} = 1.42x$$

$$DCL\,(Debt) = \frac{\$4,500,000 - \$1,800,000}{\$4,500,000 - \$1,800,000 - \$1,350,000 - \$640,000}$$

$$= \frac{\$2,700,000}{\$710,000} = 3.80x$$

$$DCL\,(Equity) = \frac{\$4,500,000 - \$1,800,000}{\$4,500,000 - \$1,800,000 - \$1,350,000 - \$400,000}$$

$$= \frac{\$2,700,000}{\$950,000} = 2.84x$$

d. The debt financing plan provides a greater earnings per share level, but provides more risk because of the increased use of debt and higher DFL and DCL. The crucial point is expectations for future sales. If sales are expected to decline or advance very slowly, the debt plan will not perform well in comparison to the equity plan. Conversely, with increasing sales, the debt plan becomes more attractive. Based on projected overall sales of $4,500,000, the debt plan should probably be favored.

5-16.   Dickinson Company has $12 million in assets. Currently half of these assets are financed with long-term debt at 10 percent and half with common stock having a par value of $8. Ms. Smith, vice-president of finance, wishes to analyze two refinancing plans, one with more debt (D) and one with more equity (E). The company earns a return on assets before interest and taxes of 10 percent. The tax rate is 45 percent.

Under Plan D, a $3 million long-term bond would be sold at an interest rate of 12 percent and 375,000 shares of stock would be purchased in the market at $8 per share and retired.

Under Plan E, 375,000 shares of stock would be sold at $8 per share and the $3,000,000 in proceeds would be used to reduce long-term debt.

a.   How would each of these plans affect earnings per share? Consider the current plan and the two new plans.
b.   Which plan would be most favorable if return on assets fell to 5 percent? Increased to 15 percent? Consider the current plan and the two new plans.
c.   If the market price for common stock rose to $12 before the restructuring, which plan would then be most attractive? Continue to assume that $3 million in debt will be used to retire stock in Plan D and $3 million of new equity will be sold to retire debt in Plan E. Also assume for calculations in part c that return on assets is 10 percent.

Solution:

Dickinson Company
Income Statements

a. Return on assets = 10%   EBIT = $1,200,000

	Current	Plan D	Plan E
EBIT	$1,200,000	$1,200,000	$1,200,000
Less: Interest	$600,000^1$	$960,000^2$	$300,000^3$
EBT	600,000	240,000	900,000
Less: Taxes (45%)	270,000	108,000	405,000
EAT	330,000	132,000	495,000
Common shares	$750,000^4$	375,000	1,125,000
EPS	$.44	$.35	$.44

(1) $6,000,000 debt @ 10%

(2) $600,000 interest + ($3,000,000 debt @ 12%)

(3) ($6,000,000 – $3,000,000 debt retired) × 10%

(4) ($6,000,000 common equity)/($8 par value) = 750,000
     shares

Plan E and the original plan provide the same earnings
per share because the cost of debt at 10 percent is equal
to the operating return on assets of 10 percent. With
Plan D, the cost of increased debt rises to 12 percent,
and the firm incurs negative leverage reducing EPS and
also increasing the financial risk to Dickinson.

b. Return on assets = 5% EBIT = $600,000

	Current	Plan D	Plan E
EBIT	$600,000	$600,000	$ 600,000
Less: Interest	600,000	960,000	300,000
EBT	0	(360,000)	300,000
Less: Taxes (45%)	---	(162,000)	135,000
EAT	0	$(198,000)	$ 165,000
Common shares	750,000	375,000	1,125,000
EPS	0	$(.53)	$.15

Return on assets = 15% EBIT = $1,800,000

	Current	Plan D	Plan E
EBIT	$1,800,000	$1,800,000	$1,800,000
Less: Interest	600,000	960,000	300,000
EBT	1,200,000	840,000	1,500,000
Less: Taxes (45%)	540,000	378,000	675,000
EAT	$ 660,000	$ 462,000	$ 825,000
Common shares	750,000	375,000	1,125,000
EPS	$.88	$1.23	$.73

If the return on assets decreases to 5%, Plan E provides the best EPS, and at 15% return, Plan D provides the best EPS. Plan D is still risky, having an interest coverage ratio of less than 2.0.

c. Return on Assets = 10% EBIT = $1,200,000

	Current	Plan D	Plan E
EBIT	$1,200,000	$1,200,000	$1,200,000
EAT	330,000	132,000	495,000
Common shares	750,000	500,000[1]	1,000,000[2]
EPS	$.44	$.26	$.50

(1) 750,000 – ($3,000,000/$12 per share)
= 750,000 – 250,000 = 500,000

(2) 750,000 + ($3,000,000/$12 per share)
= 750,000 + 250,000 = 1,000,000

As the price of the common stock increases, Plan E becomes more attractive because fewer shares can be retired under Plan D and, by the same logic, fewer shares need to be sold under Plan E.

5-17. The Lopez-Portillo Company has $10 million in assets, 80 percent financed by debt and 20 percent financed by common stock. The interest rate on the debt is 15 percent and the par value of the stock is $10 per share. President Lopez Portillo is considering two financing plans for an expansion to $15 million in assets.

Under Plan A, the debt to total assets ratio will be maintained, but new debt will cost a whopping 18 percent! Under Plan B, only new common stock at $10 per share will be issued. The tax rate is 40 percent.

a. If *EBIT* is 15 percent on total assets, compute earnings per share (*EPS*) before the expansion and under the two alternatives.
b. What is the degree of financial leverage under each of the three plans?
c. If stock could be sold at $20 per share due to increased expectations for the firm's sales and earnings, what impact would this have on earnings per share for the two expansion alternatives? Compute earnings per share for each.
d. Explain why corporate financial officers are concerned about their stock values!

Solution:

Lopez-Portillo Company

a.   Return on Assets = 12%

	Current	Plan A	Plan B
EBIT	$1,500,000	$2,250,000	$2,250,000
Less: Interest	1,200,000(a)	1,920,000(c)	1,200,000(e)
EBT	300,000	330,000	1,050,000
Less: Taxes @ 40%	120,000	132,000	420,000
EAT	$ 180,000	$ 198,000	$ 630,000
Common shares	200,000(b)	300,000(d)	700,000(f)
EPS	$.90	$.66	$.90

(a) (80% × $10,000,000) × 15% = $8,000,000 × 15% = $1,200,000

(b) (20% × $10,000,000)/$10 = $2,000,000/$10 = 200,000 shares

(c) $1,200,000 (current) + (80% × $5,000,000) × 18% = $1,200,000 + $720,000 = $1,920,000

(d) 200,000 shares (current) + (20% × $5,000,000)/$10 = 200,000 + 100,000 = 300,000 shares

(e) unchanged

(f) 200,000 shares (current) + $5,000,000/$10 = 200,000 + 500,000 = 700,000 shares

b.

$$DFL = \frac{EBIT}{EBIT - I}$$

$$DFL \text{ (Current)} = \frac{\$1,500,000}{\$1,500,000 - \$1,200,000} = 5.00x$$

$$DFL \text{ (Plan A)} = \frac{\$2,250,000}{\$2,250,000 - \$1,920,000} = 6.82x$$

$$DFL \text{ (Plan B)} = \frac{\$2,250,000}{\$2,250,000 - \$1,200,000} = 2.14x$$

c.

	Plan A	Plan B
EAT	$198,000	$630,000
Common Shares	250,000[1]	450,000[2]
EPS	$.79	$1.40

[1]   200,000 shares (current) + (20% × $5,000,000)/$20
= 200,000 + 50,000 = 250,000 shares

[2]   200,000 shares (current) + $5,000,000/$20
= 200,000 + 250,000 = 450,000 shares

Plan B would continue to provide the higher earnings per shares. The difference between plans A and B is even greater than that indicated in part (a).

d. Not only does the price of the common stock create wealth to the shareholder, which is the major objective of the financial manager, but it greatly influences the ability to fiancé projects at a high or low cost of capital. Cost of capital will be discussed in Chapter 10, and one will see the impact that the cost of capital has on capital budgeting decisions.

5-18.   Mr. Gold is in the widget business. He currently sells 1 million widgets a year at $5 each. His variable cost to produce the widgets is $3 per unit, and he has $1,500,000 in fixed costs. His sales-to-assets ratio is five times, and 40 percent of his assets are financed with 8 percent debt, with the balance financed by common stock at $10 per share. The tax rate is 40 percent.

His brother-in-law, Mr. Silverman, says he is doing it all wrong. By reducing his price to $4.50 a widget, he could increase his volume of units sold by 40 percent. Fixed costs would remain constant, and variable costs would remain $3 per unit. His sales-to-assets ratio would be 6.3 times. Furthermore, he could increase his debt-to-assets ratio to 50 percent, with the balance in common stock. It is assumed that the interest rate would go up by 1 percent and the price of stock would remain constant.

a. Compute earnings per share under the Gold plan.
b. Compute earnings per share under the Silverman plan.
c. Mr. Gold's wife, the chief financial officer, does not think that fixed costs would remain constant under the Silverman plan but that they would go up by 15 percent. If this is the case, should Mr. Gold shift to the Silverman plan, based on earnings per share?

Solution:

Gold-Silverman

a. Gold Plan

Sales ($1,000,000 units × $5)	$5,000,000
–Fixed costs	–1,500,000
–Variable costs	–3,000,000
Operating income (EBIT)	$ 500,000
–Interest[1]	32,000
EBT	$ 468,000
–Taxes @ 40%	187,200
EAT	$ 280,800
Shares[2]	60,000
Earnings Per Share	$4.68

$$\text{Assets} = \frac{\text{Sales}}{\text{Asset Turnover}} = \frac{\$5,000,000}{5} = \$1,000,000$$

[1] Debt = 40% of Assets = 40% × $1,000,000 = $400,000

Interest = 8% × $400,000 = $32,000

[2] Stock = 60% of $1,000,000 = $600,000

Shares = $600,000/$10 = $60,000

b. Silverman Plan

Sales ($1,400,000 units at $4.50)	$6,300,000
–Fixed costs	1,500,000
–Variable costs (1,400,000 units × $3)	4,200,000
Operating income (EBIT)	$ 600,000
–Interest[3]	45,000
EBT	$ 555,000
–Taxes @ 40%	222,000
EAT	$ 333,000
Shares[4]	50,000
Earnings Per Share	$6.66

$$\text{Assets} = \frac{\text{Sales}}{\text{Asset Turnover}} = \frac{\$6,300,000}{6.3} = \$1,000,000$$

[3] Debt = 50% of Assets = 50% × $1,000,000 = $500,000

Interest = 9% × $500,000 = $45,000

[4] Stock = 50% of $1,000,000 = $500,000

Shares = $500,000/$10 = $50,000

c. Silverman Plan (based on Mrs. Gold's Assumption)

Sales ($1,400,000 units at $4.50)	$6,300,000
−Fixed costs ($1,500,000 × 1.15)	1,725,000
−Variable costs (1,400,000 units × $3)	4,200,000
Operating income (EBIT)	$ 375,000
−Interest	45,000
EBT	$ 330,000
−Taxes @ 40%	132,000
EAT	$ 198,000
Shares	50,000
Earnings Per Share	$3.96

No! Gold should not shift to the Silverman Plan if Mrs. Gold's assumption is correct.

5-19.   Delsing Canning Company is considering an expansion of its facilities. Its current income statement is as follows:

Sales	$5,000,000
Less: Variable expense (50% of sales)	2,500,000
Fixed expense	1,800,000
Earnings before interest and taxes (EBIT)	700,000
Interest (10% cost)	200,000
Earnings before taxes (EBT)	500,000
Tax (30%)	150,000
Earnings after taxes (EAT)	350,000
Shares of common stock—200,000	
Earnings per share	$1.75

The company is currently financed with 50 percent debt and 50 percent equity (common stock, par value of $10). In order to expand the facilities, Mr. Delsing estimates a need for $2 million in additional financing. His investment banker has laid out three plans for him to consider:

1. Sell $2 million of debt at 13 percent.
2. Sell $2 million of common stock at $20 per share.
3. Sell $1 million of debt at 12 percent and $1 million of common stock at $25 per share.

Variable costs are expected to stay at 50 percent of sales, while fixed expenses will increase to $2,300,000 per year. Delsing is not sure how much this expansion will add to sales, but he estimates that sales will rise by $1 million per year for the next five years.

Delsing is interested in a thorough analysis of his expansion plans and methods of financing. He would like you to analyze the following:

a. The break-even point for operating expenses before and after expansion (in sales dollars).
b. The degree of operating leverage before and after expansion. Assume sales of $5 million before expansion and $6 million after expansion. Use the formula in footnote 2.
c. The degree of financial leverage before expansion and for all three methods of financing after expansion. Assume sales of $6 million for this question.
d. Compute EPS under all three methods of financing the expansion at $6 million in sales (first year) and $10 million in sales (last year).
e. What can we learn from the answer to part *d* about the advisability of the three methods of financing the expansion?

Solution:

Deising Cable Company

a. At break-even before expansion:

$PQ = FC + VC$

where PQ equals sales volume at break-even point

Sales	= Fixed costs + Variable costs
	(Variable costs = 50% of sales)

Sales	= $1,800,000 + .50 sales
.50 sales	= $1,800,000
Sales	− $3,600,000

At break-even after expansion:

Sales	= $2,300,000 + .50 sales
.50 sales	= $2,300,000
Sales	= $4,600,000

b. Degree of operating leverage, before expansion, at sales of $5,000,000

$$DOL = \frac{Q(P - VC)}{Q(P - VC) - FC} = \frac{S - TVC}{S - TVC - FC}$$

$$= \frac{\$5,000,000 - \$2,500,000}{\$5,000,000 - 2,500,000 - \$1,800,000}$$

$$= \frac{\$2,500,000}{\$700,000} = 3.57x$$

Degree of operating leverage after expansion at sales of $6,000,000

$$\text{DOL} = \frac{\$6,000,000 - \$3,000,000}{\$6,000,000 - \$3,000,000 - \$2,300,000}$$

$$= \frac{\$3,000,000}{\$700,000} = 4.29\text{x}$$

This could also be computed for subsequent years.

c. DFL before expansion:

$$\text{DFL} = \frac{\text{EBIT}}{\text{EBIT} - \text{I}}$$

$$= \frac{\$700,000}{\$700,000 - \$200,000}$$

$$= \frac{\$700,000}{\$500,000} = 1.40\text{x}$$

DFL After Expansion:

Compute EBIT and I for all three plans:

	(100% Debt) (1)	(100% Equity) (2)	(50% Debt and 50% Equity (`3)
Sales	$6,000,000	$6,000,000	$6,000,000
–TVC (.50)	3,000,000	3,000,000	3,000,000
–FC	2,300,000	2,300,000	2,300,000
EBIT	$ 700,000	$ 700,000	$ 700,000
I – Old Debt	200,000	200,000	200,000
I – New Debt	260,000	0	120,000
Total I	$ 460,000	$ 200,000	$ 320,00

$$DFL = \frac{EBIT}{EBIT - I}$$

(1)	(2)	(3)

$$\frac{\$700,000}{(\$700,000 - \$460,000)} \quad \frac{\$700,000}{(\$700,000 - \$200,000)} \quad \frac{\$700,000}{(\$700,000 - \$320,000)}$$

DFL = 2.92x   1.40x   1.84x

d. EPS @ sales of $6,000,000
(refer back to part c to get the values for EBIT and Total I)

	(100% Debt) (1)	(100% Equity) (2)	(50% Debt and 50% Equity (`3)
EBIT	$700,000	$700,000	$700,000
Total I	460,000	200,000	320,000
EBT	$240,000	$500,000	$380,000
Taxes (30%)	72,000	150,000	114,000
EAT	$168,000	$350,000	$266,000
Shares (old)	200,000	200,000	200,000
Shares (new)	0	100,000	40,000
Total Shares	200,000	300,000	240,000
EPS (EAT/ Total shares)	$.84	$1.17	$1.11

EPS @ sales of $10,000,000

	(100% Debt) (1)	(100% Equity) (2)	(50% Debt and 50% Equity (`3)
Sales	$10,000,000	$10,000,000	$10,000,000
–TVC	5,000,000	5,000,000	5,000,000
–FC	2,300,000	2,300,000	2,300,000
EBIT	$ 2,700,000	$ 2,700,000	$ 2,700,000
Total I	460,000	200,000	320,000
EBT	$ 2,240,000	$ 2,500,000	$ 2,380,000
Taxes (30%)	672,000	750,000	714,000
EAT	$ 1,568,000	$ 1,750,000	$ 1,666,000
Total Shares	200,000	300,000	240,000
EPS (EAT/ Total Shares)	$7.84	$5.83	$6.94

e. In the first year, when sales and profits are relatively low, plan 2 (100% equity) appears to be the best alternative. However, as sales expand up to $10 million, financial leverage begins to produce results as EBIT increases and Plan 1 (100% debt) is the highest yielding alternative.

Comprehensive Problem

CP 5-1.

Ryan Boot Company
Balance Sheet
December 31, 2001

Assets		Liabilities and Stockholders' Equity	
Cash...............................	$ 50,000	Accounts payable.............	$2,200,000
Marketable securities....	80,000	Accrued expenses.............	150,000
Accounts receivable......	3,000,000	Notes payable (current)....	400,000
Inventory.......................	1,000,000	Bonds (10%)....................	2,500,000
Gross plan and		Common stock (1.7 million	
equipment....................	6,000,000	shares, par value $1)......	1,700,000
Less: Accumulated		Retained earnings.............	1,180,000
depreciation.............	2,000,000		
		Total liabilities and	
Total assets....................	$8,130,00	stockholders' equity........	$8,130,000

Income Statement—2001

Sales (credit)...	$7,000,000
Fixed costs*..	2,100,000
Variable costs (0.60)...	4,200,000
Earnings before interest and taxes.........................	700,000
Less: Interest..	250,000
Earnings before taxes...	450,000
Less: Taxes @ 35%..	157,500
Earnings after taxes...	$ 292,500
Dividends (40% payout).......................................	117,000
Increased retained earnings...................................	$ 175,500

*Fixed costs include (a) lease expense of $200,000 and (b) depreciation of $500,000.

Note: Ryan Boots also has $65,000 per year in sinking fund obligations associated with its bond issue. The sinking fund represents an annual repayment of the principal amount of the bond. It is not tax deductible.

Ratios

	Ryan Boot (to be filled in)	Industry
Profit margin		5.75%
Return on assets		6.90%
Return on cquity		9.20%
Receivables turnover		4.35x
Inventory turnover		6.50x
Fixed-asset turnover		1.85x
Total-asset turnover		1.20x
Current ratio		1.45x
Quick ratio		1.10x
Debt to total assets		25.05%
Interest coverage		5.35x
Fixed charge coverage		4.62x

a. Analyze Ryan Boot Company, using ratio analysis. Compute the ratios above for Ryan and compare them to the industry data that is given. Discuss the weak points, strong points, and what you think should be done to improve the company's performance.

b. In your analysis, calculate the overall break-even point in the sales dollars and the cash break-even point. Also compute the degree of operating leverage, degree of financial leverage, and degree of combined leverage. (Use footnote 2 for DOL and footnote 3 for DCL.)

c. Use the information in parts *a* and *b* to discuss the risk associated with this company. Given the risk, decide whether a bank should loan funds to Ryan Boot.

Ryan Boot Company is trying to plan the funds needed for 2002. The management anticipates an increase in sales of 20 percent, which can be absorbed *without increasing fixed assets*.

d. What would be Ryan's needs for external funds based on the current balance sheet? Compute RNF (required new funds). Notes payable (current) and bonds are not part of the liability calculation.

e. What would be the required new funds if the company brings its ratios into line with the industry average during 2002? Specifically examine receivables turnover, inventory turnover, and the profit margin. Use the new values to recomputed the factors in RNF (assume liabilities stay the same).

f. Do not calculate, only comment on these questions. How would required new funds change if the company:

1. Were at full capacity?
2. Raised the dividend payout ratio?
3. Suffered a decreased growth in sales?
4. Faced an accelerated inflation rate?

CP Solution:

Ryan Boot Company

a. Ratio analysis		Ryan	Industry
Profit margin	$292,500/$7,000,000	4.18%	5.75%
Return on assets	$292,500/$8,130,000	3.60%	6.90%
Return on equity	$292,500/$2,880,000	10.16%	9.20%
Receivable turnover	$7,000,000/$3,000,000	2.33x	4.35x
Inventory turnover	$7,000,000/$1,000,000	7.00x	6.50x
Fixed asset turnover	$7,000,000/$4,000,000	1.75x	1.85x
Total asset turnover	$7,000,000/$8,130,000	.86x	1.20x
Current ratio	$4,130,000/$2,750,000	1.50x	1.45x
Quick ratio	$3,130,000/$2,750,000	1.14x	1.10x
Debt to total assets	$5,250,000/$8,130,000	64.58%	25.05%
Interest coverage	$700,000/$250,000	2.80x	5.35x
Fixed charge coverage	see calculation below*	1.64x	4.62x

$$* \frac{\$700,000 + 200,000\,(\text{Lease})}{\$250,000 + 200,000 + 65,000/(1-.35)} = 1.64x$$

a. The company has a lower profit margin than the industry and the problem is further compounded by the slow turnover of assets (.86x versus an industry norm of 1.20x). This leads to a much lower return on assets. The company has a higher return on equity than the industry, but this is accomplished through the firm's heavy debt ratio rather than through superior profitability.

The slow turnover of assets can be directly traced to the unusually high level of accounts receivable. The firm's accounts receivable turnover ratio is only 2.33x, versus an industry norm of 4.35x. Actually the firm does quite well with receivable turnover and its only slightly below the industry in fixed asset turnover.

The previously mentioned heavy debt position becomes more apparent when we examine times interest earned and fixed charge coverage. The latter is particularly low due to lease expenses and sinking fund obligations.

b. Break-even in sales

Sales = Fixed Costs + Variable costs
(variable costs are expressed as a percentage of sales)

$$\text{Sales}_{BE} = \$2,100,000 + .60 \text{ Sales}$$
$$.40 \, S = \$2,100,000$$
$$S = \$2,100,000/.40$$
$$S = \$5,250,000$$

Cash break-even

Sales = (Fixed costs − Non cash expenses*) + Variable costs

$$\text{Sales}_{BE} = (\$2,100,000 − \$500,000) + .60 \text{ Sales}$$
$$\text{Sales}_{BE} = \$1,600,000 + .60 \text{ Sales}$$
$$.40 \, S = \$1,600,000$$
$$S = \$1,600,000/.40$$
$$S = \$4,000,000$$

*Depreciation

$$DOL = \frac{S - TVC}{S - TVC - FC}$$

$$= \frac{\$7,000,000 - \$4,200,000}{\$7,000,000 - \$4,200,000 - \$2,100,000}$$

$$= \frac{\$2,800,000}{\$700,000} = 4x$$

$$DFL = \frac{EBIT}{EBIT - I} = \frac{\$700,000}{\$700,000 - \$250,000}$$

$$= \frac{\$700,000}{\$450,000} = 1.56x$$

$$DCL = \frac{S - TVC}{S - TVC - FC - I}$$

$$= \frac{\$7,000,000 - \$4,200,000}{\$7,000,000 - \$4,200,000 - \$2,100,000 - \$250,000}$$

$$= \frac{\$2,800,000}{\$450,000} = 6.22x$$

c. Ryan is operating at a sales volume that is $1,750,000 above the traditional break-even point and $3,000,000 above the cash break-even point. This can be viewed as somewhat positive.

However, the firm has a high degree of leverage, which indicates any reduction in sales volume could have a very negative impact on profitability. The DOL of 4x is associated with heavy fixed assets and relatively high fixed costs. The DFL of 1.56x is attributed to high debt reliance. Actually, if we were to include the lease payments of $200,000 with the interest payments of $250,000, the DFL would be almost 3x.

The banker would have to question the potential use of the funds and the firm's ability to pay back the loan. Actually, the firm already appears to have an abundant amount of assets, so hopefully a large expansion would not take place here. There appears to be a need to reduce accounts receivable rather than increase the level.

One possible use of the funds might be to pay off part of the current notes payable of $400,000. This might be acceptable if the firm can demonstrate the ability to meet its future obligations. The banker should request to see pro forma financial statements and projections of future cash flow generation. The loan might only be acceptable if the firm can bring down its inventory position back in line and improve its profitability.

d. Required new funds $= \dfrac{A}{S}(\Delta S) - \dfrac{L}{S}(\Delta S) - PS_2(1-D)$

$$RNF = \dfrac{\$4,130,000}{\$7,000,000}(\$7,000,000 \times 20\%) - \dfrac{\$2,350,000}{\$7,000,000}$$

$$(\$7,000,000 \times 20\%) - 4.18\%(\$8,400,000)(1-.4)$$

$$RNF = .590\,(\$1,400,000) - .336\,(\$1,400,000) - \$351,120\,(.6)$$
$$= \$826,000 - \$470,400 - \$210,672$$
$$= \$144,928$$

e. Required funds if selected industry ratios were applied

Receivables = Sales/Receivable turnover

Receivables = $7,000,000/4.35

Receivables = $1,609,195

Revised A (assets)
$$= \$50,000 + \$80,000 + \$1,609,195 + \$1,000,000$$
$$= \$2,739,195$$

Profit Margin = 5.75%

$$RNF = \frac{A}{S}(\Delta S) - \frac{L}{S}(\Delta S) - PS_2(1 - D)$$

$$RNF = \frac{\$2,739,195}{\$7,000,000}(\$7,000,000 \times 20\%) - \frac{\$2,350,000}{\$7,000,000}$$

$$(\$7,000,000 \times 20\%) - 5.75\% (\$8,400,000) (1 - .4)$$

RNF = .391 ($1,400,000) − .336 ($1,400,000) − $483,000 (.6)
   = $547,400 − $470,400 − $289,800
   = $212,800

Required new funds (RNF) is negative, indicating there will actually be an excess of funds equal to $212,180. This is due to the much more rapid turnover of inventory and the higher profit margin.

f. (1) If Ryan Boots were at full capacity, more funds would be needed to expand plant and equipment.

(2) More funds would be needed to offset the larger payout of earnings to dividends.

(3) Fewer funds would be required as sales grow less rapidly. Fewer new assets would be needed to support sales growth.

(4) As inflation increased so would the cost of new assets, especially inventory and plant and equipment. Even if sales prices could be increased, more assets would be required to support the same physical level of sales. Increased profits alone would not make up for the higher level of assets required and more funds would be needed.

Chapter 6

Discussion Questions

6-1.   Explain how rapidly expanding sales can drain the cash resources of a firm.

Rapidly expanding sales will require a buildup in assets to support the growth. In particular, more and more of the increase in current asset will be permanent in nature. A nonliquidating aggregate stock of current assets will be necessary to allow for floor displays, multiple items for selection, and other purposes. All of these "asset" investments can drain the cash resources of the firm.

6-2.   Discuss the relative volatility of short- and long-term interest rates.

Figure 6-10 shows the long-run view of short- and long-term interest rates. Normally, short-term rates are much more volatile than long-term rates.

6-3.   What is the significance to working capital management of matching sales and production?

If sales and production can be matched, the level of inventory and the amount of current assets needed can be kept to a minimum; therefore, lower financing costs will be incurred. Matching sales and production has the advantage of maintaining smaller amounts of current assets than level production, and therefore less financing costs are incurred. However, if sales are seasonal or cyclical, workers will be laid off in a declining sales climate and machinery (fixed assets) will be idle. Here lies the tradeoff between level and seasonal production: Full utilization of fixed assets with skilled workers and more financing of current assets versus unused capacity, training and retraining workers, with lower financing for current assets.

6-4.   How is a cash budget used to help manage current assets?

A cash budget helps minimize current assets by providing a forecast of inflows and outflows of cash. It also encourages the development of a schedule as to when inventory is produced and maintained for sales (production schedule), and accounts receivables are collected. The cash budget allows us to forecast the level of each current asset and the timing of the buildup and reduction of each.

6-5.   "The most appropriate financing pattern would be one in which asset buildup and length of financing terms are perfectly matched." Discuss the difficulty involved in achieving this financing pattern.

Only a financial manager with unusual insight and timing could design a plan in which asset buildup and the length of financing terms are perfectly matched.

One would need to know exactly what part of current assets are temporary and what part are permanent. Furthermore, one is never quite sure how much short-term or long-term financing is available at all times. Even if this were known, it would be difficult to change the financing mix on a continual basis.

6-6.   By using long-term financing to finance part of temporary current assts, a firm may have less risk but lower returns than a firm with a normal financing plan. Explain the significance of this statement.

By establishing a long-term financing arrangement for temporary current assets, a firm is assured of having necessary funding in good times as well as bad, thus we say there is low risk. However, long-term financing is generally more expensive than short-term financing and profits may be lower than those which could be achieved with a synchronized or normal financing arrangement for temporary current assets.

6-7.   A firm that uses short-term financing methods for a portion of permanent current assets is assuming more risk but expects higher returns than a firm with a normal financing plan. Explain.

By financing a portion of permanent current assets on a short-term basis, we run the risk of inadequate financing in tight money periods. However, since short-term financing is less expensive than long-term funds, a firm tends to increase its profitability over the long run (assuming it survives). In answer to the preceding question, we stressed less risk and less return; here the emphasis is on risk and high return.

6-8.   What does the term *structure of interest rates* indicate?

The term structure of interest rates shows the relative level of short-term and long-term interest rates at a point in time. It is often referred to as a yield curve.

6-9.   What are three theories for describing the shape of the term structure of interest rates (the yield curve)? Briefly describe each theory.

Liquidity premium theory, the market segmentation theory, and the expectations theory.

The liquidity premium theory indicates that long-term rates should be higher than short-term rates. This premium of long-term rates over short-term rates exists because short-term securities have greater liquidity, and therefore higher rates have to be offered to potential long-term bond buyer to entice them to hold these less liquid and more price sensitive securities.

The market segmentation theory states that Treasury securities are divided into market segments by the various financial institutions investing in the market. The changing needs, desires, and strategies of these investors tend to strongly influence the nature and relationship of short- and long-term rates.

The expectations hypothesis maintains that the yields on long-term securities are a function of short-term rates. The result of the hypothesis is that when long-term rates are much higher than short-term rates, the market is saying that is expects short-term rates to rise. Conversely, when long-term rates are lower than short-term rates, the market is expecting short-term rates to fall.

6-10.   Since the middle 1960s, corporate liquidity has been declining. What reasons can you give for this trend?

The decrease is liquidity can be traced in part to more efficient inventory management such as just-in-time inventory and point of sales terminals that provide better inventory control. The decline in working capital can also be attributed to electronic cash flow transfer systems, and the ability to sell accounts receivables through securitization of assets (this is more fully explained in the next chapter). It might also be that management is simply willing to take more liquidity risk as interest rates declined.

Problems

6-1.   Austin Electronics expects sales next year to be $900,000 if the economy is strong, $650,000 if the economy is steady, and $375,000 if the economy is weak. The firm believes there is a 15 percent probability the economy will be strong, a 60 percent probability of a steady economy, and a 25 percent probability of a weak economy.

What is the expected level of sales for next year?

Solution:

Austin Electronics

State of Economy	Sales	Probability	Expected Outcome
Strong	$900,000	.15	$135,000
Steady	650,000	.60	390,000
Weak	375,000	.25	93,750
		Expected level of sales =	$618,750

6-2.   Cobb Tie Shops, Inc., expects sales next year to be $300,000. Inventory and accounts receivable will increase $60,000 to accommodate this sales level. The company has a steady profit margin of 10 percent with a 30 percent dividend payout. How much external financing will the firm have to seek? Assume there is no increase in liabilities other than that which will occur with the external financing.

Solution:

Cobb Tie Shops, Inc.

$300,000	Sales
.10	Profit margin
30,000	Net income
− 9,000	Dividends (30%)
$ 21,000	Increase in retained earnings
$ 60,000	Increase in assets
− 21,000	Increase in retained earnings
$ 39,000	External funds needed

6-3. Antonio Banderos and Scarfs sell headwear that is very popular in the fall-winter season. Units sold are anticipated as:

October	1,000
November	2,000
December	4,000
January	3,000
	10,000 units

If seasonal production is used, it is assumed that inventory buildup will directly match sales for each month and there will be no inventory buildup.

Antonio thinks the above assumption is too optimistic and decides to go with level production to avoid being out of merchandise. He will produce the 10,000 units over 4 months at a level of 2,500 per month.

a. What is the ending inventory at the end of each month? Compare the unit sales to the units produced and keep a running total.

b. If the inventory costs $5 per unit and will be financed at the bank at a cost of 10%, what is the monthly financing cost and the total for the 4 months?

Solution:

Antonio Banderos and Scarfs

a.

	Units Sold	Units Produced	Change in inventory	Ending Inventory
October	1,000	2,500	+1,500	1,500
November	2,000	2,500	+ 500	2,000
December	4,000	2,500	−1,500	500
January	3,000	2,500	− 500	0

b.

	Ending Inventory	Cost per Unit ($5)	Inventory Financing Cost at (10%)
October	1,500	7,500	750
November	2,000	10,000	1,000
December	500	2,500	250
January	0	0	0
		Total Financing Cost =	$2,000

6-4.   Boatler Used Cadillac Co. requires $800,000 in financing over the next two years. The firm can borrow the funds for two years at 9 percent interest per year. Mr. Boatler decides to do economic forecasting and determines that if he utilizes short-term financing instead, he will pay 6.75 percent interest in the first year and 10.55 percent interest in the second year. Determine the total two-year interest cost under each plan. Which plan is less costly?

Solution:
Boatler Used Cadillac Co.

Cost of Two Year Fixed Cost Financing
$800,000 borrowed × 9% per annum x 2 years = $144,000 interest cost

Cost of Two Year Variable Short-term Financing

1st year $800,000 × 6.75% per annum   = $54,600 interest cost

2nd year $800,000 × 10.55% per annum = $\underline{$84,400}$ interest cost

$\qquad\qquad\qquad\qquad\qquad\qquad\qquad$ 138,400 total interest cost

The short-term plan is less costly.

6-5.   Stern Educational TV, Inc., has decided to buy a new computer system with an expected life of three years at a cost of $200,000. The company can borrow $200,000 for three years at 12 percent annual interest or for one year at 10 percent annual interest.

a. How much would the firm save in interest over the three-year life of the computer system if the one-year loan is utilized, and the loan is rolled over (reborrowed) each year at the same 10 percent rate? Compare this to the 12 percent three-year loan.

b. What if interest rates on the 10 percent loan go up to 15 percent in the second year and 18 percent in the third year? What would be the total interest cost compared to the 12 percent, three-year loan?

Solution:

Stern Educational TV, Inc.

a. **If Rates Are Constant**

$200,000 borrowed × 12% per annum × 3 years = $72,000 interest cost (long-term)

$200,000 borrowed × 10% per annum × 3 years = $60,000 interest cost (short-term)

$72,000 − $60,000 = $12,000 interest savings borrowing short-term

b. **If Short-term Rates Change**

1st year	$200,000 × .10 = $20,000
2nd year	$200,000 × .15 = $30,000
3rd year	$200,000 × .18 = $36,000
	Total = $86,000

$86,000 − $72,000 = $14,000 extra interest costs borrowing short-term.

6-6. Assume that Hogan Surgical Instruments Co. has $2,000,000 in assets. If it goes with a low liquidity plan for the assets, it can earn a return of 18 percent, but with a high liquidity plan, the return will be 14 percent. If the firm goes with a short-term financing plan, the financing costs on the $2,000,000 will be 10 percent, and with a long-term financing plan, the financing costs on the $2,000,000 will be 12 percent. (Review Table 6-11 for parts *a*, *b*, and *c* of this problem.)

a. Compute the anticipated return after financing costs on the most aggressive asset-financing mix.
b. Compute the anticipated return after financing costs on the most conservative asset-financing mix.
c. Compute the anticipated return after financing costs on the two moderate approaches to the asset-financing mix.
d. Would you necessarily accept the plan with the highest return after financing costs? Briefly explain.

Solution:

Hogan Surgical Instruments Company

a. **Most aggressive**

Low liquidity	$2,000,000 × 18% =	$360,000
Short-term financing	–2,000,000 × 10% =	200,000
Anticipated return		$160,000

b. **Most conservative**

High liquidity	$2,000,000 × 14% =	$280,000
Long-term financing	–2,000,000 × 12% =	240,000
Anticipated return		$ 40,000

c. **Moderate approach**

Low liquidity	$2,000,000 × 18% =	$360,000
Long-term financing	–2,000,000 × 12% =	240,000
		$120,000

Or

High liquidity	$2,000,000 × 14% =	$280,000
Short-term financing	–2,000,000 × 10% =	200,000
		$ 80,000

d. You may not necessarily select the plan with the highest return. You must also consider the risk inherent in the plan. Of course, some firms are better able to take risks than others. The ultimate concern must be for maximizing the overall valuation of the firm through a judicious consideration of risk-return options.

6-7.   Winfrey Diet Food Corp. has $4,500,000 in assets.

Temporary current assets	$1,000,000
Permanent current assets	1,500,000
Fixed assets	2,000,000
Total assets	$4,500,000

Short-term rates are 8 percent. Long-term rates are 13 percent. Earnings before interest and taxes are $960,000. The tax rate is 40 percent.

If long-term financing is perfectly matched (synchronized) with long-term asset needs, and the same is true of short-term financing, what will earnings after taxes be? For an example of perfectly matched plans, see Figure 6-5.

Solution:
Winfrey Diet Food Corporation

Long-term financing equals:

Permanent current assets	$1,500,000
Fixed assets	2,000,000
	$3,500,000

Short-term financing equals:

Temporary current assets	$1,000,000

Long-term interest expense = 13% × $3,500,000 =	$ 455,000
Short-term interest expense = 8% × 1,000,000 =	80,000
Total interest expense	$ 535,000

Earnings before interest and taxes	$ 960,000
Interest expense	535,000
Earnings before taxes	$ 425,000
Taxes (40%)	170,000
Earnings after taxes	$ 255,000

6-8.   In problem 7, assume the term structure of interest rates becomes inverted, with short-term rates going to 12 percent and long-term rates 4 percentage points lower than short-term rates.

If all other factors in the problem remain unchanged, what will earnings after taxes be?

Solution:

Winfrey Diet Food Corporation (Continued)

Long-term interest expense = 8% × $3,500,000 = $280,000

Short-term interest expense = 12% × 1,000,000 = 120,000

Total interest expense $400,000

Earnings before interest and taxes	$960,000
Interest expense	400,000
Earnings before taxes	$560,000
Taxes (40%)	224,000
Earnings after taxes	$336,000

6-9.   Collins Systems, Inc., is trying to develop an asset-financing plan. The firm has $300,000 in temporary current assets and $200,000 in permanent current assets. Collins also has $400,000 in fixed assets. Assume a tax rate of 40 percent.

a. Construct two alternative financing plans for the firm. One of the plans should be conservative, with 80 percent of assets financed by long-term sources and the rest financed by short-term sources. The other plan should be aggressive, with only 30 percent of assets financed by long-term sources and the remaining assets financed by short-term sources. The current interest rate is 15 percent on long-term funds and 10 percent on short-term financing. Also compute the annual interest payments under each plan.

b. Given that Collin's earnings before interest and taxes are $180,000, calculate earnings after taxes for each of your alternatives.

Solution:

Collins Systems Inc.

a. Temporary current assets $300,000
   Permanent current assets   200,000
   Fixed assets   400,000
   Total assets $900,000

Conservative

Amount	% of Total		Interest Rate	Interest Expense	
$900,000 × .80	=	$720,000	× .15 =	$108,000	Long-term
$900,000 × .20	=	$180,000	× .10 =	18,000	Short-term
			Total interest charge	$126,000	

Amount	% of Total		Interest Rate	Interest Expense	
$900,000 × .30	=	$270,000	× .15 =	$ 40,500	Long-term
$900,000 × .70	=	$630,000	× .10 =	63,000	Short-term
			Total interest charge	$103,000	

	Conservative	Aggressive
EBIT	$180,000	$180,000
–Int	126,000	103,500
EBT	54,000	76,500
Tax 40%	21,600	30,600
EAT	$ 32,400	$ 45,900

6-10.   Lear, Inc., has $800,000 in current assets, $350,000 of which are considered permanent current assets. In addition, the firm has $600,000 invested in fixed assets.

a. Lear wishes to finance all fixed assets and half of its permanent current assets with long-term financing costing 10 percent. Short-term financing currently costs 5 percent. Lear's earnings before interest and taxes are $200,000. Determine Lear's earnings after taxes under this financing plan. The tax rate is 30 percent.

b. As an alternative, Lear might wish to finance all fixed assets and permanent current assets plus half of its temporary current assets with long-term financing. The same interest rates apply as in part *a*. Earnings before interest and taxes will be $200,000. What will be Lear's earnings after taxes? The tax rate is 30 percent.

c. What are some of the risks and cost considerations associated with each of these alternative financing strategies?

Solution:

Lear, Inc.

a. Current   −   permanent current   =   temporary current
   assets   assets   assets
   $800,000 − $350,000   = $450,000

$$\text{Long-term interest expense} = 10\% \ [\$600,000 + \tfrac{1}{2} \ (\$350,000)]$$
$$= 10\% \times (\$775,000)$$
$$= \$77,500$$

$$\text{Short-term interest expense} = 5\% \ [\$450,000 + \tfrac{1}{2} \ (\$350,000)]$$
$$= 5\% \times (\$625,000)$$
$$= \$31,250$$

Total interest expense $= \$77,500 + \$31,250$
                            $= \$108,750$

Earnings before interest and taxes	$200,000
Interest expense	108,750
Earnings before taxes	$ 91,250
Taxes (30%)	27,375
Earnings after taxes	$ 63,875

b. Alternative financing plan

$$\text{Long-term interest expense} = 10\% \, [\$600,000 + \$350,000 \\ + \tfrac{1}{2} \, (\$450,000)] \\ = 10\% \, (\$1,175,000) \\ = \$117,500$$

$$\text{Short-term interest expense} = 5\% \, [\tfrac{1}{2} \, (\$450,000)] \\ = 5\% \, (225,000) \\ = \$11,250$$

$$\text{Total interest expense} = \$117,500 + \$11,250 \\ = \$128,750$$

Earnings before interest and taxes	$200,000
Interest	128,750
Earnings before taxes	$ 71,250
Taxes (30%)	21,375
Earnings after taxes	$ 49,875

c. The alternative financing plan which calls for more financing by high-cost debt is more expensive and reduces aftertax income by $14,000. However, we must not automatically reject this plan because of its higher cost since it has less risk. The alternative provides the firm with long-term capital which at times will be in excess of its needs and invested in marketable securities. It will not be forced to pay higher short-term rates on a large portion of its debt when short-term rates rise and will not be faced with the possibility of no short-term financing for a portion of its permanent current assets when it is time to renew the short-term loan.

6-11.   Using the expectations hypothesis theory for the term structure of interest rates, determine the expected return for securities with maturities of two, three, and four years based on the data below. Do an analysis similar to that in the right-hand portion of Table 6-6.

1-year T-bill at beginning of year 1 .... 5%
1-year T-bill at beginning of year 2 .... 6%
1-year T-bill at beginning of year 3 .... 8%
1-year T-bill at beginning of year 4 .... 10%

Solution:

2 year security $(5\% + 6\%)/2 = 5.5\%$
3 year security $(5\% + 6\% + 8\%)/3 = 6.33\%$
4 year security $(5\% + 6\% + 8\% + 10\%)/4 = 7.25\%$

6-12.   Carmen's Beauty Salon has estimated monthly financing requirements for the next six months as follows:

January	$8,000	April	$8,000
February	2,000	May	9,000
March	3,000	June	4,000

Short-term financing will be utilized for the next six months. Projected annual interest rates are:

January	8.0%	April	15.0%
February	9.0%	May	12.0%
March	12.0%	June	12.0%

a. Compute total dollar interest payments for the six months. To convert an annual rate to a monthly rate, divide by 12. Then multiply this value times the monthly balance. To get your answer sum up the monthly interest payments.

b. If long-term financing at 12 percent had been utilized throughout the six months, would the total-dollar interest payments be larger or smaller? Compute the interest owed over the six months and compare your answer to that in part *a*.

Solution:

Carmen's Beauty Salon

a. Short-term financing

Month	Rate	On Monthly Basis	Amount	Actual Interest
January	8%	.67%	$8,000	$ 53.60
February	9%	.75%	$2,000	$ 15.00
March	12%	1.00%	$3,000	$ 30.00
April	15%	1.25%	$8,000	$100.00
May	12%	1.00%	$9,000	$ 90.00
June	12%	1.00%	$4,000	$ 40.00
				$328.60

b. Long-term financing

Month	Rate	On Monthly Basis	Amount	Actual Interest
January	12%	1%	$8,000	$ 80.00
February	12%	1%	$2,000	$ 20.00
March	12%	1%	$3,000	$ 30.00
April	15%	1%	$8,000	$ 80.00
May	12%	1%	$9,000	$ 90.00
June	12%	1%	$4,000	$ 40.00
				$340.00

Total dollar interest payments would be larger under the long-term financing plan as described in part b.

6-13.   In problem 12, what long-term interest rate would represent a break-even point between using short-term financing as described in part *a* and long-term financing? Hint: Divide the interest payments in 11*a* by the amount of total funds provided for the six months and multiply by 12.

Solution:

Carmen's Beauty Salon (Continued)

Divide the total interest payments in part (a) of $328.60 by the total amount of funds extended $34,000 ($8,000 + 2,000 + 3,000 + 8,000 + 9,000 + 4,000) and multiply by 12.

$$\frac{interest}{principal} = \frac{\$328.60}{\$34,000} = .966\% \text{ monthly rate}$$

$$12 \times .966\% = 11.59\% \text{ annual rate}$$

6-14.   Garza Electronics expects to sell 500 units in January, 250 units in February, and 1,000 units in March. December's ending inventory is 700 units. Expected sales for the year are 7,200 units. Garza has decided on a level production schedule of 600 units (7,200 units for the year/12 months = 600 units per month). What is the expected unit volume of end-of-month inventory for January, February, and March? Show the beginning inventory, production, and sales for each of the three months that is used to derive the ending inventory.

Solution:

Garza Electronics

	Beginning Inventory	+ Production	− Sales	= Ending Inventory
January	700	+ 600	− 500	= 800
February	800	+ 600	− 250	= 1,150
March	1,150	+ 600	− 1,100	= 650

6-15.   Bombs Away Video Games Corporation has forecasted the following monthly sales:

January	$95,000	July	$ 40,000
February	88,000	August	40,000
March	20,000	September	50,000
April	20,000	October	80,000
May	15,000	November	100,000
June	30,000	December	118,000

Total sales = $696,000

Bombs Away Video Games sells the popular Strafe and Capture video game cartridge. It sells for $5 per unit and costs $2 per unit to produce. A level production policy is followed. Each month's production is equal to annual sales (in units) divided by 12.

Of each month's sales, 30 percent are for cash and 70 percent are on account. All accounts receivable are collected in the month after the sale is made.

a. Construct a monthly production and inventory schedule in units. Beginning inventory in January is 20,000 units. (Note: To do part *a*, you should work in terms of units of production and units of sales.)
b. Prepare a monthly schedule of cash receipts. Sales in the December before the planning year are $100,000. Work part *b* using dollars.
c. Determine a cash payments schedule for January through December. The production costs of $2 per unit are paid for in the month in which they occur. Other cash payments, besides those for production costs, are $40,000 per month.
d. Prepare a monthly cash budget for January through December using the cash receipts schedule from part *b* and the cash payments schedule from part *c*. The beginning cash balance is $5,000, which is also the minimum desired.

Solution:

Bombs Away Video Games Corporation

a. Production and inventory schedule in units

	Beginning Inventory	+	Production[1]	−	Sales[2]	=	Ending Inventory
Jan.	20,000	+	11,600		19,000	=	12,600
Feb.	12,600		11,600		17,600		6,600
Mar.	6,600		11,600		4,000		14,200
Apr.	14,200		11,600		4,000		21,800
May	21,800		11,600		3,000		30,400
June	30,400		11,600		6,000		36,000
July	36,000		11,600		8,000		39,600
Aug.	39,600		11,600		8,000		43,200
Sept.	43,200		11,600		10,000		44,800
Oct.	44,800		11,600		16,000		40,400
Nov.	40,400		11,600		20,000		32,000
Dec.	32,000		11,600		23,600		20,000

[1] Total annual sales = $696,000

$696,000/$5 per unit = 139,200 units

139,200 units/12 months = 11,600 per month

[2] Monthly dollar sales/$5 price = unit sales

b.

Cash Receipts Schedule

	Jan.	Feb.	Mar.	Apr.	May	June
Sales (in dollars)	$95,000	$88,000	$20,000	$20,000	$15,000	$30,000
30% Cash sales	28,500	26,400	6,000	6,000	4,500	9,000
70% Prior month's sales	70,000*	66,500	61,600	14,000	14,000	10,500
Total cash receipts	$98,500	$92,900	$67,600	$20,000	$18,500	$19,500

*based on December sales of $100,000

	July	Aug.	Sept.	Oct.	Nov.	Dec.
Sales (in dollars)	$40,000	$40,000	$50,000	$80,000	$100,000	$118,000
30% Cash sales	12,000	12,000	15,000	24,000	30,000	35,400
70% Prior month's sales	21,000	28,000	28,000	35,000	56,000	70,000
Total cash receipts	$33,000	$40,000	$43,000	$59,000	$86,000	$105,400

c.

Cash Payments Schedule
Constant production

	Jan.	Feb.	Mar.	Apr.	May	June
11,600 units × $2	$23,200	$23,200	$23,200	$23,200	$23,200	$23,200
Other cash payments	40,000	40,000	40,000	40,000	40,000	40,000
Total cash payments	$63,200	$63,200	$63,200	$63,200	$63,200	$63,200

	July	Aug.	Sept.	Oct.	Nov.	Dec.
11,600 units × $2	$23,200	$23,200	$23,200	$23,200	$23,200	$23,200
Other cash payments	40,000	40,000	40,000	40,000	40,000	40,000
Total cash payments	$63,200	$63,200	$63,200	$63,200	$63,200	$63,200

d.

Cash Budget

	Jan.	Feb.	Mar.	Apr.	May	June
Net cash flow	$35,300	$29,700	$ 4,400	($43,200)	($44,700)	($43,700)
Beginning cash	5,000	40,300	70,000	74,400	31,200	5,000
Cumulative cash balance	40,300	70,000	74,400	31,200	(13,500)	(38,700)
Monthly loan or (repayment)	-0-	-0-	-0-	-0-	18,500	43,700
Cumulative loan	-0-	-0-	-0-	-0-	18,500	62,200
Ending cash balance	40,300	70,000	74,400	31,200	5,000	5,000

	July	Aug.	Sept.	Oct.	Nov.	Dec.
Net cash flow	($30,200)	($23,200)	($20,200)	($4,200)	$22,800	$42,200
Beginning cash	5,000	5,000	5,000	5,000	5,000	5,000
Cumulative cash balance	(25,200)	(18,200)	(15,200)	800	27,800	47,200
Monthly loan or (repayment)	30,200	23,200	20,200	4,200	(22,800)	(42,200)
Cumulative loan	92,400	115,600	135,800	140,000	117,200	75,000
Ending cash balance	5,000	5,000	5,000	5,000	5,000	5,000

6-16.   Esquire Products, Inc., expects the following monthly sales:

January	$24,000	May.................	$ 4,000	September	$25,000
February	15,000	June.................	2,000	October	30,000
March	8,000	July	18,000	November	38,000
April	10,000	August	22,000	December......	20,000

Total sales = $216,000

Cash sales are 40 percent in a given month, with the remainder going into accounts receivable. All receivables are collected in the month following the sale. Esquire sells all of its goods for $2 each and produces them for $1 each. Esquire uses level production, and average monthly production is equal to annual production divided by 12.

a. Generate a monthly production and inventory schedule in units. Beginning inventory in January is 8,000 units. (Note: To do part *a*, you should work in terms of units of production and units of sales.)

b. Determine a cash receipts schedule for January through December. Assume that dollar sales in the prior December were $20,000. Work part *b* using dollars.

c. Determine a cash payments schedule for January through December. The production costs ($1 per unit produced) are paid for in the month in which they occur. Other cash payments (besides those for production costs) are $7,000 per month.

d. Construct a cash budget for January through December using the cash receipts schedule from part *b* and the cash payments schedule from part *c*. The beginning cash balance is $3,000, which is also the minimum desired.

e. Determine total current assets for each month. Include cash, accounts receivable, and inventory. Accounts receivable equal sales minus 40 percent of sales for a given month. Inventory is equal to ending inventory (part *a*) times the cost of $1 per unit.

Solution:

Esquire Products, Inc.

a.   Production and inventory schedule in units

	Beginning Inventory	+	Production[1]	–	Sales[2]	=	Ending Inventory
Jan.	8,000	+	9,000		12,000	=	5,000
Feb.	5,000		9,000		7,500		6,500
Mar.	6,500		9,000		4,000		11,500
Apr.	11,500		9,000		5,000		15,500
May	15,500		9,000		2,000		22,500
June	22,500		9,000		1,000		30,500
July	30,500		9,000		9,000		30,500
Aug.	30,500		9,000		11,000		28,500
Sept.	28,500		9,000		12,500		25,000
Oct.	25,000		9,000		15,000		19,000
Nov.	19,000		9,000		19,000		9,000
Dec.	9,000		9,000		10,000		8,000

[1] $216,000 sales/$2 price = 108,000 units
    108,000 units/12 months = 9,000 units per month
[2] Monthly dollar sales/$2 = number of units

b.

Cash Receipts Schedule (take dollar values from problem statement)

	Jan.	Feb.	Mar.	Apr.	May	June
Sales (in dollars)	$24,000	$15,000	$8,000	$10,000	$4,000	$2,000
40% Cash sales	9,600	6,000	3,200	4,000	1,600	800
60% Prior month's sales	12,000*	14,400	9,000	4,800	6,000	2,400
Total receipts	$21,600	$20,400	$12,200	$8,800	$7,600	$3,200

*based on December sales of $20,000

	July	Aug.	Sept.	Oct.	Nov.	Dec.
Sales (in dollars)	$18,000	$22,000	$25,000	$30,000	$38,000	$20,000
40% Cash sales	7,200	8,800	10,000	12,000	15,200	8,000
60% Prior month's sales	1,200	10,800	13,200	15,000	18,000	22,800
Total receipts	$8,400	$19,600	$23,200	$27,000	$33,200	$30,800

S-211

c.

Cash Payments Schedule
Constant production

	Jan.	Feb.	Mar.	Apr.	May	June
9,000 units × $1	$ 9,000	$ 9,000	$ 9,000	$ 9,000	$ 9,000	$ 9,000
Other cash payments	7,000	7,000	7,000	7,000	7,000	7,000
Total payments	$16,000	$16,000	$16,000	$16,000	$16,000	$16,000

	July	Aug.	Sept.	Oct.	Nov.	Dec.
9,000 units × $1	$ 9,000	$ 9,000	$ 9,000	$ 9,000	$ 9,000	$ 9,000
Other cash payments	7,000	7,000	7,000	7,000	7,000	7,000
Total cash payments	$16,000	$16,000	$16,000	$16,000	$16,000	$16,000

d.

Cash Budget

	Jan.	Feb.	Mar.	Apr.	May	June
Cash flow	$5,600	$ 4,400	($3,800)	($ 7,200)	($ 8,400)	($12,800)
Beginning cash	3,000	8,600	13,000	9,200	3,000	3,000
Cumulative cash balance	8,600	13,000	9,200	2,000	(5,400)	(9,800)
Monthly loan or (repayment)	-0-	-0-	-0-	1,000	8,400	12,800
Cumulative loan	-0-	-0-	-0-	1,000	9,400	22,200
Ending cash balance	$8,600	$13,000	$9,200	$3,000	$3,000	$3,000

	July	Aug.	Sept.	Oct.	Nov.	Dec.
Cash flow	($ 7,600)	$3,600	$ 7,200	$11,000	$17,200	$14,800
Beginning cash	3,000	3,000	3,000	3,000	3,000	12,200
Cumulative cash balance	(4,600)	6,600	10,200	14,000	20,200	27,000
Monthly loan or (repayment)	7,600	(3,600)	(7,200)	(11,000)	(8,000)	-0-
Cumulative loan	29,800	26,200	19,000	8,000	-0-	-0-
Ending cash balance	$3,000	$3,000	$3,000	$3,000	$12,200	$27,000

e.

	Cash	Assets Accounts Receivable	Inventory	Total Current
Jan.	$ 8,600	$14,400	$ 5,000	$28,000
Feb.	13,000	9,000	6,500	28,500
Mar.	9,200	4,800	11,500	25,500
Apr.	3,000	6,000	15,500	24,500
May	3,000	2,400	22,500	27,900
June	3,000	1,200	30,500	34,700
July	3,000	10,800	30,500	44,300
Aug.	3,000	13,200	28,500	44,700
Sept.	3,000	15,000	25,000	43,000
Oct.	3,000	18,000	19,000	40,000
Nov.	12,200	22,800	9,000	44,000
Dec.	27,000	12,000	8,000	47,000

The instructor may wish to point out how current assets are at relatively high levels and illiquid during June through October. In November and particularly December, the asset levels remain high, but they become increasingly more liquid as inventory diminishes relative to cash.

6-17. Pick a day within the past week and construct a yield curve for that day. Pick a day approximately a year ago and construct a yield curve for that day. How are interest rates different? *The Wall Street Journal* and the *Federal Reserve Bulletin* should be of help in setting up this problem.

Solution:

Library assignment. Answers will vary with the state of the economy.

Chapter 7

Discussion Questions

7-1.   In the management of cash and marketable securities, why should the primary concern be for safety and liquidity rather than maximization of profit?

Cash and marketable securities are generally used to meet the transaction needs of the firm and for contingency purposes. Because the funds must be available when needed, the primary concern should be with safety and liquidity rather than the maximum profits.

7-2.   Briefly explain how a corporation may use float to its advantage.

Float represents the difference between a corporation's recorded cash balances and the amount credited to the corporation by the bank. It is the latter item that is of particular interest to us. To the extent a corporation can accelerate check collections to the bank account and slow down check payments from its bank account, the cash balance at the bank may exceed the recorded amount on the company books. The differential or float may be thought of as a short-term source of funds to the corporation.

7-3.   Why does float exist and what effect do electronic funds transfer systems have on float?

Float exists because of the delay time in check processing. Electronic funds transfer, or the electronic movement of funds between computer terminals, would eliminate the need for checks and thus eliminate float.

7-4.   How can a firm operate with a negative cash balance on its corporate books?

A firm could operate with a negative balance on the corporate books, as indicated in Table 7-2, knowing float will carry them through at the bank. Checks written on the corporate books may not clear until many days later at the bank. For this reason, a negative account balance on the corporate books of $100,000 may still represent a positive balance at the bank.

7-5.   Explain the similarities and differences of lockbox systems and regional collection offices.

Both lockbox systems and regional collection offices allow for the rapid processing of checks that originate at distant points. The difference is that a regional collection center requires the commitment of corporate resources and personnel to staff an office, while a lockbox system requires only the use of a post office box and the assistance of a local bank. Clearly, the lockbox system is less expensive.

7-6.   Why would a financial manager want to slow down disbursements?

By slowing down disbursements or the processing of checks against the corporate account, the firm is able to increase float and also to provide a source of short-term financing.

7-7.   Use *The Wall Street Journal* or some other financial publication to find the going interest rates for the list of marketable securities in Table 7-3. Which security would you choose for a short-term investment? Why?

The answer to this question may well depend upon the phase of the business cycle at the time the question is considered. In normal times, small CDs and savings accounts may prove adequate. However, in a tight money period, wide differentials may be established between the various instruments and maximum returns may be found in Treasury bills, large CDs, commercial paper, and money market funds.

7-8.   Why are Treasury bills a favorite place for financial managers to invest excess cash?

Treasury bills are popular because of the large and active market in which they trade. Because of this, the investor may literally pinpoint the maturity desired choosing anywhere from one day to a year. The "T-bill" market provides maximum liquidity and can absorb almost any dollar amount of business.

7-9.   Explain why the bad debt percentage or any other similar credit-control percentage is not the ultimate measure of success in the management of accounts receivable. What is the key consideration?

An investment in accounts receivable requires a commitment of funds as is true of any other investment. The key question is: Will the dollar returns from the resource commitment provide a sufficient rate of return to justify the investment? There is no such thing as too many or too few bad debts, only too low a return on capital.

7-10.   What are three quantitative measures that can be applied to the collection policy of the firm?

The average collection period, the ratio of bad debts to credit sales and the aging of accounts receivable.

7-11.   What are the 5 Cs of credit that are sometimes used by bankers and others to determine whether a potential loan will be repaid?

The 5 C's of credit are character, capital, capacity, conditions, and collateral.

7-12.   What does the EOQ formula tell us? What assumption is made about the usage rate for inventory?

The EOQ or economic order point tells us at what size order point we will minimize the overall inventory costs to the firm, with specific attention to inventory ordering costs and inventory carrying costs. It does not directly tell us the average size of inventory on hand and we must determine this as a separate calculation. It is generally assumed, however, that inventory will be used up at a constant rate over time, going from the order size to zero and then back again. Thus, average inventory is half the order size.

7-13.   Why might a firm keep a safety stock? What effect is it likely to have on carrying cost of inventory? A safety stock protects against the risk of losing sales to competitors due to being out of an item. A safety stock will guard against late deliveries due to weather, production delays, equipment breakdowns and many other things that can go wrong between the placement of an order and its delivery. With more inventory on hand, the carrying cost of inventory will go UP.

7-14.   If a firm uses a just-in-time inventory system, what effect is that likely to have on the number and location of suppliers?

A just-in-time inventory system usually means there will be fewer suppliers, and they will be more closely located to the manufacturer they supply.

Problems

7-1.   Porky's Sausage Co. shows the following values on its corporate books.

Corporate Books

Initial amount	$10,000
Deposits	+80,000
Checks	−50,000
Balance	$40,000

The initial amount on the bank's books is also $10,000. However, only $70,000 in deposits have been recorded and only $25,000 in checks have cleared. Fill in the table below and indicate the amount of float.

Banks Books

Initial amount	$10,000
Deposits	
Checks	
Balance	_____
Float	

Solution:

Porky's Sausage Co.
Bank Books

Initial amount	$10,000
Deposits	+70,000
Checks	−25,000
Balance	$55,000
Float	$15,000*

*Based on the balance on the corporate books minus the balance on the bank's books.

7-2.   Oscar's checkbook shows a balance of $600. A recent statement from the bank (received last week) shows that all checks written as of the date of the statement have been paid except numbers 423 and 424, which were for $62 and $40, respectively. Since the statement date, checks 425, 426, and 427 have been written for $32, $70, and $44, respectively.

There is a 75 percent probability that checks 423 and 424 have been paid by this time. There is a 40 percent probability that checks 424, 426, and 427 have been paid.

a. What is the total value of the five checks outstanding?
b. What is the expected value of payments for the five checks outstanding?
c. What is the difference between parts *a* and *b*? This represents a type of float.

Solution:
Oscar's Checkbook

a. $62 + $40 + $32 + 70 + 44 = $248

b.

Amount		Probability check has cleared	Expected value
$62	×	75%	$ 46.50
40	×	75%	30.00
32	×	40%	12.80
70	×	40%	28.00
44	×	40%	17.60

$134.90 expected value of payment for 5 checks outstanding

c. (a − b) = $248.00 − $134.90 = $113.10 float

7-3. Beth's Society Clothiers, Inc., has collection centers across the country to speed up collections. The company also makes payments from remote disbursement centers so the firm's checks will take longer to clear the bank. Collection time has been reduced by two and one-half days and disbursements time increased by one and one-half days because of these policies. Excess funds are being invested in short-term instruments yielding 6 percent per annum.

a. If the firm has $4 million per day in collections and $3 million per day in disbursements, how many dollars has the cash management system freed up?

b. How much can the firm earn in dollars per year on short-term investments made possible by the freed-up cash?

Solution:

Beth's Society Clothiers, Inc.

a. $4,000,000 daily collections
   × 2.5 days speed up = $10,000,000 additional collections
   $3,000,000 daily disbursements
   × 1.5 days slow down = $ 4,500,000 delayed disbursement
                          $14,500,000 freed-up funds

b. $14,500,000   freed-up funds
   ×   6%   interest rate
   $ 870,000   interest on freed-up cash

7-4.   Neon Lights Company of Kansas City shops lamps and lighting appliances throughout the country. Ms. Neon has determined that through the establishment of local collection centers around the country, she can speed up the collection of payments by 1.5 days. Furthermore, the cash management of her bank has indicated to her that she can defer her payments on her accounts by ½ a day without offending suppliers. The bank has a remote disbursement center in Florida.

a. If Neon Light Company has $2 million per day in collections and $1 million per day in disbursements, how many dollars will the cash management system free up?
b. If Neon Light Company can earn 9 percent per annum on freed up funds, how much will the income be?
c. If the total cost of the new system is $375,000, should it be implemented?

Solution:
Neon Light Company of Kansas City

a. $2,000,000 daily collections
    × 1.5 days speed up = $3,000,000 additional collections

    $1,000,000 daily disbursements
    × .5 days slow down = $500,000 delayed disbursements
                          $3,500,000 freed-up funds

b. $3,500,000   freed-up funds
    ×   9%   interest rate
    $ 315,000   interest on freed-up cash

c. No. The income of $315,000 is $60,000 less than the last of $375,000.

7-5.   Sanders' Prime Time Lighting Co. has annual credit sales of $1,800,000 and accounts receivable of $210,000. Compute the value of the average collection period.

Solution:

Sander's Prime Time Lighting Co.

$$\text{Average collection period} = \frac{\text{Accounts Receivable}}{\text{Average daily credit sales}}$$

$$= \frac{\$210,000}{\$1,800,000/360}$$

$$= \frac{\$210,000}{\$5,000}$$

$$= 42 \text{ days}$$

7-6.   Barney's Antique Shop has annual credit sales of $1,080,000 and an average collection period of 40 days in 1996. Assume a 360-day year.

What is the company's average accounts receivable balance? Accounts receivable are equal to the average daily credit sales times the average collection period.

Solution:

Barney's Antique Shop

$$\frac{\$1,080,000 \text{ annual credit sales}}{360 \text{ days per year}} = \$3,000 \text{ credit sales a day}$$

$3,000 average daily credit sales	$\times$	40 average collection period	= $120,000 average accounts receivable balance

7-7.   In Problem 6, if accounts receivable change in 2001 to $140,000, while credit sales are $1,440,000, should we assume the firm has a more or a less lenient credit policy? Hint: Recompute the average collection period.

Solution:
Barney's Antique Shop (Continued)

$$\text{Average collection period} = \frac{\text{Accounts Receivable}}{\text{Average daily credit sales}}$$

$$= \frac{\$140,000}{\$1,440,000/360}$$

$$= \frac{\$140,000}{\$4,000}$$

$$= 35 \text{ days}$$

Since the firm has a shorter average collection period, it appears that the firm does not have a more lenient credit policy.

7-8.   Mervyn's Fine Fashions has an average collection period of 40 days. The accounts receivable balance is $80,000. What is the value of its credit sales?

Solution:
Mervyn's Fine Fashion

$$\text{Average collection period} = \frac{\text{Accounts Receivable}}{\text{Average daily credit sales}}$$

$$40 \text{ days} = \frac{\$80,000}{\dfrac{\text{Credit sales}}{360}}$$

$$\frac{\text{credit sales}}{360} = \frac{\$80,000}{40}$$

$$\text{Credit sales}/360 = \$2,000$$

$$\text{Credit sales} = \$2,000 \times 360 = \$720,000$$

7-9.   Route Canal Shipping Company has the following schedule for aging of accounts receivable:

Age of Receivables, April 30, 2001

(1) Month of Sales	(2) Age of Account	(3) Amounts	(4) Percent of Amount Due
April	0-30	$105,000	_____
March	31-60	60,000	_____
February	61-90	90,000	_____
January	91-120	45,000	_____
Total receivables		$300,000	100%

a. Fill in column (4) for each month.
b. If the firm had $1,440,000 in credit sales over the four-month period, compute the average collection period. Average daily sales should be based on a 120-day period.

c. If the firm likes to see its bills collection in 30 days, should it be satisfied with the average collection period?
d. Disregarding your answer to part *c* and considering the aging schedule for accounts receivable, should the company be satisfied?
e. What additional information does the aging schedule bring to the company that the average collection period may not show?

Solution:

Route Canal Shipping Company

Age of Receivables, April 30, 2001

a.

(1)	(2)	(3)	(4)
	Age of		Percent of
Month of Sales	Account	Amounts	Amount Due
April	0-30	$105,000	35%
March	31-60	60,000	20%
February	61-90	90,000	30%
January	91-120	45,000	15%
Total receivables		$300,000	100%

b. $\text{Average collection period} = \dfrac{\text{Accounts receivable}}{\text{Average daily credit sales}}$

$$= \frac{\$300,000}{\$1,440,000/120}$$

$$= \frac{\$300,000}{\$12,000}$$

$$= 25 \text{ days}$$

c. Yes, the average collection of 25 days is less than 30 days.

d. No. The aging schedule provides additional insight that 65 percent of the accounts receivable are over 30 days old.

e. It goes beyond showing how many days of credit sales accounts receivables represent, to indicate the distribution of accounts receivable between various time frames.

7-10.   Midwest Tires has expected sales of 12,000 tires this year, an ordering cost of $6 per order, and carrying costs of $1.60 per tire.
a.   What is the economic ordering quantity?
b.   How many orders will be placed during the year?
c.   What will the average inventory be?

Solution:

Midwest Tires

a. $EOQ = \sqrt{\dfrac{2SO}{C}} = \sqrt{\dfrac{2 \times 12,000 \times \$6}{\$1.60}}$

$= \sqrt{\dfrac{\$144,000}{\$1.60}} = \sqrt{90,000} = 300 \text{ tires}$

b. 12,000 tires/300 tires = 40 orders

c. EOQ/2 = 300/2 = 150 tires (average inventory)

7-11.   Fisk Corporation is trying to improve its inventory control system and has installed an on-line computer at its retail stores. Fisk anticipates sales of 75,000 units per year, an ordering cost of $8 per order, and carrying costs of $12.0 per unit.

a. What is the economic ordering quantity?
b. How many orders will be placed during the year?
c. What will the average inventory be?
d. What is the total cost of ordering and carrying inventory?

Solution:

Fisk Corp.

a. $EOQ = \sqrt{\dfrac{2SO}{C}} = \sqrt{\dfrac{2 \times 75,000 \times \$8}{\$1.20}} = 1,000 \text{ units}$

b. 75,000 units/1,000 units = 75 orders

c. EOQ/2 = 1,000/2 = 500 units (average inventory)

d. 75 orders × $8 ordering cost .... = $ 600

500 inventory × $1.20 carrying cost per unit ..... =   600

Total costs .... = $1,200

7-12. (See Problem 11 for basic data.) In the second year, Fisk Corporation finds that it can reduce ordering costs to $2 per order but that carrying costs stay the same at $1.20. Also, volume remains at 75,000 units.

a. Recompute a, b, c, and d in Problem 9 for the second year.
b. Now compare years one and two and explain what happened.

Solution:
Fisk Corp. (Continued)

a. $$EOQ = \sqrt{\frac{2SO}{C}} = \sqrt{\frac{2 \times 75,000 \times \$2}{\$1.20}}$$

$$= \sqrt{\frac{\$300,000}{\$1.20}} = \sqrt{250,000} = 500 \text{ units}$$

75,000 units/500 units = 150 orders
EOQ/2 = 500/2 = 250 units (average inventory)

150 orders × $2 ordering cost	= $300
250 inventory × $1.20 carrying cost per unit	= 300
Total costs	= $600

b. The number of units ordered declines 50%, while the number of orders doubles. The average inventory and total costs both decline by one-half. Notice that the total cost did not decline in equal percentage to the decline in ordering costs. This is because the change in EOQ and other variables (½) is proportional to the square root of the change in ordering costs (¼).

7-13.   Diagnostic Supplies has expected sales of 135,000 units per year, a carrying cost of $3 per unit, and an ordering cost of $4 per order.

  a. What is the economic order quantity?
  b. What is average inventory? What is the total carrying cost?
  c. Assume an additional 80 units of inventory will be required as safety stock. What will the new average inventory be? What will the new total carrying cost be?

Solution:
Diagnostic Supplies

a. $EOQ = \sqrt{\dfrac{2SO}{C}} = \sqrt{\dfrac{2 \times 135,000 \times \$4}{\$3}}$

$= \sqrt{\dfrac{\$1,080,000}{\$3}} = \sqrt{\$360,000} = 600 \text{ units}$

b. EOQ/2 = 600/2 = 300 units (average inventory)
   300 units × $3 carrying cost/unit = $900 total carrying cost

c. $\text{Average inventory} = \dfrac{EOQ}{2} + \text{Safety Stock}$

$= \dfrac{600}{2} + 80 = 300 + 80 = 380$

380 inventory × $3 carrying cost per year
= $1,140 total carrying cost

7-14.   Wisconsin Snowmobile Corp. is considering a switch to level production. Cost efficiencies would occur under level production, and aftertax costs would decline by $30,000, but inventory costs would increase by $250,000. Wisconsin Snowmobile would have to finance the extra inventory at a cost of 13.5 percent.

a. Should the company go ahead and switch to level production?
b. How low would interest rates need to fall before level production would be feasible?

Solution:
Wisconsin Snowmobile Corporation

a. Inventory increases by $250,000
      × interest expense   13.5%
   Increased costs $ 33,750

   Savings   30,000
   Less: Increased costs   ($ 33,750)
      Loss   ($ 3,750)

Don't switch to level production.

b. If interest rates fall to 12% or less, the switch would be feasible.

$$\frac{\$30,000 \text{ savings}}{\$250,000 \text{ increased inventory}} = 12\%$$

7-15.   Johnson Electronics is considering extending trade credit to some customers previously considered poor risks. Sales would increase by $100,000 if credit is extended to these new customers. Of the new accounts receivable generated, 10 percent will prove to be uncollectible. Additional collection costs will be 3 percent of sales, and production and selling costs will be 79 percent of sales. The firm is in the 40 percent tax bracket.

a. Compute the incremental income after taxes.
b. What will Johnson's incremental return on sales be if these new credit customers are accepted?
c. If the receivable turnover ratio is 6 to 1, and no other asset buildup is needed to serve the new customers, what will Johnson's incremental return on new average investment be?

Solution:
Johnson Electronics

a.

Additional sales	$100,000
Accounts uncollectible (10% of new sales)	− 10,000
Annual incremental revenue......................	$ 90,000
Collection costs (3% of new sales)............	− 3,000
Production and selling costs	
(79% of new sales)..................................	− 79,000
Annual income before taxes	$ 8,000
Taxes (40%)...	− 3,200
Incremental income after taxes..................	$ 4,800

b. Incremental return on sales $= \dfrac{\text{Incremental income}}{\text{Incremental sales}}$

$$= \$4,800 / \$100,000 = 4.8\%$$

c. Receivable turnover = Sales/Receivable turnover = 6x
    Receivables   = Sales/Receivable turnover
                         = $100,000/6
                         = $16,666.67

Incremental return on new average investment =
$4,800/$16,666.67   = 28.80%

7-16.   Henderson Office Supply is considering a more liberal credit policy to increase sales, but expects that 8 percent of the new accounts will be uncollectible. Collection costs are 5 percent of new sales; production and selling costs are 78 percent; and accounts receivable turnover is five times. Assume income taxes of 30 percent and an increase in sales of $60,000. No other asset buildup will be required to service the new accounts.

a.   What is the level of accounts receivable to support this sales expansion?
b.   What would be Henderson's incremental aftertax return on investment?
c.   Should Henderson liberalize credit if a 15 percent aftertax return on investment is required?

Assume that Henderson also needs to increase its level of inventory to support new sales and that inventory turnover is four times.

d.   What would be the total incremental investment in accounts receivable and inventory to support a $60,000 increase in sales?
e.   Given the income determined in part *b* and the investment determined in part *d*, should Henderson extend more liberal credit terms?

Solution:

Henderson Office Supply

a. Investment in accounts receivable $= \dfrac{\$60,000}{5} = \$12,000$

b.

Added sales..	$ 60,000
Accounts uncollectible (8% of new sales)	− 4,800
Annual incremental revenue......................	$ 55,200
Collection costs (5% of new sales).............	− 3,000
Production and selling costs	
(78% of new sales).................................	− 46,800
Annual income before taxes	$ 5,400
Taxes (30%)..	− 1,620
Incremental income after taxes.................	$ 3,780

Return on incremental investment $= \dfrac{\$3,780}{12,000} = 31.5\%$

c. Yes! 31.5% exceeds the required return of 15%.

d. Investment in inventory $= \dfrac{\$60,000}{4} = \$15,000$

Total incremental investment

Inventory	$15,000
Accounts receivable	12,000
Incremental investment	$27,000

$3,780/$27,000 = 14% return on investment

e. No! 14% is less than the required return of 15%.

7-17.   Comiskey Fence Co. is evaluating the extension of credit to a new group of customers. Although these customers will provide $180,000 in additional credit sales, 12 percent are likely to be uncollectible. The company will also incur $15,700 in additional collection expense. Production and marketing costs represent 70 percent of sales. The firm is in a 34 percent tax bracket and has a receivables turnover of 5 times. No other asset buildup will be required to service the new customers. The firm has a 10 percent desired return.

a. Should Comiskey Fence Co. extend credit to these customers?
b. Should credit be extended if 15 percent of the new sales prove uncollectible?
c. Should credit be extended if the receivables turnover drops to 1.5, and 12 percent of the accounts are uncollectible (as in part *a*)?

Solution:
Comiskey Fence Co.

a. Added sales $180,000
    Accounts uncollectible (12% of new sales)   21,600
    Annual incremental revenue   158,400
    Collection costs   15,700
    Production and selling costs
     (70% of new sales)   126,000
    Annual income before taxes   16,700
    Taxes (34%)   5,678
    Incremental income after taxes .... $ 11,022

$$\text{Receivable turnover} = 5.0x \quad \frac{\$180,000}{5.0} = \begin{array}{c}\$36,000 \text{ in} \\ \text{new receivables}\end{array}$$

$$\text{Return on incremental investment} = \frac{\$11,022}{\$36,000} = 30.62\%$$

Yes, extend credit to these customers since the incremental return of 30.62% is greater than 10%.

b. Same as above except accounts uncollectible are $15%
of $180,000 or $27,000. This is $5,400 more than the
value in part a. This means a reduction in incremental
income after taxes of $3,564 to $7,458. The value can
also be computed as:

Added sales..	$180,000
Accounts uncollectible (15% of new sales)	27,000
Annual incremental revenue.......................	$153,000
Collection costs...	15,700
Production and selling costs	
(70% of new sales).................................	126,000
Annual income before taxes	11,300
Taxes (34%)...	3,842
Incremental income after taxes..................	$ 7,458

$$\text{Return on incremental investment} = \frac{\$7,458}{\$36,000} = 20.72\%$$

Yes, extend credit.

c. If receivable turnover drops to 1.5x, the investment in
accounts receivable would equal $180,000/1.5 =
$120,000. The return on incremental investment,
assuming a 12% uncollectible rate, is 9.19%.

$$\text{Return on incremental investment} = \frac{\$11,022}{\$120,000} = 9.19\%$$

The credit should not be extended. 9.19% is less than the
desired 10%.

7-18.   Reconsider problem 17. Assume the average collection period is 120 days. All other factors are the same (including 12 percent uncollectibles). Should credit be extended?

Solution:
Comiskey Fence Company (Continued)

Fist compute the new accounts receivable balance.

Accounts receivable = average collection × average daily
                                    period   sales

$$120 \text{ days} \times \frac{180,000}{360 \text{ days}} = 120 \times \$500 = \$60,000$$

or

Accounts receivable = sales/accounts receivable turnover

$$\text{Accounts receivable turnover} = \frac{360 \text{ days}}{120 \text{ days}} = 3x$$

$$\$180,000/3 = \$60,000$$

Then compute return on incremental investment.

$$\frac{\$11,022}{\$60,000} = 18.37\%$$

Yes, extend credit. 18.37% is greater than 10%.

(Problems 19-22 are a series and should be taken in order.)

7-19. Dome Metals has credit sales of $144,000 yearly with credit terms of net 30 days, which is also the average collection period. Dome does not offer a discount for early payment, so its customers take the full 30 days to pay.

What is the average receivables balance? Receivables turnover?

Solution:

Dome Metals

Sales/360 days = average daily sales
$144,000/360 = $400
Accounts receivable balance = $400 × 30 days = $12,000

$$\text{Receivable turnover} = \frac{\text{Sales}}{\text{Receivables}} = \frac{\$144,000}{\$12,000} = 12$$

or

$$360 \text{ days}/30 = 12x$$

7-20. If Dome offered a 2 percent discount for payment in 10 days and every customer took advantage of the new terms, what would the new average receivables balance be? Use the full sales of $144,000 for your calculation of receivables.

Solution:

$400 × 10 days = $4,000 new receivable balance

7-21. If Dome reduces its bank loans, which cost 10 percent, by the cash generated from reduced receivables, what will be the net gain or loss to the firm (don't forget the 2 percent discount)? Should it offer the discount?

Solution:

Old receivables – new receivables = Funds freed by
              with discount   discount

$12,000   – $4,000   = $8,000 discount

Savings on loan = 10% × $8,000..........	=	$ 800
Discount on sales = 2% × $144,000.....	=	(2,880)
Net change in income from discount....		$(2,080)

No! Don't offer the discount since the income from reduced bank loans do not offset the loss on the discount.

7-22.   Assume that the new trade terms of 2/10, net 30 will increase sales by 15 percent because the discount makes Dome's price competitive. If Dome earns 20 percent on sales before discounts, should it offer the discount? (Consider the same variables as you did for problems 17 through 19 as well as increased sales.)

Solution:

New sales	$= \$144,000 \times 1.15$	$= \$165,600$
Change in sales	$= \$165,600 - \$144,000 =$	$\$21,600$
Sales per day	$= \$165,600/360$	$= \$460$
Average receivables balance	$= \$460 \times 10$	$= \$4,600$

Increase profit on new sales	$= 20\% \times \$21,600 =$	$\$4,320$
Reduced profit because of discount	$= 2\% \times \$165,600 =$	$(3,312)$
Savings in interest cost $(\$12,000 - \$4,600) \times 10\% =$		740
Net change in income..		$\$1,748$

Yes, offer the discount because total profit increases.

Comprehensive Problem

CP 7-1.   Logan Distributing Company of Atlanta sells fans and heaters to retail outlets throughout the Southeast. Joe Logan, the president of the company, is thinking about changing the firm's credit policy to attract customers away from competitors. The present policy calls for a 1/10, net 30 cash discount. The new policy would call for a 3/10, net 50 cash discount. Currently, 30 percent of Logan customers are taking the discount, and it is anticipated that this number would go up to 50 percent with the new discount policy. It is further anticipated that annual sales would increase from a level of $400,000 to $600,000 as a result of the change in the cash discount policy.

The increased sales would also affect the inventory level carried by Logan. The average inventory carried by Logan is based on a determination of an EOQ. Assume sales of fans and heaters increase from 15,000 to 22,500 units. The ordering cost for each order is $200, and the carrying cost per unit is $1.50 (these values will not change with the discount). The average inventory is based on EOQ/2. Each unit in inventory has an average cost of $12.

Cost of goods sold is equal to 65 percent of net sales, general and administrative expenses are 15 percent of net sales, and interest payments of 14 percent will only be necessary for the increase in the accounts receivable and inventory balances. Taxes will be 40 percent of before-tax income.

a. Compute the accounts receivable balance before and after the change in the cash discount policy. Use the net sales (total sales minus cash discounts) to determine the average daily sales.

b. Determine EOQ before and after the change in the cash discount policy. Translate this into average inventory (in units and dollars) before and after the change in the cash discount policy.

c. Complete the income statement below.

	Before Policy Change	After Policy Change
Net sales (sales – cash discounts)		
Cost of goods sold		
Gross profit		
General and administrative expense		
Operating profit		
Interest on increase in accounts receivable and inventory (12%)		
Income before taxes		
Taxes		
Income after taxes		

d. Should the new cash discount policy be utilized? Briefly comment.

CP Solution:

Logan Distributing Company

a. Accounts receivable = average collection × average daily
$$\text{period} \qquad \text{sales}$$

Before

Average collection period

$.30 \times 10$	$=$	3
$.70 \times 30$	$=$	$\underline{21}$
		24 days

Average daily sales

$$\frac{\text{Credit sales} - \text{discount}}{360\,\text{days}} = \frac{\$400{,}000 - (.01)(.30)(\$400{,}000)}{360\,\text{days}}$$

$$= \frac{\$400{,}000 - \$1{,}200}{360\,\text{days}}$$

$$= \frac{\$398{,}800}{360\,\text{days}}$$

Average daily sales $= \$1{,}107.78$

Accounts receivable = 24 days × $1,107.78 = $26,586.72
before policy change

After

Average collection period

.50 × 10 = 5

.50 × 50 = 25

30 days

Average daily sales

$$\frac{\text{Credit sales} - \text{discount}}{360\,\text{days}} = \frac{\$600,000 - (.03)(.50)(\$600,000)}{360\,\text{days}}$$

$$= \frac{\$600,000 - \$9,000}{360\,\text{days}}$$

$$= \frac{\$591,000}{360\,\text{days}}$$

Average daily sales = $1,641.67

Accounts receivable = 30 days × $1,641.67 = $49,250.10
after policy change

b. **Before**

$$\text{EOQ} = \frac{2SO}{C}$$

$$\sqrt{\frac{2 \times 15,000 \times \$200}{\$1.50}} = \sqrt{\frac{\$6,000,000}{\$1.50}} = \sqrt{4,000,000} = 2,000 \text{ units}$$

After

$$\sqrt{\frac{2 \times 22,500 \times \$200}{\$1.50}} = \sqrt{\frac{\$9,000,000}{\$1.50}} = \sqrt{6,000,000} = 2,449.49 \text{ units}$$

Average inventory

Before

$$\frac{2,000}{2} = 1,000 \text{ units} \qquad 1,000 \text{ units} \times \$12 = \$12,000$$

After

$$\frac{2,449.49}{2} = \begin{array}{l} 1,224.75 \text{ units} \\ \text{or } 1,225 \text{ (rounded)} \end{array} \qquad \begin{array}{l} 1,224.75 \text{ units} \times \$12 = \\ \qquad \$14,697 \text{ or} \\ \qquad \$14,700 \\ \qquad \text{(rounded)} \end{array}$$

	Before Policy Change	After Policy Change
Net sales (sales – cash discount)	$398,800	$591,000
Cost of goods sold (65%)	259,220	384,150
Gross Profit	139,580	206,850
General and admin. Expense (15%)	59,820	88,650
Operating profit	79,760	118,200
* Interest on increase in accounts receivable and inventory (14%)		3,550.45
Income before taxes	79,760	114,649.55
Taxes (40%)	31,904	45,859.82
Income after taxes	$ 47,856	$68,789.73

$$*14\% \times AR \quad = 14\% \times (\$49,250.10 - \$26,586.72)$$
$$\qquad\qquad\quad = 14\% \times \$22,663.38 = \qquad \$3,172.87$$
$$14\% \times INV \quad = 14\% \times (\$14,697 - \$12,000)$$
$$\qquad\qquad\quad = 14\% \times \$2,697 \qquad = \qquad \underline{\$\ \ 377.58}$$
$$\qquad\qquad\qquad\qquad\qquad\qquad\qquad\qquad \$3,550.45$$

d. The new cash discount policy should be utilized. The interest cost on the increased accounts receivable and inventory is small in comparison to the increased operating profit from the policy change.

Chapter 8

Discussion Questions

8-1.   Under what circumstances would it be advisable to borrow money to take a cash discount?

It is advisable to borrow in order to take a cash discount when the cost of borrowing is less than the cost of foregoing the discount. If it cost us 36 percent to miss a discount, we would be much better off finding an alternate source of funds for 8 to 10 percent.

8-2.   Discuss the relative use of credit between large and small firms. Which group is generally in the net creditor position, and why?

Larger firms tend to be in a net creditor position because they have the financial resources to be suppliers to credit. The smaller firm must look to the larger manufacturer or wholesaler to help carry the firm's financing requirements.

8-3.   How have new banking laws influenced competition?

New banking laws allowed more competition and gave banks the right to expand across state lines to create larger, more competitive markets. They also increased bank mergers.

8-4.   What is the prime interest rate? How does the average bank customer fare in regard to the prime interest rate?

The prime rate is the rate that a bank charges its most creditworthy customers. The average customer can expect to pay one or two percent (or more) above prime.

8-5.   What does LIBOR mean? Is LIBOR normally higher or lower than the U.S. prime interest rate?

LIBOR stands for London Interbank Offered Rate. As indicated in Figure 8-1, it is consistently below the prime rate.

8-6. What advantages do compensating balances have for banks? Are the advantages to banks necessarily disadvantages to corporations?

The use of a compensating balance or minimum required account balance allows the banker to generate a higher return on a loan because not all funds are actually made available to the borrower. A $125,000 loan with a $25,000 compensating balance requirement means only $100,000 is being provided on a net basis. This benefit to the lender need not be a disadvantage to the borrower. The borrower may, in turn, receive a lower quoted interest rate and certain gratuitous services because of the compensating balance requirement.

8-7. A borrower is often confronted with a stated interest rate and an effective interest rate. What is the difference, and which one should the financial manager recognize as the true cost of borrowing?

The stated interest rate is the percentage rate unadjusted for time or method of repayment. The effective interest rate is the true rate and considers all these variables. A 5 percent stated rate for 90 days provides a 20 percent effective rate. The financial manager should recognize the effective rate as the true cost of borrowing. The effective rate is also referred to as the APR (Annual Percentage Rate).

8-8. Commercial paper may show up on corporate balance sheets as either a current asset or a current liability. Explain this statement.

Commercial paper can be either purchased or issued by a corporation. To the extent one corporation purchases another corporation's commercial paper as a short-term investment, it is a current asset. Conversely, if a corporation issues its own commercial paper, it is a current liability.

8-9. What are the advantages of commercial paper in comparison with bank borrowing at the prime rate? What is a disadvantage?

In comparison to bank borrowing, commercial paper can generally be issued at below the prime rate. Furthermore, there are no compensating balance requirements, though the firm is required to maintain approved credit lines at a bank. Finally, there is a certain degree of prestige associated with the issuance of commercial paper.

The drawback is that commercial paper may be an uncertain source of funds. When money gets tight or confidence in the commercial paper market diminishes, funds may not be available. There is no loyalty factor such as that which exists between a bank and its best borrowers.

8-10.   What is the difference between pledging accounts receivable and factoring accounts receivable?

Pledging accounts receivable means receivables are used as collateral for a loan; factoring account receivables means they are sold outright to a finance company.

8-11.   What is an asset-backed public offering?

A public offering is backed by an asset (accounts receivable) as collateral. Essentially a firm sells its receivables into the securities markets.

8-12.   Briefly discuss three types of lender control used in inventory financing.

Three types of lender control used in inventory financing are:

a. Blanket inventory – lien-general claim against inventory or collateral. No specific items are marked or designated.
b. Trust receipt – borrower holds the inventory in trust for the lender. Each item is marked and has a serial number. When the inventory is sold, the trust receipt is canceled and the funds go into the lender's account.
c. Warehousing – the inventory is physically identified, segregated, and stored under the direction of an independent warehouse company that controls the movement of the goods. If done on the premises of the warehousing firm, it is termed public warehousing. An alternate arrangement is field warehousing whereby the same procedures are conducted on the borrower's property.

8-13.   What is meant by hedging in the financial futures market to offset interest rate risks?

Hedging means to engage in a transaction that partially or fully reduces a prior risk exposure. In selling a financial futures contract, if interest rates go up, one is able to buy back the contract at a profit. This will help to offset the higher interest charges to a corporation or other business entity.

Problems

8-1.   Compute the cost of not taking the following cash discounts.

     a. 2/10, net 50.
     b. 2/15, net 40.
     c. 3/10, net 45.
     d. 3/10, net 180.

Solution:

$$\text{Cost of not taking a cash discount} = \frac{\text{Discount \%}}{100\% - \text{Disc. \%}} \times \frac{360}{\text{Final due date} - \text{Discont period}}$$

a. Cost of lost discount $= \dfrac{2\%}{98\%} \times \dfrac{360}{50-10} = 2.04\% \times 9.00 = 18.36\%$

b. Cost of lost discount $= \dfrac{2\%}{98\%} \times \dfrac{360}{40-15} = 2.04\% \times 14.40 = 29.38\%$

c. Cost of lost discount $= \dfrac{3\%}{97\%} \times \dfrac{360}{45-10} = 3.09\% \times 10.29 = 31.80\%$

d. Cost of lost discount $= \dfrac{3\%}{97\%} \times \dfrac{360}{180-10} = 3.09\% \times 2.12 = 6.55\%$

8-2. Regis Clothiers can borrow from its bank at 11 percent to take a cash discount. The terms of the cash discount are 2/15, net 60. Should the firm borrow the funds?

Solution:

Regis Clothiers

First, compute the cost of not taking the cash discount and compare this figure to the cost of the loan.

$$\text{Cost of not taking a cash discount} = \frac{\text{Discount \%}}{100\% - \text{Disc.\%}} \times \frac{360}{\text{final due date} - \text{discount period}}$$

$$= \frac{2\%}{98\%} \times \frac{360}{60 - 15}$$

$$= 2.04\% \times 8 = 16.32\%$$

The cost of not taking the cash discount is greater than the cost of the loan (16.32% vs. 11%). The firm should borrow the money and take the cash discount.

8-3. Your bank will lend you $2,000 for 45 days at a cost of $25 interest. What is your effective rate of interest?

Solution:

$$\text{Effective rate} = \frac{\text{Interest}}{\text{Principal}} \times \frac{\text{Days in the year (360)}}{\text{Days loan is outstanding}}$$

$$= \frac{\$25}{\$2,000} \times \frac{360}{45}$$

$$= 1.25\% \times 8 = 10\%$$

8-4.   Sol Pine is going to borrow $3,000 for one year at 8 percent interest. What is the effective rate of interest if the loan is discounted?

Solution:

Sol Pine

$$\text{Effective rate on a discounted loan} = \frac{\text{Interest}}{\text{Princ.} - \text{Int.}} \times \frac{\text{Days per year (360)}}{\text{Days loan is outstanding}}$$

$$= \frac{\$240}{\$3,000 - \$240} \times \frac{360}{360} = \frac{\$240}{\$2,760} \times 1$$

$$= 8.70\%$$

8-5.   Mary Ott is going to borrow $5,000 for 90 days and pay $140 interest. What is the effective rate of interest if the loan is discounted?

Solution:

Mary Ott

$$\text{Effective rate on a discounted loan} = \frac{\text{Interest}}{\text{Princ.} - \text{Int.}} \times \frac{\text{Days per year (360)}}{\text{Days loan is outstanding}}$$

$$= \frac{\$140}{\$5,000 - \$140} \times \frac{360}{90} = \frac{\$140}{\$4,860} \times 4$$

$$= 2.88\% \times 4 = 11.52\%$$

8-6.   McGriff Dog Food Company normally takes 20 days to pay for average daily credit purchases of $9,000. Its average daily sales are $10,000, and it collects accounts in 25 days.

a. What is its net credit position? That is, compute its accounts receivable and accounts payable and subtract the latter from the former.

Accounts receivable = Average daily credit sales × Average collection period

Accounts payable = Average daily credit purchases × Average payment period

b. If the firm extends its average payment period from 20 days to 32 days (and all else remains the same), what is the firm's new net credit position? Has it improved its cash flow?

Solution:
McGriff Dog Food Company

a. Net credit position = Accounts Receivable – Accounts payable

   Accounts receivable = average daily × average collection

                              credit sales   period

   $10,000 × 25 = $250,000

   Accounts payable = average daily × average payment

                              credit purchases   period

   Payment Period   = $9,000 × 20 = $180,000

   Net Credit Position = $250,000 – $180,000 = $70,000

b. Accounts Receivable will remain at $250,000
   Accounts Payable = $9,000 × 32 =   288,000
   Net Credit Position   ($ 38,000)

   The firm has improved its cash flow position. Instead of extending $70,000 more in credit (funds) than it is receiving, it has reversed the position and is the net recipient of $38,000 in credit.

8-7.   Logan Drilling Corp. plans to borrow $200,000 for one year. Northern National Bank will lend the money at 10 percent interest and require a compensating balance of 20 percent. What is the effective rate of interest?

Solution:

Logan Drilling Company

Effective rate of interest with 20% compensating balance =

$$\frac{\text{Interest rate}}{(1-C)} = \frac{10\%}{(1-.2)} = \frac{10\%}{.8} = 12.5\%$$

$$\frac{\text{Interest}}{\text{Principal} - \text{Compensating balance}} \times \frac{\text{Days of the Year (360)}}{\text{Days loan is outstanding}}$$

$$= \frac{\$20,000}{\$200,000 - \$40,000} \times \frac{360}{360} = \frac{\$20,000}{\$160,000} \times 1 = 12.5\%$$

8-8. Computer Graphics Company needs $250,000 in funds for a project.

a. With a compensating balance requirement of 20%, how much will the firm need to borrow?
b. Given your answer to part *a* and a stated interest rate of 10 percent on the total amount borrowed, what is the effective rate on the $250,000 actually being used?

Solution:

Computer Graphics Company

a. Amount to be borrowed $= \dfrac{\text{Amount needed}}{(1-C)}$

$$= \dfrac{\$250,000}{(1-.20)} = \dfrac{\$250,000}{.80}$$

$$= \$312,500$$

b. $\begin{array}{ll} \$312,500 & \text{total amount borrowed} \\ \underline{\quad 10\%} & \text{Interest rate} \\ \$\,31,250 & \text{Interest} \end{array}$

$\dfrac{\$31,250}{\$250,000} = 12.5\%$ Effective rate

8-9.   The Dade Company is borrowing $300,000 for one year and paying $27,000 in interest to Miami National Bank. The bank requires a 20 percent compensating balance. What is the effective rate of interest? What would be the effective rate if the company were required to make 12 monthly payments to retire the loan? The principal, as used in Formula 8-6, refers to funds the firm can effectively utilize (Amount borrowed—Compensating balance).

Solution:

The Dade Company

Effective rate of interest with 20% compensating balance =

$$\frac{\text{Interest}}{\text{Principal} - \text{Compensating balance}} \times \frac{\text{Days in the year} \left(360\right)}{\text{Days loan is outstanding}}$$

$$= \frac{\$27,000}{\$300,000 - \$60,000} \times \frac{360}{360} = \frac{\$27,000}{\$240,000} \times 1 = 11.25\%$$

Installment loan with compensating balance

$$\frac{2 \times \text{Annual no. payments} \times \text{Interest}}{\left(\text{Total no. of payments} + 1\right) \times \text{Principal}}$$

$$= \frac{2 \times 12 \times \$27,000}{\left(12 + 1\right) \times \left(\$300,000 - \$60,000\right)}$$

$$= \frac{\$648,000}{13 \times \$240,000} = \frac{\$648,000}{\$3,120,000} = 20.77\%$$

8-10.   Randall Corporation plans to borrow $200,000 for one year at 12 percent from the Waco State Bank. There is a 20 percent compensating balance requirement. Randall Corporation keeps minimum transaction balances of $10,000 in the normal course of business. This idle cash counts toward meeting the compensating balance requirement.

What is the effective rate of interest?

Solution:

Randall Corporation

Effective rate of interest =

$$\frac{\text{Interest}}{\text{Principal} - \text{Compensating balance}} \times \frac{\text{Days in the year} \left(360\right)}{\text{Days loan is outstanding}}$$

$$\frac{\$24,000}{\$200,000 - \$30,000 \,*} \times \frac{360}{360} = \frac{\$24,000}{\$170,000} = 14.12\%$$

$$*(\$40,000 - \$10,000)$$

8-11.   The treasurer for the Macon Blue Sox baseball team is seeking at $20,000 loan for one year from the 4th National Bank of Macon. The stated interest rate is 10 percent, and there is a 15 percent compensating balance requirement. The treasurer always keeps a minimum of $1,500 in the baseball team's checking accounts. These funds count toward meeting any compensating balance requirements.

What will be the effective rate of interest on this loan?

Solution:

Macon Blue Sox Baseball Team

Effective rate of interest =

$$\frac{\text{Interest}}{\text{Principal} - \text{Compensating balance}} \times \frac{\text{Days in the year} \left(360\right)}{\text{Days loan is outstanding}}$$

$$= \frac{\$2,000}{\$20,000 - \$1,500*} \times \frac{360}{360} = \frac{\$2,000}{\$18,500} = 10.81\%$$

$$*(\$3,000 - \$1,500)$$

8-12.   Your company plans to borrow $5 million for 12 months, and your banker gives you a stated rate of 14 percent interest. You would like to know the effective rate of interest for the following types of loans. (Each of the following parts stands alone.)

a. Simple 14 percent interest with a 10 percent compensating balance.
b. Discounted interest.
c. An installment loan (12 payments).
d. Discounted interest with a 5 percent compensating balance.

Solution:

a. Simple interest with a 10% compensating balance

$$\frac{\$700,000}{\$5,000,000 - \$500,000} \times 1 = \frac{\$700,000}{\$4,500,000} = 15.56\%$$

b. Discounted interest

$$\frac{\$700,000}{\$5,000,000 - \$700,000} \times 1 = \frac{\$700,000}{\$4,300,000} = 16.28\%$$

c. An installment loan with 12 payments

$$\frac{2 \times 12 \times \$700,000}{13 \times \$5,000,000} = \frac{\$16,800,000}{\$65,000,000} = 25.85\%$$

d. Discounted interest with a 5% compensating balance

$$\$700,000/(\$5,000,000 - \$700,000 - \$250,000) =$$

$$\$700,000/\$4,050,000 = 17.28\%$$

8-13.   If you borrow $4,000 at $55 interest for one year, what is your effective interest rate for the following payment plans?

    a. Annual payment.
    b. Semiannual payments.
    c. Quarterly payments.
    d. Monthly payments.

Solution:

a. $500/$4,000 = 12.5\%$

Use formula 8-6 for b, c, and d.

Rate on installment loan =

$$\frac{2 \times \text{Annual no. of payments} \times \text{Interest}}{(\text{Total no. of payments} + 1) \times \text{Principal}}$$

b. $(2 \times 2 \times \$500)/(3 \times \$4,000) = \$2,000/\$12,000$ $= 16.67\%$

c. $(2 \times 4 \times \$500)/(5 \times \$4,000) = \$4,000/\$20,000$ $= 20.00\%$

d. $(2 \times 12 \times \$500)/(13 \times \$4,000) = \$12,000/\$52,000$ $= 23.08\%$

8-14. Lewis and Clark Camping Supplies Inc. is borrowing $45,000 from Western State Bank. The total interest is $12,000. The loan will be paid by making equal monthly payments for the next three years.

What is the effective rate of interest on this installment loan?

Solution:
Lewis and Clark Camping Supplies

Rate on installment loan =

$$\frac{2 \times \text{Annual no. of payments} \times \text{Interest}}{(\text{Total no. of payments} + 1) \times \text{Principal}}$$

$$= \frac{2 \times 12 \times \$12,000}{(36 + 1) \times \$45,000} = \frac{\$288,000}{\$1,665,000} = 17.30\%$$

8-15.　　　Mr. Hugh Warner is a very cautious businessman. His supplier offers trade credit terms of 3/10, net 80. Mr. Warner never takes the discount offered, but he pays his suppliers in 70 days rather than the 80 days allowed so he is sure the payments are never late.

What is Mr. Warner's cost of not taking the cash discount?

Solution:

Hugh Warner

$$\text{Cost of not taking a cash discount} = \frac{\text{Discount \%}}{100\% - \text{Disc. \%}} \times \frac{360}{\text{Final due date} - \text{Discount period}}$$

$$= \frac{3\%}{100\% - 3\%} \times \frac{360}{(70 - 10)}$$

$$= 3.09\% \times 6 = 18.54\%$$

In this problem, Mr. Warner has the use of funds for 60 extra days (70-10), instead of 70 extra days (80-10). Mr. Warner's suppliers are offering terms of 3/10, net 80. Mr. Warner is effectively accepting terms of 3/10, net 70.

8-16.   The Reynolds Corporation buys from its suppliers on terms of 2/10, net 55, Reynolds has not been utilizing the discounts offered and has been taking 55 days to pay its bills.

Mr. Duke, Reynolds Corporation vice president, has suggested that the company begin to take the discounts offered. Duke proposes that the company borrow from its bank at a stated rate of 14 percent. The bank requires a 20 percent compensating balance on these loans. Current account balances would not be available to meet any of this compensating balance requirement.

Do you agree with Duke's proposal?

Solution:

Reynolds Corporation

$$\text{Cost of not taking a cash discount} = \frac{\text{Discount \%}}{100\% - \text{Disc.}\%} \times \frac{360}{\text{Final due date} - \text{Discount period}}$$

$$= \frac{2\%}{98\%} \times \frac{360}{(55-10)} = 2.04\% \times 8 = 16.32\%$$

Effective rate of interest with a 20% compensating balance requirement:

$$= \text{Interest rate}/(1 - C)$$
$$= 14\%/(1 - .2)$$
$$= 14\%/(.8) = 17.5\%$$

The effective cost of the loan, 17.5%, is more than the cost of passing up the discount, 16.32%. Reynolds Corporation should continue to pay in 55 days and pass up the discount.

8-17. In problem 16, if the compensating balance requirement were 10 percent instead of 20 percent, would you change your answer? Do the appropriate calculation.

Solution:

Reynolds Corporation (Continued)

Effective rate of interest with a 10% compensating balance requirement:

$$= \frac{\text{Interest rate}}{(1-C)} = \frac{14\%}{(1-.1)} = \frac{14\%}{(.9)} = 15.56\%$$

The answer now changes. The effective cost of the loan, 15.56%, is less than the cost of passing up the discount. Reynolds Corporation should borrow the funds and take the discount.

8-18. Neveready Flashlights, Inc. needs $300,000 to take a cash discount of 2/10, net 70. A banker will loan the money for 60 days at an interest cost of $5,500.

a. What is the effective rate on the bank loan?
b. How much would it cost (in percentage terms) if the firm did not take the cash discount, but paid the bill in 70 days instead of 10 days?
c. Should the firm borrow the money to take the discount?
d. If the banker requires a 20 percent compensating balance, how much must the firm borrow to end up with the $300,000?
e. What would be the effective interest rate in part b if the interest charge for 60 days were $6,850? Should the firm borrow with the 20 percent compensating balance? (The firm has no funds to count against the compensating balance requirement.)

Solution:

Neveready Flashlights, Inc.

a. Effective rate of interest $= \dfrac{\$5,500}{\$300,000} \times \dfrac{360}{60}$

$$= 1.83\% \times 6 = 10.98\%$$

b. Cost of lost discount $= \dfrac{2\%}{98\%} \times \dfrac{360}{(70-10)}$

$$= 2.04\% \times 6 = 12.24\%$$

c. Yes, because the cost of borrowing is less than the cost of losing the discount.

d. $\dfrac{\$300,000}{(1-C)} = \dfrac{\$300,000}{(1-.20)} = \dfrac{\$300,000}{.80} = \$375,000$ Amount needed to be borrowed

e. Effective interest rate $= \dfrac{\$6,850}{\$375,000 - \$75,000} \times \dfrac{360}{60}$

$$= \dfrac{\$6,850}{\$300,000} \times 6 = 2.28\% \times 6$$

$$= 13.68\%$$

No, do not borrow with a compensating balance of 20 percent since the effective rate is greater than the savings from taking the cash discount.

8-19.　　　Summit Record Company is negotiating with two banks for a $100,000 loan.

Fidelity Bank requires a 20 percent compensating balance, discounts the loan, and wants to be paid back in four quarterly payments. Southwest Bank requires a 10 percent compensating balance, does not discount the loan, but wants to be paid back in 12 monthly installments. The stated rate for both banks is 9 percent. Compensating balances will be subtracted from the $100,000 in determining the available funds in part a.

a.　Which loan should Summit accept?
b.　Recompute the effective cost of interest, assuming that Summit ordinarily maintains at each bank $20,000 in deposits that will serve as compensating balances.
c.　Does your choice of banks change if the assumption in part b is correct?

Solution:
Summit Record Company

a. Fidelity Bank

Effective interest rate

$$= \frac{2 \times 4 \times \$9,000}{(\$100,000 - \$20,000 - \$9,000) \times (4 + 1)}$$

$$= \$72,000 / \$355,000 = 20.28\%$$

Southwest Bank

Effective interest rate

$$= \frac{2 \times 12 \times \$9,000}{(\$100,000 - \$10,000) \times (12 + 1)}$$

$$= \$216,000 / \$1,170,000 = 18.46\%$$

Choose Southwest Bank since it has the lowest effective interest rate.

b. The numerators stay the same as in part (a) but the denominator increases to reflect the use of more money because compensating balances are already maintained at both banks.

Fidelity Bank

$$\text{Effective interest rate} = \$72{,}000/(\$100{,}000 - \$9{,}000) \times 5$$
$$= \$72{,}000/\$455{,}000 = 15.82\%$$

Southwest Bank

$$\text{Effective interest rate} = \$216{,}000/(\$100{,}000 \times 13)$$
$$= \$216{,}000/\$1{,}300{,}000 = 16.62\%$$

c. Yes. If compensating balances are maintained at both banks in the normal course of business, then Fidelity Bank should be chosen over Southwest Bank. The effective cost of its loan will be less.

8-20.   Charmin Paper Company sells to the 12 accounts listed below.

Account	Receivable Balance Outstanding	Average Age of the Account over the Last Year
A..............	$ 60,000	28
B..............	120,000	43
C..............	70,000	10
D..............	20,000	52
E	50,000	42
F	220,000	34
G..............	30,000	16
H..............	300,000	65
I	40,000	33
J..............	90,000	50
K..............	210,000	14
L	60,000	35

Capital Financial Corporation will lend 90 percent against account balances that have averaged 30 days or less; 80 percent for account balances between 31 and 40 days; and 70 percent for account balances between 41 and 45 days. Customers that take over 45 days to pay their bills are not considered acceptable accounts for a loan.

The current prime rate is 8.5 percent, and Capital charges 3.5 percent over prime to Charmin as its annual loan rate.

a. Determine the maximum loan for which Charmin Paper Company could qualify.
b. Determine how much one month's interest expense would be on the loan balance determined in part *a*.

Solution:

Charmin Paper Company

a.

0-30 days		Amount
A		$ 60,000
C		70,000
G		30,000
K		210,000
	Total	370,000
	loan %	90%
	loan	$333,000

31-40 days		Amount
F		$220,000
I		40,000
L		60,000
	Total	$320,000
	loan %	80%
	loan	$256,000

41-45 days		Amount
B		$120,000
E		50,000
	Total	$170,000
	loan %	70%
	loan	$119,000

Maximum Loan = $333,000 + $256,000 + $119,000 = $708,000

b.

Loan balances	$708,000	
Interest, 12% annual	(1%)	per month
One month's interest	$ 7,080	

8-21.

The treasurer for Pittsburgh Iron Works wishes to use financial futures to hedge her interest rate exposure. She will sell five Treasury futures contracts at $107,000 per contract. It is July and the contracts must be closed out in December of this year. Long-term interest rates are currently 7.3 percent. If they increase to 8.5 percent, assume the value of the contracts will go down by 10 percent. Also if interest rates do increase by 1.2 percent, assume the firm will have additional interest expense on its business loans and other commitments of $63,000. This expense, of course, will be separate from the futures contracts.

a. What will be the profit or loss on the futures contract if interest rates go to 8.5 percent?
b. Explain why a profit or loss took place on the futures contracts.
c. After considering the hedging in part a, what is the net cost to the firm of the increased interest expense of $63,000? What percent of this $63,000 cost did the treasurer effectively hedge away?
d. Indicate whether there would be a profit or loss on the futures contracts if interest rates went down.

Solution:

Pittsburgh Iron Works

a. Sales price, December Treasury bond contract
   (Sale takes place in July) $107,000
   Purchase price, December Treasury bond contract
      (10% price decline) .9 × $107,000 =   96,300
   Gain per contract $ 10,700
   Number of contracts   5
   Profit on futures contracts $ 53,500

b. A profit took place because the value of the bond went down due to increasing rates. This meant the subsequent purchase price was less than the initial sales price.

c. Increased interest cost $63,000
    Profit from hedging   53,500
    Net cost $ 9,500

$$\frac{\text{Net Cost}}{\text{Increased interest cost}} = \frac{\$9,500}{\$63,000} = 15.08\%$$

The net cost is 15.08%. This means 84.92% of the increased interest cost was hedged away.

d. If interest rates went down, there would be a loss on the futures contracts. The lower interest rates would lead to higher bond prices and a purchase price that exceeded the original sales price.

Chapter 9

Discussion Questions

9-1.   How is the future value (Appendix A) related to the present value of a single sum (Appendix B)?

The future value represents the expected worth of a single amount, whereas the present value represents the current worth.

$$FV = PV (1 + I)^n \text{ future value} \qquad PV = FV\left(\frac{1}{(1+i)^n}\right)\text{Present value}$$

9-2.   How is the present value of a single sum (Appendix B) related to the present value of an annuity (Appendix D)?

The present value of a single amount is the discounted value for one future payment, whereas the present value of an annuity represents the discounted value of a series of consecutive payments of equal amount.

9-3.   Why does money have a time value?

Money has a time value because funds received today can be reinvested to reach a greater value in the future. A person would rather receive $1 today than $1 in ten years, because a dollar received today, invested at 6 percent, is worth $1.791 after ten years.

9-4.   Does inflation have anything to do with making a dollar today worth more than a dollar tomorrow?

Inflation makes a dollar today worth more than a dollar in the future. Because inflation tends to erode the purchasing power of money, funds received today will be worth more than the same amount received in the future.

9-5.   Adjust the annual formula for a future value of a single amount at 12 percent for 10 years to a semiannual compounding formula. What are the interest factors (FV_{IF}) before and after? Why are they different?

$$FV = PV \times FV_{IF} \text{(Appendix A)}$$

    $i = 12\%, n = 10$ 3.106 Annual

    $i = 6\%, n = 20$ 3.207 Semiannual

The more frequent compounding under the semiannual compounding assumption increases the future value.

9-6.   If, as an investor, you had a choice of daily, monthly, or quarterly compounding, which would you choose? Why?

The greater the number of compounding periods, the larger the future value. The investor should choose daily compounding over monthly or quarterly.

9-7.   What is a deferred annuity?

A deferred annuity is an annuity in which the equal payments will begin at some future point in time.

9-8.   List five different financial applications of the time value of money.

Different financial applications of the time value of money:

Equipment purchase or new product decision,
Present value of a contract providing future payments,
Future worth of an investment,
Regular payment necessary to provide a future sum,
Regular payment necessary to amortize a lone,
Determination of return on an investment,
Determination of the value of a bond.

Problems

9-1.   You invest $2,500 a year for 3 years at 8%.

    a. What is the value of your investment after 1 year? Multiply $2,500 × 1.08.

    b. What is the value of your investment after 2 years? Multiply your answer to part a by 1.08.

    c. What is the value of your investment after 3 years? Multiply your answer to part b by 1.08. This gives you your final answer.

    d. Confirm that your final answer is correct by going to Appendix A (future value of a $1), and looking up the future value for n = 3, and I = 8%. Multiply this tabular value by $2,500 and compare your answer to the answer in part c. There may be a slight difference due to rounding.

Solution:

Future Value

a. $2,500 × 1.08 = $2,700

b. $2,700 × 1.08 = $2,916

c. $2,916 × 1.08 = $3,149.28

d. Appendix A (8%, 3 periods)

    $FV = PV \times FV_{IF}$

    $2,500 × 1.260 = $3,150

9-2.   What is the present value of:

a. $8,000 in 10 years at 6 percent?
b. $16,000 in 5 years at 12 percent?
c. $25,000 in 15 years at 8 percent?
d. $1,000 in 40 periods at 20 percent?

Solution:

Appendix B
$PV = FV \times PV_{IF}$

a. $ 8,000 \times .558 = \$4,464$

b. $\$16,000 \times .567 = \$9,072$

c. $\$25,000 \times .315 = \$7,875$

d. $ 1,000 \times .001 = \$1$

9-3.   If you invest $12,000 today, how much will you have:

a. In 6 years at 7 percent?
b. In 15 years at 12 percent?
c. In 25 years at 10 percent?
d. In 25 years at 10 percent (compounded semiannually)?

Solution:

Appendix A
$FV = PV \times FV_{IF}$

a. $\$12,000 \times 1.501 = \$ 18,012$

b. $\$12,000 \times 5.474 = \$ 65,688$

c. $\$12,000 \times 10.835 = \$130,020$

d. $\$12,000 \times 11.467 = \$137,604$ (5%, 50 periods)

9-4.   How much would you have to invest today to receive:

a. $12,000 in 6 years at 12 percent?
b. $15,000 in 15 years at 8 percent?
c. $5,000 each year for 10 years at 8 percent?
d. $40,000 each year for 40 years at 5 percent?

Solution:

Appendix B (a and b)
$PV = FV \times PV_{IF}$

a. $\$12,000 \times \quad .507 = \$ \ 6,084$

b. $\$15,000 \times \quad .315 = \$ \ 4,725$

Appendix D (c and d)

c. $\$ \ 5,000 \times \ 6.710 = \$ 33,550$

d. $\$40,000 \times 17.159 = \$686,360$

9-5.   If you invest $8,000 per period for the following number of periods, how much would you have?

a. 7 years at 9 percent
b. 40 years at 11 percent

Solution:

Appendix C
$FV_A = A \times FV_{IFA}$

a. $\$8,000 \times \quad 9.20 = \$ \quad 73,600$

b. $\$8,000 \times 581.83 = \$4,654,640$

9-6.   You invest a single amount of $12,000 for 5 years at 10 percent. At the end of 5 years you take the proceeds and invest them for 12 years at 15 percent. How much will you have after 17 years?

Solution:

Appendix A
$$FV = PV \times FV_{IF}$$
$12,000 \times 1.611 = \$ 19,332$

Appendix A
$$FV = PV \times FV_{IF}$$
$19,332 \times 5.350 = \$103,426$

9-7.   Mrs. Crawford will receive $6,500 a year for the next 14 years from her trust. If an 8 percent interest rate is applied, what is the current value of the future payments?

Solution:

Appendix D
$$PV_A = A \times PV_{IFA} \ (8\%, \ 14 \ periods)$$
$$= \$6,500 \times 8.244 = \$53,586$$

9-8.   John Longwaite will receive $100,000 in 50 years. His friends are very jealous of him. If the funds are discounted back at a rate of 14 percent, what is the present value of his future "pot of gold"?

Solution:

Appendix B
$$PV = FV \times PV_{IF} \ (14\%, \ 50 \ periods)$$
$$= \$100,000 \times .001 = \$100$$

9-9.   Carrie Tune will receive $19,500 a year for the next 20 years as a result of the new song she has written. If a 10 percent rate is applied, should she be willing to sell out her future rights now for $160,000?

Solution:

Appendix D

$$PV_A = A \times PV_{IFA} \ (10\%, 20 \text{ periods})$$

$$PV_A = \$19,500 \times 8.514 = \$166,023$$

No, the present value of the annuity is worth more than $160,000.

9-10.   General Mills will receive $27,500 for the next 10 years as a payment for a weapon he invented. If a 12 percent rate is applied, should he be willing to sell out his future rights now for $160,000.

Solution:

Appendix D

$$PV_A = A \times PV_{IFA} \ (12\%, 10 \text{ periods})$$

$$PV_A = \$27,500 \times 5.650 = \$155,375$$

Yes, the present value of the annuity is worth less than $160,000.

9-11.   Al Lopez invests $2,000 in a mint condition Nolan Ryan baseball card. He expects the card to increase in value by 20 percent a years for the next five years. After that, he anticipates a 15 percent annual increase for the next three years. What is the projected value of the card after eight years?

Solution:

Appendix A

$$FV = PV \times FV_{IF} \text{ (20\%, 5 periods)}$$
$$= \$2,000 \times 2,488 = \$4,976$$
$$FV = PV \times FV_{IF} \text{ (15\%, 3 periods)}$$
$$= \$4,976 \times 1.521 = \$7,568.50$$

9-12.   Martha Reed has been depositing $1,500 in her savings account every December since 1992. Her account earns 6 percent compounded annually. How much will she have in December of 2001? (Assume that a deposit is made in 2001. Make sure to count the years carefully.)

Solution:

Appendix C

$$FV_A = A \times FV_{IFA} \text{ (6\%, n = 10)}$$
$$FV_A = \$1,500 \times 13.181 = \$19,771.50$$

9-13.   At a growth (interest) rate of 8 percent annually, how long will it take for a sum to double? To triple? Select the year that is closest to the correct answer.

Solution:

Appendix A

If the sum is doubling, then the tabular value must equal 2.

In Appendix A, looking down the 8% column, we find the factor closest to 2 (1.999) on the 9-year row. The factor closest to 3 (2.937) is on the 14-year row.

9-14.   If you owe $30,000 payable at the end of five years, what amount should your creditor accept in payment immediately if she could earn 11 percent on her money?

Solution:

Appendix B
$$PV = FV \times PV_{IF} \text{ (11\%, 5 periods)}$$
$$PV = \$30,000 \times .593 = \$17,790$$

9-15.   Mr. Flint retired as president of the Color Tile Company but is current on a consulting contract for $45,000 per year for the next 10 years.

a. If Mr. Flint's opportunity cost (potential return) is 10 percent, what is the present value of his consulting contract?
b. Assuming that Mr. Flint will not retire for two more years and will not start to receive his 10 payments until the end of the third year, what would be the value of his deferred annuity?

Solution:
Using a Two Step Procedure

Appendix D

a. $PV_A = A \times PV_{IFA}$ (i = 10%, 10 periods)

$= \$45,000 \times 6.145 = \$276,525$

Appendix B

b. $PV = FV \times PV_{IF}$ (i = 10%, 2 periods)

$\$276,525 \times .826 = \$228,410$

Alternative Solution

Appendix D

a. $PV_A = A \times PV_{IFA}$ (10%, 10 periods)

$PV_A = \$45,000 \times 6.145 = \$276,525$

b. Deferred annuity-Appendix D

$PV_A = \$45,000 (6.814 - 1.736)$ where n = 12; n = 2 and i = 10%

$= \$45,000 (5.078)$

$= \$228,510$ (or use a two step solution)

The answer is slightly different from the answer above due to rounding in the tables.

9-16.   Cousin Bertha invested $100,000 10 years ago at 12 percent, compounded quarterly. How much has she accumulated?

Solution:

Appendix A

$FV = PV \times FV_{IF}$ (3%, 40 periods)

$FV = \$100,000 \times 3.262 = \$326,200$

9-17.   Determine the amount of money in a savings account at the end of 5 years, given an initial deposit of $3,000 and an 8 percent annual interest rate when interest is compounded (*a*) annually, (*b*) semiannually, and (*c*) quarterly.

Solution:

Appendix A

$FV = PV \times FV_{IF}$

a. $\$3,000 \times 1.469 = \$4,407$

b. $\$3,000 \times 1.480 = \$4,440$

c. $\$3,000 \times 1.486 = \$4,458$

9-18.   As stated in the chapter, the annuity payments are assumed to come at the end of each payment period (termed an ordinary annuity). However, an exception occurs when the annuity payments come at the beginning of each period (termed an annuity due). To find the present value of an annuity due, you subtract one from n an add 1 to the tabular value. To find the future value of an annuity, you add 1 to n and subtract 1 from the tabular value. For example, to find the future value of a $100 payment at the beginning of each period for five periods at 10 percent, you would go to Appendix C for $n = 6$ and $I = 10\%$. You look up a value of 7.716 and subtract 1 from it for an answer of 6.716 or $671.60 ($100 \times 6.716$).

What is the future value of a 10-year annuity of $2,000 per period where payments come at the beginning of each period. The interest rate is 8 percent.

Solution:

Appendix C

$$FV_A = A \times FV_{IFA}$$

$n = 11, i = 8\%$ $16.645 - 1 = 15.645$

$FV_A = \$2,000 \times 15.645 = \$31,290$

9-19.   Your grandfather has offered you a choice of one of the three following alternatives: $5,000 now; $1,000 a year for each years; or $12,000 at the end of eight years. Assuming you could earn 11 percent annually, which alternative should you choose? If you could earn 12 percent annually, would you still choose the same alternative?

Solution:

(first alternative) Present value of $5,000 received now:
$5,000

(second alternative) Present value of annuity of $1,000 for eight years: Appendix D

$$PV_A = A \times PV_{IFA}$$
$$= \$1,000 \times PV_{IFA} (11\%, 8 \text{ years})$$
$$= \$1,000 \times 5.146$$
$$= \$5,146$$

(third alternative) Present value of $12,000 received in eight years: Appendix B

$$PV = FV \times PV_{IF}$$
$$= \$12,000 \times PV_{IF} (11\%, 8 \text{ years})$$
$$= \$12,000 \times .434$$
$$= \$5,208$$

Select $12,000 to be received in eight years.

Revised answers based on 12%.

(first alternative) Present value of $5,000 received today:
$5,000

(second alternative) Present value of annuity of $1,000 at 12% for 8 years: Appendix D

$$PV_A = A \times PV_{IFA}$$
$$= \$1,000 \times PV_{IFA} \ (12\%, 8 \ \text{years})$$
$$= \$1,000 \times 4.968$$
$$= \$4,968$$

(third alternative) Present value of $12,000 received in 8 years at 12%: Appendix B

$$PV = FV \times PV_{IF}$$
$$= \$12,000 \times PV_{IF} \ (12\%, 8 \ \text{years})$$
$$= \$12,000 \times .404$$
$$= \$4,848$$

Select $5,000 now.

9-20.   You need $23,956 at the end of nine years, and your only investment outlet is a 7 percent long-term certificate of deposit (compounded annually). With the certificate of deposit, you make an initial investment at the beginning of the first year.

a.   What single payment could be made at the beginning of the first year to achieve this objective?
b.   What amount could you pay at the end of each year annually for nine years to achieve this same objective?

Solution:

a. Appendix B

$$PV = FV \times PV_{IF} \ (7\%, 9 \ \text{periods})$$
$$PV = \$23,956 \times .544 = \$13,032.06$$

b. Appendix C

$$A = FV_A / FV_{IFA}$$
$$A = \$23,956 / 11.978 = \$2,000$$

9-21.   Beverly Hills started a paper route on January 1, 1995. Every three months, she deposits $300 in her bank account, which earns 8 percent annually but is compounded quarterly. On December 31, 1998, she used the entire balance in her bank account to invest in a certificate of deposit at 12 percent annually. How much will she have on December 31, 2001?

Solution:

Appendix C

$FV_A = A \times FV_{IFA}$ (2%, 16 periods)

$FV_A = \$300 \times 18.639 = \$5,591.70$ after four years

Appendix A

$FV = PV \times FV_{IF}$ (12%, 3 periods)

$FV = \$5,591.70 \times 1.405$

$FV = \$7,856.34$ after three more years

9-22. On January 1, 1999, Mr. Dow bought 100 shares of stock at $12 per share. On December 31, 2001, he sold the stock for $18 per share.

What is his annual rate of return? Interpolate to find the answer.

Solution:

Appendix B

$$PV_{IF} = \frac{PV}{FV}$$

$$PV_{IF} = \frac{\$12}{\$18} = .667 \text{ Return is between } 14\% - 15\% \text{ for 3 years}$$

PV_{IF} at 14%	.675
PV_{IF} at 15%	$-.658$
	.017

PF_{IF} at 14%	.675
PV_{IF} computed	$-.667$
	.008

14% + (.008/.017) (1%)
14% + .471 (1%)
14.47%

9-23.   Tom Phillips has just invested $8,760 for his son (age one). This money will be used for his son's education 17 years from now. He calculates that he will need $60,000 by the time the boy goes to school.

What rate of return will Mr. Phillips need in order to achieve this goal?

Solution:

Appendix B

$$PV_{IF} = \frac{PV}{FV} \text{ (17 periods)}$$

$$PV_{IF} = \frac{\$8,760}{\$60,000} = .146 \quad \text{Rate of return} = 12\%$$

9-24.   C. D. Rom has just given an insurance company $30,000. In return, he will receive an annuity of $3,200 for 20 years.

At what rate of return must the insurance company invest this $30,000 in order to make the annual payments? Interpolate.

Solution:

Appendix D

$$PV_{IFA} = PV_A/A \text{ (20 periods)}$$
$$= \$30,000/\$3,200$$
$$= 9.375 \text{ is between 8\% and 9\% for 20 periods}$$

PV_{IFA} at 8%	9.818
PV_{IFA} at 9%	−9.129
	.689

PV_{IFA} at 8%	9.818
PV_{IFA} computed	−9.375
	.443

$$8\% + (.443/.689)(1\%)$$
$$8\% + .643(1\%) = 8.64\%$$

9-25.   Frank Bell has just retired from the telephone company. His total pension funds have an accumulated value of $200,000, and his life expectancy is 16 more years. His pension fund manager assumes he can earn a 12 percent return on his assets.

What will be his yearly annuity for the next 16 years?

Solution:

Appendix D

$$
\begin{aligned}
A &= PV_A/PV_{IFA}\ (12\%,\ 16\ \text{periods}) \\
&= \$200,000/6.974 \\
&= \$28,677.95
\end{aligned}
$$

9-26.   Dr. Oats, a nutrition professor, invests $80,000 in a piece of land that is expected to increase in value by 14 percent per year for the next five years. She will then take the proceeds and provide herself with a 10-year annuity. Assuming a 14 percent interest rate for the annuity, how much will this annuity be?

Solution:

Appendix A

$$
\begin{aligned}
FV &= PV \times FV_{IF}\ (14\%,\ 5\ \text{periods}) \\
FV &= \$80,000 \times 1.925 = \$154,000
\end{aligned}
$$

Appendix D

$$
\begin{aligned}
A &= PV_A/PV_{IFA}\ (14\%,\ 10\ \text{periods}) \\
A &= \$154,000/5.216 = \$29,524.54
\end{aligned}
$$

9-27.   You wish to retire in 20 years, at which time you want to have accumulated enough money to receive an annuity of $12,000 for 25 years after retirement. During the period before retirement you can earn 8 percent annually, while after retirement you can earn 10 percent on your money.

What annual contributions to the retirement fund will allow you to receive the $12,000 annuity?

Solution:

Determine the present value of an annuity during retirement: Appendix D

$$PV_A = A \times PV^{IFA} (10\%, 25 \text{ years})$$
$$= \$12,000 \times 9.077 = \$108,924$$

To determine the annual deposit into an account earning 8% that is necessary to accumulate $108,924 after 20 years, use the Future Value of an Annuity table: Appendix C

$$A = FV_A/FV_{IFA} (8\%, 20 \text{ years})$$

$$= \frac{\$108,924}{45.762} = \$2,380.23 \text{ annual contribution}$$

9-28.
Judy Green has purchased an annuity to begin payment at the end of 2003 (the date of the first payment). Assume it is now the beginning of 2001. The annuity is for $12,000 per year and is designed to last eight years.

If the discount rate for the calculation is 11 percent, what is the most she should have paid for the annuity?

Solution:

Appendix D will give a factor for a 8 years annuity when the appropriate discount rate is 11 percent (5.146). The value of the annuity at the beginning of the year it starts (2003) is:

$$PV_A = A \times PV_{IFA} \text{ (11\%, 8 periods)}$$
$$= \$12,000 \times 5.146$$
$$= \$61,752$$

The present value at the beginning of 2001 is found using Appendix B (2 years at 11%). The factor is .812. Note we are discounting from the beginning of 2003 to the beginning of 2001.

$$PV = PV \times PV_{IF} \text{ (11\%, 2 periods)}$$
$$= \$61,752 \times .812$$
$$= \$50,142.62$$

The maximum that should be paid for the annuity is $50,142.62.

9-29.   If you borrow $9,725 and are required to pay back the loan in five equal annual installments of $2,500, what is the interest rate associated with the loan?

Solution:

Appendix D
$$PV_{IFA} = PV_A/A \text{ (5 periods)}$$
$$= \$9,725/\$2,500$$
$$= 3.890$$

Interest rate = 9 percent

9-30.   Tom Busby owes $20,000 now. A lender will carry the debt for four more years at 8 percent interest. That is, in this particular case, the amount owed will go up 8 percent per year for four years. The lender then will require Busby to pay off the loan over 12 years at 11 percent interest. What will his annual payments be?

Solution:

Appendix A
$$FV = PV \times FV_{IFA} \text{ (8\%, 4 periods)}$$
$$FV = \$20,000 \times 1.360$$
$$= \$27,200$$

Appendix D
$$A = PV_A/PV_{IFA} \text{ (11\%, 12 periods)}$$
$$= \$27,200/6.492$$
$$= \$4,189.77$$

9-31.   If your aunt borrows $50,000 from the bank at 10 percent interest over the eight-year life of the loan, what equal annual payments must be made to discharge the loan, plus pay the bank its required rate of interest (round to the nearest dollar)? How much of her first payment will be applied to interest? To principal? How much of her second payment will be applied to each?

Solution:

Appendix D
$$A = PV_A/PV_{IFA} \ (10\%, \ 8 \ \text{periods})$$
$$= \$50,000/5.335$$
$$= \$9,372.07$$

First payment:
$\$50,000 \times .10$	$= \$5,000$ interest
$\$9,372.07 - \$5,000$	$= \$4,372.07$ applied to principal

Second payment: First determine remaining principal
$\$50,000 - \$4,372.07$	$= \$45,627.93$
$\$45,627.93 \times .10$	$= \$4,562.79$ interest
$\$9,372.07 - \$4,562.79$	$= \$4,809.28$ applied to principal

9-32.   Jim Thomas borrows $70,000 at 12 percent interest toward the purchase of a home. His mortgage is for 30 years.

a. How much will his annual payments be? (Although home payments are usually on a monthly basis, we shall do our analysis on an annual basis for ease of computation. We get a reasonably accurate answer.)
b. How much interest will he pay over the life of the loan?
c. How much should he be willing to pay to get out of a 12 percent mortgage and into a 10 percent mortgage with 30 years remaining on the mortgage? Suggestion: Find the annual savings and then discount them back to the present at the current interest rate (10 percent).

Solution:

Appendix D

a. $A = PV_A/PV_{IFA}$ (12%, 30 periods)
  $= \$70{,}000/8.055$
  $= \$8{,}690.25$

b.
$ 8,690.25	annual payments
× 30	years
$260,707.50	total payment
− 70,000.00	repayment of principal
$190,707.50	

Appendix D

c. New payments at 10%

$A = PV_A/PV_{IFA}$ (10%, 30 periods)
  $= \$70{,}000/9.427$
  $= \$7{,}425.48$

Difference between old and new payments

$8,690.25	old
7,425.48	new
$1,264.77	difference

P.V. of difference-Appendix D

$PV_A = A \times PV_{IFA}$ (assumes 10% discount rate, 30 periods)
  $= \$1{,}264.77 \times 9.427$
  $= \$11{,}922.99$ Amount that could be paid to refinance

9-33.   You are chairperson of the investment fund for the Continental Soccer League. You are asked to set up a fund of semiannual payments to be compounded semiannually to accumulate a sum of $200,000 after ten years at an 8 percent annual rate (20 payments). The first payment into the fund is to take place six months from today, and the last payment is to take place at the end of the tenth year.

a. Determine how much the semiannual payment should be. (Round to whole numbers.)

On the day after the sixth payment is made (the beginning of the fourth year) the interest rate goes up to a 10 percent annual rate, and you can earn a 10 percent annual rate on funds that have been accumulated as well as all future payments into the fund. Interest is to be compounded semiannually on all funds.

b. Determine how much the revised semiannual payments should be after this rate change (there are 14 payments and compounding dates). The next payment will be in the middle of the fourth year. (Round all values to whole numbers.)

Solution:

Appendix C

a. A $= FV_A/FV_{IFA}$

            $= \$200,000/29.778$ (4%, 20 periods)

            $= \$6,716$

b. First determine how much the old payments are equal to after 6 periods at 4%. Appendix C.

FV_A $= A \times FV_{IFA}$ (4%, 6 periods)

           $= \$6,716 \times 6.633$

           $= \$44,547$

Then determine how much this value will grow to after 14 periods at 5%.

Appendix A

$$FV = PV \times FV_{IF} \text{ (5\%, 14 periods)}$$
$$= \$44{,}547 \times 1.980$$
$$= 88{,}203$$

Subtract this value from $200,000 to determine how much you need to accumulate on the next 14 payments.

$200,000
− 88,203
$111,797

Determine the revised semi-annual payment necessary to accumulate this sum after 14 periods at 5%.

Appendix C

$$A = FV_A / FV_{IFA}$$
$$A = \$111{,}797 / 19.599$$
$$A = \$5{,}704$$

9-34.   Your younger sister, Jennifer, will start college in five years. She has just informed your parents that she wants to go to Eastern State U., which will cost $18,000 per year for four years (cost assumed to come at the end of each year). Anticipating Jennifer's ambitions, your parents started investing $3,000 per year five years ago and will continue to do so for five more years.

How much more will your parents have to invest each year for the next five years to have the necessary funds for Jennifer's education? Use 10 percent as the appropriate interest rate throughout this problem (for discounting or compounding). Round all values to whole numbers.

Solution:

Present value of college costs

Appendix D
$$PV_A = A \times PV_{IFA} \ (10\%, \ 4 \ \text{periods})$$
$$= \$18,000 \times 3.170$$
$$= \$57,060$$

Accumulation based on investing \$3,000 per year for 10 years.

Appendix C
$$FV_A = A \times FV_{IFA} \ (10\%, \ 10 \ \text{periods})$$
$$= \$3,000 \times 15.937$$
$$= \$47,811$$

Additional funds required 5 years from now.

\$57,060	PV of college costs
47,811	Accumulation based on \$3,000 per year
\$ 9,249	Additional funds required

Added contribution for the next 5 years

Appendix C
$$A = FV_A / FV_{IFA} \ (10\%, \ 5 \ \text{periods})$$
$$= \$9,249/6.105$$
$$= \$1,515$$

9-35.

Jennifer (from problem 34) is now 18 years old (five years have passed), and she wants to get married instead of going to college. Your parents have accumulated the necessary funds for her education.

Instead of her schooling, your parents are paying $7,000 for her current wedding and plan to take year-end vacations costing $2,000 per year for the next three years.

How much money will your parents have at the end of three years to help you with graduate school, which you will start then? You plan to work on a master's perhaps a Ph.D. If graduate school costs $18,930 per year, approximately how long will you be able to stay in school based on these funds? Use 10 percent as the appropriate interest rate throughout this problem. (Round all values to whole numbers.)

Solution:

Funds available after the wedding

$57,060	Funding available before the wedding
– 7,000	Wedding
$50,060	Funds available after the wedding

Less present value of vacation

Appendix D

$$PV_A = A \times PV_{IFA} \ (10\%, 3 \text{ periods})$$
$$= \$2,000 \times 2.487 = \$4,974$$

$50,060	
– 4,974	
$45,086	Remaining funds for graduate school

Appendix A

$$FV = PV \times FV_{IF} \ (10\%, \ 3 \ \text{periods})$$

$$= \$45{,}086 \times 1.331$$

$$= \$60{,}009 \ \text{Funds available for starting graduate school}$$

Number of years of graduate education

Appendix D

$$PV_{IFA} = \frac{PV_A}{A} \ (10\%)$$

$$= \frac{\$60{,}009}{\$18{,}930} = 3.170 \ (\text{rounded})$$

with $i = 10\%$, $n = 4$ for 3.170, the answer is 4 years.

Chapter 10

Discussion Questions

10-1.   How is valuation of any financial asset related to future cash flows?

The valuation of a financial asset is equal to the present value of future cash flows.

10-2.   Why might investors demand a lower rate of return for an investment in Exxon as compared to Armco Steel or Boston Chicken, Inc.?

Because Exxon has less risk than Armco Steel or Boston Chicken. Exxon has relatively high returns and a strong market position; the latter two firms have had financial difficulties.

10-3.   What are the three factors that influence the required rate of return by investors?

The three factors that influence the demanded rate of return are:

a. The real rate of return
b. The inflation premium
c. The risk premium

10-4.   If inflationary expectations increase, what is likely to happen to yield to maturity on bonds in the marketplace? What is also likely to happen to the price of bonds?

If inflationary expectations increase, the yield to maturity (required rate of return) will increase. This will mean a lower bond price.

10-5.   Why is the remaining time to maturity an important factor in evaluating the impact of a change in yield to maturity on bond prices?

The longer the time period remaining to maturity, the greater the impact of a difference between the rate the bond is paying and the current yield to maturity (required rate of return). For example, a two percent ($20) differential is not very significant for one year, but very significant for 20 years. In the latter case, it will have a much greater effect on the bond price.

10-6.   What are the three adjustments that have to be made in going from annual to semiannual bond analysis?

The three adjustments in going from annual to semiannual bond analysis are:

1. Divide the annual interest rate by two.
2. Multiply the number of years by two.
3. Divide the annual yield to maturity by two.

10-7.   Why is a change in required yield for preferred stock likely to have a greater impact on price than a change in required yield for bonds?

The longer the life of an investment, the greater the impact of a change in the required rate of return. Since preferred stock has a perpetual life, the impact is likely to be at a maximum.

10-8.   What type of dividend pattern for common stock is similar to the dividend payment for preferred stock?

The no-growth pattern for common stock is similar to the dividend on preferred stock.

10-9.   What two conditions must be met to go from Formula 10-8 to Formula 10-9 in using the dividend valuation model?

$$P_0 = \frac{D_1}{K_e - g} \qquad (10-9)$$

To go from Formula (10-8) to Formula (10-9):

The firm must have a constant growth rate (g).
The discount rate (K_e) must exceed the growth rate (g).

10-10.   What two components make up the required rate of return on common stock?

The two components that make up the required return on common stock are:

a. The dividend yield D_1/P_0.
b. The growth rate (g). This actually represents the anticipated growth in dividends, earnings, and stock price over the long term.

10-11.   What factors might influence a firm's price-earnings ratio?

The price-earnings ratio is influenced by the earnings and sales growth of the firm, the risk (or volatility in performance), the debt-equity structure of the firm, the dividend policy, the quality of management, and a number of other factors. Firms that have bright expectations for the future tend to trade at high P/E ratios while the opposite is true of low P/E firms.

10-12.   How is the supernormal growth pattern likely to vary from the normal, constant growth pattern?

A supernormal growth pattern is represented by very rapid growth in the early years of a company or industry that eventually levels off to more normal growth. The supernormal growth pattern is often experienced by firms in emerging industries, such as in the early days of electronics or microcomputers.

10-13.   What approaches can be taken in valuing a firm's stock when there is no cash dividend payment?

In valuing a firm with no cash dividend, one approach is to assume that at some point in the future a cash dividend will be paid. You can then take the present value of future cash dividends.

A second approach is to take the present value of future earnings as well as a future anticipated stock price. The discount rate applied to future earnings is generally higher than the discount rate applied to future dividends.

Problems

(For the first 11 bond problems, assume interest payments are on an annual basis.)

10-1.   The Lone Star Company has $1,000 par value bonds outstanding at 9 percent interest. The bonds will mature in 20 years. Compute the current price of the bonds if the present yield to maturity is:

a. 6 percent.
b. 8 percent.
c. 12 percent.

Solution:
Lone Star Company

a. 6 percent yield to maturity

Present Value of Interest Payments

$PV_A = A \times PV_{IFA}$ (n = 20, I = 6%)   Appendix D

$PV_A = 90 \times 11.470 = \$1,032.30$

Present Value of Principal Payment at Maturity

$PV = FV \times PV_{IF}$ (n = 20, I = 6%)   Appendix B

$PV = 1,000 \times .312 = \$312$

Total Present Value

Present Value of Interest Payments	$1,032.30
Present Value of Principal Payments	312.00
Total Present Value or Price of the Bond	$1,344.30

b. 8 percent yield to maturity

$$PV_A = A \times PV_{IFA} \ (n = 20, I = 8\%)$$ Appendix D
$$PV_A = \$90 \times 9.818 = \$883.62$$

$$PV = FV \times PV_{IF} \ (n = 20, I = 8\%)$$ Appendix B
$$PV = \$1,000 \times .215 = \$215$$

$$
\begin{array}{r}
\$ \ \ 883.62 \\
\underline{215.00} \\
\$1,098.62
\end{array}
$$

c. 12 percent yield to maturity

$$PV_A = A \times PV_{IFA} \ (n = 20, I = 12\%)$$ Appendix D
$$PV_A = \$90 \times 7.469 = \$672.21$$

$$PV = FV \times PV_{IF} \ (n = 20, I = 12\%)$$ Appendix B
$$PV = \$1,000 \times .104 = \$104$$

$$
\begin{array}{r}
\$672.21 \\
\underline{104.00} \\
\$776.21
\end{array}
$$

10-2. Applied Software has $1,000 par value bonds outstanding at 12 percent interest. The bonds will mature in 25 years. Compute the current price of the bonds if the present yield to maturity is:

a. 11 percent.
b. 13 percent.
c. 16 percent.

Solution:

Applied Software

a. 11 percent yield to maturity

Present Value of Interest Payment

$PV_A = A \times PV_{IFA}$ (n = 25, i = 11%) Appendix D

$PV_A = \$120 \times 8.422 = \$1,010.64$

Present Value of Principal Payment at Maturity

$PV = FV \times PV_{IF}$ (n = 25, i = 11%) Appendix B

$PV = \$1,000 \times .074 = \$74$

Total Present Value

Present Value of Interest Payments	$1,010.64
Present Value of Principal Payments	74.00
Total Present Value or Price of the Bond	$1,084.64

b. 13 percent yield to maturity

$PV_A = A \times PV_{IFA}$ (n = 25, i = 13%) Appendix D

$PV_A = \$120 \times 7.330 = \$879.60$

$PV = FV \times PV_{IF}$ (n = 25, i = 13%) Appendix B

$PV = \$1,000 \times .047 = \$47$

$879.60
47.00
$926.60

c. 16 percent yield to maturity

$$PV_A = A \times PV_{IFA} \ (n = 25, i = 16\%)$$ Appendix D

$$PV_A = \$120 \times 6.097 = \$731.64$$

$$PV = FV \times PV_{IF} \ (n = 25, i = 16\%)$$ Appendix B

$$PV = \$1,000 \times .024 = \$24.00$$

$$\begin{array}{r} \$731.64 \\ \underline{24.00} \\ \$755.64 \end{array}$$

10-3.   Essex Biochemical Co. has a $1,000 par value bond outstanding that pays 10 percent annual interest. The current yield to maturity on such bonds in the market is 7 percent. Compute the price of the bonds for these maturity dates:

a.   30 years.
b.   15 years.
c.   1 year.

Solution:

Essex Biochemical

a. 30 years to maturity

Present Value of Interest Payment

$$PV_A = A \times PV_{IFA} \ (n = 30, i = 7\%)$$ Appendix D

$$PV_A = \$100 \times 12.409 = \$1,240.90$$

$$PV = FV \times PV_{IF} \ (n = 30, i = 7\%)$$ Appendix B

$$PV = \$1,000 \times .131 = \$131$$

Total Present Value

Present Value of Interest Payments	$1,240.90
Present Value of Principal Payments	131.00
Total Present Value or Price of the Bond	$1,371.90

b. 15 years to maturity

$$PV_A = A \times PV_{IFA}\ (n = 15,\ i = 7\%) \qquad \text{Appendix D}$$

$$PV_A = \$100 \times 9.108 = \$910.80$$

$$PV = FV \times PV_{IF}\ (n = 15,\ i = 7\%) \qquad \text{Appendix B}$$

$$PV = \$1,000 \times .362 = \$362$$

$$
\begin{aligned}
&\$\ 910.80 \\
&\ \ \underline{362.00} \\
&\$1,272.80
\end{aligned}
$$

c. 1 year to maturity

$$PV = FV \times PV_{IF} \qquad \text{Appendix D}$$

$$PV = \$100 \times .935 = \$93.50$$

$$PV = FV \times PV_{IF} \qquad \text{Appendix B}$$

$$PV = \$1,000 \times .935 = \$935$$

$$
\begin{aligned}
&\$\ \ \ 93.50 \\
&\ \ \underline{935.00} \\
&\$1,028.00
\end{aligned}
$$

10-4.   The Hartford Telephone Company has a $1,000 par value bond outstanding that pays 11 percent annual interest. The current yield to maturity on such bonds in the market is 14 percent. Compute the price of the bonds for these maturity dates:

a. 30 years.
b. 15 years.
c. 1 year.

Solution:

Hartford Telephone Company

a. 30 years to maturity

$$PV_A = A \times PV_{IFA} \ (n = 30, i = 14\%) \qquad \text{Appendix D}$$
$$PV_A = \$110 \times 7.003 = \$770.33$$

$$PV = FV \times PV_{IF} \ (n = 30, i = 14\%) \qquad \text{Appendix B}$$
$$PV = \$1,000 \times 0.02 = \$20$$

$$\begin{array}{r} \$770.33 \\ \underline{20.00} \\ \$790.33 \end{array}$$

b. 15 years to maturity

$$PV_A = A \times PV_{IFA} \ (n = 15, i = 14\%) \qquad \text{Appendix D}$$
$$PV_A = \$110 \times 6.142 = \$675.62$$

$$PV = FV \times PV_{IF} \ (n = 15, i = 14\%) \qquad \text{Appendix B}$$
$$PV = \$1,000 \times .140 = \$140$$

$$\begin{array}{r} \$675.62 \\ \underline{140.00} \\ \$815.62 \end{array}$$

c. 1 year to maturity

$$PV_A = A \times PV_{IFA} \ (n = 1, \ i = 14\%) \qquad \text{Appendix D}$$

$$PV_A = \$110 \times .877 = \$96.47$$

$$PV = FV \times PV_{IF} \ (n = 1, \ i = 14\%) \qquad \text{Appendix B}$$

$$PV = \$1{,}000 \times .877 = \$877.00$$

$$
\begin{aligned}
& \$\ \ 96.47 \\
& \underline{\ \ 877.00} \\
& \$973.47
\end{aligned}
$$

10-5.   For Problem 4 graph the relationship in a manner similar to the bottom half.
Bond maturity effect of Figure 10-2 in the chapter. Also explain why the
pattern of price change takes place.

Solution:

Hartford Telephone Company (continued)

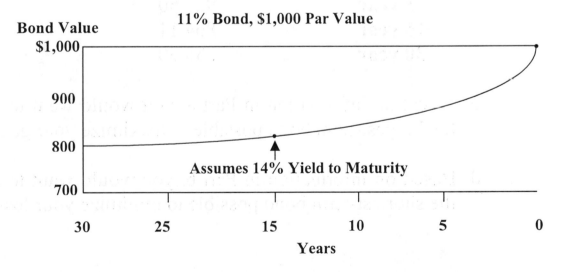

As the time to maturity becomes less and less, the
importance of the difference between the rate the bond pays
and the yield to maturity becomes less significant.
Therefore, the bond trades closer to par value.

10-6.   Using Table 10-2

   a. Assume the interest rate in the market (yield to maturity) goes down to 8%
       for the 10% bonds. Using column 2, indicate what the bond price will be
       with a 5-year, a 15-year, and a 30-year time period.
   b. Assume the interest rate in the market (yield to maturity) goes up to 12%
       for the 10% bonds. Using column 3, indicate what the bond price will be
       with a 5-year, a 10-year, and a 30-year period.
   c. Based on the information in part *a*, if you think interest rates in the market
       are going down, which bond would you choose to own?
   d. Based on information in part *b*, if you think interest rates in the market are
       going up, which bond would you choose to own?

Solution:

   a.   **Maturity**   **Bond price**
           5 year $1,080.30
          15 year   1,170.90
          30 year   1,224.80

   b.   **Maturity**   **Bond price**
          5 year   927.50
         15 year   864.11
         30 year   838.50

c. Based on information in Part a, you would want to own
    the longest-term bond possible to maximize your gain.

d. Based on information in Part b, you would want to own
    the shortest-term bond possible to minimize your loss.

10-7.   Ron Rhodes calls his broker to inquire about purchasing a bond of Golden Years Recreation Corporation. His broker quotes a price of $1,170. Ron is concerned that the bond might be overpriced based on the facts involved. The $1,000 par value bond pays 13 percent interest, and it has 18 years remaining until maturity. The current yield to maturity on similar bonds is 11 percent.

Do you think the bond is overpriced? Do the necessary calculations.

Solution:

Ron Rhodes – Golden Years Recreation Corporation

Present Value of Interest Payments

$PV_A = A \times PV_{IFA}$ (n = 18, i = 11%)   Appendix D

$PV_A = \$130 \times 7.702 = \$1,001.26$

Present Value of Principal Payment at Maturity

$PV = FV \times PV_{IF}$ (n = 18, i = 11%)   Appendix B

$PV = \$1,000 \times .153 = \$153$

$$\begin{array}{r} \$1,001.26 \\ \underline{153.00} \\ \$1,154.26 \end{array}$$

The bond has a value of $1,154.26. This indicates his broker is quoting too high a price at $1,170.

10-8.   Tom Cruise Lines, Inc., issued bonds 5 years ago at $1,000 per bond. These bonds had a 25-year life when issued and the annual interest payment was then 12 percent. This return was in line with the required returns by bondholders at that point as described below:

Real rate of return	3%
Inflation premium	5
Risk premium	4
Total return	12%

Assume that five years later the inflation premium is only 3 percent and is appropriately reflected in the required return (or yield to maturity) of the bonds. The bonds have 20 years remaining until maturity.

Compute the new price of the bond.

Solution:

Tom Cruise Lines, Inc.

First compute the new required rate of return (yield to maturity).

Real rate of return	3%
Inflation premium	3
Risk premium	4
Total return	10%

Then use this value to find the price of the bond.

Present Value of Interest Payments

$PV_A = A \times PV_{IFA}$ (n = 20, i = 10%)   Appendix D

$PV_A = \$120 \times 8.514 = \$1,021.68$

Present Value of Principal Payment at Maturity

$PV = FV \times PV_{IF}$ (n = 20, i = 10%)   Appendix B

$PV = \$1,000 \times .149 = \$149$

$$\begin{array}{r} \$1,021.68 \\ \underline{149.00} \\ \$1,170.68 \end{array}$$

10-9.   Further analysis of problem 8:

a.   Find the present value of 2 percent × $1,000 (or $20) for 20 years at 10
     percent. The $20 is assumed to be an annual payment.
b.   Add this value to $1,000.
c.   Explain why the answer to problem 7b and problem 6 are basically the
     same. (There is a slight difference due to rounding in the tables.)

Solution:
Further Analysis of Problem 8

a. $PV_A = A \times PV_{IFA}$ (n = 20, I = 10%)   Appendix D

   $PV_A = \$20 \times 8.514 = \$170.28$

b. $1,000.00
      170.28
    ‾‾‾‾‾‾‾‾‾
    $1,170.28

c. The answer to problem 9b of $1,170.28 and problem 6 of
    $1,170.68 are basically the same because in both cases
    we are valuing the present value of a $20 differential
    between actual return and required return for 20 years.

    In problem 9b we take the present value of the $20
    differential to arrive at $170.28. We then add this value
    to the $1,000.00 par value to determine a value of
    $1,170.28.

    In problem 8, we accomplish the same goal by valuing
    all future benefits at a two percent differential between
    actual return and required return to arrive at $1,170.68.

10-10.   Wilson Oil Company issued bonds five years ago at $1,000 per bond. These bonds had a 25 year life when issued and the annual interest payment was then 8 percent. This return was in line with the required returns by bondholders at that point in time as described below:

Real rate of return 2%
Inflation premium 3
Risk premium... 3
   Total return... 8%

Assume that 10 years later, due to bad publicity, the risk premium is now 6 percent and is appropriately reflected in the required return (or yield to maturity) of the bonds. The bonds have 15 years remaining until maturity. Compute the new price of the bond.

Solution:

Wilson Oil Company

First compute the new required rate of return (yield to maturity).

Real rate of return	2%
Inflation premium	3%
Risk premium	6%
	11% total required return

Then use this value to find the price of the bond.

Present Value of Interest Payments
$PV_A = A \times PV_{IFA}$ (n = 15, i = 11%)   Appendix D
$PV_A = \$80 \times 7.191 = \$575.28$

Present Value of Principal Payment at Maturity
$PV = FV \times PV_{IF}$ (n = 15, i = 11%)   Appendix B
$PV = \$1,000 \times .209 = \$209.00$

$$
\begin{array}{r}
\$575.28 \\
\underline{209.00} \\
\text{Bond Price} = \quad \$784.28
\end{array}
$$

10-11.   Lance Whittingham IV specializes in buying deep discount bonds. These represent bonds that are trading at well below par value. He has his eye on a bond issued by the Leisure Time Corporation. The $1,000 par value bond pays 4 percent annual interest and has 16 years remaining to maturity. The current yield to maturity on similar bonds is 10 percent.

a. What is the current price of the bonds?
b. By what percent will the price of the bonds increase between now and maturity?
c. What is the annual compound rate of growth in the value of the bonds? (An approximate answer is acceptable.)

Solution:

Lance Whittingham IV – Leisure Time Corporation

a. Current price of the bonds

Present Value of Interest Payments

$PV_A = A \times PV_{IFA}$ (n = 16, i = 10%)   Appendix D

$PV_A = \$40 \times 7.824 = \$312.96$

Present Value of Principal Payment at Maturity

$PV = FV \times PV_{IF}$ (n = 16, i = 10%)   Appendix B

$PV = \$1,000 \times .218 = \$218$

$$\begin{array}{r} \$312.96 \\ \underline{218.00} \\ \$530.96 \end{array}$$

b. Percent increase at maturity

Maturity Value	$1,000.00
Current price	− 530.96
Dollar increase	$ 469.04

$$\text{Percent increase} = \frac{\text{dollar increase}}{\text{current price}} = \frac{\$469.04}{530.96} = 88.34\%$$

c. Compound rate of growth

The bond will grow by 88.34 percent over 16 years. Using Appendix A, the future value of $1, we see the growth rate is between 4 and 5 percent (4.03 percent based on interpolation).

10-12. Bonds issued by the Coleman Manufacturing Company have a par value of $1,000, which, of course, is also the amount of principal to be paid at maturity. The bonds are currently selling for $850. They have 10 years remaining to maturity. The annual interest payment is 8 percent ($80).

Compute the approximate yield to maturity, using Formula 10-2.

Solution:

Coleman Manufacturing Company

Approximate Yield to Maturity is represented by Y'

$$Y' = \frac{\text{Annual interest payment} + \dfrac{\text{Principal payment} - \text{Price of the bond}}{\text{Number of years till maturity}}}{0.6\,(\text{Price of the bond}) + 0.4\,(\text{Principal payment})}$$

$$= \frac{\$80 + \dfrac{\$1,000 - 850}{10}}{0.6\,(\$850) + 0.4\,(\$1,000)}$$

$$= \frac{\$80 + \dfrac{\$150}{10}}{\$510 + 400}$$

$$= \frac{\$80 + 15}{\$910} = \frac{\$95}{\$910} = 10.44\%$$

10-13.

Bonds issued by the Tyler Food Corporation have a par value of $1,000, are selling for $1,080, and have 20 years remaining to maturity. The annual interest payment is 12.5 percent ($125).

Compute the approximate yield to maturity, using Formula 10-2.

Solution:

Tyler Food Corporation

Approximate Yield to Maturity is represented by Y'

$$Y' = \frac{\text{Annual interest payment} + \dfrac{\text{Principal payment} - \text{Price of the bond}}{\text{Number of years till maturity}}}{0.6\,(\text{Price of the bond}) + 0.4\,(\text{Principal payment})}$$

$$= \frac{\$125 + \dfrac{\$1,000 - 1,080}{20}}{0.6\,(\$1,080) + 0.4\,(\$1,000)}$$

$$= \frac{\$125 + \dfrac{\$-80}{20}}{\$648 + 400}$$

$$= \frac{\$125 - 4}{\$1,048} = \frac{\$121}{\$1,048} = 11.55\%$$

10-14.   Optional—for Problem 13, use the techniques in Appendix 10A to combine a trial-and-error approach with interpolation to find a more exact answer. You may choose to use a hand-held calculator instead.

Solution:

In using the trial and error approach in this instance, we can reasonably infer the answer is between 11 and 12 percent based on the information in problem 9. Even if we did not have this information, we could infer the yield is somewhat below 12.5 percent because the bonds are trading above the par value of $1,000. Let's begin the trial and error process at 11 percent.

Present Value of Interest Payments

$PV_A = A \times PV_{IFA}$ (n = 20, i = 11%)   Appendix D

$PV_A = \$125 \times 7.963 = \$995.38$

Present Value of Principal Payment at Maturity

$PV = FV \times PV_{IF}$ (n = 20, i = 11%)   Appendix B

$PV = \$1,000 \times .124 = \$124$

$$\begin{array}{r} \$ \ 995.38 \\ \underline{124.00} \\ \$1,119.38 \end{array}$$

The discount rate of 11 percent gives us too high a present value in comparison to the bond price of $1,080. So we next use a higher rate of 12 percent.

Present Value of Interest Payments

$PV_A = A \times PV_{IFA}$ (n = 20, i = 12%)   Appendix D

$PV_A = \$125 \times 7.469 = \$933.63$

Present Value of Principal Payment at Maturity

$$PV = FV \times PV_{IF} \ (n = 20, i = 12\%) \qquad \text{Appendix B}$$

$$PV = \$1,000 \times .104 = \$104$$

$$\begin{array}{r} \$ \ \ 933.63 \\ \underline{104.00} \\ \$1,037.63 \end{array}$$

The discount rate of 12 percent provides too low a value. The actual value falls between 11 and 12 percent. Using interpolation:

$1,119.38	PV at 11%		$1,119.38	PV at 11%
−1,037.63	PV at 12%		−1,080.00	bond price
$ 81.75			$ 39.38	

$$11\% + \frac{\$39.38}{\$81.75} \ (1\%) = 11\% + .48 \ (1\%) = 11.48\%$$

The answer is 11.48% (The answer with a hand-held calculator is 11.47%).

(For the next two problems, assume interest payments are on a semiannual basis.)

10-15. Heather Smith is considering a bond investment in Locklear Airlines. The $1,000 par value bonds have a quoted annual interest rate of 9 percent and interest is paid semiannually. The yield to maturity on the bonds is 12 percent annual interest. There are 15 years to maturity. Compute the price of the bonds based on semiannual analysis.

Solution:

Heather Smith and Locklear Airlines

$9\%/2 = 4.5\%$ semiannual interest rate

$4.5\% \times \$1,000 = \$45$ semiannual interest

$15 \times 2 = 30$ number of periods (n)

$12\%/2 = 6\%$ yield to maturity expressed on a semiannual basis

Present Value of Interest Payments

$PV_A = A \times PV_{IFA}$ (n = 30, i = 6%)   Appendix D

$PV_A = \$45 \times 13.765 = \$619.43$

Present Value of Principal Payment at Maturity

$PV = FV \times PV_{IF}$ (n = 30, i = 6%)   Appendix B

$PV = \$1,000 \times .174 = \$174$

Present Value of Interest Payments	$619.43
Present Value of Principal Payments	174.00
Total Present Value or Price of the Bond	$793.43

10-16.   You are called in as a financial analyst to appraise the bonds of Virginia Slim's Clothing Stores. The $1,000 par value bonds have a quoted annual interest rate of 13 percent, which is paid semiannually. The yield to maturity on the bonds is 10 percent annual interest. There are 25 years to maturity.

a.   Compute the price of the bonds based on semiannual analysis.
b.   With 20 years to maturity, if yield to maturity goes down substantially to 8 percent, what will be the new price of the bonds?

Solution:
Virginia Slim's Clothing Stores

a. Present Value of Interest Payments

$PV_A = A \times PV_{IFA}$ (n = 50, i = 5%)   Appendix D

$PV_A = \$65 \times 18.256 = \$1,186.64$

Present Value of Principal Payment at Maturity

$PV = FV \times PV_{IF}$ (n = 50, i = 5%)   Appendix B

$PV = \$1,000 \times .087 = \$87$

$$\begin{array}{r} \$1,186.64 \\ \underline{87.00} \\ \$1,273.64 \end{array}$$

b. $PV_A = A \times PV_{IFA}$ (n = 40, i = 4%)   Appendix D

$PV_A = \$65 \times 19.793 = \$1,286.55$

$PV = FV \times FV_{IF}$ (n = 40, i = 4%)   Appendix B

$PV = \$1,000 \times .208 = \$208$

$$\begin{array}{r} \$1,286.55 \\ \underline{208.00} \\ \$1,494.55 \end{array}$$

10-17.   The preferred stock of Denver Savings and Loan pays an annual dividend of $5.60. It has a required rate of return of 8 percent. Compute the price of the preferred stock.

Solution:

Denver Savings and Loan

$$P_p = \frac{D_p}{K_p} = \frac{\$5.60}{0.08} = \$70$$

10-18.   X-Tech Company issued preferred stock many years ago. It carries a fixed dividend of $5.00 per share. With the passage of time, yields have soared from the original 5 percent to 12 percent (yield is the same as required rate of return).

a.   What was the original issue price?
b.   What is the current value of this preferred stock?
c.   If the yield on the Standard & Poor's Preferred Stock Index declines, how will the price of the preferred stock be affected?

Solution:

X-Tech Company

a. Original price

$$P_p = \frac{D_p}{K_p} = \frac{\$5.00}{0.05} = \$100$$

b. Current value

$$\frac{\$5.00}{0.12} = \$41.67$$

c. The price of preferred stock will increase as yields decline. Since preferred stock is a fixed income security, its price is inversely related to yields as would be true with bond prices. The present value of an income stream has a higher present value as the discount rate declines, and a lower present value as the discount rate increases.

10-19.   Grant Hillside Homes, Inc., has preferred stock outstanding that pays an annual dividend of $9.80. Its price is $110. What is the required rate of return (yield) on the preferred stock?

Solution:

Grant Hillside Homes, Inc.

$$K_p = \frac{D_p}{P_p} = \frac{\$9.80}{\$110.00} = 8.91\%$$

(All of the following problems pertain to the common stock section of the chapter.)

10-20.   Stagnant Iron and Steel currently pays a $4.20 annual cash dividend (D_0). They plan to maintain the dividend at this level for the foreseeable future as no future growth is anticipated.

Of the required rate of return by common stockholders (K_e) is 12 percent, what is the price of the common stock?

Solution:

Stagnant Iron & Steel

$$P_0 = \frac{D_0}{K_e} = \frac{\$4.20}{0.12} = \$35$$

10-21.   Laser Optics will pay a common stock dividend of $1.60 at the end of the year (D_1). The required rate of return on common stick (K_e) is 13 percent. The firm has a constant growth rate (g) of 7 percent.

Compute the current price of the stock (P_0).

Solution:

Laser Optics

$$P_0 = \frac{D_1}{K_{e-g}} = \frac{\$1.60}{0.13 - 0.07} = \frac{\$1.60}{0.06} = \$26.67$$

10-22. Ecology Labs, Inc., will pay a dividend of $3 per share in the next 12 months (D_1). The required rate of return (K_e) is 10 percent and the constant growth rate is 5 percent.

    a. Compute P_0.
        (In the remaining questions for problem 19 all variables remain the same except the one specifically changed. Each question is independent of the others.)
    b. Assume K_e, the required rate of return, goes up to 12 percent, what will be the new value of P_0?
    c. Assume the growth rate (g) goes up to 7 percent, what will be the new value of P_0?
    d. Assume D_1 is $3.50, what will be the new value of P_0?

Solution:
Ecology Labs, Inc.

$$P_0 = \frac{D_1}{K_{e\text{-}g}}$$

a. $\dfrac{\$3.00}{0.10 - 0.05} = \dfrac{\$3.00}{0.05} = \$60.00$

b. $\dfrac{\$3.00}{0.12 - 0.05} = \dfrac{\$3.00}{0.07} = \$42.86$

c. $\dfrac{\$3.00}{0.10 - 0.07} = \dfrac{\$3.00}{0.03} = \$100.00$

d. $\dfrac{\$3.50}{0.10 - 0.05} = \dfrac{\$3.50}{0.05} = \$70.00$

10-23.   Sterling Corp. paid a dividend of $.80 last year. Over the next 12 months, the dividend is expected to grow at a rate of 10 percent, which is the constant growth rate for the firm (g). The new dividend after 12 months will represent D_1. The required rate of return (K_e) is 14 percent.

Compute the price of the stock (P_0).

Solution:

Sterling Corp.

$$P_0 = \frac{D_1}{K_{e-g}}$$

$$D_1 = D_0 (1+g) = \$.80 (1.10) = \$.88$$

$$P_0 = \frac{\$0.88}{0.14 - 0.10} = \frac{\$.88}{0.04} = \$22$$

10-24.   Justin Cement Company has had the following pattern of earnings per share over the last five years:

Year	Earnings per Share
1997	$4.00
1998	4.20
1999	4.41
2000	4.63
2001	4.86

The earnings per share have grown at a constant rate (on a rounded basis) and will continue to do so in the future. Dividends represent 40 percent of earnings.

Project earnings and dividends for the next year (2002).

If the required rate of return (K_e) is 13 percent, what is the anticipated stock price (P_0) at the beginning of 2002?

Solution:

Justin Cement Company

Earnings have been growing at a rate of 5 percent per year.

	Base Period	
1998	$4.20/4.00	5% growth
1999	$4.41/4.20	5% growth
2000	$4.63/4.41	5% growth
2001	$4,86/4.63	5% growth

The projected EPS for 2002 is $5.10 ($4.86 × 1.05)

Dividends for 2002 represent 40% of earnings or $2.04 ($5.10 × 40%)

This is the value for D_1.

K_e (required rate of return) is 13% and the growth rate is 5%.

$$P_0\,(2002) = \frac{D_1}{K_{e-g}} = \frac{\$2.04}{0.13 - 0.05} = \frac{\$2.04}{0.08} = \$25.50$$

10-25.   A firm pays a $3.80 dividend at the end of year one (D_1), has a stock price of $50, and a constant growth rate (g) of 4 percent.

Compute the required rate of return (K_e).

Solution:

$$K_e = \frac{D_1}{P_0} + g$$

$$K_e = \frac{\$3.80}{\$50.00} + 4\% = 7.6\% + 4\% = 11.6\%$$

10-26.   A firm pays a $1.50 dividend at the end of year one (D_1), has a stock price of $60 ($P_0$), and a constant growth rate (g) of 8 percent.

a. Compute the required rate of return (K_e).

Indicate whether each of the following changes would make the required rate of return (K_e) go up or down. (Each question is separate from the others. That is, assume only one variable changes at a time.) No actual numbers are necessary.

b. The dividend payment increases.
c. The expected growth rate increases.
d. The stock price increases.

Solution:

a. $K_e = \dfrac{D_1}{P_0} + g$

$$K_e = \frac{\$1.50}{\$60.00} + 8\% = 2.5\% + 8\% = 10.5\%$$

b. If the dividend payment increases, the dividend yield (D_1/P_0) will go up, and the required rate of return (K_e) will also go up.

c. If the expected growth rate (g) increases, the required rate of return (K_e) will go up.

d. If the stock price increases, the dividend yield (D_1/P_0) will go down, and the required rate of return (K_e) will also go down.

10-27.   Hunter Petroleum Corporation paid a $2 dividend last year. The dividend is expected to grow at a constant rate of 5 percent over the next three years. The required rate of return is 12 percent (this will also serve as the discount rate in this problem). Round all values to three places to the right of the decimal point where appropriate.

a.   Compute the anticipated value of the dividends for the next three years. That is, compute D_1, D_2, and D_3; for example, D_1 is $2.10 ($2.00 × 1.05).

b.   Discount each of these dividends back to the present at a discount rate of 12 percent and then sum them.

c.   Compute the price of the stock at the end of the third year (P_3).

$$P_3 = \frac{D_4}{K_e - g}$$

(D_4 is equal to D_3 times 1.05)

d.   After your have computed P_3, discount it back to the present at a discount rate of 12 percent for three years.

e.   Add together the answers in part b and part d to get P_0, the current value of the stock. This answer represents the present value of the first three periods of dividends, plus the present value of the price of the stock after three periods (which, in turn, represents the value of all future dividends).

f.   Use Formula 10-9 to show that it will provide approximately the same answer as part e.

$$P_0 = \frac{D_1}{K_e - g}$$

For Formula 10-9 use $D_1 = $2.10, $K_e = 12$ percent, and $g = 5$ percent. (The slight difference between the answers to part e and part f is due to rounding.)

Solution:

Hunter Petroleum Corporation

a. D_1 $2.00 \ (1.05) = 2.10$

   D_2 $2.10 \ (1.05) = 2.205$

   D_3 $2.205 \ (1.05) = 2.315$

b.

	Dividends	PV(12%)	PV of Dividends
D_1	$2.10	.893	$1.875
D_2	$2.205	.797	1.757
D_3	$2.315	.712	1.648
			$5.280

c. $P_3 = \dfrac{D_4}{K_{e-g}}$ $D_4 = \$2.315 \ (1.05) = \$2.431$

   $P_3 = \dfrac{\$2.431}{.12 - .05} = \dfrac{2.431}{.07} = \$34.729$

d. PV of P_3 for $n = 3$, $i = 12\%$

   $\$34.729 \times .712 = \$24.727$

e. answer to part b (PV of dividends) $ 5.280

   answer to part d (PV of P_3)   24.727

   current value of the stock $30.007

f. $P_0 = \dfrac{D_1}{K_{e-g}} = \dfrac{\$2.10}{.12 - .05} = \dfrac{\$2.10}{.07} = \$30.00$

Appendix

10A-1   Bonds issued by the Peabody Corporation have a par value of $1,000, are selling for $890, and have 18 years to maturity. The annual interest payment is 8 percent.

Find yield to maturity by combining the trial and error approach with interpolation, as shown in this appendix. (Use an assumption of annual interest payments.)

Solution:

Peabody Corporation

Since the bond is trading below par value at $890, we can assume the yield to maturity must be above the quoted interest rate of 8 percent. (The yield to maturity would be 8 percent at a bond value of $1,000.) As a first approximation, we will try 9 percent.

Present Value of Interest Payments

$PV_A = A \times PV_{IFA}$ (n = 18, i = 9%)   Appendix D

$PV_A = \$80 \times 8.756 = \$700.48$

Present Value of Principal Payment at Maturity

$PV = FV \times PV_{IF}$ (n = 18, i = 9%)

$PV = \$1,000 \times .212 = \$212$

$$\begin{array}{r} \$700.48 \\ \underline{212.00} \\ \$912.48 \end{array}$$

The discount rate of 9 percent gives us too high a present value in comparison to the bond price of $890. So we next use a higher discount rate of 10 percent.

Present Value of Interest Payments

$$PV_A = A \times PV_{IFA} \ (n = 18, \ i = 10\%) \qquad \text{Appendix D}$$

$$PV_A = \$80 \times 8.201 = \$656.08$$

Present Value of Principal Payment at Maturity

$$PV = FV \times PV_{IF} \ (n = 18, \ i = 10\%)$$

$$PV = \$1,000 \times .180 = \$180$$

$$\begin{array}{r} \$656.08 \\ \underline{180.00} \\ \$836.08 \end{array}$$

The discount rate of 10 percent provides a value lower than the price of the bond. The actual value for the bond must fall between 9% and 10%. Using interpolation, the answer is:

$912.48	PV at 9%		$912.48	PV at 9%
−836.08	PV at 10%		−890.00	Bond price
$ 76.40			$ 22.48	

$$9\% + \frac{\$22.48}{76.40} \left(1\%\right) = 9\% + .29 \left(1\%\right) = 9.29\%$$

10B-1.   The McMillan Corporation paid a dividend of $2.40 per share of stock over the last 12 months. The dividend is expected to grow at a rate of 25 percent over the next three years (supernormal growth). It will then grow at a normal, constant rate of 6 percent for the foreseeable future. The required rate of return is 14 percent (this will also serve as the discount rate). Round to two places to the right of the decimal point throughout the problem.

a. Compute the anticipated value of the dividends for the next three years (D_1, D_2, and D_3).

b. Discount each of these dividends back to the present at a discount rate of 14 percent and then sum them.

c. Compute the price of the stock at the end of the third year (P_3).

$$P_3 = \frac{D_4}{K_e - g}$$ [Review Appendix 10B for the definition of D_4]

d. After you have computed P_3, discount it back to the present at a discount rate of 14 percent for three years.

e. Add together the answers in part b and part d to get the current value of the stock. (This answer represents the present value of the first three periods of dividends plus the present value of the price of the stock after three periods.)

Solution:

McMillan Corporation

a. D_1 $2.40 (1.25) = $3.00
    D_2 $3.00 (1.25) = $3.75
    D_3 $3.75 (1.25) = $4.69

b. **Supernormal dividends**	**Discount rate $Ke = 14\%$**	**Present value of dividends during the supernormal growth period**
D_1 $3.00	.877	$2.63
D_2 $3.75	.769	2.88
D_3 $4.69	.675	3.17
		$8.68

c. $P_e = \dfrac{D_4}{K_{e-g}}$

$$D_4 = D_3\,(1.06) = \$4.69\,(1.06) = \$4.97$$

$$P_3 = \dfrac{\$4.97}{.14 - .06} = \dfrac{\$4.97}{0.08} = \$62.13$$

d. PV of P_3 for $n = 3$, $i = 14\%$
   $\$62.13 \times .675 = \$41.94$

e. Answer to part b (PV of dividends) $ 8.68
    Answer to part d (PV of P_3)   41.94
    Current value of the stock $50.62

Chapter 11

Discussion Questions

11-1.   Why do we use the overall cost of capital for investment decisions even when only one source of capital will be used (e.g., debt)?

Though an investment financed by low-cost debt might appear acceptable at first glance, the use of debt could increase the overall risk of the firm and eventually make all forms of financing more expensive. Each project must be measured against the overall cost of funds to the firm.

11-2.   How does the cost of a source of capital relate to the valuation concepts presented previously in Chapter 10?

The cost of a source of financing directly relates to the required rate of return for that means of financing. Of course, the required rate of return is used to establish valuation.

11-3.   In computing the cost of capital, do we use the historical costs of existing debt and equity or the current costs as determined in the market? Why?

In computing the cost of capital, we use the current costs for the various sources of financing rather than the historical costs. We must consider what these funds will cost us to finance projects in the future rather than their past costs.

11-4.   Why is the cost of debt less than the cost of preferred stock if both securities are priced to yield 10 percent in the market?

Even though debt and preferred stock may be both priced to yield 10 percent in the market, the cost of debt is less because the interest on debt is a tax-deductible expense. A 10 percent market rate of interest on debt will only cost a firm in a 35 percent tax bracket an aftertax rate of 6.5 percent. The answer is the yield multiplied by the difference of (one minus the tax rate).

11-5.   What are the two sources of equity (ownership) capital for the firm?

The two sources of equity capital are retained earnings and new common stock.

11-6.   Explain why retained earnings has an opportunity cost associated with it?

Retained earnings belong to the existing common stockholders. If the funds are paid out instead of reinvested, the stockholders could earn a return on them. Thus, we say retaining funds for reinvestment carries an opportunity cost.

11-7.   Why is the cost of retained earnings the equivalent of the firm's own required rate of return on common stock (K_e)?

Because stockholders can earn a return at least equal to their present investment. For this reason, the firm's rate of return (K_e) serves as a means of approximating the opportunities for alternate investments.

11-8.   Why is the cost of issuing new common stock (K_n) higher than the cost of retained earnings (K_e)?

In issuing new common stock, we must earn a slightly higher return than the normal cost of common equity in order to cover the distribution costs of the new security. In the case of the Baker Corporation, the cost of new common stock was six percent higher.

11-9.   How are the weights determined to arrive at the optimal weighted average cost of capital?

The weights are determined by examining different capital structures and using that mix which gives the minimum cost of capital. We must solve a multidimensional problem to determine the proper weights.

11-10.   Explain the traditional, U-shaped approach to the cost of capital.

The logic of the U-shaped approach to cost of capital can be explained through Figure 11-1. It is assumed that as we initially increase the debt-to-equity mix the cost of capital will go down. After we reach an optimum point, the increase use of debt will increase the overall cost of financing to the firm. Thus we say the weighted average cost of capital curve is U-shaped.

11-11.   It has often been said that if the company can't earn a rate of return greater than the cost of capital it should not make investments. Explain.

If the firm cannot earn the overall cost of financing on a given project, the investment will have a negative impact on the firm's operations and will lower the overall wealth of the shareholders.

Clearly, it is undesirable to invest in a project yielding 8 percent if the financing cost is 10 percent.

11-12.   What effect would inflation have on a company's cost of capital? (Hint: Think about how inflation influences interest rates, stock prices, corporate profits, and growth.)

Inflation can only have a negative impact on a firm's cost of capital-forcing it to go up. This is true because inflation tends to increase interest rates and lower stock prices, thus raising the cost of dent and equity directly and the cost of preferred stock indirectly.

11-13.   What is the concept of marginal cost of capital?

The marginal cost of capital is the cost of incremental funds. After a firm reaches a given level of financing, capital costs will go up because the firm must tap more expensive sources. For example, new common stock may be needed to replace retained earnings as a source of equity capital.

Appendix

11A-1.   How does the capital asset pricing model help explain changing costs of capital?

The capital asset pricing model explains the relationship between risk and return, and the price adjustment of capital assets to changes in risk and return. As investors react to their economic environment and their willingness to take risk, they change the prices of financial assets like common stock, bonds, and preferred stock. As the prices of these securities adjust to investors' required returns, the company's cost of capital is adjusted accordingly.

11A-2.   How does the SML react to changes in the rate of interest, changes in the rate of inflation, and changing investor expectations?

The SML, Security Market Line, reflects the risk-return tradeoffs of securities. As interest rates increase, the SML moves up parallel to the old SML. Now investors require a higher minimum return on risk free assets and an equally higher rate for all levels of risk. A change in the rate of inflation has a similar impact. The risk free rate goes up to provide the appropriate inflation premium and there is an upward shift in the SML.

In regard to changing investor expectations, as investors become more risk averse, the SML increases its slope. The more risk taken, the greater the return premium that is desired (see figure 11A-4).

Problems

11-1.　　　Telecom Systems can issue debt yielding 8 percent. The company is in a 35 percent bracket.

What is the aftertax cost of debt?

Solution:
Telecom Systems

$$K_d = Yield\,(1 - T)$$
$$= 8\%\,(1 - .35)$$
$$= 8\%\,(.65)$$
$$= 5.20\%$$

11-2.　　　Calculate the aftertax cost of debt under each of the following conditions.

	Yield	Corporate Tax Rate
a.	6.0%	16%
b.	12.6%	35%
c.	9.4%	24%

Solution:

$$K_d = Yield\,(1 - T)$$

	Yield	(1 – T)	Yield (1 – T)
a.	6.0%	(1 – .16)	5.04%
b.	12.6%	(1 – .35)	8.19%
c.	9.4%	(1 – .24)	7.14%

11-3.   The Goodsmith Charitable Foundation, which is tax-exempt, issued debt last year at 8 percent to help finance a new playground facility in Los Angeles. This year the cost of debt is 20 percent higher; that is, firms that paid 10 percent for debt last year would be paying 12 percent this year.

a. If the Goodsmith Charitable Foundation borrowed money this year, what would the aftertax cost of debt be, based on their cost last year and the 20 percent increase?
b. If the Foundation was found to be taxable by the IRS (at a rate of 35 percent) because it was involved in political activities, what would the aftertax cost of debt be?

Solution:
Goldsmith Charitable Foundation

a. K_d $= \text{Yield} (1 - T)$
   Yield $= 8\% \times 1.20 = 9.6\%$

   K_d $= 9.6\% (1 - 0) = 9.6\% (1) = 9.6\%$
b. K_d $= 9.6\% (1 - .35) = 9.6\% (.65) = 6.24\%$

11-4.   Royal Jewelers, Inc. has an aftertax cost of debt of 6 percent. With a tax rate of 40 percent, what can you assume the yield on the debt is?

Solution:
Regal Jewelers, Inc.

$$K_d = \text{Yield} (1 - T)$$

$$\text{Yield} = \frac{K_d}{(1 - T)}$$

$$\text{Yield} = \frac{6\%}{(1 - .40)} = \frac{6\%}{.60} = 10\%$$

11-5. Airborne Airlines, Inc. has $1,000 par value bond outstanding with 25 years to maturity. The bond carries an annual interest payment of $78 and is currently selling for $875. Airborne is in the 30 percent tax bracket. The firm wishes to know what the after tax cost of a new bond issue is likely to be. The yield to maturity on the new issue will be the same as the yield to maturity on the old issue because the risk and maturity date will be similar.

a. Compute the approximate yield to maturity (Formula 11-1) on the old issue and use this as the yield for the new issue.

b. Make the appropriate tax adjustment to determine the aftertax cost of debt.

Solution:

Airborne Airlines, Inc.

a.

$$Y' = \frac{\text{Annual interest payment} + \dfrac{\text{Principal payment} - \text{Price of the bond}}{\text{Number of years to maturity}}}{.6\,(\text{Price of bond}) + .4\,(\text{Principal payment})}$$

$$= \frac{\$78 + \dfrac{\$1,000 - \$875}{25}}{.6\,(\$875) + .4\,(\$1,000)}$$

$$= \frac{\$78 + \dfrac{\$125}{25}}{\$525 + \$400}$$

$$= \frac{\$78 + \$5}{\$925}$$

$$= \frac{\$83}{\$925} = 8.97\%$$

b. K_d = Yield $(1 - T)$

= 8.97% $(1 - .30)$

= 8.97% $(.70)$

= 6.28%

11-6.   Russell Container Corporation has a $1,000 par value bond outstanding with 20 years to maturity. The bond carries an annual interest payment of $95 and is currently selling for $920 per bond. Russell Corp. is in a 25 percent tax bracket. The firm wishes to know what the aftertax cost of a new bond issue is likely to be. The yield to maturity on the new issue will be the same as the yield to maturity on the old issue because the risk and maturity date will be similar.

a. Compute the approximate yield to maturity (Formula 11-1) on the old issue and use this as the yield for the new issue.
b. Make the appropriate tax adjustment to determine the aftertax cost of debt.

Solution:
Russell Container Corporation

a.

$$Y' = \frac{\text{Annual interest payment} + \dfrac{\text{Principal payment} - \text{Price of the bond}}{\text{Number of years to maturity}}}{.6\,(\text{Price of bond}) + .4\,(\text{Principal payment})}$$

$$= \frac{\$95 + \dfrac{\$1,000 - \$920}{20}}{.6\,(\$920) + .4\,(\$1,000)}$$

$$= \frac{\$95 + \dfrac{\$86}{20}}{\$552 + \$400}$$

$$= \frac{\$95 + \$4}{\$952}$$

$$= \frac{\$99}{\$952} = 10.40\%$$

b. K_d = Yield $(1 - T)$
          = 10.40% $(1 - .25)$
          = 10.40% $(.75)$
          = 7.80%

11-7.   For Russell Container Corporation, described in problem 6, assume that the yield on the bonds goes up by one percentage point and that the tax rate is now 35 percent.

a.   What is the new aftertax cost of debt?
b.   Has the aftertax cost of debt gone up or down from problem 4? Explain why.

Solution:

Russell Container Corporation (Continued)

a. K_d = Yield $(1 - T)$
   = 11.40% $(1 - .35)$
   = 11.40% $(.65)$
   = 7.41%

b. It has gone down. Although the before-tax yield is higher, the larger tax deduction (35 percent versus 25 percent) more than offsets the higher rate.

11-8.   New Jersey Bell Telephone Co. is planning to issue debt that will mature in the year 2024. In many respects the issue is similar to currently outstanding debt of the corporation. Using Table 11-2 in the chapter, identify:

a.   The yield to maturity on similarly outstanding debt for the firm, in terms of maturity.
b.   Assume that because the new debt will be issued at par, the required yield to maturity will be 0.15 percent higher than the value determined in part *a*. Add this factor to the answer in *a*. (New issues at par sometimes require a slightly higher yield than old issues that are trading below par. There is less leverage and fewer tax advantages.)
c.   If the firm is in a 30 percent tax bracket, what is the aftertax cost of debt?

Solution:
New Jersey Bell Telephone

a. 8.36%
b. 8.36% + .15% = 8.51%
c. K_d = Yield $(1 - T)$
   = 8.51% $(1 - .30)$
   = 8.51% $(.70)$
   = 5.96%

11-9. Medco Corporation can sell preferred stock for $80 with an estimated flotation cost of $3. It is anticipated that the preferred stock will pay $6 per share in dividends.

a. Compute the cost of preferred stock for Medco Corp.
b. Do we need to make a tax adjustment for the issuing firm?

Solution:
Medco Corporation

a. $K_p = \dfrac{D_p}{P_p - F}$

$= \dfrac{\$6}{\$80 - \$3} = \dfrac{\$6}{\$77} = 7.79\%$

b. No tax adjustment is required. Preferred stock dividends are not a tax deductible expense for the issuing firm (the dividends, of course, are 70 percent tax exempt to a corporate recipient).

11-10. The Meredith Corporation issued $100 par value preferred stock 10 years ago. The stock provided an 8 percent yield at the time of issue. The preferred stock is now selling for $75.

What is the current yield or cost of preferred stock? (Disregard flotation costs.)

Solution:
Meredith Corporation

$Yield = \dfrac{D_p}{P_p} = \dfrac{\$8}{\$75} = 10.67\%$

11-11.   The treasurer of Riley Coal Co. is asked to compute the cost of fixed income securities for her corporation. Even before making the calculations, she assumes the aftertax cost of debt is at least 2 percent less than that for preferred stock. Based on the following facts, is she correct?

Debt can be issued at a yield of 10.6 percent, and the corporate tax rate is 35 percent. Preferred stock will be priced at $50, and pay a dividend of $4.40. The floatation cost on the preferred stock is $2.

Solution:

Riley Coal Inc.

Aftertax cost of debt

$$K_d = \text{Yield} (1 - T)$$
$$= 10.6\% (1 - .35) = 10.6\% (.65) = 6.89\%$$

Aftertax cost of preferred stock

$$K_p = \frac{D_p}{P_p - F} = \frac{\$4.40}{\$50 - \$2} = \frac{\$4.40}{\$48} = 9.17\%$$

Yes, the treasurer is correct. The difference is 2.28% (6.89% versus 9.17%).

11-12.   Barton Electronics wants you to calculate its cost of common stock. During the next 12 months, the company expects to pay dividends (D_1) of $1.20 per share, and the current price of its common tock is $30 per share. The expected growth rate is 9 percent.

a.   Compute the cost of retained earnings (K_e). Use Formula 11-6.
b.   If a $2 floatation cost is involved, compute the cost of new common stock (K_n). Use Formula 11-7.

Solution:

Barton Electronics

a. $K_e = \dfrac{D_1}{P_0} + g$

$$= \frac{\$1.20}{\$30} + 9\% = 4\% + 9\% = 13\%$$

b. $K_n = \dfrac{D_1}{P_0 - F} + g$

$$= \frac{\$1.20}{\$30 - \$2} + 9\% = \frac{\$1.20}{\$28} + 9\%$$

$$= 4.29\% + 9\% = 13.29\%$$

11-13.   Compute K_e and K_n under the following circumstances:

a. $D_1 = \$4.60$, $P_0 = \$60$, $g = 6\%$, $F = \$3.00$.
b. $D_1 = \$0.25$, $P_0 = \$20$, $g = 9\%$, $F = \$1.50$.
c. E_1 (earnings at the end of period one) = $6, payout ratio equals 30 percent, $P_0 = \$24$, $g = 4.5\%$, $F = \$1.60$.
d. D_0 (dividend at the beginning of the first period) = $3, growth rate for dividends and earnings (g) = 8%, $P_0 = \$50$, $F = \$3$.

Solution:

a. $K_e = \dfrac{D_1}{P_0} + g$

$= \dfrac{\$4.60}{\$60} + 6\% = 7.67\% + 6\% = 13.67\%$

$K_n = \dfrac{D_1}{P_0 - F} + g$

$= \dfrac{\$4.60}{\$60 - \$3} + 6\% = \dfrac{\$4.60}{\$57} + 6\%$

$= 8.07\% + 6\% = 14.07\%$

b. $K_e = \dfrac{D_1}{P_0} + g$

$\qquad = \dfrac{\$.25}{\$20} + 9\% = 1.25\% + 9\% = 10.25\%$

$K_n = \dfrac{D_1}{P_0 - F} + g$

$\qquad = \dfrac{\$.25}{\$20 - \$1.50} + 9\% = \dfrac{\$.25}{\$18.50} + 9\%$

$\qquad = 1.35\% + 9\% = 10.35\%$

c. $D_1 = 30\% \times E_1 = 30\% \times \$6.00 = \$1.80$

$K_e = \dfrac{D_1}{P_0} + g$

$\qquad = \dfrac{\$1.80}{\$24} + 4.5\% = 7.5\% + 4.5\% = 12\%$

$K_n = \dfrac{D_1}{P_0 - F} + g$

$\qquad = \dfrac{\$1.80}{\$24 - \$1.60} + 4.5\%$

$\qquad = \dfrac{\$1.80}{\$22.40} + 4.5\% = 8.04\% + 4.5\% = 12.54\%$

d. $D_1 = D_0 (1+g) = \$3.00 \times (1.08) = \$3.24$

$$K_e = \frac{D_1}{P_0} + g$$

$$= \frac{\$3.24}{\$50} + 8\% = 6.48\% + 8\% = 14.48\%$$

$$K_n = \frac{D_1}{P_0 - F} + g$$

$$= \frac{\$3.24}{\$50 - \$3} + 8\% = \frac{\$3.24}{\$47} + 8\%$$

$$= 6.89\% + 8\% = 14.89\%$$

11-14.   O'Neal's Men's Shops, Inc., specializes in large-size clothing. Business has been good, as indicated by the six-year growth in earnings per share. The earnings have grown from $1.00 to $1.87.

   a.   Use Appendix A at the back of the text to determine the compound annual rate of growth in earnings ($n = 6$).
   b.   Based on the growth rate determined in part *a*, project earnings for next year (E_1). (Round to two places to the right of the decimal point.)
   c.   Assume the dividend payout ratio is 40 percent. Compute (D_1). (Round to two places to the right of the decimal point.)
   d.   The current price of the stock is $18. Using the growth rate (g) from part *a* and D_1 from part *c*, compute K_e.
   e.   If the floatation cost if $1.50, compute the cost of new common stock (K_n).

Solution:
O'Neal's Men's Shops, Inc.

a. FV_{IF} (Appendix A) $= \dfrac{\$1.87}{1.00} = 1.87 \ (n = 6) \ i = 11\%$

b. $E_1 = E_o (1 + g)$
$= \$1.87 (1.11)$
$= \$2.08$

c. $D_1 = E_1 \times 40\%$
$= \$2.08 \times 40\%$
$= \$.83$

d. $K_e = \dfrac{D_1}{P_o} + g$

$= \dfrac{\$.83}{\$18} + 11\%$

$= 4.61\% + 11\%$

$= 15.61\%$

e. $K_n = \dfrac{D_1}{P_0 - F} + g$

$= \dfrac{\$.83}{\$18 - \$1.50} + 11\%$

$= \dfrac{\$.83}{\$16.50} + 11\%$

$= 5.03\% + 11\% = 16.03\%$

11-15.   United Business Forms' capital structure is as follows:

Debt..	35%
Preferred stock	15
Common equity......................	50

The aftertax cost of debt is 7 percent; the cost of preferred stock is 10 percent; and the cost of common equity (in the form of retained earnings) is 13 percent.

Calculate United Business Forms' weighted average cost of capital in a manner similar to Table 11-1.

Solution:
United Business Forms

	Cost (aftertax)	Weights	Weighted Cost
Debt (K_d)	7.0%	35%	2.45%
Preferred stock (K_p)...	10.0	15	1.50
Common equity (K_e) (retained earnings)...	13.0	50	6.50
Weighted average cost of capital (K_a)			10.45%

11-16.   As an alternative to the capital structure shown in problem 15 for United
              Business Forms, an outside consultant has suggested the following
              modifications.

Debt	65%
Preferred stock	5
Common equity	30

Under this new, more debt-oriented arrangement, the aftertax cost of debt is 9.8
percent; the cost of preferred stock is 12 percent; and the cost of common equity
(in the form of retained earnings) is 15.5 percent.

Recalculate United Business Forms' weighted average cost of capital. Which
plan is optimal in terms of minimizing the weighted average cost of capital?

Solution:
United Business Forms (Continued)

	Cost (aftertax)	Weights	Weighted Cost
Debt (K_d)	9.8%	65%	6.37%
Preferred stock (K_p)	12.0	5	0.60
Common equity (K_e) (retained earnings)	15.5	30	<u>4.65</u>
Weighted average cost of capital (K_a)			11.62%

The plan presented in Problem 11-13 is the better
alternative. Even though the second plan has more
relatively cheap debt, the increased costs of all forms of
financing more than offset this factor.

11-17.   Given the following information, calculate the weighted average cost of capital for Hamilton Corp. Line up the calculations in the order shown in Table 11-1.

Percent of capital structure:

Debt..	30%
Preferred stock	15
Common equity..............................	55

Additional information:

Bond coupon rate	13%
Bond yield to maturity	11%
Dividend, expected common	$3.00
Dividend, preferred.........................	$10.00
Price, common	$50.00
Price, preferred..............................	$98.00
Flotation cost, preferred..................	$5.50
Growth rate	8%
Corporate tax rate...........................	30%

Solution:
The Hamilton Corp.

$$K_d = \text{Yield} (1 - T)$$
$$= 11\% (1 - 0.30)$$
$$= 11\% (.70)$$
$$= 7.7\%$$

The bond yield of 11% is used rather than the coupon rate of 13% because bonds are priced in the market according to competitive yields to maturity. The new bond would be sold to reflect yield to maturity.

$$K_p = \frac{D_p}{P_p - F}$$

$$= \frac{\$10.00}{\$98 - \$5.50} = \frac{\$10.00}{\$92.50} = 10.81\%$$

$$K_e = \frac{D_1}{P_0} + g$$

$$= \frac{\$3}{\$50} + 8\% = 6\% + 8\% = 14\%$$

	Cost (aftertax)	Weights	Weighted Cost
Debt (K_d)	7.70%	30%	2.31%
Preferred stock (K_p)...	10.81	15	1.62
Common equity (K_e) (retained earnings)...	13.00	55	7.70
Weighted average cost of capital (K_a)			11.63%

11-18.   Given the following information, calculate the weighted average cost of capital for the Hadley Corporation. Line up the calculations in the order shown in Table 11-1.

Percent of capital structure:

Preferred stock	10%
Common equity.............................	60%
Equity...	30%

Additional information:

Corporate tax rate............................	34%
Dividend, preferred.........................	$9.00
Dividend, expected common	$3.50
Price, preferred...............................	$102.00
Growth rate	6%
Bond yield.......................................	10%
Flotation cost, preferred..................	$3.20
Price, common	$70.00

Solution:
Hadley Corporation

$$K_d = \text{Yield } (1 - T)$$
$$= 10\% \, (1 - .34)$$
$$= 10\% \, (.66)$$
$$= 6.6\%$$

$$K_p = D_p/(P_p - F)$$
$$= \$9/(\$102 - 3.20) = \$9/\$98.80 = 9.11\%$$

$$K_e = (D_1/P_0) + g$$
$$= (\$3.50/\$70.00) + 6\% = 5\% + 6\% = 11\%$$

	Cost (aftertax)	Weights	Weighted Cost
Debt (K_d)	6.60%	30%	1.98%
Preferred stock (K_p)...	9.11	10	0.91
Common equity (K_e) (retained earnings)...	11.00	60	6.60
Weighted average cost of capital (K_a)			9.49%

11-19.   Brook's Window Shielde, Inc. is trying to calculate its cost of capital for use in a capital budgeting decision. Ms. Glass, the vice president of finance, has given you the following information and has asked you to compute the weighted average cost of capital.

The company currently has outstanding a bond with an 11.2 percent coupon rate and another bond with a 7.5 percent rate. The firm has been informed by its investment banker that bonds of equal risk and credit rating are now selling to yield 12.4 percent.

The common stock has a price of $54 and an expected dividend (D_1) of $2.70 per share. The firm's historical growth rate of earnings and dividends per share has been 14.5 percent, but security analysts on Wall Street expect this growth to slow to 12 percent in future years.

The preferred stock is selling at $50 per share and carries a dividend of $4.75 per share. The corporate tax rate is 35 percent. The flotation cost is 2.8 percent of the selling price for preferred stock. The optimum capital structure for the firm seems to be 35 percent debt, 10 percent preferred stock, and 55 percent common equity in the form of retained earnings.

Compute the cost of capital for the individual components in the capital structure, and then calculate the weighted average cost of capital (similar to Table 11-1).

Solution:

Brook's Window Shielde, Inc.

$$K_d = \text{Yield}\,(1 - T)$$
$$= 12.4\%\,(1 - .35) = 12.4\%\,(.65) = 8.06\%$$

$$K_p = D_p/(P_p - F)$$
$$= \$4.75/(\$50 - \$1.40) = \$4.75/\$48.60 = 9.77\%$$

$$K_e = (D_1/P_o) + g$$
$$= (\$2.70/\$54) + 12\% = 5\% + 12\% = 17\%$$

	Cost (aftertax)	Weights	Weighted Cost
Debt (K_d)	8.06%	35%	2.82%
Preferred stock (K_p)...	9.77	10	0.98
Common equity (K_e) (retained earnings)...	17.00	55	<u>9.35</u>
Weighted average cost of capital (K_a)			13.15%

11-20.   Northwest Utility Company faces increasing needs for capital. Fortunately, it has an Aa3 credit rating. The corporate tax rate is 35 percent. Northwest's treasurer is trying to determine the corporation's current weighted average cost of capital in order to assess the profitability of capital budgeting projects. Historically, the corporation's earning and dividends per share have increased about 6.2 percent annually and this should continue in the future. Northwest's common stock is selling at $60 per share, and the company will pay a $4.50 per share dividend (D_1).

The company's $100 preferred stock has been yielding 8 percent in the current market. Flotation costs for the company have been estimated by its investment banker to be $2.00 for preferred stock.

The company's optimum capital structure is 50 percent debt, 10 percent preferred stock, and 40 percent common equity in the form of retained earnings. Refer to the table below on bond issues for comparative yields on bonds of equal risk to Northwest.

Data on Bond Issues

Issue	Moody's Rating	Price	Yield to Maturity
Utilities:			
Southwest Electric Power—7 ¼ 2023	Aa2	$ 875.18	8.24%
Pacific Bell—7 3/8 2025	Aa3	882.25	8.43
Pennsylvania Power & Light—8 ½ 2022	A2	950.66	8.99
Industrials:			
Johnson & Johnson—6 ¾ 2023	Aaa	840.24	8.14
Dillard's Department Stores—7 ⅞ 2023	A2	920.92	8.44
Marriott Corp.—10 2012	B2	1,015.10	9.99

Compute the answers to the following questions from the information given.

a. Cost of debt, K_d (use the accompanying table—relate to the utility bond credit rating for yield).
b. Cost of preferred stock, K_p.
c. Cost of common equity in the form of retained earnings, K_e.
d. Weighted average cost of capital.

Solution:

Northwest Utility Company

a. The student must realize that the cost of debt is related to the cost of debt for other debt issues of the same risk class. Although, in actuality, the rate Northwest might pay will not be exactly equal to Pacific Bell, it should be close enough to serve as an approximation. Both are utilities that are rates Aa3.

$$K_d = \text{Yield} (1 - T)$$
$$= 8.43\% (1 - .35) = 8.43\% (.65) = 5.48\%$$

b.
$$K_p = D_p/(P_p - F)$$
$$= \$8/(\$100 \ \$2.00) = \$8/\$98 = 8.16\%$$

c.
$$K_e = (D_1/P_o) + g$$
$$= (\$4.50/\$60) + 6.2\% = 7.5\% + 6.2\% = 13.70\%$$

d.

	Cost (aftertax)	Weights	Weighted Cost
Debt (K_d)	5.48%	50%	2.74%
Preferred stock (K_p)...	8.16	10	.82
Common equity (K_e) (retained earnings)...	13.70	40	5.48
Weighted average cost of capital (K_a)			9.04%

11-21.   The Nolan Corporation finds that it is necessary to determine its marginal cost of capital. Nolan's current capital structure calls for 45 percent debt, 15 percent preferred stock, and 40 percent common equity. Initially common equity will be in the form of retained earnings (K_e) and then new common stock (K_n). The costs of the various sources of financing are as follows: debt, 5.6 percent; preferred stock, 9 percent; retained earnings, 12 percent; and new common stock, 13.2 percent.

    a. What is the initial weighted average cost of capital? (Include debt, preferred stock, and common equity in the form of retained earnings, K_e.)

    b. If the firm has $12 million in retained earnings, at what size capital structure will the firm run out of retained earnings?

    c. What will the marginal cost of capital be immediately after that point? (Equity will remain at 40 percent of the capital structure, but will all be in the form of new common stock, K_n.)

    d. The 5.6 percent cost of debt referred to above applies only to the first $18 million of debt. After that the cost of debt will be 7.2 percent. At what size capital structure will there be a change in the cost of debt?

    e. What will the marginal cost of capital be immediately after that point? (Consider the facts in both parts *c* and *d*.)

Solution:

Nolan Corporation

a.

	Cost (aftertax)	Weights	Weighted Cost
Debt (K_d)	5.60%	45%	2.52%
Preferred stock (K_p)...	9.00	15	1.35
Common equity (K_e) (retained earnings)...	12.00	40	4.80
Weighted average cost of capital (K_a)			8.67%

b. $X = \dfrac{\text{Retained earnings}}{\text{\% of retained earnings within the capital structure}}$

$\quad = \dfrac{\$12\text{ million}}{.40} = \$30\text{ million}$

c.

	Cost (aftertax)	Weights	Weighted Cost
Debt (K_d)	5.60%	45%	2.52%
Preferred stock (K_p)...	9.00	15	1.35
New common stock (K_n)	13.20	40	<u>5.28</u>
Marginal cost of capital (K_{mc})			9.15%

d. $Z = \dfrac{\text{Amount of lower cost debt}}{\text{\% of debt within the capital structure}}$

$\quad = \dfrac{\$18\,\text{million}}{.45} = \$40\,\text{million}$

e.

	Cost (aftertax)	Weights	Weighted Cost
Debt (K_d)	7.20%	45%	3.24%
Preferred stock (K_p)...	9.00	15	1.35
New common stock (K_n)	13.20	40	<u>5.28</u>
Marginal cost of capital (K_{mc})			9.87%

11-22.   The McGee Corporation finds it is necessary to determine its marginal cost of capital. McGee's current capital structure calls for 40 percent debt, 5 percent preferred stock, and 55 percent common equity. Initially, common equity will be in the form of retained earnings (K_e) and then new common stock (K_n). The costs of the various sources of financing are as follows: debt, 7.4 percent; preferred stock, 10.0 percent; retained earnings, 13.0 percent; and new common stock, 14.4 percent.

a. What is the initial weighted average cost of capital? (Include debt, preferred stock, and common equity in the form of retained earnings, K_e.)
b. If the firm has $27.5 million in retained earnings, at what size capital structure will the firm run out of retained earnings?
c. What will the marginal cost of capital be immediately after that point? (Equity will remain at 55 percent of the capital structure, but will all be in the form of new common stock, K_n.)
d. The 7.4 percent cost of debt referred to above applies only to the first $32 million of debt. After that the cost of debt will be 8.6 percent. At what size capital structure will there be a change in the cost of debt?
e. What will the marginal cost of capital be immediately after that point? (Consider the facts in both parts c and d.)

Solution:

The McGee Corporation

a.

	Cost (aftertax)	Weights	Weighted Cost
Debt (K_d)	7.40%	40%	2.96%
Preferred stock (K_p)...	10.00	5	.50
Common equity (K_e) (retained earnings)...	13.00	55	7.15
Weighted average cost of capital (K_a)			10.61%

b. $X = \dfrac{\text{Retained earnings}}{\% \text{ of retained earnings within the capital structure}}$

$= \dfrac{\$27.5 \text{ million}}{.55} = \$50 \text{ million}$

c.

	Cost (aftertax)	Weights	Weighted Cost
Debt (K_d)	7.40%	40%	2.96%
Preferred stock (K_p)...	10.00	5	.50
New common stock (K_n)	14.40	55	<u>7.92</u>
Marginal cost of capital (K_{mc})			11.38%

d. $Z = \dfrac{\text{Amount of lower cost debt}}{\text{\% of debt within the capital structure}}$

$= \dfrac{\$32\ \text{million}}{.40} = \$80\ \text{million}$

e.

	Cost (aftertax)	Weights	Weighted Cost
Debt (K_d)	8.60%	40%	3.44%
Preferred stock (K_p)...	10.00	5	.50
New common stock (K_n)	14.40	55	<u>7.92</u>
Marginal cost of capital (K_{mc})			11.86%

Comprehensive Problems

CP 11-1.   Southern Textiles is in the process of expanding its productive capacity to introduce a new line of products. Current plans call for a possible expenditure of $100 million on four projects of equal size ($25 million), but different returns. Project A will increase the firm's processed yarn capacity and has an expected return of 15 percent after taxes. Project B will increase the capacity for woven fabrics and carries a return of 13.5 percent. Project C, a venture into synthetic fibers, is expected to earn 11.2 percent, and Project D, an investment into dye and textile chemicals, is expected to show a 10.5 percent return.

The firm's capital structure consists of 40 percent debt and 60 percent common equity and this will continue in the future. There is no preferred stock.

Southern Textiles has $15 million in retained earnings. After a capital structure with $15 million in retained earnings is reached (in which retained earnings represent 60 percent of the financing), all additional equity financing must come in the form of new common stock.

Common stock is selling for $30 per share and underwriting costs are estimated at $3 if new shares are issued. Dividends for the next year will be $1.50 per share ($D_1$), and earnings and dividends have grown consistently at 9 percent per year.

The yield on comparative bonds has been hovering at 11 percent. The investment banker feels that the first $20 million of bonds could be sold to yield 11 percent while additional debt might require a 2 percent premium and be sold to yield 13 percent. The corporate tax rate is 34 percent.

a. Based on the two sources of financing, what is the initial weighted average cost of capital? (Use K_d and K_e.)
b. At what size capital structure will the firm run out of retained earnings?
c. What will the marginal cost of capital be immediately after that point?
d. At what size capital structure will there be a change in the cost of debt?
e. What will the marginal cost of capital be immediately after that point?
f. Based on the information about potential returns on investments in the first paragraph and information on marginal cost of capital (in parts *a*, *c*, and *e*), how large a capital investment budget should the firm use?
g. Graph the answer determined in part *f*.

Garner Data Systems is a very large company with common stock listed on the New York Stock Exchange and bonds traded over-the-counter. As of the current balance sheet, it has three bond issues outstanding:

	Expiration
$50 million of 9% series	2013
$100 million of 6% series	2010
$150 million of 4% series	2004

The vice president of finance is planning to sell $150 million of bonds to replace the debt due to expire in 2004. At present market yields on similar Baa bonds are 11.2 percent. Garner also has $60 million of 6.9 percent noncallable preferred stock outstanding, and it has no intentions of selling any preferred stock at any time in the future. The preferred stock is currently priced at $68 per share, and its dividend per share is $6.30.

The company has had very volatile earnings, but its dividends per share have had a very stable growth rate of 8.5 percent and this will continue. The expected dividend (D_1) is $2.10 per share, and the common stock is selling for $60 per share. The company's investment banker has quoted the following flotation costs to Garner: $1.80 per share for preferred stock and $3 per share for common stock.

On the advice of its investment banker, Garner has kept its debt at 50 percent of assets and its equity at 50 percent. Garner sees no need to sell either common or preferred stock in the foreseeable future as it has generated enough internal funds for its investment needs when these funds are combined with debt financing. Garner's corporate tax rate is 35 percent.

Compute the cost of capital for the following:

a. Bond (debt) (K_d).
b. Preferred stock (K_p).
c. Common equity in the form of retained earnings (K_e).
d. New common stock (K_n)
e. Weighted average cost of capital.

CP Solution:

Marginal Cost of
Capital and Investment Returns

Southern Textiles

a. K_d = Yield $(1 - T)$
   = $11\% (1 - .34) = 11\% (.66) = 7.26\%$

   K_e = $(D_1/P_o) + g$
   = $(\$1.50/\$30.00) + 9.0\% = 5.0\% + 9.0\% = 14.0\%$

	Cost (aftertax)	Weights	Weighted Cost
Debt (K_d)	7.26%	40%	2.90%
Common equity (K_e) (retained earnings)...	14.00	60	8.40
Weighted average cost of capital (K_a)			11.30%

b. $X = \dfrac{\text{Retained earnings}}{\text{\% of retained earnings within the capital structure}}$

$= \dfrac{\$15 \text{ million}}{.60} = \$25 \text{ million}$

c. First compute K_n

K_n = $(D_1/(P_o - F)) + g$
   = $(\$1.50/(\$30 - \$3)) + 9\%$
   = $(\$1.50/\$27) + 9\% = 5.56\% + 9\% = 14.56\%$

	Cost (aftertax)	Weights	Weighted Cost
Debt (K_d)	7.26%	40%	2.90%
New common stock (K_n)	14.56	60	8.74
Marginal cost of capital (K_{mc})			11.64%

d. $Z = \dfrac{\text{Amount of lower cost debt}}{\text{\% of debt within the capital structure}}$

$\quad = \dfrac{\$20\,\text{million}}{.40} = \$50\,\text{million}$

e. First compute the new value for K_d

$\quad K_d \;=\; \text{Yield } (1 - T)$

$\quad\quad = \; 13\% \,(1 - .34) = 13\% \,(.66) = 8.58\%$

	Cost (aftertax)	Weights	Weighted Cost
Debt (K_d)	8.58%	40%	3.43%
New common stock (K_n)	14.56	60	8.74
Marginal cost of capital (K_{mc})			12.17%

f. The answer is $50 million.

	Return on Investment		Marginal Cost of Capital
1st $25 million	15.0%	>	11.30%
$25 million - $50 million	13.5%	>	11.63%
$50 million - $75 million	11.2%	<	12.17%
$75 million - $100 million	10.5%	<	12.17%

g. Percent

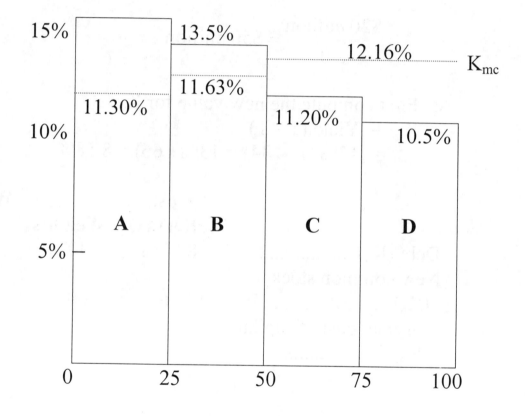

Amount of Capital ($ millions)

Top of bar represents return on investment
Dotted line represents marginal cost of capital (K_{mc})
Invest up to $50 million

Cost of Capital with Changing Financial Needs

Garner Data Systems

a. The before tax cost of debt will be equal to the market rate of 11.2%. The student must realize that the historical cost of the three bonds does not influence the cost of debt.

$$K_d = \text{Yield } (1 - T)$$
$$= 11.2\% (1 - .35) = 11.2\% (.65) = 7.28\%$$

b. The fact that the preferred stock carries a coupon rate of 6.9% does not influence K_p, which is dependent upon current prices and the dividend.

$$K_p = (D_p)/(P_p - F)$$
$$= \$6.30/(\$68 - \$1.80) = (\$6.30)/(\$66.20) = 9.52\%$$

c. $K_e = (D_1/P_o) + g$
$$= \$2.10/\$60.00 + 8.5\% = 3.5\% + 8.5\% = 12.00\%$$

d. $K_n = (D_1/P_o - F)) + g$
$$= \$2.10/(\$60 - \$3.00) + 8.5\%$$
$$= \$2.10/\$57.00 + 8.5\% = 3.68\% + 8.5\% = 12.18\%$$

e. Only those sources of capital that are expected to be used as long-run optimum components of the capital structure should be included in the weighted average cost of capital. The firm states that all their funds can be supplied by retained earnings (50%), therefore, we do not need to include new common stock or preferred stock in our calculation of the weighted cost of capital.

	Cost (aftertax)	Weights	Weighted Cost
Debt (K_d)	7.28%	50%	3.64%
Common equity (K_e) (retained earnings)...	12.00	50	<u>6.00</u>
Weighted average cost of capital (K_a)			9.64%

Appendix

11A-1   Assume that R_f = 6 percent and K_m = 10 percent. Compute K_j for the following betas, using Formula 11A-2.

    a. 0.7
    b. 1.4
    c. 1.7

Solution:

a. K_j
$$
\begin{aligned}
&= R_f + \beta\,(K_m - R_f) \\
&= 6\% + .7\,(10\% - 6\%) \\
&= 6\% + .7\,(4\%) \\
&= 6\% + 2.8\% \\
&= 8.8\%
\end{aligned}
$$

b. K_j
$$
\begin{aligned}
&= 6\% + 1.4\,(10\% - 6\%) \\
&= 6\% + 1.4\,(4\%) \\
&= 6\% + 5.6\% \\
&= 11.6\%
\end{aligned}
$$

c. K_j
$$
\begin{aligned}
&= 6\% + 1.7\,(10\% - 6\%) \\
&= 6\% + 1.7\,(4\%) \\
&= 6\% + 6.8\% \\
&= 12.8\%
\end{aligned}
$$

11A-2. In the preceding problem, assume an increase in interest rates changes R_f to 7.0 percent, and the market risk premium $(K_m - R_f)$ changes to 6.5 percent. Compute K_j for the three betas of 0.7, 1.4, and 1.7.

Solution:

a. K_j $= 7\% + .7\,(6.5\%)$
$= 7\% + 4.55\%$
$= 11.55\%$

b. K_j $= 7\% + 1.4\,(6.5\%)$
$= 7\% + 9.1\%$
$= 16.1\%$

c. K_j $= 7\% + 1.7\,(6.5\%)$
$= 7\% + 11.05\%$
$= 18.05\%$

Chapter 12

Discussion Questions

12-1.   What are the important administrative considerations in the capital budgeting process?

Important administrative considerations relate to: the search for and discovery of investment opportunities, the collection of data, the evaluation of projects, and the reevaluation of prior decisions.

12-2.   Why does capital budgeting rely on analysis of cash flows rather than on net income?

Cash flow rather than net income is used in capital budgeting analysis because the primary concern is with the amount of actual dollars generated. For example, depreciation is subtracted out in arriving at net income, but this noncash deduction should be added back in to determine cash flow or actual dollars generated.

12-3.   What are the weaknesses of the payback method?

The weaknesses of the payback method are:
a.   There is no consideration of inflows after the cutoff period.
b.   The concept fails to consider the time value of money.

12-4.   What is normally used as the discount rate in the net present value method?

The cost of capital as determined in Chapter 11.

12-5.   What does the term *mutually exclusive investments* mean?

The selection of one investment precludes the selection of other alternative investments.

12-6.   If a corporation has projects that will earn more than the cost of capital, should it ration capital?

From a purely economic viewpoint, a firm should not ration capital. The firm should be able to find additional funds and increases its overall profitability and wealth through accepting investments to the point where marginal return equals marginal cost.

12-7.   What is the net present value profile? What three points should be determined to graph the profile?

The net present value profile allows for the graphic portrayal of the net present value of a project at different discount rates. Net present values are shown along the vertical axis and discount rates are shown along the horizontal axis.

The points that must be determined to graph the profile are:
a. The net present value at zero discount rate.
b. The net present value as determined by a normal discount rate.
c. The internal rate of return for the investment.

12-8.   How does an asset's ADR (asset depreciation range) relate to its MACRS category?

The ADR represents the asset depreciation range or the expected physical life of the asset. Generally, the *midpoint* of the range or life is utilized. The longer the ADR midpoint, the longer the MACRS category in which the asset is placed. However, most assets can still be written off more rapidly than the midpoint of the ADR. For example, assets with ADR midpoints of 10 years to 15 years can be placed in the 7-year MACRS category for depreciation purposes.

Problems

12-1.   Assume a corporation has earnings before depreciation and taxes of $100,000, and depreciation of $50,000, and that it has a 30 percent tax bracket. Compute its cash flow using the format below.

Earnings before depreciation and taxes	_____
Depreciation	_____
Earnings before taxes	_____
Taxes @ 30%	_____
Earnings after taxes	_____
Depreciation	_____
Cash flow	_____

Solution:

Earnings before depreciation and taxes	$100,000
Depreciation	− 50,000
Earnings before taxes	50,000
Taxes @ 30%	15,000
Earnings after taxes	35,000
Depreciation	+ 50,000
Cash flow	$ 85,000

12-2.   a. In problem 1, how much would *cash flow* be if there were only $10,000 in depreciation? All other factors are the same.
          b. How much *cash flow* is lost due to the reduced depreciation between problems 1 and 2a?

Solution:

a.

Earnings before depreciation and taxes	$100,000
Depreciation	– 10,000
Earnings before taxes	90,000
Taxes @ 30%	27,000
Earnings after taxes	63,000
Depreciation	+ 10,000
Cash flow	$ 73,000

b.

Cash flow (problem 1)	$85,000
Cash flow (problem 2a)	73,000
Difference in cash flow	$12,000

12-3. Assume a $50,000 investment and the following cash flows for two alternatives.

Year	Investment A	Investment B
1	$10,000	$20,000
2	11,000	25,000
3	13,000	15,000
4	16,000	
5	30,000	

Which alternative would you select under the payback method?

Solution:

Payback for Investment A		Payback for Investment B	
$50,000 – $10,000	1 year	$50,000 – $20,000	1 year
40,000 – 11,000	2 years	30,000 – 25,000	2 years
29,000 – 13,000	3 years	5,000/15,000	.33 years
16,000 – 16,000	4 years		

Payback Investment A = 4.00 years
Payback Investment B = 2.33 years
Investment B would be selected because of the faster payback.

12-4. Referring back to problem 3, if the inflow in the fifth year for investment A were $30,000,000 instead of $30,000, would your answer change under the payback method?

Solution:

The $30,000,000 inflow would still leave the payback period for Investment A at 4 years. It would remain inferior to Investment B under the payback method.

12-5.   The Short-Line Railroad is considering a $100,000 investment in either of two companies. The cash flows are as follows:

Year	Electric Co.	Water Works
1	$70,000	$15,000
2	15,000	15,000
3	15,000	70,000
4-10	10,000	10,000

a. Using the payback method, what will the decision be?
b. Explain why the answer in part *a* can be misleading.

Solution:
Short-Line Railroad
a.

Payback for Electric Co.		Payback for Water Works	
$100,000 – $70,000	1 year	$100,000 – $15,000	1 year
30,000 – 15,000	2 years	85,000 – 15,000	2 years
15,000 – 15,000	3 years	70,000 – 70,000	3 years

Payback (Electronic Co.) = 3 years
Payback (Water Works) = 3 years

b. The answer in part a is misleading because the two investments seem to be equal with the same payback period of three year. Nevertheless, the Electronic Co. is a superior investment because it covers large cash flows in the first year, while the large recovery for Water Works is not until the third years. The problem is that the payback method does not consider the time value of money.

12-6.   Diaz Camera Company is considering two investments both of which cost
         $10,000. The cash flows are as follows:

Year	Project A	Project B
1	$6,000	$5,000
2	4,000	3,000
3	3,000	8,000

a. Which of the two projects should be chosen based on the payback method?
b. Which of the two projects should be chosen based on the net present value
    method? Assume a cost of capital of 10 percent.
c. Should a firm normally have more confidence in answer *a* or answer *b*?

Solution:
Diaz Camera Company

a. Payback Method

Payback for Project A	Payback for Project B
2 years	2 ¼ years

Under the Payback Method, you should select Project A
because of the shorter payback period.

b. Net Present Value Method

Year	Cash Flow	Project A PV_{IF} at 10%	Present Value
1	$6,000	.909	$ 5,454
2	$4,000	.826	$ 3,304
3	$3,000	.751	$ 2,253

Present Value of Inflows	$11,011
Present Value of Outflows	10,000
Net Present Value	$ 1,011

		Project B	
Year	Cash Flow	PV$_{IF}$ at 10%	Present Value
1	$5,000	.909	$ 4,545
2	$3,000	.826	$ 2,478
3	$8,000	.751	$ 6,008

Present Value of Inflows	$13,031
Present Value of Outflows	10,000
Net Present Value	$ 3,031

Under the net present value method, you should select Project B because of the higher net present value.

c. A company should normally have more confidence in answer b because the net present value considers all inflows as well as the time value of money. The heavy late inflow for Project B was partially ignored under the payback method.

12-7. You buy a new piece of equipment for $11,778, and you receive a cash inflow of $2,000 per year for 10 years. What is the internal rate of return?

Solution:

Appendix D

$$PV_{IFA} = \frac{\$11,778}{\$2,000} = 5.889$$

IRR $= 11\%$

For n = 10, we find 5.889 under the 11% column.

12-8.   King's Department Store is contemplating the purchase of a new machine at a cost of $13,869. The machine will provide $3,000 per year in cash flow for six years. King's has a cost of capital of 12 percent.

Using the internal rate of return method, evaluate this project and indicate whether it should be undertaken.

Solution:

King's Department Store

Appendix D

PV_{IFA} $= \$13,869/\$3,000 = 4.623$

IRR $= 8\%$

For n = 6, we find 4.623 under the 8% column.

The machine should not be purchased since its return is under 12 percent.

12-9.   Home security system is analyzing the purchase of manufacturing equipment that will cost $40,000. The annual cash inflows for the next three years will be:

Year	Cash Flow
1	$20,000
2	18,000
3	13,000

a.   Determine the internal rate of return using interpolation.
b.   With a cost of capital of 12 percent, should the machine be purchased?

Solution:
Home Security Systems

a.   Step 1   Average the inflows.

$20,000
9,000
13,000
$51,000 ÷ 3 = $17,000

Step 2   Divide the inflows by the assumed annuity in Step 1.

$$\frac{Investment}{Annuity} = \frac{\$40,000}{17,000} = 2.353$$

Step 3   Go to Appendix D for the 1st approximation. The value in Step 2 (for n = 3) falls between 13% and 14%.

Step 4   Try a first approximation of discounting back the inflows. Because the inflows are biased toward the early years, we will use the higher rate of 14%.

Year	Cash Flow	PV$_{IF}$ at 14%	Present Value
1	$20,000	.877	$17,540
2	$18,000	.769	$13,842
3	$13,000	.675	$ 8,775
			$40,157

Step 5   Since the NPV is slightly over $40,000, we need to try a higher rate. We will try 15%.

Year	Cash Flow	PV$_{IF}$ at 15%	Present Value
1	$20,000	.870	$17,400
2	$18,000	.756	$13,608
3	$13,000	.658	$ 8,554
			$39,562

Because the NPV is now below $40,000, we know the IRR is between 14% and 15%. We will interpolate.

$40,157.............. PV @ 14% $40,157.............. PV @ 14%
$\underline{-39,562}$.............. PV @ 15% $\underline{-40,000}$.............. Cost
$ 595 $ 157

$$14\% + (\$157/\$595)(1\%) = .264$$
$$14\% + .264(1\%) = 14.264\%\ IRR$$
The IRR is 14.264%

If the student skipped from 14% to 16%, the calculations to find the IRR would be as follows:

Year	Cash Flow	PV_{IF} at 16%	Present Value
1	$20,000	.862	$17,240
2	$18,000	.743	$13,374
3	$13,000	.641	$ 8,333
			$38,947

$40,157.............. PV @ 14% $40,157.............. PV @ 14%
–38,947.............. PV @ 16%   –40,000.............. Cost
$ 1,210 $ 157

$$14\% + (\$157/\$1,210)\,(2\%) = .130\,(2\%)$$
$$14\% + (.130)\,(2\%) = 14.260\%$$

This answer is very close to the previous answer, the difference is due to rounding.

b. Since the IRR of 14.265% (or 14.260%) is greater than the cost of capital of 12%, the project should be accepted.

12-10.   Altman Hydraulic Corporation will invest $160,000 in a project that will produce the following cash flows. The cost of capital is 11 percent. Should the project be undertaken? Use the net present value. (Note that the third year's cash flow is negative.)

Year	Cash Flow
1	$ 54,000
2	66,000
3	(66,000)
4	57,000
5	120,000

Solution:

Altman Hydraulic Corporation

Year	Cash Flow	PV$_{IF}$ at 11%	Present Value
1	$54,000	.901	$ 48,654
2	66,000	.812	53,592
3	(60,000)	.731	(43,860)
4	57,000	.659	37,563
5	120,000	.593	71,160

Present value of inflows	$167,109
Present value of outflows	160,000
Net present value	$ 7,109

The net present value is positive and the project should be undertaken

12-11.   Hamilton Control Systems will invest $90,000 in a temporary project that will generate the following cash inflows for the next three years.

Year	Cash Flow
1	$23,000
2	38,000
3	60,000

The firm will be required to spend $15,000 to close down the project at the end of the three years. If the cost of capital is 10 percent, should the investment be undertaken? Use the net present value method.

Solution:
Hamilton Control Systems

Present Value of inflows

Year	Cash Flow	× PV$_{IF}$ at 10%	Present Value
1	$23,000	.909	$20,907
2	38,000	.826	31,388
3	60,000	.751	45,060
			$97,355

Present Value of outflows

0	$90,000	1.000	$ 90,000
3	15,000	.751	11,265
			$101,265

Present Value of inflows	$ 97,355
Present Value of outflows	101,265
Net present value	($ 3,910)

12-12. Cellular Labs will invest $150,000 in a project that will not begin to produce returns until after the 3rd year. From the end of the 3rd year until the end of the 12th year (10 periods), the annual cash flow will be $40,000. If the cost of capital is 12 percent, should this project be undertaken?

Solution:

Cellular Labs

Present Value of Inflows

Find the Present Value of a Deferred Annuity

A = $40,000, n = 10, i = 12%

PV_A = A × PV_{IFA} (Appendix D)

PV_A = $40,000 × 5.650 = $226,000

Discount from Beginning of the third period (end of second period to present):

FV = $226,000, n = 2, i = 12%

PV = FV × PV_{IF} (Appendix B)

PV = $226,000 × .797 = $180,122

Present value of inflows	$180,122
Present value of outflows	150,000
Net present value	$ 30,122

The net present value is positive and the project should be undertaken.

12-13. The Hudson Corporation makes an investment of $14,400 which provides the following cash flows:

Year	Cash Flow
1	$7,000
2	7,000
3	4,000

a. What is the net present value at an 11 percent discount rate?
b. What is the internal rate of return? Use the interpolation procedure in this chapter.
c. In this problem would you make the same decision under both parts *a* and *b*?

Solution:

Hudson Corporation

a. Net Present Value

Year	Cash Flow	11% PV_{IF}	Present Value
1	$7,000	.901	$ 6,307
2	7,000	.812	5,684
3	4,000	.731	2,924

Present value of inflows	$14,915
Present value of outflows	14,400
Net present value	$ 515

b. Internal Rate of Return

We will average the inflows to arrive at an assumed annuity value.

$ 7,000
  7,000
  4,000
$18,000/3 = $6,000

We divide the investment by the assumed annuity value.

$$\frac{\$14,400}{6,000} = 2.4 \quad PV_{IFA}$$

Using Appendix D for n = 3, the first approximation appears to fall between 12% and 13%. Since the heavy inflows are in the early years, we will try 13 percent.

Year	Cash Flow	13% PV$_{IF}$	Present Value
1	$7,000	.885	$ 6,195
2	7,000	.783	5,481
3	4,000	.693	2,772

Present value of inflows $14,448

Since 13% is not high enough to get $14,400 as the present value, we will try 15%. (We could have only gone up to 14%, but we wanted to be sure to include $14,400 in this calculation. Of course, students who use 14% are doing fine).

Year	Cash Flow	15% PV$_{IF}$	Present Value
1	$7,000	.870	$ 6,090
2	7,000	.756	5,292
3	4,000	.658	2,632

Present value of inflows $14,014

The correct answer must fall between 13% and 15%. We interpolate.

$14,448.............. PV @ 13% $14,448.............. PV @ 14%
 14,014.............. PV @ 15%   14,400.............. Cost
$ 434 $ 48

$$13\% + \frac{\$48}{\$434} \ (2\%) = 13\% + .11 \ (2\%) = 13\% + .22\% = 13.22\%$$

As an alternative answer, students who use 14% as the second trial and error rate will show to following:

Year	Cash Flow	×	14% PV$_{IF}$	Present Value
1	$7,000		.877	$ 6,139
2	7,000		.769	5,383
3	4,000		.675	2,700

Present value of inflows $14,222

The correct answer falls between 13% and 14%. We interpolate.

$14,448.............. PV @ 13% $14,448.............. PV @ 13%
 14,222.............. PV @ 14%   14,400.............. Cost
$ 226 $ 48

$$13\% + \frac{\$48}{\$226} \ (1\%) = 13\% + .21 \ (1\%) = 13\% + .21\% = 13.21\%$$

c. Yes, both the NPV is greater than 0 and the IRR is greater than the cost of capital.

12-14.   The Pan American Bottling Co. is considering the purchase of a new machine that would increase the speed of bottling and save money. The net cost of this machine is $45,000. The annual cash flows have the following projections.

Year	Cash Flow
1	$15,000
2	20,000
3	25,000
4	10,000
5	5,000

a. If the cost of capital is 10 percent, what is the net present value of selecting the new machine?
b. What is the internal rate of return?
c. Should the project be accepted? Why?

Solution:
Pan American Bottling Co.

a. Net Present Value

Year	Cash Flow	10% PV_{IF}	Present Value
1	$15,000	.900	$13,635
2	20,000	.826	16,520
3	25,000	.751	18,775
4	10,000	.683	6,830
5	5,000	.621	3,105

Present value of inflows	$58,865
Present value of outflows	−45,000
Net present value	$13,865

b. Internal Rate of Return

We will average the inflows to arrive at an assumed annuity.

$15,000
 20,000
 25,000
 10,000
  5,000
$75,000/5 = $15,000

We divide the investment by the assumed annuity value.

$$\frac{\$45,000}{\$15,000} = 3 \text{ PV}_{IFA}$$

Using Appendix D for n = 5, 20% appears to be a reasonable first approximation (2.991). We try 20%.

Year	Cash Flow	20% PV$_{IF}$	Present Value
1	$15,000	.833	$12,495
2	20,000	.694	13,880
3	25,000	.579	14,475
4	10,000	.484	4,820
5	5,000	.402	2,010

Present value of inflows $47,680

Since 20% is not high enough, we try the next highest rate at 25%.

Year	Cash Flow	25% PV$_{IF}$	Present Value
1	$15,000	.800	$12,000
2	20,000	.640	12,800
3	25,000	.512	12,800
4	10,000	.410	4,100
5	5,000	.328	1,640
	Present value of inflows		$43,340

The correct answer must fall between 20% and 25%. We interpolate.

$47,680............. PV @ 20% $47,680.............. PV @ 20%

 43,340............. PV @ 25%   45,000.............. Cost

$ 4,340 $ 2,680

$$20\% + \frac{\$2,680}{\$4,340}\ (5\%) = 20\% + .62\ (5\%) = 20\% + 3.10\% = 23.10\%$$

c. The project should be accepted because the net present value is positive and the IRR exceeds the cost of capital.

12-15.   You arc asked to evaluate the following two projects for the Norton Corporation. Using the net present value method, combined with the profitability index approach described in footnote 2 of this chapter, which project would you select? Use a discount rate of 10 percent.

Project X (Videotapes of the Weather Report) ($10,000 investment)		Project Y (Slow-Motion Replays of Commercials); ($30,000 investment)	
Year	Cash Flow	Year	Cash Flow
1	$5,000	1	$15,000
2	3,000	2	8,000
3	4,000	3	9,000
4	3,600	4	11,000

Solution:

Norton Corporation

NPV for Project X

Year	Cash Flow	PV_{IF} at 10%	Present Value
1	$5,000	.909	$ 4,545
2	3,000	.826	2,478
3	4,000	.751	3,004
4	3,600	.683	2,459

Present value of inflows	$12,486
Present value of outflows (Cost)	−10,000
Net present value	$ 2,486

$$\text{Profitablity index (X)} = \frac{\text{Present value of inflows}}{\text{Present value of outflows}}$$

$$= \frac{\$12,486}{\$10,000} = 1.2486$$

NPV for Project Y

Year	Cash Flow	PV_{IF} at 10%	Present Value
1	$15,000	.909	$13,635
2	8,000	.826	6,608
3	9,000	.751	6,759
4	11,000	.683	7,513

Present value of inflows	$34,515
Present value of outflows (Cost)	−30,000
Net present value	$ 4,515

$$\text{Profitablity index (Y)} = \frac{\text{Present value of inflows}}{\text{Present value of outflows}}$$

$$= \frac{\$34,515}{\$30,000} = 1.1505$$

You should select Project X because it has the higher profitability index. This is true in spite of the fact that it has a lower net present value. The profitability index may be appropriate when you have different size investments.

12-16.   Turner Video will invest $48,500 in a project. The firm's cost of capital is 9 percent. The investment will provide the following inflows.

Year	Inflow
1	$10,000
2	12,000
3	16,000
4	20,000
5	24,000

The internal rate of return is 14 percent.

a. If the reinvestment assumption of the net present value method is used, what will be the total value of the inflows after five years? (Assume the inflows come at the end of each year.)

b. If the reinvestment assumption of the internal rate of return method is used, what will be the total value of the inflows after five years?

c. Generally, is one investment assumption likely to be better than another?

Solution:

Turner Video

a. Reinvestment assumption of NPV

Year	Inflows	Rate	No. of Periods	Future Value Factor	Value
1	$10,000	9%	4	1.412	$14,120
2	12,000	9%	3	1.295	15,540
3	16,000	9%	2	1.188	19,008
4	20,000	9%	1	1.090	21,800
5	24,000	–	0	1.000	24,000
					$94,468

b. Reinvestment assumption of IRR

Year	Inflows	Rate	No. of Periods	Future Value Factor	Value
1	$10,000	14%	4	1.689	$16,890
2	12,000	14%	3	1.482	17,784
3	16,000	14%	2	1.300	20,800
4	20,000	14%	1	1.140	22,800
5	24,000	–	0	1.000	24,000
					$102,274

c. No. However, for investments with a very high IRR, it may be unrealistic to assume that reinvestment can take place at an equally high rate. The net present value method makes the more conservative assumption of reinvestment at the cost of capital.

12-17. The Suboptimal Glass Company uses a process of capital rationing in its decision making. The firm's cost of capital is 13 percent. It will only invest $60,000 this year. It has determined the internal rate of return for each of the following projects.

Project	Project Size	Internal Rate of Return
A	$10,000	15%
B...............	30,000	14
C...............	25,000	16.5
D	10,000	17
E...............	10,000	23
F...............	20,000	11
G	15,000	16

a. Pick out the projects that the firm should accept.
b. If Projects D and E were mutually exclusive, how would that affect your overall answer? That is, which projects would you accept in expending the $60,000?

Solution:
Suboptimal Glass Company

You should rank the investments in terms of IRR.

Project	IRR	Project Size	Total Budget
E	23%	$10,000	$ 10,000
D	17	10,000	20,000
C	16.5	25,000	45,000
G	16	15,000	60,000
A	15	10,000	70,000
B	14	30,000	100,000
F	11	20,000	120,000

a. Because of capital rationing, only $60,000 worth of projects can be accepted. The four projects to accept are E, D, C and G. Projects A and B provide positive benefits also, but cannot be undertaken under capital rationing.

b. If Projects D and E are mutually exclusive, you would select Project E in preference to D. You would then include Project A with the freed up funds. In summary, you would accept E, C, G and A. The last project would replace D and is of the same $10,000 magnitude.

12-18.   Keller Construction Company is considering two new investments. Project E calls for the purchase of earth-moving equipment. Project H represents the investment in a hydraulic lift. Keller wishes to use a new present value profile in comparing the projects. The investment and cash flow patterns are as follows:

Project E ($20,000 investment)		Project H ($20,000 investment)	
Year	Cash Flow	Year	Cash Flow
1	$ 5,000	1	$16,000
2	6,000	2	5,000
3	7,000	3	4,000
4	10,000		

a. Determine the net present value of the projects based on a zero discount rate.

b. Determine the net present value of the projects based on a 9 percent discount rate.

c. The internal rate of return on Project E is 13.25 percent, and the internal rate of return on Project H is 16.30 percent. Graph a net present value profile for the two investments similar to Figure 12-3. (Use a scale up to $8,000 on the vertical axis, with $2,000 increments. Use a scale up to 20 percent on the horizontal axis, with 5 percent increments.)

d. If the two projects are not mutually exclusive, what would your acceptable or rejection decision be if the cost of capital (discount rate) is 8 percent? (Use the net present value profile for your decision; no actual numbers are necessary.)

e. If the two projects are mutually exclusive (the selection of one precludes the selection of the other), what would be your decision if the cost of capital is (1) 6 percent, (2) 13 percent, (3) 18 percent? Once again, use the net present value profile for your answer.

Solution:

Keller Construction Company

a. Zero discount rate

Project E

$$\underset{\text{Inflows}}{8{,}000 = (\$5{,}000 + \$6{,}000 + \$7{,}000 + \$10{,}000)} \underset{\text{Outflow}}{- \$20{,}000}$$

Project H

$$\underset{\text{Inflows}}{\$5{,}000 = (\$16{,}000 + \$5{,}000 + \$4{,}000)} \underset{\text{Outflow}}{- \$20{,}000}$$

b. 9% discount rate

Project E

Year	Cash Flow	PV_{IF} at 9%	Present Value
1	$ 5,000	.917	$4,585
2	6,000	.842	5,052
3	7,000	.772	5,404
4	10,000	.708	7,080

Present value of inflows	$22,121
Present value of outflows	20,000
Net present value	$ 2,121

Project H

Year	Cash Flow	PV_{IF} at 9%	Present Value
1	$16,000	.917	$14,672
2	5,000	.842	4,210
3	4,000	.772	3,088

Present value of inflows	$21,970
Present value of outflows	20,000
Net present value	$ 1,970

c. Net Present Value Profile

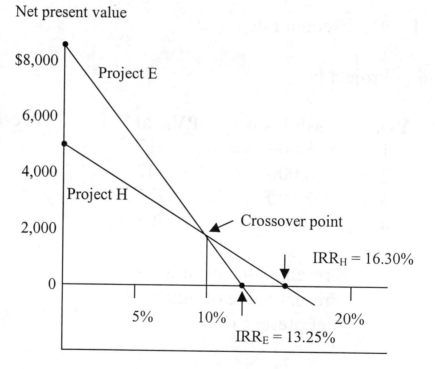

d. Since the projects are not mutually exclusive, they both can be selected if they have a positive net present value. At an 8% rate, they should both be accepted. As a side note, we can see Profit E is superior to Project H.

e. With mutually exclusive projects, only one can be accepted. Of course, that project must still have a positive net present value. Based on the visual evidence, we see:

(i)   6% cost of capital—select Project E
(ii) 13% cost of capital—select Project H
(iii) Do not select either project

12-19.   Davis Chili Company is considering an investment of $15,000, which produces the following inflows.

Year	Cash Flow
1	$8,000
2	7,000
3	4,000

You are going to use the net present value profile to approximate the value for the internal rate of return. Please follow these steps.

a. Determine the net present value profile to approximate the value for the internal rate of return. Please follow these steps.
b. Determine the net present value of the project based on a 10 percent discount rate.
c. Determine the net present value of the project based on a 20 percent discount rate (it will be negative).
d. Draw a net present value profile for the investment and observe the discount rate at which the net present value is zero. This is an approximation of the internal rate of return based on the interpolation procedure presented in this chapter. Compare your answers in parts *d* and *e*.
e. Actually compute the internal rate of return based on the interpolation procedure presented in this chapter. Compare your answers in parts *d* and *e*.

Solution:

Davis Chili Company

a. NPV @ 0% discount rate

$$\begin{array}{cc} \text{Inflows} & \text{Outflow} \\ \$4,000 = (\$8,000 + \$7,000 + \$4,000) - \$15,000 \end{array}$$

b.

Year	Cash Flow	PV_{IF} at 10%	Present Value
1	$8,000	.909	$ 7,272
2	7,000	.826	5,782
3	4,000	.751	3,004

Present value of inflows	$16,058
Present value of outflows	15,000
Net present value	$ 1,058

c.

Year	Cash Flow	PV_{IF} at 20%	Present Value
1	$8,000	.833	$ 6,664
2	7,000	.694	4,858
3	4,000	.579	2,316

Present value of inflows	$13,838
Present value of outflows	15,000
Net present value	($ 1,162)

d. Net Present Value Profile

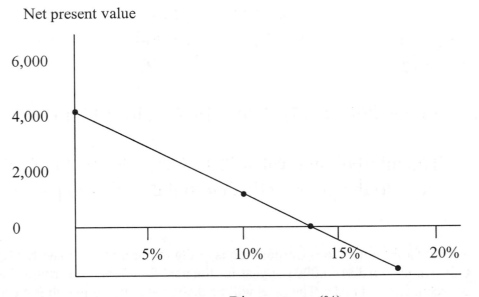

Net present value

Discount rate (%)

e. The answer appears to be slightly above 14%. We will use 14% as the first approximation.

Year	Cash Flow	PV$_{IF}$ at 14%	Present Value
1	$8,000	.877	$ 7,016
2	7,000	.769	5,383
3	4,000	.675	2,700

Present value of inflows $15,099

The second approximation is at 15%.

Year	Cash Flow	PV$_{IF}$ at 15%	Present Value
1	$8,000	.870	$ 6,960
2	7,000	.756	5,292
3	4,000	.658	2,632

Present value of inflows $14,884

We interpolate between 14% and 15%.

$15,099	PV @ 14%	$15,099	PV @ 14%
14,884	PV @ 15%	15,000	Cost
$ 215		$ 99	

$$14\% + (\$99/\$215)\,(1\%) = 14\% + .46 = 14.46\%$$

The interpolation value of 14.46% appears to be very close to the graphically determined value in part d.

12-20.   Telstar Communications Corporation is going to purchase an asset for $300,000 that will produce $140,000 per year for the next four years in earnings before depreciation and taxes. The asset will be depreciated using the three-year MACRS depreciation schedule in Table 12-9. (This represents four years of depreciation based on the half-year convention.) The firm is in a 35 percent tax bracket. Fill in the schedule below for the next four years.

Earnings before depreciation and taxes   _____
Depreciation   _____
Earnings before taxes   _____
Taxes   _____
Earnings after taxes   _____
+ Depreciation   _____
Cash flow   _____

Solution:

Telstar Communications Corporation

First determine annual depreciation.

Year	Depreciation Base	Percentage Depreciation (Table 12-9)	Annual Depreciation
1	$300,000	.333	$ 99,900
2	300,000	.445	133,500
3	300,000	.148	44,400
4	300,000	.074	22,200
			$300,000

Then determine the annual cash flow. Earnings before depreciation and taxes (EBDT) will be the same for each year, but depreciation and cash flow will differ.

	1	2	3	4
EBDT	$140,000	$140,000	$140,000	$140,000
– D	99,900	133,500	44,400	22,200
EBT	40,100	6,500	95,600	117,800
T (35%)	14,035	2,275	33,460	41,230
EAT	26,065	4,225	62,140	76,570
+ D	99,900	133,500	44,400	22,200
Cash Flow	$125,965	$137,725	$106,540	$ 98,770

12-21.   Assume $60,000 is going to be invested in each of the following assets. Using Tables 12-8 and 12-9, indicate the dollar amount of the first year's depreciation.

    a.   Office furniture
    b.   Automobile
    c.   Electric and gas utility property
    d.   Sewage treatment plant

Solution:

a. Office furniture – Based on Table 12-8, this falls under 7-year MACRS depreciation. Then examining Table 12-9, the first year depreciation rate is .143. Thus:

$$\$60,000 \times .143 = \$8,580$$

b. Automobile – This falls under 5-year MACRS depreciation. The first year depreciation rate is .200.

$$\$60,000 \times .200 = \$12,000$$

c. Electric and gas utility property – This falls under 20-year MACRS depreciation. The first year depreciation rate is .038.

$$\$60,000 \times .038 = \$2,280$$

d. Sewage treatment plant – This falls under 15-year MACRS depreciation. The first year depreciation rate is .050.

$$\$60,000 \times .050 = \$3,000$$

12-22.   The Summit Petroleum Corporation will purchase an asset that qualifies for three-year MACRS depreciation. The cost is $80,000 and the asset will provide the following stream of earnings before depreciation and taxes for the next four years:

Year 1	$36,000
Year 2	40,000
Year 3	31,000
Year 4	19,000

The firm is in a 35 percent tax bracket and has an 11 percent cost of capital. Should it purchase the asset? Use the net present value method.

Solution:
Summit Petroleum Corporation

First determine annual depreciation.

Year	Depreciation Base	Percentage Depreciation (Table 12-9)	Annual Depreciation
1	$80,000	.333	$26,640
2	80,000	.445	35,600
3	80,000	.148	11,840
4	80,000	.074	5,920
			$80,000

Then determine the annual cash flow.

	1	2	3	4
EBDT	$36,000	$40,000	$31,000	$19,000
– D	26,640	35,600	11,840	5,920
EBT	9,360	4,400	19,160	13,080
T (35%)	3,276	1,540	6,706	4,578
EAT	6,084	2,860	12,454	8,502
+ D	26,640	35,600	11,840	5,920
Cash Flow	$32,724	$38,460	$24,294	$14,422

Then determine the net present value.

Year	Cash Flow (inflows)	PV_{IF} at 11%	Present Value
1	$32,724	.901	$29,484
2	38,460	.812	31,230
3	24,294	.731	17,759
4	14,422	.659	9,504

Present value of inflows	$87,977
Present value of outflows	80,000
Net present value	$ 7,977

The asset should be purchased based on the new present value.

12-23.   Propulsion Labs will acquire new equipment that falls under the five-year MACRS category. The cost is $200,000. If the equipment is purchased, the following earnings before depreciation and taxes will be generated for the next six years.

Year 1	$75,000
Year 2	70,000
Year 3	55,000
Year 4	35,000
Year 5	25,000
Year 6	21,000

The firm is in a 30 percent tax bracket and has a 14 percent cost of capital. Should Propulsion Labs purchase the equipment? Use the net present value method.

Solution:

Propulsion Labs

First determine annual depreciation.

Year	Depreciation Base	Percentage Depreciation (Table 12-9)	Annual Depreciation
1	$200,000	.200	$ 40,000
2	200,000	.320	64,000
3	200,000	.192	38,400
4	200,000	.115	23,000
5	200,000	.115	23,000
6	200,000	.058	11,600
			$200,000

Then determine the annual cash flow.

	1	2	3	4	5	6
EBDT	$75,000	$70,000	$55,000	$35,000	$25,000	$21,000
– D	40,000	64,000	38,400	23,000	23,000	11,600
EBT	35,000	6,000	16,600	12,000	2,000	9,400
T (30%)	10,500	1,800	4,980	3,600	600	2,820
EAT	24,500	4,200	11,620	8,400	1,400	6,580
+ D	40,000	64,000	38,400	23,000	23,000	11,600
Cash Flow	$64,500	$68,200	$50,020	$31,400	$24,400	$18,180

Then determine the net present value.

Year	Cash Flow (inflows)	PV$_{IF}$ at 14%	Present Value
1	$64,500	.877	$ 56,567
2	68,200	.769	52,446
3	50,020	.675	33,764
4	31,400	.592	18,589
5	24,400	.519	12,664
6	18,180	.456	8,290

Present value of inflows	$182,320
Present value of outflows	200,000
Net present value	($17,680)

The equipment should not be purchased.

12-24.   Universal Electronics is considering the purchase of manufacturing equipment with a 10-year midpoint in its asset depreciation range (ADR). Carefully refer to Table 12-8 to determine in what depreciation category the asset falls. (Hint: It is not 10 years.) The asset will cost $90,000 and it will produce earnings before depreciation and taxes of $32,000 per year for three years, and then $12,000 a year for seven more years. The firm has a tax rate of 34 percent. With a cost of capital of 11 percent, should it purchase the asset? Use the net present value method. In doing your analysis, if you have years in which there is no depreciation, merely enter a zero for depreciation.

Solution:
Universal Electronics

Because the manufacturing equipment has a 10-year midpoint of its asset depreciation range (ADR), it falls into the seven-year MACRS category as indicated in Table 12-8. Furthermore, we see that most types of manufacturing equipment fall into the seven-year MACRS category.

With seven-year MACRS depreciation, the asset will be depreciated over eight years (based on the half-year convention). Also, we observe that the equipment will produce earnings for 10 years, so in the last two years there will be no depreciation write-off.

We first determine the annual depreciation.

Year	Depreciation Base	Percentage Depreciation (Table 12-9)	Annual Depreciation
1	$90,000	.143	$12,870
2	90,000	.245	22,050
3	90,000	.175	15,750
4	90,000	.125	11,250
5	90,000	.089	8,010
6	90,000	.089	8,010
7	90,000	.089	8,010
8	90,000	.045	4,050
			$90,000

Annual Cash Flow

	1	2	3	4	5	6	7	8	9	10
EBDT	$32,000	$32,000	$32,000	$12,000	$12,000	$12,000	$12,000	$12,000	$12,000	$12,000
– D	12,870	22,050	15,750	11,250	8,010	8,010	8,010	4,050	0	0
EBT	$19,130	$ 9,950	$16,250	$ 750	$ 3,990	$ 3,990	$ 3,990	$ 7,950	$12,000	$12,000
T (34%)	6,504	3,383	5,525	255	1,357	1,357	1,357	2,703	4,080	4,080
EAT	$12,626	$ 6,567	$10,725	$ 495	$ 2,633	$ 2,633	$ 2,633	$ 5,247	$ 7,920	$ 7,920
+ D	12,870	22,050	15,750	11,250	8,010	8,010	8,010	4,050	0	0
Cash Flow	$25,496	$28,617	$26,475	$11,745	$10,643	$10,643	$10,643	$ 9,297	$ 7,920	$ 7,920

S-413

Next determine the net present value.

Year	Cash Flow (inflows)	PV$_{IF}$ at 11%	Present Value
1	$25,496	.901	$ 22,972
2	28,617	.812	23,237
3	26,475	.731	19,353
4	11,745	.659	7,740
5	10,643	.593	6,311
6	10,643	.535	5,694
7	10,643	.482	5,130
8	9,297	.434	4,035
9	7,920	.391	3,097
10	7,920	.352	2,788

Present value of inflows	$100,357
Present value of outflows	90,000
Net present value	$ 10,357

New asset should be purchased.

12-25.   The Bagwell Ball Bearing Company has a proposed contract with the First Military Base Facility of Texas. The initial investment in land and equipment will be $90,000. Of this amount, $60,000 is subject to five-year MACRS depreciation. The balance is in nondepreciable property (land). The contract covers a six-year period. At the end of six years the nondepreciable assets will be sold for $30,000. The depreciated assets will have zero resale value.

The contract will require an additional investment of $40,000 in working capital at the beginning of the first year and, of this amount, $20,000 will be returned to the Bagwell Ball Bearing Company after six years.

This investment will produce $32,000 in income before depreciation and taxes for each of the six years. The corporation is in a 35 percent tax bracket and has a 10 percent cost of capital.

Should the investment be undertaken? Use the net present value method.

Solution:

Bagwell Ball Bearing Company

Although there are some complicating features in the problem, we are still comparing the present value of cash flows to the total initial investment.

The initial investment is:

Land and Equipment...............	$ 90,000
Working capital	40,000
Initial investment	$130,000

In computed the present value of the cash flows, we first determine annual depreciation based on a $60,000 depreciation base.

Year	Depreciation Base	Percentage Depreciation (Table 12-9)	Annual Depreciation
1	$60,000	.200	$12,000
2	60,000	.320	19,200
3	60,000	.192	11,520
4	60,000	.115	6,900
5	60,000	.115	6,900
6	60,000	.058	3,480
			$60,000

We then determine the annual cash flow. In addition to normal cash flow from operations; we also consider the funds generated in the sixth year from the sale of the nondepreciable property (land) and from the recovery of working capital.

Then determine the annual cash flow.

Annual Cash Flow

	1	2	3	4	5	6
EBDT	$32,000	$32,000	$32,000	$32,000	$32,000	$32,000
– D	12,000	19,200	11,520	6,900	6,900	3,480
EBT	20,000	12,800	20,480	25,100	25,100	28,520
T (35%)	7,000	4,480	7,168	8,785	8,785	9,982
EAT	13,000	8,320	13,312	16,315	16,315	18,538
+ D	12,000	19,200	11,520	6,900	6,900	3,480
Sale of non-depreciable assets						30,000
+ Recovery of working capital						20,000
Cash Flow	$25,000	$27,520	$24,832	$23,215	$23,215	$72,018

We then determine the net present value.

Year	Cash Flow (inflows)	PV_{IF} at 10%	Present Value
1	$25,000	.909	$ 22,725
2	27,520	.826	22,732
3	24,832	.751	18,649
4	23,215	.683	15,856
5	23,215	.621	14,417
6	72,018	.564	40,618

Present value of inflows $134,997
Present value of outflows   130,000
Net present value $ 4,997

The investment should be undertaken.

12-26. An asset was purchased three years ago for $120,000. It falls into the five-year category for MACRS depreciation. The firm is in a 35 percent tax bracket. Compute the following:

a. Tax loss on the sale and the related tax benefit if the asset is sold now for $12,560.
b. Gain and related tax on the sale if the asset is sold now for $51,060. (Refer to footnote 3.)

Solution:

First determine the book value of the asset.

Year	Depreciation Base	Percentage Depreciation (Table 12-9)	Annual Depreciation
1	$120,000	.200	$24,000
2	120,000	.320	38,400
3	120,000	.192	23,040

Total depreciation to date $85,440

Purchase price	$120,000
– Total depreciation to date	85,440
Book value	$ 34,560

a. $12,560 sales price

Book value	$ 34,560
Sales price	12,560
Tax loss on the sale	$ 22,000

Tax loss on the sale	$ 22,000
Tax rate	35%
Tax benefit	$ 7,700

b. $51,060 sales price

Sales price	$ 51,060
Book value	34,560
Taxable gain	16,500
Tax rate	35%
Tax obligation	$ 5,775

Comprehensive Problems

CP 12-1. Hercules Exercising Equipment Co. purchased a computerized measuring device two years ago for $60,000. The equipment falls into the five-year category for MACRS depreciation and can currently be sold for $23,800.

A new piece of equipment will cost $150,000. It also falls into the five-year category for MACRS depreciation.

Assume the new equipment would provide the following stream of added cost savings for the next six years.

Year	Cost Savings
1	$57,000
2	49,000
3	47,000
4	45,000
5	42,000
6	31,000

The tax rate is 34 percent and the cost of capital is 12 percent.

a. What is the book value of the old equipment?
b. What is the tax loss on the sale of the old equipment?
c. What is the tax benefit from the sale?
d. What is the cash inflow from the sale of the old equipment?
e. What is the net cost of the new equipment? (Include the inflow from the sale of the old equipment.)
f. Determine the depreciation schedule for the new equipment.
g. Determine the depreciation schedule for the remaining years of the old equipment.
h. Determine the incremental depreciation between the old and new equipment and the related tax shield benefits.
i. Compute the aftertax benefits of the cost savings.
j. Add the depreciation tax shield benefits and the aftertax cost savings, and determine the present value. (See Table 12-17 as an example.)
k. Compare the present value of the incremental benefits (*j*) to the net cost of the new equipment (*e*). Should the replacement be undertaken?

CP Solution:

Replacement Decision Analysis

Hercules Exercising Equipment Co.

a.

Year	Depreciation Base	Percentage Depreciation (Table 12-9)	Annual Depreciation
1	$60,000	.200	$12,000
2	60,000	.320	19,200

Total depreciation to date $31,200

Purchase price	$60,000
– Total depreciation to date	31,200
Book value	$28,800

b.	Book value	$28,800
	Sales price	23,800
	Tax loss on the sale	$ 5,000

c.	Tax loss on the sale	$ 5,000
	Tax rate	35%
	Tax benefit	$ 1,750

d.	Sales price of the old equipment	$23,800
	Tax benefit from the sale	1,750
	Cash inflow from the sale of the old equipment	$25,550

e.	Price of the new equipment	$150,000
	– Cash inflow from the sale of the old equipment	25,550
	Net cost of the new equipment	$124,450

f. Depreciation schedule on the new equipment.

Year	Depreciation Base	Percentage Depreciation (Table 12-9)	Annual Depreciation
1	$150,000	.200	$ 30,000
2	150,000	.320	48,000
3	150,000	.192	28,800
4	150,000	.115	17,250
5	150,000	.115	17,250
6	150,000	.058	8,700
			$150,000

g. Depreciation schedule for the remaining years of the old equipment.

Year*	Depreciation Base	Percentage Depreciation (Table 12-9)	Annual Depreciation
1	$60,000	.192	$11,520
2	60,000	.115	6,900
3	60,000	.115	6,900
4	60,000	.058	3,480

*The next four years represent the last four years on the old equipment.

h. Incremental depreciation and tax shield benefits.

(1)	(2)	(3)	(4)	(5)	(6)
	Depreciation on new	Depreciation on old	Incremental	Tax	Tax Shield
Year	Equipment	Equipment	Depreciation	Rate	Benefits
1	$30,000	$11,520	$18,480	.35	$ 6,468
2	48,000	6,900	41,100	.35	14,385
3	28,800	6,900	21,900	.35	7,665
4	17,250	3,480	13,770	.35	4,819
5	17,250		17,250	.35	6,038
6	8,700		8,700	.35	3,045

i. Aftertax cost savings

Year	Savings	(1-Tax Rate)	After tax Savings
1	$57,000	.65	$37,050
2	49,000	.65	31,850
3	47,000	.65	30,550
4	45,000	.65	29,250
5	42,000	.65	27,300
6	31,000	.65	20,150

j. Present value of the total incremental benefits.

(1) Year	(2) Tax Shield Benefits from Depreciation	(3) After Tax Cost Savings	(4) Total Annuity Benefits	(5) Present Value Factor 12%	(6) Present Value
1	$ 6,468	$37,050	$43,518	.893	$ 38,862
2	14,385	31,850	46,235	.797	36,849
3	7,665	30,550	38,215	.712	27,209
4	4,819	29,250	34,069	.636	21,668
5	6,038	27,300	33,338	.567	18,903
6	3,045	20,150	23,195	.507	11,760

Present value of incremental Benefits $155,251

k. Present value of incremental benefits $155,251
    Net cost of new equipment   124,450
    Net present value $ 30,801

Based on the present value analysis, the equipment should be replaced.

CP 12-2.   The Lancaster Corporation purchased a piece of equipment three years ago for $250,000. It has an asset depreciation range (ADR) midpoint of eight years. The old equipment can be sold for $97,920.

A new piece of equipment can be purchased for $360,000. It also has an ADR of eight years.

Assume the old and new equipment would provide the following operating gains (or losses) over the next six years.

Year	New Equipment	Old Equipment
1................	$100,000	$36,000
2................	86,000	26,000
3................	80,000	19,000
4................	72,000	18,000
5................	62,000	16,000
6................	43,000	(9,000)

The firm has a 36 percent tax rate and a 9 percent cost of capital. Should the new equipment be purchased to replace the old equipment?

CP Solution:
Replacement Decision Analysis

Lancaster Corporation

Book Value of Old Equipment

(ADR of 8 years indicates the use of the 5-year MACRS schedule)

Year	Depreciation Base	Percentage Depreciation (Table 12-9)	Annual Depreciation
1	$250,000	.200	$ 50,000
2	250,000	.320	80,000
3	250,000	.192	48,000

Total depreciation to date $178,000

Purchase price	$250,000
– Total depreciation to date	178,000
Book value	$ 72,000

Tax Obligation on the Sale

Sales price	$97,920
Book value	72,000
Taxable gain	25,920
Tax rate	36%
Taxes	$ 9,331

Cash Inflow From the Sale of the Old Equipment

Sales price	$97,920
Taxes	9,331
	$88,589

Net Cost of the New Equipment

Purchase price	$360,000
– Cash inflow from the sale of the old equipment	88,589
Net cost	$271,411

Depreciation Schedule of the New Equipment.

(ADR of 8 years indicates the use of 5-year MACRS Schedule)

Year	Depreciation Base	Percentage Depreciation (Table 12-9)	Annual Depreciation
1	$360,000	.200	$ 72,000
2	360,000	.320	115,200
3	360,000	.192	69,120
4	360,000	.115	41,400
5	360,000	.115	41,400
6	360,000	.058	20,880
			$360,000

Depreciation Schedule for the Remaining Years of the Old Equipment.

Year*	Depreciation Base	Percentage Depreciation (Table 12-9)	Annual Depreciation
1	$250,000	.115	$28,750
2	250,000	.115	28,750
3	250,000	.058	14,500

*The next three years represent the last three years of the old equipment.

Incremental Depreciation and Tax Shield Benefits.

(1)	(2) Depreciation on new Equipment	(3) Depreciation on old Equipment	(4) Incremental Depreciation	(5) Tax Rate	(6) Tax Shield Benefits
Year					
1	$ 72,000	$28,750	$43,250	.36	$15,570
2	115,200	28,750	86,450	.36	31,122
3	69,120	14,500	54,620	.36	19,663
4	41,400		41,400	.36	14,904
5	41,400		41,400	.36	14,904
6	20,880		20,880	.36	7,517

Aftertax cost savings

New Equipment	Old Equipment	Cost Savings	(1 – Tax Rate)	Aftertax Savings
$100,000	$36,000	$64,000	.64	$40,960
86,000	26,000	60,000	.64	38,400
80,000	19,000	61,000	.64	39,040
72,000	18,000	54,000	.64	34,560
62,000	16,000	46,000	.64	29,440
43,000	(9,000)	52,000	.64	33,280

Present value of the total incremental benefits.

(1) Year	(2) Tax Shield Benefits from Depreciation	(3) After Tax Cost Savings	(4) Total Annuity Benefits	(5) Present Value Factor 12%	(6) Present Value
1	$15,570	$40,960	$56,530	.917	$ 51,838
2	31,122	38,400	69,522	.842	58,538
3	19,663	39,040	58,703	.772	45,319
4	14,904	34,560	49,464	.708	35,021
5	14,904	29,440	44,344	.650	28,824
6	7,517	33,280	40,797	.596	24,315

Present value of incremental Benefits $243,855

Net Present Value

Present value of incremental benefits $243,855
Net cost of new equipment   271,411
Net present value   ($27,556)

Based on the present value analysis, the equipment should not be replaced.

Chapter 13

Discussion Questions

13-1.   If corporate managers are risk-averse, does this mean they will not take risks? Explain.

Risk-averse corporate managers are not unwilling to take risks, but will require a higher return from risky investments. There must be a premium or additional compensation for risk taking.

13-2.   Discuss the concept of risk and how it might be measured.

Risk may be defined in terms of the variability of outcomes from a given investment. The greater the variability, the greater the risk. Risk may be measured in terms of the coefficient of variation, in which we divide the standard deviation (or measure of dispersion) by the mean. We also may measure risk in terms of beta, in which we determine the volatility of returns on an individual stock relative to a stock market index.

13-3.   When is the coefficient of variation a better measure of risk than the standard deviation?

The standard deviation is an absolute measure of dispersion while the coefficient of variation is a relative measure and allows us to relate the standard deviation to the mean. The coefficient of variation is a better measure of dispersion when we wish to consider the relative size of the standard deviation or compare two or more investments of different size.

13-4.   Explain how the concept of risk can be incorporated into the capital budgeting process.

Risk may be introduced into the capital budgeting process by requiring higher returns for risky investments. One method of achieving this is to use higher discount rates for riskier investments. This risk-adjusted discount rate approach specifies different discount rates for different risk categories as measured by the coefficient of variation or some other factor. Other methods, such as the certainty equivalent approach, also may be used.

13-5.   If risk is to be analyzed in a qualitative way, place the following investment decisions in order from the lowest risk to the highest risk:

a. New equipment.
b. New market.
c. Repair of old machinery.
d. New product in a foreign market.
e. New product in a related market.
f. Addition to a new product line.

Referring to Table 13-3, the following order would be correct:

repair old machinery (c)
new equipment (a)
addition to normal product line (f)
new product in related market (e)
completely new market (b)
new product in foreign market (d)

13-6.   Assume a company, correlated with the economy, is evaluating six projects, of which two are positively correlated with the economy, two are negatively correlated, and two are not correlated with it at all. Which two projects would you select to minimize the company's overall risk?

In order to minimize risk, the firm that is positively correlated with the economy should select the two projects that are negatively correlated with the economy.

13-7.   Assume a firm has several hundred possible investments and that it wants to analyze the risk-return trade-off for portfolios of 20 projects. How should it proceed with the evaluation?

The firm should attempt to construct a chart showing the risk-return characteristics for every possible set of 20. By using a procedure similar to that indicated in Figure 13-11, the best risk-return trade-offs or efficient frontier can be determined. We then can decide where we wish to be along this line.

13-8.   Explain the effect of the risk-return trade-off on the market value of common stock.

High profits alone will not necessarily lead to a high market value for common stock. To the extent large or unnecessary risks are taken, a higher discount rate and lower valuation may be assigned to our stock. Only by attempting to match the appropriate levels for risk and return can we hope to maximize our overall value in the market.

13-9.   What is the purpose of using simulation analysis?

Simulation is one way of dealing with the uncertainty involved in forecasting the outcomes of capital budgeting projects or other types of decisions. A Monte Carlo simulation model uses random variables for inputs. By programming the computer to randomly select inputs from probability distributions, the outcomes generated by a simulation are distributed about a mean and instead of generating one return or net present value, a range of outcomes with standard deviations are provided.

Problems

13-1.   Lowe Technology Corp. is evaluating the introduction of a new product. The possible levels of unit sales and the probabilities of their occurrence are given.

Possible Market Reaction	Sales in Units	Probabilities
Low response	20	.10
Moderate response	40	.20
High response...........................	65	.40
Very high response...................	80	.30

a. What is the expected value of unit sales for the new product?
b. What is the standard deviation of unit sales?

Solution:

Lowe Technology Corp.

a. $$\overline{D} = \sum DP$$

D	P	DP
20	.10	2
40	.20	8
65	.40	26
80	.30	24
		$60 = \overline{D}$

b. $$\sigma = \sqrt{\sum (D - \overline{D})^2 P}$$

D	$\overline{D}$	$(D - \overline{D})$	$(D - \overline{D})^2$	P	$(D - \overline{D})^2 P$
20	60	−40	1,600	.10	160
40	60	−20	400	.20	80
65	60	+5	25	.40	10
80	60	+20	400	.30	120
					370

$$\sqrt{370} = 19.24 = \sigma$$

13-2.   Shack Homebuilders, Limited, is evaluating a new promotional campaign that could increase home sales. Possible outcomes and probabilities of outcomes are shown below. Compute the coefficient of variation.

Possible Outcomes	Additional Sales in Units	Probabilities
Ineffective campaign	40	.20
Normal response	60	.50
Extremely effective	140	.30

Solution:

Shack Homebuilders, Limited

Coefficient of variation (V) = standard deviation/expected value.

$$\overline{D} = \sum DP$$

D	P	DP
40	.20	8
60	.50	30
140	.30	$\underline{42}$
		$80 = \overline{D}$

$$\sigma = \sqrt{\sum (D - \overline{D})^2 P}$$

D	$\overline{D}$	$(D - \overline{D})$	$(D - \overline{D})^2$	P	$(D - \overline{D})^2 P$
40	80	−40	1,600	.20	320
60	80	−20	400	.50	200
140	80	+60	3,600	.30	$\underline{1,080}$
					1,600

$$\sqrt{1,600} = 40 = \sigma$$

$$V = \frac{40}{80} = .50$$

13-3.   Possible outcomes for three investment alternatives and their probabilities of occurrence are given below.

	Alternative 1		Alternative 2		Alternative 3	
	Outcomes	Probability	Outcomes	Probability	Outcomes	Probability
Failure	50	.2	90	.3	80	.4
Acceptable	80	.4	160	.5	200	.5
Successful	120	.4	200	.2	400	.1

Rank the three alternatives in terms of risk from lowest to highest (compute the coefficient of variation).

Solution:

Alternative 1	Alternative 2	Alternative 3
$D \times P = DP$	$D \times P = DP$	$D \times P = DP$
$\$\ 50\quad .2\quad \$10$	$\$\ 90\quad .3\quad \$\ 27$	$\$\ 80\quad .4\quad \$\ 32$
$80\quad .4\quad 32$	$160\quad .5\quad 80$	$200\quad .5\quad 100$
$120\quad .4\quad \underline{48}$	$200\quad .2\quad \underline{40}$	$400\quad .1\quad \underline{40}$
$\overline{D} = \$90$	$\overline{D} = \$147$	$\overline{D} = \$172$

Standard Deviation Alternative 1

D	$\overline{D}$	$(D-\overline{D})$	$(D-\overline{D})^2$	P	$(D-\overline{D})^2 P$
$\$\ 50$	$\$90$	$\$\text{–}40$	$\$1,600$	.2	$\$320$
80	90	-10	100	.4	40
120	90	$+30$	900	.4	$\underline{360}$
					$\$720$

$$\sqrt{720} = \$26.83 = \sigma$$

Alternative 2

$ 90	$147	$–57	$3,249	.3	$ 974.70
160	147	+13	169	.5	84.50
200	147	+53	2,809	.2	561.80
					$1,621.00

$$\sqrt{1,621} = \$40.26 = \sigma$$

Alternative 3

$ 80	$172	$–92	$ 8,464	.4	$3,385.60
200	172	+28	784	.5	392.00
400	172	+228	51,984	.1	5,198.40
					$8,976.00

$$\sqrt{8,976} = \$94.74 = \sigma$$

Rank by Coefficient of Variation

Coefficient of variation (V) = standard deviation/expected value

$$\underline{V}$$

Alternative 2 $\dfrac{40.26}{147} = .274$

Alternative 1 $\dfrac{26.83}{90} = .298$

Alternative 3 $\dfrac{94.74}{172} = 551$

13-4. Five investment alternatives have the following returns and standard deviations of returns.

Alternative	Returns: Expected Value	Standard Deviation
A...............	$ 1,000.............	$ 590
B...............	3,000.............	600
C...............	3,000.............	750
D...............	5,000.............	2,300
E...............	10,000.............	800

Using the coefficient of variation, rank the five alternatives from lowest risk to highest risk.

Solution:

Coefficient of variation (V) = standard deviation/expected value

		Ranking from lowest to highest
A	$590/$1,000 = .59	E (.08)
B	$600/$3,000 = .20	B (.20)
C	$750/$3,000 = .25	C (.25)
D	$2,300/$5,000 = .46	D (.46)
E	$800/$10,000 = .08	A (.59)

13-5. In problem 4, if you were to choose between Alternative B and C only, would you need to use the coefficient of variation? Why?

Solution:

You would not need to use the coefficient of variation. Since B and C have the same expected value, they can be evaluated based solely on their standard deviations of return. C has a larger standard deviation and so is riskier than B for the same expected return.

13-6.   Tim Trepid is highly risk-averse while Mike Macho actually enjoys taking a risk.

  a.   Which one of the four investments should Tim choose? Compute the
       coefficients of variation to help you in your choice.
  b.   Which one of the four investments should Mike choose?

Investments	Returns – Expected Value	Standard Deviation
Buy stocks	$ 8,800	$ 5,600
Buy bonds	7,000	2,060
Buy commodity futures	16,900	22,000
Buy options	11,600	12,400

Solution:

Coefficient of variation (V) = standard deviation/expected value.

Buy stocks	$5,600/8,800 = .636
Buy bonds	$2,060/7,000 = .294
Buy commodity futures	$22,000/16,900 = 1.302
Buy options	$12,400/11,600 = 1.069

a. Tim should buy the bonds because bonds have the lowest
   coefficient of variation.

b. Mike should buy the commodity futures because they
   have the highest coefficient of variation.

13-7. Wildcat Oil Company was set up to take large risks and is willing to take the greatest risk possible. Richmond Construction Company is more typical of the average corporation and is risk-averse.

a. What of the following four projects should Wildcat Oil Company choose? Compute the coefficients of variation to help you make your decision.
b. What one of the four projects should Richmond Construction Company choose based on the same criteria?

Projects	Returns – Expected Value	Standard Deviation
A	$262,000	$138,000
B	674,000	403,000
C	88,000	108,000
D	125,000	207,000

Solution:

Wildcat Oil Company and Richmond Construction Company

Coefficient of variation (V) = standard deviation/expected value.

Project A	$138,000/262,000 = .527
Project B	$403,000/674,000 = .598
Project C	$108,000/88,000 = 1.227
Project D	$207,000/125,000 = 1.656

a. Wildcat Oil Company should choose Project D because it has the largest coefficient of variation.

b. Richmond Construction Company should choose Project A because it has the smallest coefficient of variation.

13-8. Kyle's Shoe Stores, Inc., is considering opening an additional suburban outlet. An aftertax cash flow of $100 per week is expected from two stores that are being evaluated. Both stores have positive net present values.

Which store site would you select based on the distribution of these cash flows? Use the coefficient of variation as your measure of risk.

Site A		Site B	
Probability	**Cash Flows**	**Probability**	**Cash Flows**
.2.............	50	.1.............	20
.3.............	100	.2.............	50
.3.............	110	.4.............	100
.2.............	135	.2.............	150
		.1.............	180

Solution:

Kyle's Shoe Stores, Inc.

Standard Deviations of Sites A and B

Site A

D	$\bar{D}$	$(D-\bar{D})$	$(D-\bar{D})^2$	P	$(D-\bar{D})^2 P$
$ 50	$100	$–50	$2,500	.2	$500
100	100	–0–	–0–	.3	–0–
110	100	+10	100	.3	30
135	100	+35	1,225	.2	245
					$775

$$\sqrt{775} = \$27.84 = \sigma_A$$

Site B

D	$\overline{D}$	$(D - \overline{D})$	$(D - \overline{D})^2$	P	$(D - \overline{D})^2 P$
$ 20	$100	$-80	$6,400	.1	$ 640
50	100	-50	2,500	.2	500
100	100	-0-	-0-	.4	-0-
150	100	+50	2,500	.2	500
180	100	+80	6,400	.1	640
					$2,280

$$\sqrt{2,280} = \$47.75 = \sigma_B$$

$V_A = \quad \$27.84/\$100 = .2784$
$V_B = \quad \$47.75/\$100 = .4775$

Site A is the preferred site since it has the smaller coefficient of variation. Because both alternatives have the same expected value, the standard deviation alone would have been enough for a decision. A will be just as profitable as B but with less risk.

13-9.   Micro Systems is evaluating a $50,000 project with the following cash flows.

Year	Cash Flows
1	$ 9,000
2	12,000
3	18,000
4	16,000
5	24,000

The coefficient of variation for the project is .726.

Based on the following table of risk-adjusted discount rates, should the project be undertaken? Select the appropriate discount rate and then compute the net present value.

Coefficient of Variation	Discount Rate
0 – .25	6%
.26 – .50	8%
.51 – .75	12%
.76 – 1.00	16%
1.01 – 1.25	20%

Solution:

Micro Systems

Year	Inflows	PV_{IF} @ 12%	PV
1	$ 9,000	.893	$ 8,037
2	12,000	.797	9,564
3	18,000	.712	12,816
4	16,000	.636	10,176
5	24,000	.567	13,608

PV of Inflows	$54,201
Investment	50,000
NPV	$ 4,201

Based on the positive net present value, the project should be undertaken.

13-10.   Payne Medical Labs is evaluating two new products to introduce into the marketplace. Product 1 (a new form of plaster cast) is relatively low in risk for this business and will carry a 10 percent discount rate. Product 2 (a knee joint support brace) has a less predictable outcome and will require a higher discount rate of 15 percent. Either investments will require an initial capital outlay of $90,000. The inflows from projected business over the next five years are given below. Which product should be selected, using net present value analysis?

Year	Product 1	Product 2
1	$25,000	$16,000
2	30,000	22,000
3	38,000	34,000
4	31,000	29,000
5	19,000	70,000

Solution:

Payne Medical Labs

Product 1

Year	Inflows	PV$_{IF}$ @ 10%	PV
1	$25,000	.909	$22,725
2	30,000	.826	24,780
3	38,000	.751	28,538
4	31,000	.683	21,173
5	19,000	.621	11,799
	PV of Inflows		$109,015
	Investment		90,000
	NPV		$ 19,015

Product 2

Year	Inflows	PVIF @ 15%	PV
1	$16,000	.870	$13,920
2	22,000	.756	16,632
3	34,000	.658	22,372
4	29,000	.572	16,588
5	70,000	.497	34,790
			$104,302
			90,000
			$ 14,302

Select Method 1

The instructor may wish to point out that Problem 2 has higher undiscounted total cash flows than Product 1 (the numbers are $171,000 versus $143,000), but has a lower NPV because of the higher discount rate.

13-11. Debby's Dance Studios is considering the purchase of new sound equipment that will enhance the popularity of its aerobics dancing. The equipment will cost $25,000. Debby is not sure how many members the new equipment will attract, but she estimates that her increased annual cash flows for each of the next five years will have the following probability distribution. Debby's cost of capital is 11 percent.

Cash Flow	(Probability)
$3,600	.2
5,000	.3
7,400	.4
9,800	.1

a. What is the expected value of the cash flow? The value you compute will apply to each of the 5 years.
b. What is the expected net present value?
c. Should Debby buy the new equipment?

Solution:

Debby's Dance Studios

a. Expected Cash Flow

Cash Flow		P	
$3,600	×	.2	$ 720
5,000	×	.3	1,500
7,400	×	.4	2,960
9,800	×	.1	980
			$6,160

b. Net Present Value   (Appendix D)

$6,160 × 3.696 $(PV_{IFA}$ @ 11%, n = 5) =

$22,767	Present Value of inflows
25,000	Present Value of outflows
$(2,233)	Net Present Value

c. Debby should not buy this new equipment because the net present value is negative.

13-12.   Highland Mining and Minerals Co. is considering the purchase of two gold
mines. Only one investment will be made. The Australian gold mine will cost
$1,600,000 and will produce $300,000 in years 5 through 15 and $500,000 in
years 16 through 25. The U.S. gold mine will cost $2,000,000 and will produce
$250,000 per year for the next 25 years. The cost of capital is 10 percent.

a. Which investment should be made? (Note: In looking up present value
factors for this problem, you need to work with the concept of a deferred
annuity for the Australian mine. The returns in years 5 through 15 actually
represent 11 years; the returns in years 16 through 25 represent 10 years.)
b. If the Australian mine justifies an extra 5 percent premium over the normal
cost of capital because of its riskiness and relative uncertainty of flows, does
the investment decision change?

Solution:
Highland Mining and Minerals Co.

a. Calculate the net present value for each project.

The Australian Mine

Years	Cash Flow	n Factor	PV_{IFA} @ 10%	Present Value
5-15	$300,000	(15 – 4)	(7.606 – 3.170)	$1,330,800
16-25	$500,000	(25 – 15)	(9.077 – 7.606)	$ 735,500

Present Value of inflows	$2,066,300
Present Value of outflows	$1,600,000
Net Present Value	$ 466,300

The U.S. Mine

Years	Cash Flow	n Factor	PV$_{IFA}$ @ 10%	Present Value
1-25	$250,000	(25)	9.077	$2,269,250

Present Value of inflows	$2,269,250
Present Value of outflows	$2,000,000
Net Present Value	$ 269,250

Select the Australian Mine.

b. Recalculate the net present value of the Australian Mine at a 15 percent discount rate..

Years	Cash Flow	n Factor	PV$_{IFA}$ @ 15%	Present Value
5-15	$300,000	(15 – 4)	(5.847 – 2.855)	$ 897,600
16-25	$500,000	(25 – 15)	(6.464 – 5.847)	$ 308,500

Present Value of inflows	$1,206,100
Present Value of outflows	$1,600,000
Net Present Value	$(393,900)

Now the decision should be made to reject the purchase of the Australian Mine and purchase the U.S. Mine.

13-13. Mr. Sam Golff desires to invest a portion of his assets in rental property. He has narrowed his choices down to two apartment complexes, Palmer Heights and Crenshaw Village. After conferring with the present owners, Mr. Golff has developed the following estimates of the cash flows for these properties.

Palmer Heights		Crenshaw Village	
Yearly Aftertax Cash Inflow (in thousands)	Probability	Yearly Aftertax Cash Inflow (in thousands)	Probability
$10	.1	$15	.2
15	.2	20	.3
30	.4	30	.4
45	.2	40	.1
50	.1		

a. Find the expected cash flow from each apartment complex.
b. What is the coefficient of variation for each apartment complex?
c. Which apartment complex has more risk?

Solution:

Mr. Sam Golff

a.
$$\overline{D} = \sum DP$$

Palmer Heights **Crenshaw Village**

D	P	DP	D	P	DP
10	.1	$ 1.0	15	.2	$ 3.0
15	.2	3.0	20	.3	6.0
30	.4	12.0	30	.4	12.0
45	.2	9.0	40	.1	4.0
50	.1	5.0	Expected Cash		$25.0
Expected Cash		$30.0	Flow		(thousands)
Flow		(thousands)			

b. First find the standard deviation and then the coefficient of variation.

$$V = \frac{\sigma}{\overline{D}}$$

Palmer Heights

D	$\bar{D}$	$(D-\bar{D})$	$(D-\bar{D})^2$	P	$(D-\bar{D})^2 P$
$10	$30	$–20	$400	.10	40
15	30	–15	225	.20	45
30	30	0	0	.40	0
45	30	+15	225	.20	45
50	30	+20	400	.10	40
					170

$$\sqrt{170} = \$13.04 \text{ (thousands)} = \sigma$$

$$V = \$13.04/\$30 = .435$$

Crenshaw Village

D	$\bar{D}$	$(D-\bar{D})$	$(D-\bar{D})^2$	P	$(D-\bar{D})^2 P$
$15	$25	$–10	$100	.20	20.0
20	25	–5	25	.30	7.5
30	25	+5	25	.40	10.0
40	25	+15	225	.10	22.5
					$60.0

$$\sqrt{60} = \$7.75 \text{ (thousands)} = \sigma$$

$$V = \$7.75/\$25 = .310$$

c. Based on the coefficient of variation, Palmer Heights has more risk (.435 vs. .310).

13-14. Referring to Problem 13, Mr. Golff is likely to hold the complex of his choice for 25 years, and he will use this time period for decision-making purposes. Either apartment complex can be acquired for $200,000. Mr. Golff uses a risk-adjusted discount rate when considering investments. His scale is related to the coefficient of variation.

Coefficient of Variation	Discount Rate	
0-0.20	5%	
0.21-0.40	9	(cost of capital)
0.41-0.60	13	
Over 0.90	16	

a. Compute the risk-adjusted net present values for Palmer Heights and Crenshaw Village. You can get the coefficient of correlation and cash flow figures (in thousands) from the previous problem.

b. Which investment should Mr. Golff accept if the two investments are mutually exclusive? If the investments are not mutually exclusive and no capital rationing is involved, how would your decision be affected?

Solution:
Mr. Sam Golff (Continued)

a. Risk-adjusted net present value

	Palmer Heights With V = .435, discount rate = 13%	**Crenshaw Village** With V = .310, discount rate = 9%
Expected Cash Flow	$ 30,000	$25,000
IF$_{PVA}$ (n = 25)	7.330	9.823
Present Value of Inflows	$219,900	$245,575
Present Value of Outflows	200,000	$200,000
Net Present Value	$ 19,900	$ 45,575

b. If these two investments are mutually exclusive, he should accept Crenshaw Village because it has a higher net present value.

If the investments are non-mutually exclusive and no capital rationing is involved, they both should be undertaken.

13-15.   Allison's Dresswear Manufacturers is preparing a strategy for the fall season. One alternative is to expand its traditional ensemble of wool sweaters. A second option would be to enter the cashmere sweater market with a new line of high-quality designer label products. The marketing department has determined that the wool and cashmere sweater lines offer the following probability of outcomes and related cash flows.

	Expand Wool Sweaters Line		Enter Cashmere Sweaters Line	
Expected Sales	Probability	Present Value of Cash Flows from Sales	Probability	Present Value of Cash Flows from Sales
Fantastic	.2	$180,000	.4	$300,000
Moderate	.6	130,000	.2	230,000
Low	.2	85,000	.4	0

The initial cost to expand the wool sweater line is $110,000. To enter the cashmere sweater line the initial cost in designs, inventory, and equipment is $125,000.

a. Diagram a complete decision tree of possible outcomes similar to Figure 13-8. Note that you are dealing with thousands of dollars rather than millions. Take the analysis all the way through the process of computing expected NPV (last column for each investment).
b. Given the analysis in part *a*, would you automatically make the investment indicated?

Solution:

a.

Allison's Dresswear Manufacturers

	(1)	(2)	(3)	(4)	(5)	(6)
	Expected Sales	Probability	Present Value of cash flows from sales	Initial cost	NPV (3) – (4)	Expected NPV (2) × (5)
Expand Wool Sweaters Line	Fantastic	.2	$180,000	$110,000	$70,000	$14,000
	Moderate	.6	130,000	110,000	20,000	12,000
	Low	.2	85,000	110,000	(25,000)	(5,000)
					Expected NPV	$21,000
Enter Cashmere Sweaters Line	Fantastic	.4	$300,000	$125,000	$175,000	$70,000
	Moderate	.2	230,000	125,000	105,000	21,000
	Low	.4	0	125,000	(125,000)	(50,000)
					Expected NPV	$41,000

b. The indicated investment, based on the expected NPV, is in the Cashmere sweater line. However, there is more risk in this alternative so further analysis may be necessary. It is not an automatic decision.

13-16.   When returns from a project can be assumed to be normally distributed, such as those shown in Figure 13-6 (represented by a symmetrical, bell-shaped curve), the areas under the curve can be determined from statistical tables based on standard deviations. For example, 68.26 percent of the distribution will fall within one standard deviation of the expected value $(\overline{D} \pm 1\sigma)$. Similarly 95.44 percent will fall within two standard deviations $(\overline{D} \pm 2\sigma)$, and so on. An abbreviated table of areas under the normal curve is shown here.

Number of σ's from Expected Value	+ or −	+ and −
0.5	0.1915	0.3830
1.0	0.3413	0.6826
1.5	0.4332	0.8664
1.96	0.4750	0.9500
2.0	0.4772	0.9544

Assume Project A has an expected value of $30,000 and a standard deviation (σ) of $6,000.

a. What is the probability that the outcome will be between $24,000 and $36,000?
b. What is the probability that the outcome will be between $21,000 and $39,000?
c. What is the probability that the outcome will be at least $18,000?
d. What is the probability that the outcome will be less than $41,760?
e. What is the probability that the outcome will be less than $27,000 or greater than $39,000?

Solution:

a. expected value = $30,000, σ = $6,000

$24,000 − $36,000
expected value ± 1 σ
.6826

b. $21,000 − $39,000
expected value ± 1.5 σ
.8664

c. at least $18,000

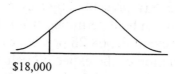

$18,000

$$\frac{\$18,000 - \$30,000}{\$6,000} = \frac{-\$12,000}{\$6,000} = -2$$

.4772
.5000
.9772
Distribution
under the curve

d. Less than $41,760

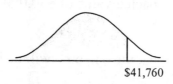

$41,760

$$\frac{\$41,760 - \$30,000}{\$6,000} = \frac{\$11,760}{\$6,000} = 1.96$$

.4750
.5000
.9750
Distribution
under the curve

e. Less than $27,000 or greater than $39,000

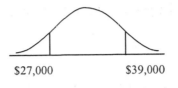

$27,000 $39,000

Area

$$\frac{\$27,000 - \$30,000}{\$6,000} = \frac{-\$3,000}{\$6,000} = -.5 \qquad .1915 \qquad .5000 - .1915 = .3085$$

$$+$$

$$\frac{\$39,000 - \$30,000}{\$6,000} = \frac{\$9,000}{\$6,000} = 1.5 \qquad .4332 \qquad .5000 - .4332 = \frac{.0668}{.3753}$$

Distribution under the curve is .3753.

13-17.   The Oklahoma Pipeline Company projects the following pattern of inflows from an investment. The inflows are spread over time to reflect delayed benefits. Each year is independent of the others.

Year 1		Year 5		Year 10	
Cash Inflow	Probability	Cash Inflow	Probability	Cash Inflow	Probability
65..............	.20	50....................	.25	40...................	.30
80..............	.60	80....................	.50	80...................	.40
95..............	.20	110....................	.25	120...................	.30

The expected value for all three years is $80.

a. Compute the standard deviation for each of the three years.
b. Diagram the expected values and standard deviations for each of the three years in a manner similar to Figure 13-6 in this chapter.
c. Assuming a 6 percent and a 12 percent discount rate, complete the table below for present value factors.

Year	PV_{IF} 6 Percent	PV_{IF} 12 Percent	Difference
1..........	.943	.893	.050
5..........	____	____	____
10.........	____	____	____

d. Is the increasing risk over time, as diagrammed in part b, consistent with the larger differences in PV_{IF}s over time as computed in part c?

e. Assume the initial investment is $135. What is the net present value of the investment at a 12 percent discount rate? Should the investment be accepted?

Solution:

Oklahoma Pipeline Company

a. Standard deviation—year 1

D	$\overline{D}$	$(D-\overline{D})$	$(D-\overline{D})^2$	P	$(D-\overline{D})^2 P$
$65	80	−15	225	.20	45
80	80	0	0	.60	0
95	80	+15	225	.20	45
					90

$$\sqrt{90} = 9.49 = \sigma$$

Standard deviation—year 5

D	$\overline{D}$	$(D-\overline{D})$	$(D-\overline{D})^2$	P	$(D-\overline{D})^2 P$
50	80	−30	900	.25	225
80	80	0	0	.50	0
110	80	+30	900	.25	225
					450

$$\sqrt{450} = 21.21 = \sigma$$

Standard deviation—year 10

D	$\overline{D}$	$(D-\overline{D})$	$(D-\overline{D})^2$	P	$(D-\overline{D})^2 P$
40	80	−40	1,600	.30	480
80	80	0	0	.40	0
120	80	+40	1,600	.30	480
					960

$$\sqrt{960} = \$30.98 = \sigma$$

b. Risk over time

Dollars

$80 ────────────────────────────── Expected Cash flow ($80)

1 yr.   5 yr.   10 yr.

Time

c.

Year	(1) PV$_{IF}$ 6%	(2) PV$_{IF}$ 12%	(3) PV$_{IF}$ Difference
1	.943	.893	.050
5	.747	.567	.180
10	.558	.322	.236

d. Yes. The larger risk over time is consistent with the larger differences in the present value interest factors (IF$_{PV}$) over time. In effect, future uncertainty is being penalized by a lower present value interest factor (IF$_{PV}$). This is one of the consequences of using progressively higher discount rates to penalize for risk.

Year	Inflow	PV$_{IF}$ (12%)	PV
1	$80	.893	$ 71.4
5	80	.567	$ 45.4
10	80	.322	$ 25.8

PV of inflows	$142.6
Investment	$135.0
NPV	$7.6

Accept the investment.

13-18. Treynor Pie Co. is a food company specializing in high calorie snack foods. It is seeking to diversify its food business and lower its risks. It is examining three companies—a gourmet restaurant chain, a baby food company, and a nutritional products firm. Each of these companies can be bought at the same multiple of earnings. The following represents information about the companies.

Company	Correlation with Treynor Pie Company	Sales ($ millions)	Expected Earnings ($ millions)	Standard Deviation in Earnings ($ millions)
Treynor Pie Company	+ 1.0	$100	$8	$2.0
Gourmet restaurant	+ .6	60	6	1.2
Baby food company	+ .2	50	4	1.8
Nutritional products company	− .7	70	5	3.4

a. Using the last two columns, compute the coefficient of variation for each of the four companies. Which company is the least risky? Which company is the most risky?

b. Discuss which of the acquisition candidates is most likely to reduce Treynor Pie Company's risk? Explain why.

Solution:

Treynor Pie Co.

a. Coefficient of variation $(V) = \dfrac{\text{standard deviation}}{\text{expected value}}$

(millions)

Treynor Pie Co.	$2/$8	= .25
Gourmet Restaurant	$1.2/$6	= .20
Baby Food	$1.8/$4	= .45
Nutritional Products	$3.4/$5	= .68

The Gourmet Restaurant chain is the least risky with a coefficient of variation of .20, while the nutritional products firm has the highest risk with a coefficient of variation of .68.

b. Because the nutritional products firm is highly negatively correlated (–.7) with Treynor Pie Co., it is most likely to reduce risk. It would appear that the demand for high calorie snack foods moves in the opposite direction as the demand for nutritional items.

Thus, Treynor Pie Co. would reduce its risk to the largest extent by acquiring the company with the highest coefficient of variation (.68) as computed in part a. This would appear to represent a paradox, but it is not. It simply reflects the fact that the interaction between two companies is much more important than the individual risk of the companies.

13-19.   Transoceanic Airlines is examining a resort motel chain to add to its operation. Prior to the acquisition, the normal expected outcomes for the firm are as follows:

	Outcomes ($ millions)	Probability
Recession	$30	.30
Normal economy	50	.40
Strong economy	70	.30

After the acquisition, the expected outcomes for the firm would be:

	Outcomes ($ millions)	Probability
Recession	$ 10	.30
Normal economy	50	.40
Strong economy	100	.30

a. Compute the expected value, standard deviation, the coefficient of variation prior to the acquisition.

After the acquisition, these values are as follows:

Expected value	53.0 ($ millions)
Standard deviation	34.9 ($ millions)
Coefficient of variation	.658

b. Comment on whether this acquisition appears desirable to you.
c. Do you think the firm's stock price is likely to go up as a result of this acquisition?
d. If the firm were actually interested in reducing its risk exposure, which of the following three industries would you advise it to consider for an acquisition? Briefly comment on your answer.
    (1) Major travel agency
    (2) Oil company
    (3) Gambling casino

Solution:

Transoceanic Airlines

a.
$$\overline{D} = \sum DP$$

D	P	PD
$30	.30	9
50	.40	20
70	.30	21
		$50 ($ million)

$$\sigma = \sqrt{\sum (D - \overline{D})^2 P}$$

D	$\overline{D}$	$(D - \overline{D})$	$(D - \overline{D})^2$	P	$(D - \overline{D})^2 P$
$30	50	−20	400	.30	120
50	50	0	0	.40	0
70	50	+20	400	.30	120
					240

$$\sqrt{240} = \$15.5 \quad (\$million)$$

$$V = \$15.5/\$50 = .310$$

b. No, it does not appear to be desirable. Although the expected value is $3 million higher, the coefficient of variation is more than twice as high (.658 vs. 310). The slightly added return probably does not adequately compensate for the added risk.

c. Probably not. There may be a higher discount rate applied to the firm's earnings to compensate for the additional risk. The stock price may actually go down.

d. The oil company may provide the best diversification benefits. The performance of oil companies and airlines tend to go in opposite directions. If oil prices are high, oil companies benefit, but airlines are hurt. The opposite effect is true when oil prices are low. A major travel agency or gambling casino would probably not provide much in the way of risk reduction benefits. They are both closely associated with entertainment and travel.

13-20. Ms. Sharp is looking at a number of different types of investments for her portfolio. She identifies eight possible investments.

	Return	Risk		Return	Risk
(a)	11%	1.5%	(e)	14%	5.0%
(b)	11	2.1	(f)	15	5.0
(c)	13	3.0	(g)	15	5.8
(d)	13	4.2	(h)	16	7.0

a. Graph the data points in a manner similar to Figure 13-11. Use the axes on the top below for your data.

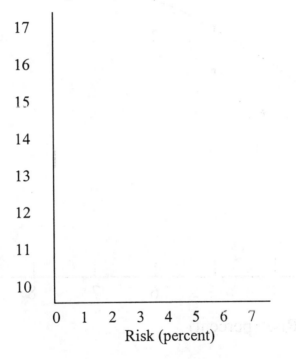

b. Draw a curved line representing the efficient frontier.
c. What two objectives do points on the efficient frontier satisfy?
d. Is there one point on the efficient frontier that is best for all investors?

Solution:

Ms. Sharp

a., b.

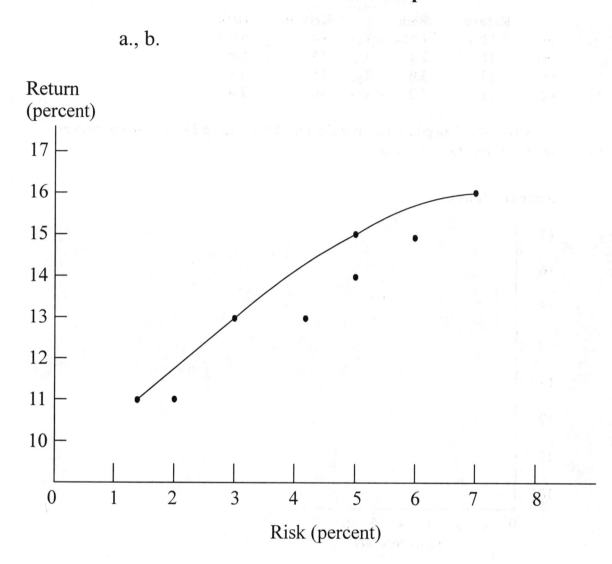

c. Achieve the highest possible return for a given risk level.
   Allow the lowest possible risk at a given return level.

d. No. Each investor must assess his or her own preferences
   about their risk and return trade-off.

Comprehensive Problems

CP 13-1.   Gibson Appliance Co. is a very stable billion-dollar company with a sales growth of about 7 percent per year in good or bad economic conditions. Because of this stability (a coefficient of correlation with the economy of + .4, and a standard deviation of sales of about 5 percent from the mean), Mr. Hoover, the vice president of finance, thinks the company could absorb a small risky company that would add quite a bit of return without increasing the company's risk very much. He is trying to decide which of the two companies he will buy, using the figures below. Gibson's cost of capital is 12 percent.

Genetic Technology Co. (cost $80 million)		Silicon Microchip Co. (cost $80 million)	
Cash Flow for 10 years ($ millions)	Probability	Cash Flows for 10 years ($ millions)	Probability
$ 2	.2	$ 5	.2
8	.3	7	.2
16	.2	18	.3
25	.2	24	.3
40	.1		

a. What is the expected cash flow from both companies?
b. Which company has the lower coefficient of variation?
c. Compute the net present value of each company.
d. Which company would you pick, based on net present values?
e. Would you change your mind if you added the risk dimensions to the problem? Explain.
f. What if Genetic Technology Co. had a coefficient of correlation with the economy of −.2 and Silicon Microchip Co. had one of + .5? Which of these companies would give you the best portfolio effects for risk reduction?
g. What might be the effect of the acquisitions on the market value of Gibson Appliance Co.'s stock?

CP Solution:

Portfolio Effect of a Merger

Gibson Appliance Co.

a.

Genetic Technology Co.   **Silicon Microchip Co.**

D	P	DP	D	P	DP
$ 2	.2	.4	$ 5	.2	1.0
8	.3	2.4	7	.2	1.4
16	.2	3.2	18	.3	5.4
25	.2	5.0	24	.3	7.2
40	.1	4.0			

Expected Value of $15.0   Expected Value of $15.0
Cash Flows   (million)   Cash Flows   (million)

b. Coefficient of variation for Genetic Technology Co.

D	$\overline{D}$	$(D-\overline{D})$	$(D-\overline{D})^2$	P	$(D-\overline{D})^2 P$
$ 2	$15	$–13	$169	.2	$33.8
8	15	–7	49	.3	14.7
16	15	+1	1	.2	.2
25	15	+10	100	.2	20.0
40	15	+25	625	.1	65.5
					$131.2

$$\sqrt{131.2} = \$11.45 \ (\text{million}) = \sigma$$

$$\text{Coefficient of variation} = \$11.45/\$15 = .763$$
$$(\text{million})$$

Coefficient of variation for Silicon Microchip Co.

D	$\overline{D}$	$(D-\overline{D})$	$(D-\overline{D})^2$	P	$(D-\overline{D})^2 P$
$ 5	$15	$-103	$100	.2	$20.0
7	15	-8	64	.2	12.8
18	15	+3	9	.3	2.7
24	15	+9	81	.3	24.3
					$59.8

$$\sqrt{59.8} = \$7.73 \ (\text{million}) = \sigma$$

Coefficient of variation = $\$7.73/\$15 = .515$

Silicon Microchip has a lower coefficient of variation, $.515 < .763$.

c. For both companies the annual expected value is $15 million for 10 years. The cost is $80 million for either company.

Gibson has a cost of capital of 12%.

$15 million $\times$ PV$_{IFA}$ (n = 10, i = 12%)   Appendix D

$15 $\times$ 5.650 = $84.750 PV of inflows

  80.000 PV of outflows

  $ 4.750 Net Present Value (million)

d. Based on present values, you could pick either company.

e. The only way one will win out over the other is if risk factors are considered. Since Genetic Technology Co. has the higher coefficient of variation, we would select the lower risk company—Silicon Microchip. If Gibson Appliance Co. uses risk-adjusted cost of capital concepts, it would use a higher cost of capital for the cash flows generated by Genetic Technology Co. and this would reduce its NPV.

f. Since Gibson Appliance Co. has a correlation coefficient with the economy of +.4, the selection of Genetic Technology Co. would offer the most risk reduction because its correlation coefficient with the economy is –.2.

g. Because Gibson Appliance Co. is a stable billion-dollar company, this investment of $80 million would probably not have a great impact on the stock price in the short run. There could be some positive movement in the stock price if investors perceive less risk from portfolio diversification. This would be particularly true for a merger with Genetic Technology Co. You can use this question to discuss risk-return trade-offs and market reactions.

CP 13-2.   Kennedy Trucking Company is considering the purchase of 60 new diesel trucks that are 15 percent more fuel-efficient that the ones the firm is now using. Mr. Hoffman, the president, has found that the company uses an average of 10 million gallons of diesel fuel per year at a price of $1.25 per gallon. If he can cut fuel consumption by 15 percent, he will save $1,875,000 per year (1,500,000 gallons times $1.25).

Mr. Hoffman assumes that the price of diesel fuel is an external market force that he cannot control and that any increased costs of fuel will be passed on to the shipper through higher rates endorsed by the Interstate Commerce Commission. If this is true, then fuel efficiency would save more money as the price of diesel fuel rises (at $1.35 per gallon, he would save $2,025,000 in total if he buys the new trucks). Mr. Hoffman has come up with two possible forecasts as shown below—each of which he feels has about a 50 percent chance of coming true. Under assumption number one, diesel prices will stay relatively low; under assumption number two, diesel prices will rise considerably. Sixty new trucks will cost Kennedy Trucking $5 million. Under a special provision from the Interstate Commerce Commission, the allowable deprecation will be 25 percent in year one, 38 percent in year two, and 37 percent in year three. The firm has a tax rate of 40 percent and a cost of capital of 10 percent.

a.   First compute the yearly expected costs of diesel fuel for both assumption one (relatively low prices) and assumption two (high prices) from the forecasts below.

Forecast for assumption one (low fuel prices):

Probability (same for each year)	Price of Diesel Fuel per Gallon		
	Year 1	Year 2	Year 3
.1..............	$ .80	$ .90	$1.00
.2..............	1.00	1.10	1.10
.3..............	1.10	1.20	1.30
.2..............	1.30	1.45	1.45
.2..............	1.40	1.55	1.60

Forecast for assumption two (high fuel prices):

Probability (same for each year)	Price of Diesel Fuel per Gallon		
	Year 1	Year 2	Year 3
.1...............	$1.20	$1.50	$1.70
.3...............	1.30	1.70	2.00
.4...............	1.80	2.30	2.50
.2...............	2.20	2.50	2.80

b. What will be the dollar savings in diesel expenses each year for assumption one and for assumption two?
c. Find the increased cash flow after taxes for both forecasts.
d. Compute the net present value of the truck purchases for each fuel forecast assumption and the combined net present value (that is, weigh the NPVs by .5).
e. If you were Mr. Hoffman, would you go ahead with this capital investment?
f. How sensitive to fuel prices is this capital investment?

CP Solution:

Investment Decision Based on Probability Analysis

Kennedy Trucking Company

a. Assumption One:

	Yr. 1		Yr. 2		Yr. 3	
Probability	D	DP	D	DP	D	DP
.1	$0.80	.08	$0.90	.09	$1.00	.10
.2	1.00	.20	1.10	.22	1.10	.22
.3	1.10	.33	1.20	.36	1.30	.39
.2	1.30	.26	1.45	.29	1.45	.29
.2	.140	.28	1.55	.31	1.60	.32

Expected value $1.15/gallon $1.27/gallon $1.32/gallon

Assumption Two:

Probability	Yr. 1		Yr. 2		Yr. 3	
	D	DP	D	DP	D	DP
.1	$1.20	.12	$1.50	.15	$1.70	.17
.3	1.30	.39	1.70	.51	2.00	.60
.4	1.80	.72	2.30	.92	2.50	1.00
.2	2.20	.44	2.50	.50	2.80	.56

Expected value $1.67/gallon $2.08/gallon $2.33/gallon

b. Assumption One:

Yr.	Expected Cost/gal.	# of Gals. without Efficiency =	Cost	% Savings with Efficiency	Total $ Saved
1	$1.15	10 million	$11,500,000	15%	$1,725,000
2	1.27		12,700,000		1,905,000
3	1.32		13,200,000		1,980,000

Assumption Two:

Yr.	Expected Cost/gal.	# of Gals. without Efficiency =	Cost	% Savings with Efficiency	Total $ Saved
1	$1.67	10 million	$16,700,000	15%	$2,505,000
2	2.08		20,800,000		3,120,000
3	2.33		23,300,000		3,495,000

c. First compute annual depreciation: Then proceed to the analysis.

Year 1   25%   ×   5 mil.   =   1.25 mil.

Year 2   38%   ×   5 mil.   =   1.90 mil.

Year 3   37%   ×   5 mil.   =   1.85 mil.

Total saved equals increase in EBDT.

Assumption One:

	Year 1	Year 2	Year 3
Increase in EBDT	$1,725,000	$1,905,000	$1,980,000
– Depreciation	1,250,000	1,900,000	1,850,000
Increase in EBT	475,000	5,000	130,000
– Taxes 40 percent	190,000	2,000	52,000
Increase in EAT	285,000	3,000	78,000
+ Depreciation	1,250,000	1,900,000	1,850,000
Increased Cash Flow	$1,535,000	$1,903,000	$1,928,000

Assumption Two:

	Year 1	Year 2	Year 3
Increase in EBDT	$2,505,000	$3,120,000	$3,495,000
– Depreciation	1,250,000	1,900,000	1,850,000
Increase in EBT	1,255,000	1,220,000	1,645,000
– Taxes 40 percent	502,000	488,000	658,000
Increase in EAT	753,000	732,000	987,000
+ Depreciation	1,250,000	1,900,000	1,850,000
Increased Cash Flow	$2,003,000	$2,632,000	$2,837,000

d. Present Value:

Assumption One:

Year	Cash Flow	PV_{IF} @ 10%	Present Value
1	$1,535,000	.909	$1,395,315
2	1,903,000	.826	1,571,878
3	1,928,000	.751	1,447,928
	PV of inflows		$4,415,121
	PV of outflows		5,000,000
	NPV		$(584,879)

Assumption Two:

Year	Cash Flow	PV_{IF} @ 10%	Present Value
1	$2,003,000	.909	$1,820,727
2	2,632,000	.826	2,174,032
3	2,837,000	.751	2,130,587
	PV of inflows		$6,125,346
	PV of outflows		5,000,000
	NPV		$1,125,346

Combined NPV:

Outcome	NPV	Probability	
Assumption One	−584,879	.5	−292,440
Assumption Two	1,125,346	.5	562,673
Expected Outcome			$270,233

e. Yes – The combined expected value of the outcomes is positive.

f. Quite sensitive when that many gallons are used per year.

Chapter 14

Discussion Questions

14-1.   In addition to U.S. corporations, what government groups complete for funds in the U.S. capital markets?

The federal government, government agencies, and state and local governments all compete for funds.

14-2.   Are federally sponsored credit agency issues directly backed by the U.S. Treasury?

Federally sponsored credit agency issues are not directly backed by the U.S. Treasury.

14-3.   What is a key tax characteristic associated with state and local (municipal) securities?

They are tax exempt, meaning the interest on them is normally exempt from federal income taxes and from state income taxes in the state of issue.

14-4.   What are three forms of corporate securities discussed in the chapter?

Corporate bonds, preferred stock, and common stock are the three forms of corporate securities discussed in the chapter.

14-5.   Do corporations rely more on external or internal funds as sources of financing?

Corporations rely more heavily on external funds as sources of financing. Sixty percent of corporate funds came from external sources during the time period under study.

14-6.   Explain the role of financial intermediaries in the flow of funds through the three-sector economy.

In a three-sector economy consisting of business, households, and government, financial intermediaries such as commercial banks, mutual saving banks, insurance companies, mutual funds, pension funds, and credit unions provide the mechanism for reallocating funds from one surplus sector to a deficit sector. These institutions indirectly invest excess funds in areas of the economy where funds are needed.

14-7.   In what two ways do security markets provide liquidity?

First, they enable corporations to raise funds by selling new issues of securities rapidly and at fair competitive prices. Second, they allow the investor who purchases securities to sell them with relative ease and speed and thereby to turn a paper asset into cash.

14-8.   What is the difference between organized exchanges and over-the-counter markets?

The organized exchanges have one central location and operate as auction markets. The over-the-counter markets have no central location; instead a network of dealers all over the country is linked by computer display terminals, telephones, and teletypes.

14-9.   What the two schools of thought about the new use of decimalization?

There are two schools of thought on decimalization. One group, the market makers are concerned that their spreads (difference between the bid and asking price) will shrink and their profitability will dry up. If their profits decline too much, they may be forced out of the market and this would have an effect on the market's liquidity. The other school thinks that decimals will be easier to understand and that this should increase volume and attract more investors to the market. Additionally, as technology drives down trading costs, the market markers can afford to give up some of their profits to benefit investors. Even before the change was complete, *The Wall Street Journal* switched over to decimals.

14-10.   What is the difference between dealers on the over-the-counter (OTC) markets and brokers on the exchanges?

The difference between *dealers* in the OTC markets and *brokers* on exchanges is that dealers own the securities they trade, while brokers act as agents for the buyers and sellers.

14-11.   How would you define efficient security markets?

Markets are efficient when (1) prices adjust rapidly to new information; (2) there is a continuous market, in which each successive trade is made at a price close to the previous price; and (3) the market can absorb large dollar amounts of securities without destabilizing the price.

14-12.   The efficient market hypothesis is interpreted in a weak form, a semistrong form, and a strong form. How can we differentiate its various forms?

The weak form of efficient markets simply states that past price information is unrelated to future prices and that since no trends are predictable, investors cannot take advantage of them. The semi-strong form states that prices reflect all public information, while the strong form states that all information, both public and private, is reflected in the stock prices.

14-13.   What was the primary purpose of the Securities Act of 1933?

The primary purpose of the Securities Act of 1933 was to provide full disclosure of all pertinent information whenever a corporation sold anew issue of securities.

14-14.   What act of Congress created the Securities and Exchange Commission?

The Securities Act of 1934 created the Securities and Exchange Commission.

14-15.   What is program trading? What is the potential consequence of program trading?

Program trading means that computer-based trigger points in the market are established by these traders for unusually bid orders to buy or sell securities. If a large number of institutional investors engage in program trading at the same time (and all are either buying or selling), there is the potential for a market crash (such as on October 19, 1987) or an incredible market rise.

Chapter 15

Discussion Questions

15-1.   In what way is an investment banker a risk taker?

The investment banker is a risk taker (underwriter) in that the investment banking house agrees to buy the securities from the corporation and resell them to other security dealers and the public.

15-2.   What is the purpose of market stabilization activities during the distribution process?

Market stabilization activities are managed in an attempt to insure that the market price will not fall below a desired level during the distribution process. Syndicate members committed to purchasing the stock at a given level could be in trouble if there is a rapid decline in the price of the stock.

15-3.   Discuss how an underwriting syndicate decreases risk for each underwriter and at the same time facilitates the distribution process.

By forming a syndicate of many underwriters rather than just one, the overall risk is diffused and the capabilities for widespread distribution are enhanced. A syndicate may comprise as few as two or as many as 100 investment banking houses.

15-4.   Discuss the reason for the differences between underwriting spreads for stocks and bonds.

Common stocks often carry a larger underwriting spread than bonds because the market reaction to stocks is more uncertain.

15-5.   Explain how the price of a new security issue is determined.

The price is determined by the firm's industry, its financial characteristics, and the firm's anticipated earnings and divided-paying capability. Based on appropriate valuation techniques, a price will be tentatively assigned and will be compared to that enjoyed by similar firms in a given industry. If the industry's price-earnings ratio is 12, the firm should not stray too far from the norm. Anticipated public demand will also be a major factor in pricing a new issue.

15-6.   What is shelf registration? How does it differ from the traditional requirements for security offerings?

Shelf registration permits large companies to file one comprehensive registration statement (under SEC Rule 415). This statement outlines the firm's plans for future long-term financing. Then, when market conditions appear to be appropriate, the firm can issue the securities without further SEC approval. Shelf registration is different from the traditional requirement that security issuers file a detailed registration statement for SEC review and approval each and every time they plan a sale.

15-7.   Comment on the market performance of companies going public, both immediately after the offering has been made and some time later. Relate this to research that has been done in this area.

Due to underpricing by the investment banker, there is often a positive excess return immediately after the offering. With the passage of time, the efficiency of the market beings to become evident and long-term sustainable performance is very much dependent on the quality of the issue and market conditions.

15-8.   Discuss the benefits accruing to a company that is traded in the public securities markets.

The benefits of having a publicly traded security are:
a.   Greater ability to raise capital.
b.   Additional prestige and visibility that can be helpful in bank negotiations, executive recruitment, and the marketing of products.
c.   Increased liquidity for existing stockholders.
d.   Ease in estate planning for existing stockholders.
e.   An increased capability to engage in the merger and acquisition process.

15-9.   What are the disadvantages to being public?

The disadvantage of being public are:
a.   All information must be made available to the public through SEC and state filings. This can be very expensive for a small company.
b.   The president must be a public relations representative to the investment community.
c.   Tremendous pressure is put on the firm for short-term performance.
d.   Large downside movement in the stock can take place in a bear market.
e.   The initial cost of going public can be very expensive for a small firm.

15-10.   If a company were looking for capital by way of a private placement, where would it look for funds?

Funds for private placement can be found through insurance companies, pension funds, and wealthy individuals.

15-11.   How does a leveraged buyout work? What does the debt structure of the firm normally look like after a leveraged buyout? What might be done to reduce the debt?

The use of a leveraged buy-out implies that either management or some other investor group borrows the needed cash to repurchase all the shares of the company. After the repurchase, the company exits with a lot of debt and heavy interest expense. To reduce the debt load, assets may be sold off to generate cash. Also, returns from asset sales may be redeployed into higher return areas.

15-12.   How might a leveraged buyout eventually lead to high returns for companies?

Companies may restructure their companies and once again take them public at a large profit.

15-13.   What is privatization?

In the international markets, investment bankers take companies private that were previously owned by the government.

Problems

15-1.　　The Hamilton Corporation currently has four million shares of stock outstanding and will report earnings of $6,000,000 in the current year. The company is considering the issuance of one million additional shares that will net $30 per share to the corporation.

a. What is the immediate dilution potential for this new stock issue?
b. Assume the Hamilton Corporation can earn 10.5 percent on the proceeds of the stock issue in time to include it in the current year's results. Should the new issue be undertaken based on earnings per share?

Solution:
Hamilton Corporation

a. Earnings per share before stock issue
   $$\$6,000,000/4,000,000 = \$1.50$$

Earnings per share after stock issue
   $$\$6,000,000/5,000,000 = \$1.20$$

dilution　$1.50
　　　　　 1.20
　　　　　$ 30 per share

b. net income = $6,000,000 + .105 ($1,000,000 × $30)
　　　　　 = $6,000,000 + .105 ($30,000,000)
　　　　　 = $6,000,000 + $3,150,000
　　　　　 = $9,150,000

Earnings per share after additional income
EPS = $9,150,000/$5,000,000
　　 = $1.83

Based on the current year's results, the public offering should be undertaken. E.P.S. go from $1.50 to $1.83. Of course, other variables may also be considered.

15-2.   In problem 1, if the one million additional shares can only be issued at $23 per share and the company can earn 6.0 percent on the proceeds, should the new issue be undertaken based on earnings per share?

Solution:
Hamilton Corporation (Continued)

$$\text{net income} = \$6,000,000 + .06\ (\$23,000,000)$$
$$= \$6,000,000 + \$1,380,000 = \$7,378,000$$

Earnings per share after additional income

$$\text{EPS} = \$7,378,000/5,000,000 = \$1.48$$

No, E.P.S. would decline by 2 cents from $1.50 to $1.48.

15-3.   American Health Systems currently has six million shares of stock outstanding and will report earnings of $15 million in the current year. The company is considering the issuance of 1.5 million additional shares that will net $50 per share to the corporation.

a. What is the immediate dilution potential for this new stock issue?
b. Assume that American Health Systems can earn 12 percent on the proceeds of the stock issue in time to include it in the current year's results. Should the new issue be undertaken based on earnings per share?

Solution:
American Health Systems

a. Earnings per share before stock issue

$$\$15,000,000/6,000,000 = \$2.50$$

Earnings per share after stock issue

$$\$15,000,000/7,500,000 = \$2.00$$

dilution $2.50
            2.00
         $ .50 per share

b. net income $= \$15,000,000 + .12\,(1,500,000 \times \$50)$
$\qquad\qquad = \$15,000,000 + .12\,(\$75,000,000)$
$\qquad\qquad = \$15,000,000 + \$9,000,000$
$\qquad\qquad = \$24,000,000$

Earnings per share after additional income
EPS $= \$24,000,000/7,500,000$
$\qquad = \$3.20$

Yes, the EPS of \$3.20 is higher than \$2.50.

15-4.   In problem 3, if the 1.5 million additional shares can be issued at \$28 per share and the company can earn 10 percent on the proceeds, should the new issue be undertaken based on earnings per share?

Solution:

American Health Systems (Continued)

net income $= \$15,000,000 + .10\,(1,500,000 \times \$28)$
$\qquad\qquad = \$15,000,000 + .10\,(\$42,000,000)$
$\qquad\qquad = \$15,000,000 + \$4,200,000$
$\qquad\qquad = \$19,200,000$

Earnings per share after additional income
EPS $= \$19,200,000/7,500,000$
$\qquad = \$2.56$

Yes, the EPS of \$2.56 is higher than \$2.50.

15-5.   Walton and Company is the managing investment banker for a major new
underwriting. The price of the stock to the investment banker is $18 per share.
Other syndicate members may buy the stock for $18.25. The price to the
selected dealers group is $18.80, with a price to brokers of $19.20. Finally, the
price to the public is $19.50.

a. If Walton and Company sells its shares to the dealer group, what will the
    percentage return be?
b. If Walton and Company performs the dealer's function also and sells to
    brokers, what will the percentage return be?
c. If Walton and Company fully integrates its operation and sells directly to
    the public, what will its percentage return be?

Solution:
Walton and Company

a. $18.80   Selected dealer group's price
   18.00   Managing investing banker's price
   $ .80   Differential

   $\dfrac{\$\ .80}{18.00}$ = 4.44% Return

b. $19.20   Brokers price
   18.00   Managing investment banker's price
   $ 1.20   Differential

   $\dfrac{\$\ 1.20}{18.00}$ = 6.67% Return

c. $19.50   Public price
   18.00   Managing investment banker's price
   $ 1.50   Differential

   $\dfrac{\$\ 1.50}{18.00}$ = 8.33% Return

15-6.   The Wrigley Corporation needs to raise $30 million. The investment banking firm of Tinkers, Evers, & Chance will handle the transaction.

   a. If stock is utilized, 2,000,000 shares will be sold to the public at $15.70 per share. The corporation will receive a net price of $15 per share. What is the percentage of underwriting spread per share? What is the percentage of underwriting spread per share?
   b. If bonds are utilized, slightly over 30,000 bonds will be sold to the public at $1,001 per bond. The corporation will receive a net price of $992 per bond. What is the percentage of underwriting spread per bond? (Relate the dollar spread to the public price.)
   c. Which alternative has the larger percentage of spread? Is this the normal relationship between the two types of issues?

Solution:
Wrigley Corporation

a. Spread = $15.70 − $15.00 = $.70
% underwriting spread = $.70/$15.70 = 4.46%

b. Spread = $1,001 − $992 = $9
% underwriting spread = $9/$1,001 = .899%

c. The stock alternative has the larger percentage spread. This is normal because there is more uncertainty in the market associated with a stock offering and investment bankers want to be appropriately compensated.

15-7.   Kevin's Bacon Company, Inc. has earnings of $6 million with two million shares outstanding before a public distribution. Five hundred thousand shares will be included in the sale, of which 300,000 are new corporate shares, and 200,000 are shares currently owned by Ann Fry, the founder and CEO. The 200,000 shares that Ann is selling are referred to as a secondary offering and all proceeds will go to her.

The net price from the offering will be $15.50 and the corporate proceeds are expected to produce $1.5 million in corporate earnings.

a.   What were the corporation's earnings per share before the offering?
b.   What are the corporation's earnings per share expected to be after the offering?

Solution:

Kevin's Bacon Company

a. Earnings per share before stock issue
$6,000,000/2,000,000 = $3.00

b. Earnings per share after stock issue

Total Earnings
Before offering	$6,000,000
Incremental Earnings	1,500,000
Earnings after offering	$7,500,000

Corporate shares outstanding
Before offering	2,000,000
Incremental Shares	300,000*
Shares after offering	2,300,000

*   The 200,000 secondary shares are not included as new corporate shares.

$$\frac{\text{Earnings}}{\text{per share}} = \$7,500,000 / 2,300,000 = \$3.26$$

15-8. Becker Brothers is the managing underwriter for a one million share issue by Jay's Hamburger Heaven. Becker Brothers is "handling" 10 percent of the issue. Its price is $25 and the price to the public is $26.40.

Becker also provides the market stabilization function. During the issuance, the market for the stock turned soft, and Becker was forced to purchase 40,000 shares in the open market at an average price of $25.75. They later sold the shares at an average value of $23.

Compute Becker Brothers *overall* gain or loss from managing this issue.

Solution:

Becker Brothers

Original Distribution

$10\% \times 1,000,000 =$ 100,000 shares for Becker

$ 1.40 profit per share

$140,000 profit on original distribution

Market Stabilization

40,000 shares for Becker

$ 2.75 loss per share

$110,000 loss on market stabilization

Gain on original distribution	$140,000
Loss on market stabilization	110,000
Net gain	$ 30,000

15-9.   Trump Card Co. will issue stock at a retail (public) price of $30. The company will receive $27.60 per share.

a.   What is the spread on the issue in percentage terms?
b.   If the firm demands receiving a net price only $1.50 below the public price suggested in part a, what will the spread be in percentage terms?
c.   To hold the spread down to 3 percent based on the public price in part a, what net amount should Trump Card Co. receive?

Solution:

Trump Card Company

a. $\dfrac{\$ \text{Spread}}{\text{Public Price}} = \dfrac{\$2.40}{\$30} = 8\%$

b. $\dfrac{\$ \text{Spread}}{\text{Public Price}} = \dfrac{\$1.50}{\$30} = 5\%$

c. Public Price $30.00
    3% Spread   .90
    Net Amount Received $29.10

15-10.   Winston Sporting Goods is considering a public offering of common stock. Its investment banker has informed the company that the retail price will be $18 per share for 600,000 shares. The company will receive $16.50 per share and will incur $150,000 in registration, accounting, and printing fees.

a.   What is the spread on this issue in percentage terms? What are the total expenses of the issue as a percentage of total value (at retail)?

b.   If the firm wanted to net $18 million from this issue, how many shares must be sold?

Solution:

Winston Sporting Goods

a. $18 − $16.50   = $1.50 spread $1.50/$18.00 = 8.33% spread

    Total expenses =   ($1.50 × 600,000 shares)

                       + $150,000 (out-of-pocket)

              = $900,000 + $150,000

              = $1,050,000

    Total value   =   600,000 shares × $18 = $10,800,000

$$\frac{\text{Total expenses}}{\text{Total value}} = \frac{\$1,050,000}{\$10,800,000} = 9.72\%$$

b.   Amount needed   = $18,000,000

    Total shares to be sold to net $18,000,000

       = ($18,000,000 + issue costs)/net price per share

       = $18,150,000/$16.50 per share = 1,100,000 shares

15-11. Rogers Homebuilding is about to go public. The investment banking firm of Leland Webber and Company is attempting to price the issue. The homebuilding industry generally trades at a 20 percent discount below the P/E ratio on the Standard & Poor's 500 Stock Index. Assume that Index currently has a P/E ratio of 25. Rodgers can be compared to the homebuilding industry as follows:

	Ashley	Homebuilding industry
Growth rate in earnings per share ...	12 percent	10 percent
Consistency of performance	Increased earnings 4 out of 5 years	Increased earnings 3 out of 5 years
Debt to total assets	55 percent	40 percent
Turnover of product	Slightly below average	Average
Quality of management...................	High	Average

Assume, in assessing the initial P/E ratio, the investment banker will first determine the appropriate industry P/E based on the Standard & Poor's 500 Index. Then ½ point will be added to the P/E ratio for each case in which Rodgers is superior to the industry norm, and ½ point will be deducted for an inferior comparison. On this basis, what should the initial P/E be for Rodgers Homebuilding?

Solution:

Rodgers Homebuilding

80% of the Standard and Poor's 500 Stock Index =
80% × 25 = 20

Industry Comparisons

Growth rate in earnings per share-superior	+ ½
Consistency of performance-superior	+ ½
Debt to total assets-inferior	− ½
Turnover of product-inferior	− ½
Quality of management-superior	+ ½
Quality of management-superior	+ ½

Initial P/E ratio = 20 + ½ = 20 ½

15-12. The investment banking firm of A. Einstein & Co. will use a dividend valuation model to appraise the shares of the Modern Physics Corporation. Dividends (D_1) at the end of the current year will be $1.44. The growth rate (g) is 8 percent and the discount rate (K_e) is 12 percent.

a. Using Formula 10-9 from Chapter 10, what should be the price of the stock to the public?
b. If there is a 6 percent total underwriting spread on the stock, how much will the issuing corporation receive?
c. If the issuing corporation requires a net price of $34.50 (proceeds to the corporation) and there is a 6 percent underwriting spread, what should be the price of the stock to the public? (Round to two places to the right of the decimal point.)

Solution:

A. Einstein & Co.

a. $P_o = \dfrac{D_1}{K_e - g} = \dfrac{\$1.44}{.12 - .08} = \dfrac{\$1.44}{.04} = \$36$

b.
Public price	$36.00
Underwriting spread (6%)	2.16
Net price to the corporation	$33.84

c. Necessary public price $= \dfrac{\text{Net price}}{(1 - \text{underwriting spread})}$

$$\dfrac{\$34.50}{(1-.06)} = \dfrac{\$34.50}{.94} = \$36.70$$

15-13.   The Landers Corporation needs to raise $1 million of debt on a 25-year issue. If it places the bonds privately, the interest rate will be 11 percent. Thirty thousand dollars in out-of-pocket costs will be incurred. For a public issue, the interest rate will be 10 percent, and the underwriting spread will be 4 percent. There will be $100,000 in out-of-pocket costs.

Assume interest on the debt is paid semiannually, and the debt will be outstanding for the full 25-year period, at which time it will be repaid.

Which plan offers the higher net present value? For each plan, compare the net amount of funds initially available—inflow—to the present value of future payments of interest and principal to determine net present value. Assume the stated discount rate is 12 percent annually. Use 6 percent semiannually throughout the analysis. (Disregard taxes.)

Solution:

Landers Corporation

Private Placement

$1,000,000	debt
− 30,000	out-of-pocket costs
$ 970,000	net amount to Landers

Present value of future interest payments

interest payments (semiannually) $= 11\%/2 = 5.5\%$
interest payments $= 5.5\% \times \$1,000,000 = \$55,000$

$PV_A = A \times PV_{IFA}\ (n = 50,\ i = 6\%)$
$PV_A = \$55,000 \times 15.762$ (Appendix D)
$PV_A = \$866,910$

Present value of lump-sum payment at maturity

$$PV = FV \times PV_{IF} \ (n = 50, \ i = 6\%)$$
$$PV = \$1,000,000 \times .054 \qquad \text{(Appendix B)}$$
$$PV = \$54,000$$

Total present value of interest and maturity payments

$$
\begin{aligned}
&\$866,910 \\
&\underline{+ \ 54,000} \\
&\$920,910 \qquad \text{total present value}
\end{aligned}
$$

The net present value equals the net amount to Landers minus the present value of future payments.

$970,000	net amount to Landers
−920,000	present value of future payments
$ 49,090	net present value (private offering)

Public Issue

$1,000,000	debt
− 40,000	4% spread
− 100,000	out-of-pocket costs
$ 860,000	net amount to Landers

Present value of future interest payments

interest payments (semiannually) = 10%/2 = 5%
interest payments = 5% × \$1,000,000 = \$50,000

PV_A = A × PV_{IFA} (n = 50, i = 6%)
PV_A = \$50,000 × 15.762   (Appendix D)
PV_A = \$788,100

Present value of lump-sum payment at maturity

PV = FV × PV_{IF} (n = 50, i = 6%)
PV = \$1,000,000 × .054   (Appendix B)
PV = \$54,000

Total present value of interest and maturity payments

\$788,100
+ 54,000
\$842,100   total present value

Net present value equals the net amount to Landers minus the present value of future payments.

\$860,000   net amount to Landers
–842,100   present value of future payments
\$ 17,900   net amount to Landers

The private placement has the higher net present value (\$49,090 vs. \$17,900)

15-14. Midland Corporation has a net income of $15 million and 6 million shares outstanding. Its common stock is currently selling for $40 per share. Midland plans to sell common stock to set up a major new production facility with a net cost of $21,660,000. The production facility will not produce a profit for one year, and then it is expected to earn a 15 percent return on the investment. Stanley Morgan and Co., an investment banking firm, plans to sell the issue to the public for $38 per share with a spread of 5 percent.

a. How many shares of stock must be sold to net $21,660,000? (Note: No out-of-pocket costs must be considered in this problem.)
b. Why is the investment banker selling the stock at less than its current market price?
c. What are the earnings per share (EPS) and the price-earnings ratio before the issue (based on a stock price of $40)? What will be the price per share immediately after the sale of stock if the P/E stays constant?
d. Compute the EPS and the price (P/E stays constant) after the new production facility begins to produce a profit.
e. Are the shareholders better off because of the sale of stock and the resultant investment? What other financing strategy could the company have tried to increase earnings per share?

Solution:

Midland Corporation

a. $21,660,000 net amount to be raised.

Determine net price to the corporation

$38.00	public price
− 1.90	5% spread
$36.10	net price

Determine number of shares to be sold

$$\frac{\$21,660,000}{\$36.10} = 600,000 \text{ shares}$$

b. The new shares will increase the total number of shares outstanding and dilute EPS. This dilution effect may reduce the stock price in the market temporarily until income from the new assets becomes included in the price the market is willing to pay for the stock. By selling at below market value, the investment banker is attempting to attract investors into this temporarily dilutive situation. The investment banking firm is also reducing its own underwriting risk by pricing the issue at the lower value.

c.
EPS	$= \$15,000,000/6,000,000 = \$2.50$
P/E ratio	$= \text{Price/EPS} = \$40/\$2.50 = 16x$
EPS after offering	$= \$15,000,000/6,600,000 = \$2.27$
Price	$= \text{P/E} \times \text{EPS} = 16 \times \$2.27 = \$36.32$

d.
Net income	$= \$15,000,000 + 15\% \, (\$21,660,000)$
	$= \$15,000,000 + \$3,249,000$
	$= \$18,249,000$

EPS after contribution $= \$18,249,000/6,600,000 = \$2.77$
Price $\quad = \text{P/E} \times \text{EPS} = 16 \times \$2.77 = \$44.32$

e. In the long run, it appears that the company is better off because of the additional investment. Earnings per share are $.27 higher and the stock price also increased. If the firm had used debt financing or a combination of debt and stock, they would have increased earnings per share even more, but would have created additional financial obligations in the process.

15-15. The Presley Corporation is about to go public. It currently has aftertax earnings of $7,500,000, and 2,500,000 shares are owned by the present stockholders (the Presley family). The new public issue will represent 600,000 new shares. The new shares will be priced to the public at $20 per share, with a 5 percent spread on the offering price. There will also be $200,000 in out-of-picket costs to the corporation.

a. Compute the net proceeds to the Presley Corporation.
b. Compute the earnings per share immediately before the stock issue.
c. Compute the earnings per share immediately after the stock issue.
d. Determine what rate of return must be earned on the net proceeds to the corporation so there will not be a dilution in earnings per share during the year of going public.
e. Determine what rate of return must be earned on the proceeds to the corporation so there will be a 5 percent increase in earnings per share during the year of going public.

Solution:

Presley Corporation

a. $20 price × 95% = $19 net price

$19	net price
× 600,000	new shares
$11,400,000	proceeds before out-of-pocket costs
− 200,000	out-of-pocket costs
$11,200,000	net proceeds

b. Earnings per share before stock issue $= \dfrac{\$7,500,000}{2,500,000} = \$3.00$

c. Earnings per share after stock issue $= \dfrac{\$7,500,000}{3,100,000} = \$2.42$

d. There are now 3,100,000 shares outstanding. To maintain earnings of $3 per share, total earnings must be $9,300,000. This would imply an increase in earnings of $1,800,000 ($9,300,000 − $7,500,000).

$$\frac{\text{incremental earnings}}{\text{net proceeds}} = \frac{\$1,800,000}{\$11,200,000} = 16.07\%$$

16.07% must be earned on the net proceeds to produce EPS of $3.00.

e. $3.00 (1.05)   = $3.15 (5% increase in EPS)
   Total earnings   = $3.15 × 3,100,000 shares = $9,765,000
   incremental earnings = $9,765,000 − $7,500,000 = $2,265,000

$$\frac{\text{incremental earnings}}{\text{net proceeds}} = \frac{\$2,265,000}{\$11,200,000} = 20.22\%$$

20.22% would have to be earned to produce EPS of $3.15.

15-16.   I. B. Michaels has a chance to participate in a new public offering by Hi-Tech Micro Computers. His broker informs him that demand for the 500,000 shares to be issued is very strong. His broker's firm is assigned 15,000 shares in the distribution and will allow Michaels, a relatively good customer, 1.5 percent of its 15,000 share allocation.

The initial offering price is $30 per share. There is a strong aftermarket, and the stock goes to $33 one week after issue. At the end of the first full month after issue, Mr. Michaels is pleased to observe his shares are selling for $34.75. He is content to place his shares in a lockbox and eventually use their anticipated increased value to help send his son to college many years in the future. However, one year after the distribution, he looks up the share in *The Wall Street Journal* and finds they are trading at $28.75.

a. Compute the total dollar profit or loss on Mr. Michael's shares one week, one month, and one year after the purchase. In each case compute the profit or loss against the initial purchase price.

b. Also compute this percentage gain or loss from the initial $30 price and compare this to the results that might be expected in an investment of this nature based on prior research. Assume the overall stock market was basically unchanged during the period of observation.

c. Why might a new public issue be expected to have a strong aftermarket?

Solution:

I.B. Michaels

a. Mr. Michael's purchase = 1.5% × 15,000 shares = 225 shares

Dollar profit or loss

1 week	225 shares × ($33 – $30)	= $	675.00	profit
1 month	225 shares × ($34.75 – $30)	= $1,068.75		profit
1 year	225 shares × ($28.75 – $30)	= $	281.25	loss

b. Percentage profit or loss

1 week	$3.00/$30	= 10.00%
1 month	$4.75/$30	= 15.83%
1 year	–$1.25/$30	= –4.17%

The results are in line with prior research. The stock went up one week and one month after issue, but actually provided a negative return for one year after issue. This is consistent with the research of Reilly (footnote 1), which showed excess returns of 10.9 percent, 11.6 percent and –3.0 percent over comparable periods of study. Actually, the stock was a bit stronger than that indicated by the Reilly research for one month after issue.

c. A new public issue may be expected to have a strong aftermarket because investment bankers often underprice the issue to insure the success of the distribution.

15-17.   The management of Mitchell Labs decided to go private in 1994 by buying in all 3 million outstanding shares at $19.50 per share. By 1996, management had restructured the company by selling off the petroleum research division for $13 million, the fiber technology division for $9.5 million, and the synthetic products division for $21 million. Because these divisions had been only marginally profitable, Mitchell Labs is a stronger company after the restructuring. Mitchell is now able to concentrate exclusively on contract research and will generate earnings per share of $1.25 this year. Investment bankers have contacted the firm and indicated that if it reentered the public market, the 3 million shares it purchased to go private could now be reissued to the public at a P/E ratio of 16 times earnings per share.

a. What was the initial cost to Mitchell Labs to go private?
b. What is the total value to the company from (1) the proceeds of the divisions that were sold as well as (2) the current value of the 3 million shares (based on current earnings and an anticipated P/E of 16)?
c. What is the percentage return to the management of Mitchell Labs from the restructuring? Use answers from parts *a* and *b* to determine this value.

Solution:

Mitchell Labs

a. 3 million shares × $19.50 = $58.5 million (cost to go private)

b. Proceeds from sale of the divisions

Petroleum research division	$13.0 million
Fiber Technology division	9.5 million
Synthetic products division	21.0 million
	$43.5 million

Current value of the 3 million shares

3 million shares × (P/E × EPS)

3 million × (16 × $1.25)

3 million × $20	$60.0 million
Total value to the company	$103.5 million

c.
Total value to the company	$103.5 million
– Cost to go private	58.5 million
Profit from restructuring	$ 45.0 million

$$\frac{\text{Profit from restructuring}}{\text{Cost to go private}} = \frac{\$45.0 \ \text{million}}{\$58.5 \ \text{million}} = 76.92\%$$

Comprehensive Problem

CP 15-1.   The Bailey Corporation, a manufacturer of medical supplies and equipment, is planning to sell its shares to the general public for the first time. The firm's investment banker, Robert Merrill and Company, is working with Bailey Corporation in determining a number of items. Information on the Bailey Corporation follows:

Bailey Corporation
Income Statement
For the Year 200X

Sales (all on credit)	$42,680,000
Cost of goods sold	32,240,000
Gross profit	10,440,000
Selling and administrative expense	4,558,000
Operating profit	5,882,000
Interest expense	600,000
Net income before taxes	5,282,000
Taxes	2,120,000
Net income	$ 3,162,000

Bailey Corporation
Balance Sheet
As of December 31, 200X

Assets

Current assets		
Cash	$	250,000
Marketable securities		130,000
Accounts receivable		6,000,000
Inventory		8,300,000
Total current assets		14,680,000
Net plant and equipment		13,970,000
Total assets		$28,650,000

Liabilities and Stockholders' Equity

Current liabilities:

Accounts payable	$ 3,800,000
Notes payable	3,550,000
Total current liabilities	7,350,000
Long-term liabilities	5,260,000
Total liabilities	$12,970,000

Stockholders' equity:

Common stock (1,800,000 shares at $1 par)	$ 1,800,000
Capital in excess of pare	6,300,000
Retained earnings	7,580,000
Total stockholders' equity	15,680,000
Total liabilities and stockholders' equity	$28,650,000

a. Assume that 800,000 new corporate shares will be issued to the general public. What will earnings per share be immediately after the public offering? (Round to two places to the right of the decimal point.) Based on the price-earnings ratio of 12, what will the initial price of the stock be? Use earnings per share after the distribution in the calculation.

b. Assuming an underwriting spread of 5 percent and out-of-pocket costs of $300,000, what will net proceeds to the corporation be?

c. What return must the corporation earn on the net proceeds to equal the earnings per share before the offering? How does this compare with current return on the total assets on the balance sheet?

d. Now assume that, of the initial 800,000 share distribution, 400,000 belong to current stockholders and 400,000 are new shares, and the latter will be added to the 1,800,000 shares currently outstanding. What will earnings per share be immediately after the public offering? What will the initial market price of the stock be? Assume a price-earnings ratio of 12 and use earnings per share after the distribution in the calculation.

e. Assuming an underwriter spread of 5 percent and out-of-picket costs of $300,000, what will net proceeds to the corporation be?

f. What return must the corporation now earn on the net proceeds to equal earnings per share before the offering? How does this compare with current return on the total assets on the balance sheet?

CP Solution:

New Public Offering

Bailey Corporation

a. Earnings per share (after) $= \dfrac{\text{Earnings}}{\text{Shares}}$

$$\frac{\$3,162,000}{1,800,000 + 800,000} \qquad = \frac{\$3,162,000}{2,600,000} = \$1.22$$

Initial market price $\quad = \text{P/E} \times \text{EPS}$

$$= 12 \times \$1.22 = \$14.64$$

b. 800,000 shares × $14.64 = $11,712,000 gross proceeds

$$
\begin{array}{rl}
- & 585,600 \quad \text{5\% spread} \\
- & \underline{300,000} \quad \text{out-of-pocket costs} \\
& \$10,826,400 \quad \text{net proceeds}
\end{array}
$$

c. Earnings per share (before) $\quad = \dfrac{\text{Earnings}}{\text{Shares}}$

$$\frac{\$3,162,000}{1,800,000} = \$1.76$$

In order to earn $1.76 after the offering, the return on $10,826,400 must produce new earnings equal to X.

$$\frac{\$3,162,00 + X}{1,800,000 + 800,000} = \$1.76$$

$$\frac{\$3,162,000 + X}{2,600,000} = \$1.76$$

$3,162,000 + X = \$1.76\ (2,600,000)$

$X = \$4,576,000 - \$3,162,000$
$X = \$1,414,000$

Proof:

$$\frac{\$3,162,000 + \$1,414,000}{1,800,000 + 800,000} = \frac{\$4,576,000}{2,600,000} = \$1.76$$

thus: $\dfrac{\text{New earnings}}{\text{New proceeds}} = \dfrac{\$1,414,000}{\$10,826,400} = 13.06\%$

The firm must earn 13.06% on net proceeds to equal earnings per share before the offering.

This is greater than current return on assets of 11.04%.

$$\frac{\text{Net income}}{\text{Total assets}} = \frac{\$3,162,000}{\$28,650,000} = 11.04\%$$

d. Earnings per share (after) $= \dfrac{\text{Earnings}}{\text{Shares}}$

$$\frac{\$3,162,000}{1,800,000 + 400,000} = \frac{\$3,162,000}{2,200,000} = \$1.44$$

Initial market price = P/E × EPS

$12 \times \$1.44 = \$17.28.$

e. $400{,}000 \times \$17.28 = \$6{,}912{,}000$ gross proceeds
$$\underline{\hspace{1.2cm}} - \ 345{,}600 \quad \text{5\% spread}$$
$$\underline{\ - \ \ \ 300{,}000} \quad \text{out-of-pocket costs}$$
$$\$6{,}266{,}400 \quad \text{net proceeds}$$

f. $\dfrac{\$3{,}162{,}000 + X}{1{,}800{,}000 + 400{,}000} = \$1.76$

$\dfrac{\$3{,}162{,}000 + X}{2{,}200{,}000} = \$1.76$

$\$3{,}162{,}000 + X = \$1.76\,(2{,}200{,}000)$

$X = \$3{,}872{,}000 - \$3{,}162{,}000$

$X = \$710{,}000$

proof:

$\dfrac{\$3{,}162{,}000 + \$710{,}000}{1{,}800{,}000 + 400{,}000} = \dfrac{\$3{,}872{,}000}{2{,}200{,}000} = \$1.76$

thus:

$\dfrac{\text{New earnings}}{\text{Net proceeds}} = \dfrac{\$710{,}000}{\$6{,}266{,}400} = 11.33\%$

This is greater than the current return on assets of 11.04%.

$\dfrac{\text{Net income}}{\text{Total assets}} = \dfrac{\$3{,}162{,}000}{\$28{,}650{,}000} = 11.04\%$

Chapter 16

Discussion Questions

16-1.   Corporate debt has been expanding very dramatically since World War II. What has been the impact on interest coverage, particularly since 1977?

   In 1977, the average U.S. manufacturing corporation had its interest covered almost eight times. By the late 1990s, the ratio had been cut in half.

16-2.   What are some specific features of bond agreements?

   The bond agreement specifies such basic items as the par value, the coupon rate, and the maturity date.

16-3.   What is the difference between a bond agreement and a bond indenture?

   The bond agreement covers a limited number of items, whereas the bond indenture is a supplement that often contains over 100 pages of complicated legal wording and specifies every minute detail concerning the bond issue. The bond indenture covers such topics as pledged collateral, methods of repayment, restrictions on the corporation, and procedures for initiating claims against the corporation.

16-4.   Discuss the relationship between the coupon rate (original interest rate at time of issue) on a bond and its security provisions.

   The greater the security provisions afforded to a given class of bondholders, the lower the coupon rate.

16-5.   Take the following list of securities and arrange them in order of their priority of claims:

Preferred stock   Senior debenture
Subordinated debenture   Senior secured debt
Common stock   Junior secured debt

The priority of claims can be determined from Figure 16-2:

senior secured debt,
junior secured debt,
senior debenture,
subordinated debenture,
preferred stock,
common stock.

16-6.   What method of "bond repayment" reduces debt and increases the amount of common stock outstanding?

Bond conversion.

16-7.   What is the purpose of serial repayments and sinking funds?

The pu7rpose of serial and sinking fund payments is to provide an orderly procedure for the retirement of a debt obligation. To the extend bonds are paid off over their life, there is less risk to the security holder.

16-8.   Under what circumstances would a call on a bond be exercised by a corporation? What is the purpose of a deferred call?

A call provision may be exercised when interest rates on new securities are considerably lower than those on previously issued debt. The purpose of a deferred call is to insure that the bondholder will not have to surrender the security due to a call for at least the first five or ten years.

16-9.   Discuss the relationship between bond prices and interest rates. What impact do changing interest rates have on the price of long-term bonds versus short-term bonds?

Bond prices on outstanding issues and interest rates move in opposite directions. If interest rates go up, bond prices will go down and vice versa. Long-term bonds are particularly sensitive to interest rate changes between the bondholder is locked into the interest rate for an extended period of time.

16-10.   What is the difference between the following yields: coupon rate, current yield, yield to maturity?

The different bond yield terms may be defined as follows:

Coupon rate -   stated interest rate divided by par value.
Current yield -   stated interest rate divided by the current price of the bond.
Yield to maturity -the interest rate that will equate future interest payments and payment at maturity to a current market price.

16-11.   How does the bond rating affect the interest rate paid by a corporation on its bonds?

The higher the rating on a bond, the lower the interest payment that will be required to satisfy the bondholder.

16-12.   Bonds of different risk classes will have a spread between their interest rates. Is this spread always the same? Why?

The spread in the yield between bonds in different risk classes is not always the same. The yield spread changes with the economy. If investors are pessimistic about the economy, they will accept as much as 3% less return to go into very high-quality securities-whereas, in more normal times the spread may only-be 1 ½%.

16-13.   Explain how the bond refunding problem is similar to a capital budgeting decision.

The bond refunding problem is similar to a capital budgeting problem in that an initial investment must be made in the form of redemption and reissuing costs, and cash inflows will take place in the form of interest savings. We take the present value of the inflows to determine if they equal or exceed the outflow.

16-14.   What cost of capital is generally used in evaluating a bond refunding decision? Why?

We use the aftertax cost of new debt as the discount rate rather than the more generalized cost of capital. Because the net cash benefits are known with certainty, the refunding decision represents a riskless investment. For this reason, we use a lower discount rate.

16-15.   Explain how the zero-coupon rate bond provides return to the investor. What are the advantages to the corporation?

The zero-coupon-rate bond is initially sold at a deep discount from par value. The return to the investor is the difference between the investor's cost and the face value received at the end of the life of the bond. The advantages to the corporation are that there is immediate cash inflow to the corporation, without any outflow until the bond matures. Furthermore, the difference between the initial bond price and the maturity value may be amortized for tax purposes over the life of the bond by the corporation.

16-16.   Explain how floating rate bonds can save the investor from potential embarrassments in portfolio valuations.

Interest payments change with changing interest rates rather than with the market value of the bond. This means that the market value of a floating rate bond is almost fixed. The one exception is when interest rates dictated by the floating rate formula approach (or exceed) broadly defined limits.

16-17.   Discuss the advantages and disadvantages of debt.

The primary advantages of debt are:
a. Interest payments are tax deductible.
b. The financial obligation is clearly specified and of a fixed nature.
c. In an inflationary economy, debt may be paid back with cheaper dollars.
d. The use of debt, up to a prudent point, may lower the cost of capital to the firm.

The disadvantages are:
a. Interest and principal payment obligations are set by contract and must be paid regardless of economic circumstances.
b. Bond indenture agreements may place burdensome restrictions on the firm.
c. Debt, utilized beyond a given point, ay serve as a depressant on outstanding common stock.

16-18.   What is a Eurobond?

A Eurobond is a bond payable in the borrower's currency but sold outside the borrower's country. It is usually sold by an international syndicate.

16-19.   What do we mean by capitalizing lease payments?

Capitalizing lease payments means computing the present value of future lease payments and showing them as an asset and liability on the balance sheet.

16-20.   Explain the close parallel between a capital lease and the borrow-purchase decision from the viewpoint of both the balance sheet and the income statement.

In both cases we create an asset and liability on the balance sheet. Furthermore in both cases, for income statement purposes, we amortize the asset and write off interest (implied or actual) on the debt.

Appendix

16A-1. What is the difference between technical insolvency and bankruptcy?

Technical insolvency refers to the circumstances where a firm is unable to pay its bills as they come due. A firm may be technically insolvent even though it has a positive net worth. Bankruptcy, on the other hand, indicates that the market value of a firm's assets is less than its liabilities and the firm has a negative net worth. Under the law, either technical insolvency or bankruptcy may be adjudged as a financial failure of the business firm.

16A-2. What are the four types of out-of-court settlements? Briefly describe each.

Extension -	Creditors agree to allow the firm more time to meet its financial obligations.
Composition -	Creditors agree to accept a fractional settlement on their original claims.
Creditor committee -	A creditor committee is set up to run the business because it is believed that management can no longer conduct the affairs of the firm.
Assignment -	Liquidation of assets takes place without going through formal court action.

16A-3. What is the difference between an internal reorganization and an external reorganization under formal bankruptcy procedures?

An internal reorganization calls for an evaluation and restricting of the current affairs of the firm. Current management may be replaced and a redesign of the capital structure may be necessary. An external reorganization means that an actual merger partner will be found for the firm.

16A-4. What are the first three priority items under liquidation in bankruptcy?

(1) Cost of administering the bankruptcy procedures.

(2) Wages due workers if earned within three months of filing the bankruptcy petition. The maximum amount is $600 per worker.

(3) Tax due at the federal, state or local level.

Problems

(*Assume the par value of the bonds in the following problems is $1,000 unless otherwise specified.*)

16-1. The Garland Corporation has a bond outstanding with a $90 annual interest payment, a market price of $820, and a maturity date in five years. Find the following:

   a.   The coupon rate.
   b.   The current yield.
   c.   The approximate yield to maturity.

Solution:

Garland Corporation

a. $90 interest/$1,000 par = 9% coupon rate
b. $90 interest/$820 market price = 10.98% current yield
c. Approximate yield to maturity = (Y')

$$(Y') = \frac{\text{Annual interest payment} + \dfrac{\text{Principal payment} - \text{Price of the bond}}{\text{Number of years to maturity}}}{.6\,(\text{Price of the bond}) + .4\,(\text{Principal payment})}$$

$$= \frac{\$90 + \dfrac{\$1,000 - \$820}{5}}{.6\,(\$820) + .4\,(\$1,000)}$$

$$= \frac{\$90 + \dfrac{\$180}{5}}{\$492 + \$400}$$

$$= \frac{\$90 + \$36}{\$892}$$

$$= \frac{\$126}{\$892} = 14.13\%$$

16-2.   The Preston Corporation has a bond outstanding with a $110 annual interest payment, a market price of $1,200, and a maturity in 10 years. Find the following:

a.   The coupon rate.
b.   The current yield.
c.   The approximate yield to maturity.

Solution:
Preston Corporation

a. $110 interest/$1,000 market price = 11% coupon rate
b. $110 interest/$1,200 market price = 9.17% current yield
c.   Approximate yield to maturity = (Y')

$$(Y') = \frac{\text{Annual interest payment} + \dfrac{\text{Principal payment} - \text{Price of the bond}}{\text{Number of years to maturity}}}{.6 \,(\text{Price of the bond}) + .4 \,(\text{Principal payment})}$$

$$= \frac{\$110 + \dfrac{\$1,000 - \$1,200}{10}}{.6\,(\$1,200) + .4\,(\$1,000)}$$

$$= \frac{\$110 + \dfrac{-\$200}{10}}{\$720 + \$400}$$

$$= \frac{\$110 + \$20}{\$1,120}$$

$$= \frac{\$90}{\$1,120} = 8.04\%$$

16-3.   An investor must choose between two bonds:

Bond A pays $80 annual interest and has a market value of $800. It has 10 years to maturity.

Bond B pays $85 annual interest and has a market value of $900. It has two years to maturity.

a. Compute the current yield on both bonds.
b. Which bond should he select based on your answer to part *a*?
c. A drawback of current yield is that it does not take into consideration the total life of the bond. For example, the approximate yield to maturity on Bond A is 11.36 percent. What is the approximate yield to maturity on Bond B?
d. Has your answer changed between parts *b* and *c* of this question in terms of which bond to select?

Solution:

a. <u>Bond A</u>
   $80 interest/$800 market price = 10% current yield

   <u>Bond B</u>
   $85 interest/$900 market price = 9.44% current yield

b. Bond A. It has a higher current yield.

c. Approximate yield to maturity = (Y')   Bond B

$$(Y') = \frac{\text{Annual interest payment} + \dfrac{\text{Principal payment} - \text{Price of the bond}}{\text{Number of years to maturity}}}{.6\,(\text{Price of the bond}) + .4\,(\text{Principal payment})}$$

$$= \frac{\$85 + \dfrac{\$1,000 - \$900}{2}}{.6\,(\$900) + .4\,(\$1,000)}$$

$$= \frac{\$85 + \dfrac{-\$100}{2}}{\$540 + \$400}$$

$$= \frac{\$85 + \$50}{\$940}$$

$$= \frac{\$135}{\$940} = 14.36\%$$

d. Yes. Bond B now has the higher yield to maturity. This is because the $100 discount will be recovered over only two years. With Bond A there is a $200 discount, but a 10-year recovery period.

16-4.   The Florida Investment Fund buys 90 bonds of the Gator Corporation through a broker. The bonds pay 8 percent annual interest. The yield to maturity (market rate of interest) is 10 percent. The bonds have a 25-year maturity.

Using an assumption of semiannual interest payments:

a. Compute the price of a bond. (Refer to "semiannual interest and bond prices" in Chapter 10 for review if necessary.)
b. Compute the total value of the 90 bonds.

Solution:
Florida Investment Company

a. Present value of interest payments

$$PV_A = A \times PV_{IFA} \ (n = 50, i = 5\%) \qquad \text{Appendix D}$$
$$PV_A = \$40 \times 18.256 = \$730.24$$

Present value of principal payment at maturity

$$PV = FV \times PV_{IF} \ (n = 50, i = 5\%) \qquad \text{Appendix B}$$
$$PV = \$1,000 \times .087 = \$87.00$$

Total present value

Present value of interest payments	$730.24
Present value of payment at maturity	87.00
Total present value or price of the bond	$817.24

b. Value of 90 bonds

$$\begin{array}{r} \$817.24 \\ \times \quad 90 \\ \hline \$73,551.60 \end{array}$$

16-5.   Cox Media Corporation pays an 11 percent coupon rate on debentures that are due in 20 years. The current yield to maturity on bonds of similar risk is 8 percent. The bonds are currently callable at $1,060. The theoretical value of the bonds will be equal to the present value of the expected cash flow from the bonds.

    a. Find the theoretical market value of the bonds using semiannual analysis.
    b. Do you think the bonds will sell for the price you arrived at in part *a*? Why?

Solution:

Cox Media Corporation

a. Present value of interest payments

$$PV_A = A \times PV_{IFA} \ (n = 40, \ i = 4\%) \qquad \text{Appendix D}$$
$$PV_A = \$55 \times 19.793 = \$1,088.62$$

Present value of principal payment at maturity

$$PV = FV \times PV_{IF} \ (n = 40, \ i = 4\%) \qquad \text{Appendix B}$$
$$PV = \$1,000 \times .208 = \$208$$

Total present value

Present value of interest payments	$1,088.62
Present value of payment at maturity	208.00
Total present value or price of the bond	$1,296.62

b. No. The call price of $1,060 will keep the bonds from getting much over $1,060. Since the bonds are currently callable, investors will not want to buy the bonds at almost $1,300 and risk having them called away at $1,060.

16-6.   The yield to maturity for 15-year bonds is as follows for four different bond rating categories.

Aaa	9.4%	Aa2	10.0%
Aa1	9.6%	Aa3	10.2%

The bonds of Falter Corporation were rated as Aa1 and issued at par a few weeks ago. The bonds have just been downgraded to Aa2. Determine the new price of the bonds, assuming a 15-year maturity and semiannual interest payments. As a first step, use the table above as a guide to appropriate interest rates for bonds with different ratings.

Solution:

With a Aa1 rating at issue, the coupon rate is 9.6% annually or 4.8% semiannually. With a downgrading to Aa2, the new yield to maturity is 10% or 5% semiannually.

Present value of interest payments

$$PV_A = A \times PV_{IFA} \; (n = 30, i = 5\%) \qquad \text{Appendix D}$$
$$PV_A = \$48 \times 15.372 = \$737.86$$

Present value of principal payment at maturity

$$PV = FV \times PV_{IF} \; (n = 30, i = 5\%) \qquad \text{Appendix B}$$
$$PV = \$1,000 \times .231 = \$231$$

Total present value

Present value of interest payments	$737.86
Present value of payment at maturity	231.00
Total present value or price of the bond	$968.86

16-7. Twenty-five-year B-rated bonds of Katz Copying Machines were initially issued at a 12 percent yield. After 10 years the bonds have been upgraded to Aa2. Such bonds are currently yielding 10 percent. Use Table 16-3 to determine the price of the bonds with 15 years remaining to maturity. (You do not need the bond ratings to enter the table; just use the basic facts of the problem.)

Solution:

Katz Copying Machines

Using Table 16-3:

12% initial coupon rate, 10% current yield to maturity,
15 years remaining to maturity: $1,153.32

16-8. A previously issued A2. 15-year industrial bond provides a return one-fourth higher than the prime interest rate of 8 percent. Previously issue A 2 public utility bonds provide a yield three-eighths of a percentage point higher than previously issue A2 industrial bonds. Finally, new issues of A2 public utility bonds pay one-fourth of a percentage point more than previously issued A2 public utility bonds.

What should the interest rate be on a newly issued A2 public utility bond?

Solution:

Interest rate on previously issue A2 15-year industrial bonds	8% × 1.25 =	10.00%
Additional return on A2 15-year public utility bond		+.375%
Additional return on new issues		+.250%
Anticipated return on newly issues A2 public utility bonds		10.625%

16-9.   A 20-year, $1,000 par value zero-coupon rate bond is to be issued to yield 11 percent.

    a. What should be the initial price of the bond? (Take the present value of $1,000 for 20 years at 11 percent, using Appendix B.)

    b. If immediately upon issue, interest rates dropped to 9 percent, what would be the value of the zero-coupon rate bond?

    c. If immediately upon issue, interest rates increased to 13 percent, what would be the value of the zero-coupon rate bond?

Solution:

a. PV of $1,000 for n = 20, i = 11%, PV_{IF} = .124

$$
\begin{array}{r}
\$1,000 \\
\times\ .124 \\
\hline
\$\ \ 124
\end{array}
$$

b. PV of $1,000 for n = 20, i = 9%, PV_{IF} = .178

$$
\begin{array}{r}
\$1,000 \\
\times\ .178 \\
\hline
\$\ \ 178
\end{array}
$$

c. PV of $1,000 for n = 20, i = 13%, PV_{IF} = .087

$$
\begin{array}{r}
\$1,000 \\
\times\ .087 \\
\hline
\$\ \ \ 87
\end{array}
$$

16-10.   What is the effective yield to maturity on a zero-coupon bond that sells for $116 and will mature in 25 years at $1,000? (Compute PV_{IF} and go to Appendix B for the 25-year figure to find the answer or compute FV_{IF} and go to Appendix A for the 25-year figure. Either approach will work.)

Solution:

$$PV_{IF} = \frac{PV}{FV} = \frac{\$116}{\$1,000} = .116$$

Using Appendix B for n = 25, the yield is 9 percent

or

$$FV_{IF} = \frac{FV_{IF}}{PV_{IF}} = \frac{\$1,000}{\$116} = 8.621$$

Using Appendix A for n = 30, the yield is approximately 9 percent.

16-11.   You buy a 7 percent 30-year, $1,000 par value floating rate bond in 1996. By the year 2002, rates on bonds of similar risk are up to 9 percent. What is your one best guess as to the value of the bond?

Solution:

With a floating rate bond, the rate the bond pays changes with interest rates in the market. Therefore, the price of the bond stays constant. The one best guess is $1,000.

16-12. Twelve years ago, the Archer Corporation borrowed $6,000,000. Since then, cumulative inflation has been 80 percent (a compound rate of approximately 5 percent per year).

a. When the firm repays the original $6,000,000 loan this year, what will be the effective purchasing power of the $6,000,000? (Hint: Divide the loan amount by one plus cumulative inflation.)

b. To maintain the original $6,000,000 purchasing power, how much should the lend be repaid? (Hint: Multiply the loan amount by one plus cumulative inflation.)

c. If the lender knows he will only receive $6,000,000 in payment after 12 years, how might he be compensated for the loss in purchasing power? A descriptive answer is acceptable.

Solution:

Archer Corporation

a. $\dfrac{\text{Loan amount}}{1 + \text{Cumulative inflation}} = \dfrac{\$6,000,000}{1.80} = \$3,333,333$

b. $\$6,000,000 \times 1.80 = \$10,800,000$

A $10,800,000 loan repayment in an 80% cumulative inflationary environment will provide $6,000,000 in purchasing power to the original lender.

c. Charge a high enough interest rate to not only provide an adequate annual return on the borrowed funds, but also compensate for the loss of purchasing power.

16-13.   A $1,000 par value bond was issued 25 years ago at a 12 percent coupon rate. It currently has 15 years remaining to maturity. Interest rates on similar debt obligations are now 8 percent.

a. What is the current price of the bond? (Look up the answer in Table 16-3.)
b. Assume Ms. Russell bought the bond three years ago, when it had a price of $1,070. What is her dollar profit based on the bond's current price?
c. Further assume Ms. Russell paid 30 percent of the purchase price in cash and borrowed the rest (known as buying on margin). She used the interest payments from the bond to cover the interest costs on the loan. How much of the purchase price of $1,070 did Ms. Russell pay in cash?
d. What is Ms. Russell's percentage return on her cash investment? Divide the answer to part b by the answer to part c.
e. Explain why her return is so high.

Solution:

Ms. Russell

a. The original bond was issued at 12%
   Yield to maturity is now 8%
   15 years remain to maturity
   The bond price is $1,345.52

b. $1,345.52   Current price
    _1,070.00_   Purchase price
    $ 275.52   Dollar increase

c. Purchase Price $1,070.00
   × 30% Margin $ 321.00   Purchase price paid in cash

d. $$\frac{\text{Dollar profit}}{\text{Purchase price paid in cash}} = \frac{\$275.52}{\$321.00}$$

   85.83% represents Ms. Russell's return on her investment.

e. Ms. Russell has not only benefited from an increase in the price of the bond (due to lower interest rates), but she also has benefited from the use of leverage by buying on margin. She has controlled a $1,070 initial investment with only $321 in cash. The low cash investment tends to magnify gains (as well as losses).

16-14.   The Bowman Corporation has a $20 million bond obligation outstanding, which it is considering refunding. Though the bonds were initially issued at 12 percent, the interest rates on similar issues have declined to 10.5 percent. The bonds were originally issued for 20 years and have 15 years remaining. The new issue would be for 15 years. There is an 8 percent call premium on the old issue. The underwriting cost on the new $20,000,000 issue is $570,000, and the underwriting cost on the old issue was $400,000. The company is in a 35 percent tax bracket, and it will use a 7 percent discount rate (rounded aftertax cost of debt) to analyze the refunding decision.

Should the old issue be refunded with new debt?

Solution:

Bowman Corporation

Outflows
1. Payment of call premium
   $20,000,000 × 8%   = $1,600,000
   $1,600,000 (1 − .35) = $1,040,000

2. Underwriting cost on new issue
   Amortization of costs ($570,000/15) (.35)
   $38,000 × (.35) = $13,300 tax savings per year

Actual expenditure	$570,000
PV of future tax savings $13,300 × 9.108*	121,136
Net cost of underwriting expense on new issue	$448,864

*PV_{IFA} for n = 15, i = 7% (Appendix D)

Inflows

3. Cost savings in lower interest rates

12% (interest on old bond)×$20,000,000 = $2,400,000/year

10.5% (interest on new bond)×$20,000,000 = 2,100,000/year

Savings per year = $ 300,000

Savings per year $300,000 × (1 − .35) = $ 195,000 aftertax

$ 195,000
× 9.108 PV_{IFA} (n = 15, i = 7%)   Appendix D
$1,776,060

4. Underwriting cost on old issue

Original amount	$400,000
Amount written off over 5 years at $20,000 per year	100,000
Unamortized old underwriting cost	$300,000
Present value of deferred future write-off $20,000 × 9.108 (n = 15, i = 7%)	182,160
Immediate gain in old underwriting cost write-off	$117,840
Tax rate	× . 35
Aftertax value of immediate gain in old Underwriting cost write-off	$ 41,244

Summary

	Outflows		**Inflows**
1.	$1,040,000	3.	$1,776,060
2.	448,864	4.	41,244
	$1,488,864		$1,817,304

PV of inflows	$1,817,304
PV of outflows	1,488,864
Net present value	$ 328,440

Refund the old issue (particularly if it is perceived that interest rates will not go down even more).

16-15. The Robinson Corporation has $50 million of bonds outstanding which were issued at a coupon rate of 11 ¾ percent seven years ago. Interest rates have fallen to 10 ¾ percent. Mr. Brooks, the vice-president of finance, does not expect rates to fall any further. The bonds have 18 years left to maturity, and Brooks would like to refund the bonds with a new issue of equal amount also having 18 years to maturity. The Robinson Corporation has a tax rate of 35 percent. The underwriting cost on the old issue was 2.5 percent of the total bond value. The underwriting cost on the new issue will be 1.8 percent of the total bond value. The original bond indenture contained a five-year protection against a call, with a 9.5 percent call premium starting in the sixth year and scheduled to decline b one-half percent each year thereafter. (Consider the bond to be seven years old for purposes of computing the premium.) Assume the discount rate is equal to the aftertax cost of new debt rounded to the nearest whole number. Should the Robinson Corporation refund the old issue?

Solution:

Robinson Corporation

First compute the discount rate 10.75% $(1 - .35) = 10.75\%$ $(.65) = 6.99\%$. Round up to 7%.

Outflows

1. Payment on call provision

$50,000,000 × 9%		= $4,500,000
$4,500,000 $(1 - .35)$		= $2,925,000

2. Underwriting cost on new issue

Actual expenditure	1.8% × $50,000,000	= $900,000
Amortization of costs	($900,000/18) (.35)	=
Tax savings per year =	$50,000 (.35)	= $ 17,500

Actual expenditure	$900,000
PV of future tax savings $17,500 × 10.059*	176,033
Net cost of underwriting expense on new issue	$723,967

   *PV_{IFA} for n = 18, i = 7% (Appendix D)

Inflows

3. Cost savings in lower interest rates

11 ¾% (interest on old bond) × $50,000,000 =	$5,875,000
10 ¾% (interest on new bond) × (50,000,000 =	5,375,000
Savings per year	$ 500,000

   Savings per year $500,000 × $(1 - .35)$ = $325,000 Aftertax

$325,000

$\underline{10.059}$ PV$_{\text{IFA}}$ (n = 18, i = 7%)   Appendix D

$3,269,175   Present value of savings

4. Underwriting cost on old issue

Original amount (2.5% × $50,000,000)	$1,250,000
Amount written off over last 7 years at $50,000 per year ($1,250,000/25) × 7	350,000
Unamortized old underwriting cost	$ 900,000
Present value of deferred future write off: $50,000 × 10.059	502,950
Immediate gain in old underwriting write-off	$ 397,050
Tax rate	× .35
Aftertax value of immediate gain in old underwriting cost write-off	$ 138,968

Summary

	Outflows			Inflows
1.	$2,925,000		3.	$3,269,175
2.	723,967		4.	138,968
	$3,648,967			$3,408,143

PV of inflows	$3,408,143
PV of outflows	3,648,967
Net present value	$ (240,824)

Based on the negative net present value, the Robinson Corporation should not refund the issue.

16-16. In problem 15, what would be the aftertax cost of the call premium at the end of year 13 (in dollar value)?

Solution:

The Robinson Corporation (Continued)

Call premium (aftertax cost)

7 years of ½% deductions (7th through 13th year) = 3 ½%

9 ½%   Call premium
−3 ½%
6%   Call premium at the end of the 13th year

$50,000,000 × 6%   = $3,000,000
$ 3,000,000 (1 − .35)   = $1,950,000

16-17.   The Deluxe Corporation has just signed a 120-month lease on an asset with a 15-year life. The minimum lease payments are $2,000 per month ($24,000 per year) and are to be discounted back to the present at a 7 percent annual discount rate. The estimated fair value of the property is $175,000.

Should the lease be recorded as a capital lease or an operating lease?

Solution:
The Deluxe Corporation

Using criteria 3 and 4

The lease is less than 75% of the estimated life of the leased property.

120 months = 10 years
10/15   = 67%

However, the present value of the lease payments is greater than 909% of the fair value of the property.

$ 24,000   annual lease payments
$\underline{\quad 7.024}$ (PV$_{IFA}$ for n = 10, i = 7%)   Appendix D
$168,576   present value of lease payments

$$\frac{\$168,576}{\$175,000} = 96.3\%$$

Since one of the four criteria for compulsory treatment as a capital lease is indicated, the transaction must be treated as a capital lease.

16-18. The Ellis Corporation has heavy lease commitments. Prior to *SFAS No. 13*, it merely footnoted lease obligations in the balance sheet, which appeared as follows:

In $ millions		In $ millions	
Current assets......................	$ 50	Current liabilities.................	$ 10
Fixed assets.........................	50	Long-term liabilities............	30
		Total liabilities..................	$ 40
		Stockholders' equity.............	60
		Total liabilities and	
Total assets.........................	$100	Stockholders' equity...........	$100

The footnotes stated that the company had $10 million in annual capital lease obligations for the next 20 years.

a. Discount these annual lease obligations back to the present at a 6 percent discount rate (round to the nearest million dollars).
b. Construct a revised balance sheet that includes lease obligations, as in Table 16-8.
c. Compute total debt to total assets on the original and revised balance sheets.
d. Compute total debt to equity on the original and revised balance sheets.
e. In an efficient capital market environment, should the consequences of *SFAS No. 13*, as viewed in the answers to parts c and d, change stock prices and credit ratings?
f. Comment on management's perception of market efficiency (the viewpoint of the financial officer).

Solution:
Ellis Corp.

a. $10   million annual lease payments
        11.470   (PV$_{IFA}$ for n = 20, i = 6%)
     $114.700   million (round to $115 million)

b.

Current assets	$50 million	Current liabilities	$ 10 million
Fixed assets	50 million	Long-term liabilities	30 million
Leased property under capital lease	115 million	Obligations under capital lease	115 million
		Total liabilities	155 million
		Stockholders' equity	60 million
		Total liabilities and Stockholders' equity	
Total assets	$215 million	equity	$215 million

c.   Original   Revised

$$\frac{\text{Total debt}}{\text{Total assets}} = \frac{\$40\,\text{million}}{\$100\,\text{million}} = 40\% \qquad \frac{\$155\,\text{million}}{\$215\,\text{million}} = 72.1\%$$

d.   Original   Revised

$$\frac{\text{Total debt}}{\text{Equity}} = \frac{\$40\,\text{million}}{\$60\,\text{million}} = 66.7\% \qquad \frac{\$155\,\text{million}}{\$60\,\text{million}} = 258.3\%$$

e. No, the information was already known by financial analysts before it was brought into the balance sheet.

f. Management is concerned about whether the market is as efficient as is generally believed. They feel that newly presented information may make their performance look questionable.

16-19.   The Hardaway Corporation plans to lease a $900,000 asset to the O'Neil Corporation. The lease will be for 10 years.

a. If the Hardaway Corporation desires a 12 percent return on its investment, how much should the lease payments be?
b. If the Hardaway Corporation is able to take a 10 percent deduction from the purchase price of $900,000 and will pass the benefit along to the O'Neil Corporation in the form of lower lease payments (related to the Hardaway Corporation's lower initial net cost), how much should the revised lease payments be? Continue to assume that the Hardaway Corporation desires a 12 percent return on the 10-year lease.

Solution:

Hardaway Corporation

a. Determine 10-year annuity that will yield 12%.

$$A = PV_A/PV_{IFA} \ (i = 12\%, n = 10) \qquad \text{Appendix D}$$

$$= \frac{\$900,000}{5.650} = \$159,292$$

b. The 10% deduction reduces the net cost of $810,000.

Original cost	$900,000
10%	90,000
Net cost	$810,000

$$A = \frac{\$810,000}{5.650} = \$143,363$$

Appendix

16A-1. The trustee in the bankruptcy settlement for Titanic Boat Co. lists the following book values and liquidation values for the assets of the corporation. Liabilities and stockholders' claims are also shown at the top of page 488.

Assets

	Book Value	Liquidation Value
Accounts receivable	$1,400,000	$1,200,000
Inventory	1,800,000	900,000
Machinery and equipment	1,100,000	600,000
Building and plant	4,200,000	2,500,000
Total assets	$8,500,000	$5,200,000

Liabilities and Stockholders' Claim

Liabilities:

Accounts payable	$2,800,000
First lien, secured by machinery and equipment	900,000
Senior unsecured debt	2,200,000
Subordinated debenture	1,700,000
Total liabilities	7,600,000

Stockholders' claims:

Preferred stock	250,000
Common stock	650,000
Total stockholders' claims	900,000
Total liabilities and Stockholders' claims	$8,500,000

a. Compute the difference between the liquidation value of the assets and the liabilities.

b. Based on the answer to part *a*, will preferred stock or common stock participate in the distribution?

c. Assuming the administrative costs of bankruptcy, workers' allowable wages, and unpaid taxes add up to $400,000, what is the total of remaining asset value available to cover secured and unsecured claims?

d. After the machinery and equipment are sold to partially cover the first lien secured claim, how much will be available from the remaining asset liquidation values to cover unsatisfied secured claims and unsecured debt?

e. List the remaining asset claims of unsatisfied secured debt holders and unsecured debt holders in a manner similar to that shown at the bottom portion of Table 16A-3.

f. Compute a ratio of your answers in part *d* and part *e*. This will indicate the initial allocation ratio.

g. List the remaining claims (unsatisfied secured and unsecured) and make an initial allocation and final allocation similar to that shown in Table 16A-4. Subordinated debenture holders may keep the balance after full payment is made to senior debt holders.

h. Show the relationship of amount received to total amount of claim in a similar fashion to that of Table 16A-5. (Remember to use the sales liquidation value for machinery and equipment plus the allocation amount in part g to arrive at the total received on secured debt.)

Solution:

Titanic Boat Co.

a.

Liquidation value of assets	$5,200,000
Liabilities	7,600,000
Difference	($2,400,000)

b. Preferred and common stock will not participate in the distribution because the liquidation value of the assets does not cover creditor claims.

c.

Asset values in liquidation	$5,200,000
Administrative costs, wages and taxes	– 400,000
Remaining asset values	$4,800,000

d.

Remaining asset value	$4,800,000
Payment to secured creditors	– 600,000
Amount available to unsatisfied secured claims and unsecured debt	$4,200,000

e. Remaining claims of unsatisfied secured debt and unsecured debt holder

Secured debt (unsatisfied first lien)	$ 300,000
Accounts payable	2,800,000
Senior unsecured debt	2,200,000
Subordinated debentures	1,700,000
	$7,000,000

f. $\dfrac{\text{Amount available to unsatisfied security claims and unsecured debt (part d)}}{\text{Remaining claims of unsatisfied secured debt and unsecured debt holders (part e)}} = \dfrac{\$42,000,000}{\$7,000,000} = 60\%$

g. Allocation procedures for unsatisfied secured claims and unsecured debt.

(1) Category	(2) Amount of Claim	(3) Initial Allocation (60%)	(4) Amount Received
Secured debt (unsatisfied first lien)	$ 300,000	$ 180,000	$ 180,000
Accounts Payable	2,800,000	1,680,000	1,680,000
Senior unsecured debt	2,200,000	1,320,000	2,200,000
Subordinated debentures	1,700,000	1,020,000	140,000
	$7,000,000	$4,200,000	$4,200,000

*The subordinated debenture holders must transfer $880,000 of their initial allocation to the senior unsecured debt holders to fully provide for their payment ($1,320,000 + $880,000 = $2,200,000). This will leave $140,000 for subordinated debentures ($1,020,000 – $880,000).

h. Payments and percent of claims

Category	Total amount of claim	Amount received	Percent of claim satisfied
Secured debt (first lien)	$ 900,000	$ 780,000	86.7%
Accounts payable	2,800,000	1,680,000	60.0%
Senior unsecured debt	2,200,000	2,200,000	100.0%
Subordinated debentures	1,700,000	140,000	8.2%

16B-1.   Howell Auto Parts is considering whether to borrow funds and purchase an asset or to lease the asset under an operating lease arrangement. If the company purchases the asset, the cost will be $10,000. It can borrow funds for four years at 12 percent interest. The firm will use the three-year MACRS depreciation category (with the associated four-year write-off). Assume a tax rate of 35 percent.

The other alternative is to sign two operating leases, one with payments of $2,600 for the first two years, and the other with payments of $4,600 for the last two years. In your analysis, round all values to the nearest dollar.

a. Compute the aftertax cost of the leases for the four years.
b. Compute the annual payment for the loan (round to the nearest dollar).
c. Compute the amortization schedule for the loan. (Disregard a small difference from a zero balance at the end of the loan—due to rounding.)
d. Determine the depreciation schedule (see Table 12-9).
e. Compute the aftertax cost of the borrow-purchase alternative.
f. Compute the present value of the aftertax cost of the two alternatives. Use a discount rate of 8 percent.
g. Which alternative should be selected, based on minimizing the present value of aftertax costs?

Solution:

Howell Auto Parts

a.

(1) Year	(2) Payment	(3) Tax Shield 35% of (1)	(4) Aftertax Cost
1	$2,600	$910	$1,690
2	$2,600	910	1,690
3	$4,600	1,610	2,990
4	$4,600	1,610	2,990

b.

$$A = \frac{PV_A}{PV_{IFA}} = \frac{\$10,000}{3.037} = \$3,293 \ (n = 4, i = 12\%) \ \text{Appendix D}$$

c.

(1) Year	(2) Beginning Balance	(3) Annual Payment	(4) Annual Interest 12% of (2)	(5) Repayment on Principal (3) − (4)	(6) Ending Balance (2) − (5)
1	$10,000	$3,293	$1,200	$2,093	$7,907
2	7,907	3,293	949	2,344	5,563
3	5,563	3,293	668	2,625	2,938
4	2,938	3,293	353	2,940	(2)

d.

Year	Depreciation Base	Depreciation Percentage	Depreciation
1	$10,000	.333	$ 3,330
2	10,000	.445	4,450
3	10,000	.148	1,480
4	10,000	.074	740
			$10,000

e.

Year	(1) Payment	(2) Interest	(3) Depreciation	(4) Total Tax Deductions	(5) Tax Shield 35% × (4)	(6) Net After-Tax Cost (1) − (5)
1	$3,293	$1,200	$3,330	$4,530	$1,586	$1,707
2	3,293	949	4,450	5,399	1,890	1,403
3	3,293	668	1,480	2,148	752	2,541
4	3,293	353	740	1,093	383	2,910

f.

Year	Aftertax cost of leasing	PV Factor at 8%	Present Value	Aftertax cost of Borrow-Purchase	PV factor at 8%	Present Value
1	$1,690	.926	$1,565	$1,707	.926	$1,581
2	1,690	.857	1,448	1,403	.857	1,202
3	2,990	.794	2,374	2,541	.794	2,018
4	2,990	.735	2,198	2,910	.735	2,139
			$7,585			$6,940

g. The borrow and purchase decision has a lower present value and would be selected based on that criterion. Other factors may also be considered.

Chapter 17

Discussion Questions

17-1.   Why has corporate management become increasingly sensitive to the desires of large institutional investors?

Corporate management has become increasingly sensitive to the desires of large institutional investors because they fear these shareholders may side with corporate raiders in voting their shares in mergers or takeovers attempt.

17-2.   Why might a corporation use a special category such as founders' stock in issuing common stock?

Founders' stock may carry special voting rights that allow the original founders to maintain voting privileges in excess of their proportionate ownership.

17-3.   What is the purpose of cumulative voting? Are there any disadvantages to management?

The purpose of cumulative voting is to allow some minority representation on the board of directors. A possible disadvantage to management is that minority stockholders can challenge their actions.

17-4.   How does the preemptive right protect stockholders from dilution?

The preemptive right provides current stockholders with a first option to buy new shares. In this fashion, their voting right and claim to earnings cannot be diluted without their consent.

17-5.   If common stockholders are the *owners* of the company, why do they have the last claim on assets and a residual claim on income?

The actual owners have the last claim to any and all funds that remain. If the firm is profitable, this could represent a substantial amount. Thus, the residual claim may represent a privilege as well as a potential drawback. Generally, other providers of capital may only receive a fixed amount.

17-6.   During a rights offering, the underlying stock is said to sell "rights-on" and "ex-rights." Explain the meaning of these terms and their significance to current stockholders and potential stockholders.

When a rights offering is announced, a stock initially trades rights-on, that is, if you buy the stock you will also acquire a right toward future purchase of stock.

After a certain period of time (say four weeks), the stock goes ex-rights; thus when you buy the stock you no longer get a right toward future purchase of stock.

The significance to current and future stockholders is that they must decide if they wish to use or sell the right when the stock is trading rights-on. The stock will go down by the appropriate value of the right when the stock moves to an ex-rights designation.

17-7.   Why might management use a poison pill strategy?

A poison pill may help management defend itself against a potential takeover attempt. When another company attempts to acquire the firm, the poison pill allows current stockholders to acquire additional shares at a very low price. This increases the shares outstanding and makes it more difficult for the potential acquiring company to successfully complete the merger.

17-8.   Preferred stock is often referred to as a hybrid security. What is meant by this term as applied to preferred stock?

Preferred stock is a "hybrid" or intermediate form of security possessing some of the characteristics of debt and common stock. The fixed amount provision is similar to debt, but the noncontractual obligation is similar to common stock. Though the preferred stockholder does not have a ownership interest in the firm, the priority of claim is higher than that of the common stockholder.

17-9.   What is the most likely explanation for the use of preferred stock from a corporate viewpoint?

Most corporations that issue preferred stock do so to achieve a balance in their capital structure. It is a means of expanding the capital base of the firm without diluting the common stock ownership position or incurring contractual debt obligations.

17-10.   If preferred stick is riskier than bonds, why has preferred stock had lower yields than bonds in recent years?

Preferred stock may offer a slightly lower yield than bonds in spite of greater risk because corporate recipients' of preferred stock dividends must add only 30 percent of such dividends to taxable income; thus 70 percent of such dividends are exempt from taxation.

17-11.   Why is the cumulative feature of preferred stock particularly important to preferred stockholders?

With the cumulative feature, if preferred stock dividends are not paid in any one year, they accumulate and must be paid in total before common stockholders can receive dividends. Even though preferred stock dividends are not a contractual obligation as is true of interest on debt, the cumulative feature tends to make corporations very aware of obligations to preferred stockholders. Preferred stockholders may even receive new securities for forgiveness of missed dividend payments.

17-12.   A small amount of preferred stock is participating. What would your reaction be if someone said common stock is also participating?

The participation privileges of a few preferred stock issues mean that preferred stockholders may receive a payout over and above the quoted rate when the corporation enjoys a particularly good year. This is very similar to the situation with common stock and one can certainly say that common stock is a participation-type security.

17-13.   What is an advantage of floating rate preferred stock for the risk-averse investor?

There is less price volatility than with regular preferred stock.

17-14.   Put and X by the security that has the feature best related to the following considerations. You may wish to refer to Table 17-3.

Common Stock Preferred Stock Bonds

a. Ownership and control of the firm
b. Obligation to provide return
c. Claims to assets in bankruptcy
d. High cost of distribution
e. Highest return
f. Highest risk
g. Tax-deductible payment
h. Payment partially tax-exempt
   to corporate recipient

		Common Stock	Preferred Stock	Bonds
a.	Owners and control of the firm	X		
b.	Obligation to provide return			X
c.	Claims to assets in bankruptcy		X	
d.	Highest cost of distribution	X		
e.	Highest return	X		
f.	Highest risk	X		
g.	Tax deductible payment		X	
h.	Payment partially tax exempt to corp. viewpoint	X	X	

Problems

17-1.   Russell Stover wishes to know how many shares are necessary to elect 4 directors out of the 11 directors up for election in the Tasty Candy Company. There are 75,000 shares outstanding. (Use formula 17-1 to determine the answer.)

Solution:

Tasty Candy Company

$$\text{Shares required} = \frac{\begin{array}{c}(\text{Number of directors desired}) \times \\ (\text{Total number of shares outstanding})\end{array}}{\text{Total number of directors to be elected} + 1} + 1$$

$$= \frac{4 \times 75,000}{11 + 1} + 1 = \frac{300,000}{12} + 1$$

$$= 25,000 + 1 = 25,001 \text{ shares}$$

17-2.   Mr. R.C. Cola owns 7,001 shares of Softdrinks, Inc. There are 10 seats on the company board of directors, and the company has a total of 77,000 shares outstanding. Softdrinks, Inc., utilizes cumulative voting.

Can Mr. Cola elect himself to the board when the vote to elect 10 directors is held next week? (Use Formula 17-2 to determine if he can elect one director.)

Solution:

Softdrinks, Inc.

$$\begin{array}{c}\text{Number of} \\ \text{directors} \\ \text{that can be} \\ \text{elected}\end{array} = \frac{\begin{array}{c}(\text{Shares owned} - 1) \times \\ (\text{Total number of directors to be elected}) + 1\end{array}}{\text{Total number of shares outstanding}}$$

$$\frac{(7,001 - 1) \times (10 + 1)}{77,000} = \frac{7,000 \times 11}{77,000} = \frac{77,000}{77,000} = 1 \text{ director}$$

Yes, Mr. Cola can elect himself to the board.

17-3.   Betsy Ross owns 918 shares in Hanson Fabrics Company. There are 13 directors to be elected. Thirty-one thousand shares are outstanding. The firm has adopted cumulative voting.

   a. How many total votes can be cast?
   b. How many votes does Betsy control?
   c. What percentage of the total votes does she control?

Solution:

Hansen Fabrics Company

$$\text{Votes} = \text{Number of shares} \times \text{number of directors to be elected}$$

   a. $31,000 \times 13 = 403,000$ votes
   b. $918 \times 13 = 11,934$ votes
   c. $11,934/403,000 = 2.96\%$

17-4.   The Beasley Corporation has been experiencing declining earnings, but has just announced a 50 percent salary increase for its top executives. A dissident group of stockholders wants to oust the existing board of directors. There are currently 11 directors and 30,000 shares of stock outstanding. Mr. Wright, the president of the company, has the full support of the existing board. The dissident stockholders control proxies for 10,001 shares. Mr. Wright is worried about losing his job.

   a. Under cumulative voting procedures, how many directors can the dissident stockholders elect with the proxies they now hold?

   How many directors could they elect under majority rule with these proxies?

   b. How many shares (or proxies) are needed to elect six directors under cumulative voting?

Solution:

Beasley Corporation

a. Number of directors that can be elected

$$= \frac{(\text{Shares owned} - 1) \times (\text{Total number of directors to be elected}) + 1}{\text{Total number of shares outstanding}}$$

$$= \frac{(10,001 - 1) \times (11 + 1)}{30,000} = \frac{120,000}{30,000} = 4$$

Four directors can be elected by the dissident stockholders under cumulative voting.

None would be elected by the dissidents under majority rule because the existing board controls over 50 percent of the shares.

b. Shares required

$$= \frac{(\text{Number of directors desired}) \times (\text{Total number of shares outstanding})}{\text{Total number of directors to be elected} + 1} + 1$$

$$= \frac{6 \times 30,000}{11 + 1} + 1 = \frac{180,000}{12} + 1 = 15,001 \text{ shares}$$

17-5. Midland Petroleum is holding a stockholders' meeting next month. Ms. Ramsey is the president of the company and has the support of the existing board of directors. All 11 members of the board are up for reelection. Mr. Clark is a dissident stockholder. He controls proxies for 40,001 shares. Ms. Ramsey and her friends on the board control 60,001 shares. Other stockholders, whose loyalties are unknown, will be voting the remaining 19,998 shares. The company uses cumulative voting.

    a. How many directors can Mr. Clark be sure of electing?
    b. How many directors can Ms. Ramsey and her friends be sure of electing?
    c. How many directors could Mr. Clark elect if he obtains all the proxies for the uncommitted votes? (Uneven values must be rounded down to the nearest whole number regardless of the amount.) Will he control the board?

Solution:

Midland Petroleum

a. Number of directors that can be elected

$$= \frac{(\text{Shares owned} - 1) \times (\text{Total number of directors to be elected}) + 1}{\text{Total number of shares outstanding}}$$

$$= \frac{(10,001 - 1) \times (11 + 1)}{30,000} = \frac{120,000}{30,000} = 4$$

$$\frac{(40,001 - 1) \times (11 + 1)}{(40,001 + 60,001 + 19,998)} = \frac{40,000 \times 12}{120,000} = 4 \text{ directors}$$

Mr. Clark can be assured of electing 4 directors.

b. $$\frac{(60,001 - 1) \times (11 + 1)}{120,000} = \frac{60,000 \times 12}{120,000}$$

$$= \frac{720,000}{120,000} = 6 \text{ directors}$$

Ms. Ramsey and her friends can be assured of electing 6 directors.

c. Shares owned = shares owned and proxies of other voters

$$= \frac{(40,001+19,998-1) \times 12}{120,000} = \frac{59,998 \times 12}{120,000}$$

$$= \frac{719,976}{120,000} = 5.9998 = 5 \text{ directors (rounded down)}$$

He can only elect 5 directors. No, Ms. Ramsey will control the board.

17-6.   In problem 5, if nine directors were to be elected, and Ms. Ramsey and her friends had 60,001 shares and Mr. Clark had 40,001 shares plus half the uncommitted votes, how many directors could Mr. Clark elect?

Solution:
Midland Petroleum (Continued)

$$\frac{(40,001+9,999-1) \times (9+1)}{120,000} = \frac{49,999 \times 10}{120,000}$$

$$= \frac{499,990}{120,000} = 4.17 = 4 \text{ directors (rounde down)}$$

17-7. Mr. Michaels control proxies for 38,000 of the 70,000 outstanding shares of Northern Airlines. Mr. Baker heads a dissident group which controls the remaining 32,000 shares. There are seven board members to be elected and cumulative voting rules apply. Michaels does not understand cumulative voting and plans to cast 100,000 of his 266,000 (38,000 × 7) votes for his brother-in-law, Scott. His remaining votes will be spread evenly over three other candidates.

How many directors can Baker elect if Michaels acts as described above? Use logical numerical analysis rather than a set formula to answer the question. Baker has 224,000 votes (32,000 × 7).

Solution:

Northern Airlines

Mr. Michaels controls 266,000 votes (38,000 shares × 7 directors).

Mr. Baker controls 224,000 votes (32,000 shares × 7 directors).

If Mr. Michaels casts 100,000 votes for Scott, this will leave 55,333 votes (166,000/3) for each of the other three candidates that he favors.

Mr. Baker could elect 4 of 7 directors with less than one half of the votes because of Mr. Michaels' error in voting.

This is true because Mr. Baker could cast 56,000 votes for each of the four directors of his choice (224,000/4 = 56,000).

17-8.   Rust Pipe Co. was established in 1985. Four years later the company went public. At that time, Robert Rust, the original owner, decided to establish two classes of stock. The first represents Class A founders' stock and is entitled to 10 votes per share. The normally traded common stock, designated as Class B, is entitled to one vote per share. In late 2001, Mr. Steele was considering purchasing shares in Rust Pipe Co. While he knew the existence of founders' shares was not often present in other companies, he decided to buy the shares anyway because of a new technology Rust Pipe had developed to improve the flow of liquids through pipes.

Of the 1,200,000 total shares currently outstanding, the original founder's family owns 51,325 shares. What is the percentage of the founder's family votes compared to the Class B votes?

Solution:

Rust Pipe Company

$$\text{Founder's family votes} = \text{Shares owned} \times 10$$
$$= 51{,}325 \times 10$$
$$= 513{,}250$$

$$\text{Class B votes} = \text{total votes} - \text{founder's family shares}$$
$$= 1{,}200{,}000 - 51{,}325 = 1{,}148{,}675$$

$$\frac{\text{Founder's family votes}}{\text{Class B votes}} = \frac{513{,}250}{1{,}148{,}675} = 44.68\%$$

17-9.   Prime Bankcorp has issued rights to its shareholders. The subscription price is $50 and five rights are needed along with the subscription price to buy one of the new shares. The stock is selling for $59 rights-on.

a.   What would be the value of one right?
b.   If the stock goes ex-rights, what would the new stock price be?

Solution:
Prime Bankcorp

a. $R = \dfrac{M_o - S}{N+1}$

$= \dfrac{\$59 - \$50}{5+1} = \dfrac{\$9}{6} = \$1.50$

b. $\$59.00 - \$1.50 = \$57.50$

The stock price will decrease by the amount of the right's value.

17-10.   Computer Graphics has announced a rights offering for its shareholders. Carol Stevens owns 1,200 shares of Computer Graphics' stock. Four rights plus $60 cash are needed to buy one of the new shares. The stock is currently selling for $72 rights-on.

a.   What is the value of a right?
b.   How many of the new shares could Carol buy if she exercised all her rights? How much cash would this require?
c.   Carol does not know if she wants to exercise her rights or sell them. Would either alternative have a more positive effect on her wealth?

Solution:

Computer Graphics

a. $R = \dfrac{M_o - S}{N + 1}$

$$= \frac{\$72 - \$60}{4 + 1} = \frac{\$12}{5} = \$2.40 \quad \text{Value per right}$$

b. Carol owns 1,200 shares so she would receive 1,200 rights.

1,200 rights/4 rights per share = 300 shares

300 shares × $60 subscription price = $18,000

c. Neither exercising the rights nor selling them would have any effect on the stockholder's wealth (all things being equal).

17-11.   Todd Winningham IV has $4,000 to invest. He has been looking at Gallagher Tennis Clubs, Inc., common stock. Gallagher has issued a rights offering to its common stockholders. Six rights plus $38 cash will buy one new share. Gallagher's stock is selling for $50 ex-rights.

   a. How many rights could Todd buy with his $4,000? Alternatively, how many shares of stock could he buy with the same $4,000 at $50 per share?
   b. If Todd invests his $4,000 in Gallagher rights and the price of the stock rises to $59 per share ex-rights, what would his dollar profit on the rights be? (First compute profits per right.)
   c. If Todd invests his $4,000 in Gallagher stock and the price of the stock rises to $59 per share ex-rights, what would his total dollar profit be?
   d. What would the answer to part *b* if the price of Gallagher's stock falls to $30 per share ex-rights instead of rising to $59.
   e. What would the answer be to part *c* if the price of Gallagher's stock falls to $30 per share ex-rights?

Solution:

Gallagher Tennis Clubs, Inc.

(Todd Winningham IV)

a. $$R = \frac{M_e - S}{N}$$

$$= \frac{\$50 - \$38}{6} = \$2 \text{ per right}$$

$4,000 investment/\$2 per right   = 2,000 rights
$4,000 investment/\$50 per share = 80 shares

b. ($59 − $38)/6   = $3.50 per right value
$3.50 per right value − $2.00 = $1.50 profit per rights
$1.50 × 2,000 rights   = $3,000 total profit on rights

c. ($59 − $50)   = $9 profit per share
$9 × 80 shares   = $720 total dollar profit on the stock

d. ($30 − $38)/6   = −$1.33; the right's value = 0

Todd would lose his entire $4,000 investment.

e. ($30 − $50)   = −$20 loss per share
−$20 × 80   = −$1,600

Todd would lose $1,600 on his $4,000 investment.

17-12.　Mr. And Mrs. Anderson own five shares of Magic Tricks Corporation common stock. The market value of the stock is $60. They also have $48 in cash. They have just received word of a rights offering. One new share of stock can be purchased at $48 for each five shares currently owned (based on five rights).

a.　What is the value of a right?
b.　What is the value of the Andersons' portfolio before the rights offering? (Portfolio in this question represents stock plus cash.)
c.　If the Andersons participate in the rights offering, what will be the value of their portfolio, based on the diluted value (ex-rights) of the stock?
d.　If they sell their five rights but keep their stock at its diluted value and hold on to their cash, what will be the value of their portfolio?

Solution:

Magic Tricks Corp.

(The Andersons)

a. $R = \dfrac{M_o - S}{N + 1}$

$$= \frac{\$60 - \$48}{5 + 1} = \frac{\$12}{\$6} = \$2$$

b. Portfolio value

Stock　5 × $60　　= $300
Cash　　　　　　　　48
Total Portfolio Value　$348

c. First compute diluted value:
   Diluted value = Market value ex-rights

$$M_e = M_o - R = \$60 - \$2 = \$58$$

or

5 old shares sold at $60 per share	$300
1 new share will sell at $48	48
Total value of 6 shares	$348

Average value of 1 share (Market value ex-rights) = $58

Portfolio value

Stock	$6 \times \$58 =$	$348
Cash		0
Total portfolio value		$348

d. Portfolio Value

Stock	$5 \times \$58 =$	$290
Proceeds from sale of 5 rights ($5 \times \$2$)		10
Cash =		48
Total portfolio value		$348

17-13.   Walker Machine tools has 5 million shares of common stock outstanding. The current market price of Walker common stock is $42 per share rights-on. The company's net income this year is $15 million. A rights offering has been announced in which 500,000 new shares will be sold at $36.50 per share. The subscription price plus 10 rights is needed to buy one of the new shares.

a.   What are the earnings per share and price-earnings ratio before the new shares are sold via the rights offering?
b.   What would the earnings per share be immediately after the rights offering? What would the price-earnings ratio be immediately after the rights offering? Assume there is no change in the market value of the stock except for the change when the stock begins trading ex-rights. (Round answers to two places after the decimal point.)

Solution:
Walker Machine Tools

a. $15 million earnings/5 million shares = $3 earnings per share
$42 market price/$3 earnings per share = 14 price-earnings ratio

b. 5 million original shares + 500,000 new shares = 5,500,000 shares

$$\frac{\$15 \text{ million earnings}}{5,500,000 \text{ shares}} = \$2.73 \text{ earnings per share}$$

$$R = \frac{M_o - S}{N + 1} = \frac{\$42 - \$36.50}{10 + 1} = \frac{\$5.50}{11} = \$.50$$

$42 per share − $.50 = $41.50

$$\frac{\$41.50 \text{ market price per share}}{\$2.73 \text{ earnings per share}} = 15.20 \text{ price - earnings ratio}$$

17-14. The Neeley Corporation has some excess cash that it would like to invest in marketable securities for a long-term hold. Its vice president of finance is considering three investments (Neeley is in a 35 percent tax bracket). Which one should she select based on aftertax return: (a) Treasury bonds at a 9 percent yield; (b) corporate bonds at a 12 percent yield; or (c) preferred stock at a 10 percent yield?

Solution:

Neeley Corporation

a. Treasury bonds $\quad 9\% \times (1 - .35) = 9\% \times .65 = 5.85\%$

b. Corporate bonds $\quad 12\% \times (1 - .35) = 12\% \times .65 = 7.80\%$

c. Preferred stock $\quad$ 70% of the dividend is excluded from corporate taxes so only 30% is taxable.

$$10\% \times [1 - (.35)(.30)]$$
$$10\% \times (1 - .105)$$
$$10\% \times .895\% = 8.95\%$$

The preferred stock should be selected because it provides the highest aftertax return.

17-15.   National Health Corporation (NHC) has a cumulative preferred stock issue outstanding, which ahs a stated annual dividend of $9 per share. The company has been losing money and has not paid the preferred dividends for the last five years. There are 300,000 shares of preferred stock outstanding and 600,000 shares of common stock.

a. How much is the company behind in preferred dividends?
b. If NHC earns $11,000,000 in the coming year after taxes but before dividends, and this is all paid out to the preferred stockholders, how much will the company be in arrears (behind in payments)? Keep in mind that the coming year would represent the sixth year.
c. How much, if any, would be available in common stock dividends in the coming year if $11,000,000 is earned, as indicated in part *b*?

Solution:

National Health Corp.

a. $9 per share $\times$ 300,000 shares $\times$ 5 years $=$ $13,500,000 dividends in arrears.

b. $13,500,000 original dividends in arrears $+$ ($9 $\times$ 300,000) next year's preferred dividends $-$ $11,000,000 profit paid out in dividends.

   $13,500,000 $+$ $2,700,000 $-$ $11,000,000 $=$ $5,200,000 amount still in arrears.

c. No common stock dividends can be paid until all the preferred dividends are paid to the cumulative preferred stockholders.

17-16.   Robbins Petroleum Company is four years in arrears on cumulative preferred stock dividends. There are 850,000 preferred shares outstanding, and the annual dividend is $6.50 per share. The vice president of finance sees no real hope of paying the dividends in arrears. She is devising a plan to compensate the preferred stockholders for 90 percent of the dividends in arrears.

a. How much should the compensation be?
b. Robbins will compensate the preferred stockholders in the form of bonds paying 12 percent interest in a market environment in which the going rate of interest is 14 percent for similar bonds. The bonds will have a 15-year maturity. Using the bond valuation table in Chapter 16 (Table 16-3), indicate the market value of a $1,000 par value bond.
c. Based on market value, how many bonds must be issued to provide the compensation determined in part *a*? (Round to the nearest whole number.)

Solution:
Robbins Petroleum Company

a. $6.50 per share × 850,000 shares × 4 years =

$22,100,000 × 90% = $19,890,000 compensation

b. $875.54

c.
Compensation	$19,890,000
Bond value	$875.54
Number of bonds to provide compensation	22,717

17-17.   The treasurer of Newton Bottling Company (a corporation) currently has $100,000 invested in preferred stock yielding 8 percent. He appreciates the tax advantages of preferred stock and is considering buying $100,000 more with borrowed funds. The cost of the borrowed funds is 10 percent. He suggests this proposal to his board of directors. They are somewhat concerned by the fact that the treasurer will be paying 2 percent more for funds than the company will be earning on the investment. Newton Bottling is in a 34 percent tax bracket.

a. Compute the amount of the aftertax income from the additional preferred stock if it is purchased.
b. Compute the aftertax borrowing cost to purchase the additional preferred stock. That is, multiply the interest cost times $(1 - T)$.
c. Should the treasurer proceed with his proposal?

Solution:
Newton Bottling Company

a. Preferred Stock $100,000
    Dividend yield..................   8%
    Dividend.......................... $ 8,000
    Taxable income (30%)......   2,400
    Tax rate (34%)   816
    Aftertax income .... $ 7,184 ($8,000 – $816)

b. Loan $100,000
    Interest expense 10%
    Interest............................ $ 10,000
    x $(1 - T)$ 66%
    Aftertax borrowing cost.... $ 6,600

c. Yes, the aftertax income exceeds the aftertax borrowing cost. Of course, other factors may be considered as well.

17-18.   Referring back to the original information in problem 17, if the yield on the $100,000 of preferred stock is still 8 percent and the borrowing cost remains at 10 percent, but the tax rate is only 15 percent, is this a feasible investment?

Solution:

Newton Bottling Company (Continued)

Dividend............................	$ 8,000
Taxable income.................	2,400
Tax rate (15%)	360
Aftertax income	$ 7,640 ($8,000 – $360)

b. Interest.............................	$10,000
x (1 – T)	85 %
Aftertax borrowing cost....	$ 8,500

No, the aftertax income is now less than the aftertax borrowing cost.

17-19.   Barnes Air Conditioning, Inc. has two classes of preferred stock: floating rate
           preferred stock and straight (normal) preferred stock. Both issues have a par
           value of $100. The floating rate preferred stock pays an annual dividend yield
           of 6 percent, and the straight preferred stock pays 7 percent. Since the issuance
           of the two securities, interest rates have gone up by 2 percent for each issue.
           Both securities will pay their year-end dividend today.

     a.   What is the price of the floating rate preferred stock likely to be?
     b.   What is the price of the straight preferred stock likely to be? Refer back to
          Chapter 10 and use Formula 10-4 to answer this question.

Solution:
Barnes Air Conditioning, Inc.

a. The floating rate preferred stock should be trading at
   very close to the par value of $100 per share since
   interest rates will adjust to current market conditions
   rather than price.

b. Based on formula 10-4, the price of straight preferred
   stock will be:

$$P_p = \frac{D_p}{K_p} = \frac{\$7}{.09} = \$77.78$$

Comprehensive Problems

CP 17-1.   The Crandall Corporation currently has 100,000 shares outstanding that are selling at $50 per share. It needs to raise $900,000. Net income after taxes is $500,000. Its vice president of finance and its investment banker have decided on a rights offering, but are not sure how much to discount the subscription price from the current market value. Discounts of 10 percent, 20 percent, and 40 percent have been suggested. Common stock is the sole means of financing for the Crandall Corporation.

a. For each discount, determine the subscription price, the number of shares to be issued, and the number of rights required to purchase one share. (Round to one place after the decimal point where necessary.)
b. Determine the value of one right under each of the plans. (Round to two places after the decimal point.)
c. Compute the earnings per share before and immediately after the rights offering under a 10 percent discount from the subscription price.
d. By what percentage has the number of shares outstanding increased?
e. Stockholder X has 100 shares before the rights offering and participated by buying 20 new shares. Compute his total claim to earnings both before and after the rights offering (that is, multiply shares by the earnings per share figures computed in part c).
f. Should Stockholder X be satisfied with this claim over a longer period of time?

CP Solution:

Rights Offering and the Impact on Shareholders

Crandall Corp.

a. 10% discount-subscription price equals $45.

$$\text{Number of new shares} = \frac{\text{Required funds}}{\text{Subscription price}} = \frac{\$900,000}{\$45} = 20,000$$

$$\text{Number of rights to purchase one share} = \frac{\text{Old shares}}{\text{New shares}} = \frac{100,000}{20,000} = 5$$

20% discount-subscription price equals $40

$$\text{Number of new shares} = \frac{\text{Required funds}}{\text{Subscription price}} = \frac{\$900,000}{\$40} = 22,500$$

$$\text{Number of rights to purchase one share} = \frac{\text{Old shares}}{\text{New shares}} = \frac{100,000}{22,500} = 4.4$$

40% discount-subscription price equals $30

$$\text{Number of new shares} = \frac{\text{Required funds}}{\text{Subscription price}} = \frac{\$900,000}{\$30} = 30,000$$

$$\text{Number of rights to purchase one share} = \frac{\text{Old shares}}{\text{New shares}} = \frac{100,000}{30,000} = 3.3$$

b. $R = \dfrac{M_o - S}{N + 1}$

$$\underline{10\%}$$
$$R = \frac{\$50 - 45}{5 + 1} = \frac{\$5}{6} = \$.83 \qquad \underline{20\%} \atop R = \frac{\$50 - 40}{4.4 + 1} = \frac{\$10}{5.4} = \$1.85$$

$$\underline{40\%}$$
$$R = \frac{\$50 - 30}{3.3 + 1} = \frac{\$20}{4.3} = \$4.65$$

c. EPS before rights offering = net income/old shares
   $500,000/100,000   = $5.00

   EPS after rights offering = net income/(old + new shares)
   $500,000/120,000   = $4.17

d. 20% increase in shares outstanding (100,000 to 120,000)

e. Before   100 shares × $5.00 = $500
   After   120 shares × $4.17 = $500 (rounded)

f. No, he would expect greater earnings. He and others have put additional capital into the corporation so total claims to earnings should improve. Invested capital has increased from $5,000,000 to $5,900,000. He earned $500 before he put $900 more (20 shs. × $45) of additional funds in the corporation. Over time, earnings should increase.

CP 17-2.   Dr. Robert Grossman founded Electro Cardio Systems, Inc., (ECS) in 1992. The principal purpose of the firm was to engage in research and development of heart pump devices. Although the firm did not show a profit until 1997, by 2001 it reported aftertax earnings of $1,200,000. The company had gone public in 1995 at $10 a share. Investors were initially interested in buying the stock because of its future prospects. By year-end 2001, the stock was trading at $42 per share because the firm had made good on its promise to produce life saving heart pumps and, in the process, was now making reasonable earnings. With 850,000 shares outstanding, earnings per share were $1.41.

Dr. Grossman and the members of the board of directors were initially pleased when another firm, Parker Medical Products, began buying their stock. John Parker, the chairman and CEO of Parker Medical Products, was thought to be a shrewd investor and his company's purchase of 50,000 shares of ECS was taken as an affirmation of the success of the heart pump research firm.

However, when Parker bought another 50,000 shares, Dr. Grossman and members of the board of directors of ECS became concerned that John Parker and his firm might be trying to take over ECS.

Upon talking to his attorney, Dr. Grossman was reminded that ECS had a poison pill provision that took effect when any outside investor accumulated 25 percent or more of the shares outstanding. Current stockholders, excluding the potential takeover company, were given the privilege of buying up to 500,000 new shares of ECS at 80 percent of current market value. Thus, new shares would be restricted to friendly interests.

The attorney also found that Dr. Grossman and "friendly" members of the board of directors currently owned 175,000 shares of ECS.

a. How many more shares would Parker Medical Products need to purchase before the poison pill provision would go into effect? Given the current price of ECS stock of $42, what would be the cost to Parker to get up to that level?

b. ECS's ultimate fear was that Parker Medical Products would gain over a 50 percent interest in ECS's shares outstanding. What would be the additional cost to Parker to get to 50 percent (plus 1 share) of the stock outstanding of ECS at the current market price of ECS stock. In answering this question, assume parker had previously accumulated the 25 percent position discussed in question *a*.

c. Now assume that Parker exceeds the number of shares you computed in part *b* and gets all the way up to accumulated 625,000 shares of ECS. Under the poison pill provision, how many shares must "friendly" shareholders purchase to thwart a takeover attempt by Parker? What will be the total cost? Keep in mind that friendly interests already own 175,000 shares of ECS and to maintain control, they must own one more share than Parker.

d. Would you say the poison pill is an effective deterrent in this case? Is the poison pill in the best interest of the general stockholders (those not associated with the company)?

CP Solution:

Poison Pill Strategy

Electro Cardio Systems, Inc.

a. If Parker owns 25 percent of the shares outstanding of ECS, the poison pill will go into effect.

Since there are 850,000 shares outstanding, the trigger point is at 212,500 shares. This means Parker would have to buy <u>112,500</u> additional shares to go with its current ownership of 100,000.

The cost of 112,500 additional shares of ECS common stock at its current price of $42 per share would be $4,725,000.

b. To get a 50% + 1 share interest in ECS, Parker would need to own 425,000 (1/2 of 850,000) + 1 shares. The number is 425,001.

Since Parker has already acquired 212,500 shares of ECS, it would need to buy 212,501 more shares.

At a stock price of $42 per share, this would represent an additional cost of $8,505,042.

212,501	additional shares
$42	stock price
$8,925,042	additional cost

c. One more share than Parker would necessitate an ownership of 625,001 shares.

Since "friendly" interests to ECS already own 175,000 shares, this would mean they would need to acquire 450,001 additional shares.

Because under the poison pill provision, they can buy at 80% of current market value, the total cost of the 450,001 shares would be $15,120,033.

450,001	additional shares
$33.60	cost per share*
$15,120,033	total cost

*$42 × 80% (poison pill provision) = $33.60

d. Yes, the poison pill is an effective deterrent in this case. With 850,000 shares outstanding and the "friendly" interests already owning 175,000 shares, the most that Parker can acquire is 625,000. Since the poison pill provision allows up to 500,000 additional shares to be purchased by "friendly" interests, the "friendly" interests are assured of always owning more than 625,000 shares. Their total potential is 675,000 shares (175,000 shares currently owned plus 500,000 under the poison pill plan).

Quite likely, the poison pill is not in the best interest of the general shareholders. Without the poison pill, ECS is more likely to be a merger takeover candidate. Often a price is offered well in excess of current market value for a takeover candidate. For example, ECS, with a current price of $42, might be offered $60 or $70 per share in a takeover tender offer. General stockholders would certainly benefit from such an offer.

Chapter 18

Discussion Questions

18-1.   How does the marginal principle of retained earnings relate to the returns that a stockholder may make in other investments?

The marginal principle of retained earnings suggests that the corporation must do an analysis of whether the corporation or the stockholders can earn the most on funds associated with retained earnings. Thus, we must consider what the stockholders can earn on other investments.

18-2.   Discuss the difference between a passive and an active dividend policy.

A passive dividend policy suggests that dividends should be paid out if the corporation cannot make better use of the funds. We are looking more at alternate investment opportunities than at preferences for dividends. If dividends are considered as an active decision variable, stockholder preference for cash dividends is considered very early in the decision process.

18-3.   How does the stockholder, in general, feel about the relevance of dividends?

The stockholder would appear to consider dividends as relevant. Dividends do resolve uncertainty in the minds of investors and provide information content. Some stockholders may say that the dividends are relevant, but in a different sense. Perhaps they prefer to receive little or no dividends because of the immediate income tax and higher tax rate imposed on cash dividends.

18-4.   Explain the relationship between a company's growth possibilities and its dividend policy.

The greater a company's growth possibilities, the more funds that can be justified for profitable internal reinvestment. This is very well illustrated in Table 18-1 in which we show four-year growth rates for selected U.S. corporations and their associated dividend payout percentages. This is also discussed in the life cycle of the firm.

18-5.   Since initial contributed capital theoretically belongs to the stockholders, why are there legal restrictions on paying out the funds to the stockholders?

Creditors have extended credit on the assumption that a given capital base would remain intact throughout the life of a loan. While they may not object to the payment of dividends from past and current earnings, they must have the protection of keeping contributed capital in place.

18-6.   Discuss how desire for control may influence a firm's willingness to pay dividends.

Management's desire for control could imply that a closely held firm should avoid dividends to minimize the need for outside financing. For a larger firm, - management may have to pay dividends in order to maintain their current position through keeping stockholders happy.

18-7.   If you buy stock on the ex-dividend date, will you receive the upcoming quarterly dividend?

No, the old stockholder receives the upcoming quarterly dividend. Of course, if you continue to hold the stock, you will receive the next dividend.

18-8.   How is a stock split (versus a stock dividend) treated on the financial statements of a corporation?

For a stock split, there is no transfer of funds, but merely a –reduction in par value and a –proportionate increase in the number of shares outstanding.

Impact of a Stock Split

Before	After
Common stock (1,000,000 shares at $10 par)	(2,000,000 shares at $5 par)

18-9.   Why might a stock dividend or a stock split be of limited value to an investor?

The asset base remains the same and the stockholders' proportionate interest is unchanged (everyone got the same new share). Earnings per share will go down by the exact proportion that the number of shares increases. If the P/E ratio remains constant, the total value of each shareholder's portfolio will not increase.

The only circumstances in which a stock dividend may be of some usefulness and perhaps increase value is when dividends per share remain constant and total dividends go up, or where substantial information is provided about a growth company. A stock split may have some functionality in placing the company into a lower "stock price" trading range.

18-10.   Does it make sense for a corporation to repurchase its own stock? Explain.

A corporation can make a rational case for purchasing its own stock as an alternate to a cash dividend policy. Earnings per share will go up and if the price-earnings ratio remains the same, the stockholder will receive the same dollar benefit as through a cash dividend. Because the benefits are in the format of capital gains, the tax rate will be lower and the tax may be deferred until the stock is sold.

A corporation also may justify the repurchase of its own stock because it is at a very low price, or to maintain constant demand for the shares. Reacquired shares may be used for employee options or as a part of a tender offer in a merger or acquisition. Finns may also reacquire part of their stock as protection against a hostile takeover.

18-11.   What advantages to the corporation and the stockholder do dividend reinvestment plans offer?

Dividend reinvestment plans allow corporations to raise funds continually from present stockholders. This reduces the need for some external funds. These plans allow stockholders to reinvest dividends at low costs and to buy fractional shares, neither of which can be easily accomplished in the market by an individual. The strategy of dividend reinvestment plans allows for the compounding of dividends and the accumulation of common stock over time.

Problems

18-1.   Neil Diamond Brokers, Inc. reported earnings per share of $4.00 and paid $.90 in dividends. What is the payout ratio?

Solution:

Neil Diamond Brokers, Inc.

Payout ratio   =   earnings per share/dividends per share
                = $.90/$4.00 = 22.5%

18-2.   Sewell Enterprises earned $160 million last year and retained $100 million. What is the payout ratio?

Solution:

Sewell Enterprises

Dividends   =   (earnings – retained funds)
               = $160 mil. – $100 mill. = $60 mil.

Payout ratio   =   dividends/earnings
                = $60 mil./$160 mil. = 37.5%

18-3.   Bay View Shipping Company earned $800 million last year and had a 35 percent payout ratio. How much did the firm add to its retained earnings?

Solution:

Bay View Shipping Company

Dividends   =   earnings × payout ratio

               = $800 mil. × 35%

               = $280 mil.

Addition to retained earnings = earnings – dividends
           $520 mil.   = $800 mil. – $280 mil.

18-4.   The following companies have different financial statistics. What dividend policies would you recommend for them? Explain your reasons.

	Turtle Co.	Hare Corp.
Growth rate in sales and earnings..................	5%	20%
Cash as a percentage of total assets	15%	2%

Solution:

Turtle is not growing very fast so it doesn't need cash for growth unless it desires to change its policies. Assuming it doesn't, Turtle should have a high payout ratio.

Hare is growing very fast and needs its cash for reinvestment in assets. For this reason, Hare should have a low dividend payout.

18-5.   A financial analyst is attempting to asses the future dividend policy of Environmental Systems by examining its life cycle. She anticipates no payout of earnings in the form of cash dividends during the development stage (I). During the growth stage (II), she anticipate 10 percent of earnings will be distributed as dividends. As the firm progresses to the expansion stage (III), the payout ratio will go up to 45 percent, and eventually reach 60 percent during the maturity stage (IV).

a. Assuming earnings per share will be the following during each of the four stages, indicate the cash dividend per share (if any) during each stage.

Stage I	$ .15
Stage II	1.80
Stage III	2.60
Stage IV	3.10

b. Assume in Stage IV that an investor owns 275 shares and is in a 31 percent tax bracket, what will be the investor's aftertax income from the cash dividend?

c. In what two stages is the firm most likely to utilize stock dividends or stock splits?

Solution:

Environmental Systems

a.

	Earnings	Payout Ratio	Dividends
Stage I	$ .15	0	0
Stage II	$1.80	10%	$ .18
Stage III	2.60	45%	$1.17
Stage IV	3.10	60%	$1.86

b. Total Dividends $=$ Shares $\times$ dividends per share

$\qquad\qquad\qquad\;\; = \;\; 275 \quad \times \$1.86$

$\qquad\qquad\qquad\;\; = \;\; \$511.50$

$\quad$ Aftertax income $\;\; = \;\;$ total dividends $\times (1 - T)$

$\qquad\qquad\qquad\quad\; = \;\; \$511.50 \times (1 - .31)$

$\qquad\qquad\qquad\quad\; = \;\; \$511.50 \times (.69)$

$\qquad\qquad\qquad\quad\; = \;\; \$352.94$

c. Stock dividends or stock splits are most likely to be utilized during stage II (growth) or stage III (expansion).

18-6.   Austin Power Company has the following balance sheet:

Assets

Cash..	$ 50,000
Accounts receivable..	250,000
Fixed Assets..	700,000
Total Assets..	$1,000,000

Liabilities

Accounts payable...	$ 250,000
Notes payable...	50,000
Capital ⌐ Common stock (100,000 shares @ $2 par)....	200,000
Accounts ⎨ Capital in excess of par................................	100,000
⌐ Retained earnings...	400,000
	$1,000,000

The firm's stock sells for $11 a share.

a.   Show the effect on the capital account(s) of a two-for-one stock split.
b.   Show the effect on the capital accounts of a 10 percent stock divided. Part *b* is separate from part *a*. In part *b* do not assume the stock split has taken place.
c.   Based on the balance in retained earnings, which of the two dividend plans is more restrictive on future cash dividends?

Solution:

Austin Power Company

a. 2 for 1 stock split

    *   Common stock (200,000 shares @ $1 par) $200,000

         Capital excess of par   100,000

         Retained earnings   400,000

    *   The only account affected

b. 10% stock dividend

         Common stock (110,000 shares @ $2 par) $220,000

    *   Capital in excess of par   190,000

   ** Retained earnings   290,000

    * $100,000 + 10,000 ($11 − $2) = $100,000 + $90,000

        = $190,000

   ** $400,000 − 20,000 − 90,000 = $400,000 − 110,000

        = $290,000

c. The stock dividend. Cash dividends cannot exceed the balance in retained earnings and the balance is lower with the stock dividend ($290,000 versus $400,000).

18-7. In doing a five-year analysis of future dividends, the Dawson Corporation is considering the following two plans. The Values represent dividends per share.

Year	Plan A	Plan B
1..........	$1.50	$ .50
2..........	1.50	2.00
3..........	1.50	.20
4..........	1.60	4.00
5..........	1.60	1.70

a. How much in total dividends per share will be paid under each plan over the five years?

b. Mr. Bright, the vice president of finance, suggests that stockholders often prefer a stable dividend policy to a highly variable one. He will assume that stockholders apply a lower discount rate to dividends that are stable. The discount rate to be used for plan A is 10 percent; the discount rate for Plan B is 12 percent. Which plan will provide the higher present value for the future dividends? (Round to two places to the right of the decimal point.)

Solution:

Dawson Corporation

a. Plan A ($1.50 + 1.50 + 1.50 + 1.60 + 1.60) = $7.70
    Plan B ($.50 + 2.00 + .20 + 4.00 + 1.70) = $8.40

b. Plan A

	Dividend Per Share	×	PV_{IF} (10%)	PV
1	$1.50		.909	$1.36
2	1.50		.826	1.24
3	1.50		.751	1.13
4	1.60		.683	1.09
5	1.60		.621	.99
			Present Value of future dividends	$5.81

Plan B

	Dividend Per Share	×	PV$_{IF}$ (12%)	PV
1	$ .50		.893	$ .45
2	2.00		.797	1.59
3	.20		.712	.14
4	4.00		.636	2.54
5	1.70		.567	.96
			Present Value of future dividends	$5.68

Plan A will provide the higher present value of future dividends.

18-8.   The stock of North American Dandruff Company is selling at $80 per share. The firm pays a dividend of $2.50 per share.

a. What is the dividend yield?
b. If the firm has a payout rate of 50 percent, what is the firm's P/E ratio?

Solution:
North American Dandruff Company

a. Annual dividend yield   =   cash dividend/price
　　　　　　　　　　　　　 = $2.50/$80 = 3.125%

b. Earnings per share   =   cash dividends/.5
　　　　　　　　　　　 = $2.50/.5 = $5

　　P/E ratio   =   Price/earnings per share
　　　　　　　 = $80/$5 = 16x

18-9. The shares of the Charles Darwin Fitness Centers sell for $60. The firm has a P/E ratio of 20. Forty percent of earnings are paid out in dividends. What is the firm's dividend yield?

Solution:

Charles Darwin Fitness Centers

Earnings per share $\quad$ = Stock price/price-earnings ratio
$\qquad\qquad\qquad\qquad$ = $60/20 = $3.00

Dividends per share $\quad$ = Earnings per share × .40

$\qquad\qquad\qquad\qquad$ = $3.00 × .40 = $1.20

Dividend yield $\qquad\qquad$ = Dividends per share/price
$\qquad\qquad\qquad\qquad$ = $1.20/$60 = .02 or 2%

18-10.　　The Marsh Land Development Company has two very important stockholders: Ms. Bush, an individual investor, and the Forrester Corporation. Ms. Bush is in a 31 percent marginal tax bracket, while the Forrester Corporation is in a 35 percent tax bracket.

a.　If Ms. Bush receives a $5.00 in cash dividends, how much in taxes (per share) will she pay?

b.　If the Forrester Corporation receives $5.00 in cash dividends, how much in taxes (per share) will it pay? (Please review the partial exemption accorded to corporate recipients of cash dividends in Table 17-3 of the prior chapter.)

Solution:
Marsh Land Development Company

a. Ms. Bush

$5.00	Cash dividend
31%	Marginal tax rate
$1.55	Taxes

b. Forrester Corporation

$5.00	Cash dividend
30%	Taxable
$1.50	Taxes
35%	Marginal tax rate
$.525	Taxes

18-11.　　Max Johnson owns 200 shares of Newmont Labs, Inc., which he bought for $15 per share. He is in a 33 percent tax bracket. It is the first week in December, and he has already received the full cash dividend for the year of $1.60 per share. The stock is currently selling for $25 ½. He has decided to sell the stock and after paying broker commissions, his net proceeds will be $25 per share. His tax rate on capital gains is 20 percent.

a.　How much in total taxes will Max pay this year for his investment in Newmont Labs, Inc.? Consider dividend income as well as capital gains.

b.　Discuss the advantages of the capital gains tax over the tax on dividends.

Solution:

Newmont Labs, Inc.

a. <u>Taxes on dividends</u>

Dividend income	=	Shares × dividends per share
	=	200 × $1.60
	=	$320

Taxes	=	Dividend income × marginal tax rate
	=	$320 × 33.0%
	=	$105.60

<u>Taxes on Capital gains</u>

Sales price	$ 25
Purchase price	15
Capital gains per share	$ 10
x Number of shares	200
Total capital gains	$2,000
Capital gains tax rate	20%
Capital gains tax	$ 400

<u>Total taxes</u>

Taxes on dividends	$105.60
Taxes on capital gains	400.00
	$505.60

b. First of all the maximum tax on capital gains is lower than the maximum tax on dividend income. (20 percent versus 39.6 percent). Furthermore, the capital gains tax is not due until the year the stock is sold whereas the tax on dividends is due in the year received.

18-12.   The Ohio Freight Company's common stock is selling for $40 the day before the stock goes ex-dividend. The annual dividend yield is 6.7 percent, and dividends are distributed quarterly. Based solely on the impact of the cash dividend, by how much should the stock go down on the ex-dividend date? What will the new price of the stock be?

Solution:
Ohio Freight Company

Annual dividend   =   6.7% × $40 = $2.68
Quarterly dividend = $2.68/4 = $.67

The stock should go down by $.67 to $39.33.

18-13.   The Western Pipe Company has the following capital section in its balance sheet. Its stock is currently selling for $5 per share.

Common stock (50,000 shares at $1 par)................... $ 50,000
Capital in excess of par... 50,000
Retained earnings.. 100,000
$200,000

The firm intends to first declare a 10 percent stock dividend and then pay a 20-cent cash dividend (which also causes a reduction of retained earnings). Show the capital section of the balance sheet after the first transaction and then after the second transaction.

Solution:
Western Pipe Co.

After 1st transaction

Common stock (55,000 shares at $1 par)........... $ 55,000
Capital in excess of par 70,000
Retained earnings 75,000
$200,000

After 2nd transaction

Common stock (55,000 shares at $1 par)........... $ 55,000
Capital in excess of par 70,000
Retained earnings* 64,000
$189,000

* The cash dividend of 20¢ per share causes retained earnings to be reduced by $11,000 (55,000 × 20¢).

18-14.   Phillips Rock and Mud is trying to determine the maximum amount of cash dividends it can pay this year. Assume its balance sheet is as follows:

Assets

Cash..	$ 312,500
Accounts receivable..	800,000
Fixed Assets..	987,500
Total Assets...	$2,100,000

Liabilities

Accounts payable..	$ 445,000
Long-term payable..	280,000
Common stock (250,000 shares @ $2 par).........................	500,000
Retained earnings...	875,000
Total liabilities and stockholders' equity	$2,100,000

a. From a legal perspective, what is the maximum amount of dividends per share the firm could pay? Is this realistic?

b. In terms of cash availability, what is the maximum amount of dividends per share the firm could pay?

c. Assume the firm earned a 16 percent return on stockholders' equity last year. If the board wishes to pay out 60 percent of earnings in the form of dividends, how much will dividends per share be? (Round to two places to the right of the decimal point.)

Solution:

Phillips Rock and Mud

a. From a legal viewpoint, the firm can pay cash dividends equal to retained earnings of $875,000. Or a per share basis, this represents $3.50 per share.

$$\frac{\text{Retained earnings}}{\text{Shares}} = \frac{\$875,000}{250,000} = \$3.50$$

This would not be realistic in light of the firm's cash balance.

b. $\dfrac{\text{Cash}}{\text{Shares}} = \dfrac{\$312,500}{250,000} = \$1.25$

c. Stockholder's equity = common stock + retained earnings
   $1,375,000   = $500,000 + $875,000

Return on equity   = 16% × $1,375,000 = $220,000

Dividends   = 60% × return on equity
                    = 60% × $220,000
                    = $132,000

$$\frac{\text{Dividends}}{\text{Shares}} = \frac{\$132,000}{250,000} = \$.53$$

18-15.   The Warner Corporation has earnings of $750,000 with 300,000 shares outstanding. Its P/E ratio is 16. The firm is holding $400,000 of funds to invest or pay out in dividends. If the funds are retained, the aftertax return on investment will be 15 percent, and this will add to present earnings. The 15 percent is the normal return anticipated for the corporation and the P/E ratio would remain unchanged. If the funds are paid out in the form of dividends, the P/E ratio will increase by 10 percent because the stockholders are in a very low tax bracket and have a preference for dividends over retained earnings. Which plan will maximize the market value of the stock?

Solution:

Warner Corp.

Retain

Incremental earnings $= 15\% \times \$400,000 = \$60,000$

$$\text{Earnings Per share} = \frac{\$750,000 + \$60,000}{300,000} = \frac{\$810,000}{300,000} = \$2.70$$

Price of stock $= \text{P/E} \times \text{EPS}$

$\qquad\qquad = 16 \times \$2.70 = \$43.20$

Payout

New P/E $\qquad = \quad 1.10 \times 16 = 17.6$

Earnings per share $\qquad = \dfrac{\$750,000}{300,000} = \$2.50$

Price of stock $\qquad = \quad \text{P/E} \times \text{EPS}$

$\qquad\qquad\qquad = 17.6 \times \$2.50 = \$44.00$

The payout option provides the maximum market value.

18-16.   Omni Telecom is trying to decide whether to increase its cash dividend immediately or use the funds to increase its future growth rate. It will use the dividend valuation model originally presented in Chapter 10 for purposes of analysis. The model was shown as formula 10-9 and is reproduced below (with a slight addition in definition of terms).

$$P_0 = \frac{D_1}{K_e - g}$$

P_0 = Price of the stock today

D_1 = Dividend at the end of the first year
$D_0 \times (1 + g)$

D_0 = Dividend today

K_e = Required rate of return

g = Constant growth rate in dividends

D_0 is currently $2.00, K_e is 10 percent, and g is 5 percent.

Under Plan A, D_0 would be *immediately* increased to $2.20 and K_e and g will remain unchanged.

Under Plan B, D_0 will remain at $2.00 but g will go up to 6 percent and K_e will remain unchanged.

a. Compute P_0 (price of the stock today) under Plan A. Note D_1 will be equal to $D_0 \times (1 + g)$ or $2.20 (1.05). K_e will equal 10 percent and g will equal 5 percent.

b. Compute P_0 (price of the stock today) under Plan B. Note D_1 will be equal to $D_0 \times (1 + g)$ or $2.00 (1.06). K_e will be equal to 10 percent and g will be equal to 6 percent.

c. Which plan will produce the higher value?

Solution:

Omni Telecom

a. Plan A – increase cash dividend immediately

$$P_o = \frac{D_1}{K_e - g}$$

<u>First Compute D_1</u>

$$
\begin{aligned}
D_1 &= D_0(1+g) \\
&= \$2.20(1.05) = \$2.31
\end{aligned}
$$

<u>Then Compute the stock price</u>

$D_1 = \$2.31$, $K_e = .10$, $g = .05$

$$P_o = \frac{\$2.31}{.10 - .05} = \frac{\$2.31}{.05} = \$46.20$$

b. Plan B – increase growth rate

$$P_o = \frac{D_1}{K_e - g}$$

<u>First Compute D_1</u>

$$
\begin{aligned}
D_1 &= D_0(1+g) \\
&= \$2.00(1.06) = \$2.12
\end{aligned}
$$

<u>Then Compute the stock price</u>

$D_1 = \$2.12$, $K_e = .10$, $g = .06$

$$P_o = \frac{\$2.12}{.10-.06} = \frac{\$2.12}{.04} = \$53$$

c. Plan B, which calls for using funds to increase the growth rate, will produce a higher value.

18-17. Wilson Pharmaceuticals' stock has done very well in the market during the last three years. It has risen from $45 to $70 per share. The firm's current statement of stockholders' equity is as follows:

Common stock (4 million shares issued at par value of $10 per share).................................	$ 40,000,000
Paid-in-capital in excess of par.................................	15,000,000
Retained earnings...	45,000,000
Net worth	$100,000,000

a. What changes would occur in the statement of stockholders' equity after a two-for-one stock split?

b. What changes would occur in the statement of stockholders' equity after a three-for-one stock split?

c. Assume that Wilson earned $14 million. What would be its earnings per share before and after the two-for-one stock split? After the three-for-one stock split?

d. What would be the price per share after the two-for-one stock split? After the three-for-one stock split? (Assume that the price-earnings ratio of 20 stays the same.)

e. Should a stock split change the price-earnings ratio for Wilson?

Solution:

Wilson Pharmaceutical

a. Eight (8) million shares would be outstanding at a par value of $5 per share. Everything else will be the same.

b. Twelve (12) million shares would be outstanding at a par value of $3.33 per share. Everything else will be the same.

c. EPS before $= \$14,000,000/4,000,000$ shares
$$= \$3.50 \text{ EPS}$$

EPS after 2-1 split $= \$14,000,000/8,000,000$ shares
$$= \$1.75 \text{ EPS}$$

EPS after 3-1 split $= \$14,000,000/12,000/000$ shares
$$= \$1.17 \text{ EPS}$$

d. $\qquad$ P/E $\times$ EPS $=$ Price

Price after 2-1 split $= 20 \times \$1.75 = \$35.00$

Price after 3-1 split $= 20 \times \$1.17 = \$23.40$

e. Probably not. A stock split should not change the price-earnings ratio unless it is combined with a change in dividends to the stockholders. Generally speaking, nothing of real value has taken place. Only to the limited extent that new information content from this split increased investor's expectations would the stock split possible have an impact on the P/E ratio.

18-18.   Ace Products sells marked playing cards to blackjack dealers. It has not paid a dividend in many years, but is currently contemplating some kind of dividend. The capital accounts for the firm are as follows:

Common stock (2,000,000 shares at $5 par)..............	$10,000,000
Capital in excess of par*..	6,000,000
Retained earnings..	24,000,000
Net worth	$40,000,000

*The increase in capital in excess of par as a result of a stock dividend is equal to the new shares created times (market price – par value).

The company's stock is selling for $20 per share. The company had total earnings of $4,000,000 during the year. With 2,000,000 shares outstanding, earnings per share were $2.00. The firm has a P/E ratio of 10.

a. What adjustments would have to be made to the capital accounts for a 10 percent stock dividend?
b. What adjustments would be made to EPS and the stock price? (Assume the P/E ratio remains constant.)
c. How many shares would an investor end up with if he or she originally had 100 shares?
d. What is the investor's total investment worth before and after the stock dividend if the P/E ratio remains constant? (There may be a $1 to $2 difference due to rounding.)
e. Has Ace Products pulled a magic trick, or has it given the investor something of value? Explain.

Solution:

Ace Products

a. Common stock (2,200,000 shares at $5 par) $11,000,000
   *Capital in excess of par   9,000,000
   **Retained earnings   20,000,000
   Net worth $40,000,000

*200,000 shares × ($20 − $5) = 200,000 × $15 = $3,000,000
   $6,000,000 + 3,000,000 = $9,000,000

**$24,000,000 − $1,000,000 − $3,000,000 = $20,000,000

b. EPS after stock dividend = $4,000,000/$2,200,000 = $1.82
   Price = P/E ratio × EPS = 10 × 1.82 = $18.20

c. 100 + (100 × 10%) = 110 shares after the stock dividend

d. <u>Before</u>   <u>After</u>
   100 × $20 = $2,000   110 × $18.20 = $2,002

e. Generally speaking, nothing of real value has taken
   place. Only to the limited extent that total cash dividends
   might have increased or information been provided
   could small benefits have taken place.

18-19.   The Carlton Corporation has $4 million in earnings after taxes and 1 million shares outstanding. The stock trades at the P/E of 20. The firm has $3 million in excess cash.

a. Compute the current price of the stock.
b. If the $3 million is used to pay dividends, how much will dividends per share be?
c. If the $3 million is used to repurchase shares in the market at a price of $83 per share, how many shares will be acquired? (Round to nearest share.)
d. What will the new earnings per share be? (Round to two places to the right of the decimal.)
e. If the P/E remains constant, what will the price of the securities be? By how much, in terms of dollars, did the repurchase increase the stock price?
f. Has the stockholder's total wealth changed as a result of the stock repurchase as opposed to the cash dividends.
g. What tax advantages might there be for a stock repurchase as compared to a cash dividend?
h. What are some other reasons a corporation may wish to repurchase its own shares in the market?

Solution:
Carlton Corporation

a. Price   =   P/E × EPS
   EPS   = $4 mil./1 mil. = $4
   Price   =   20 × $4 = $80

b. $3 mil./1 mil.   = $3 dividends per share

c. $3,000,000/$83   =   36,145 shares reacquired

d. Shares outstanding after repurchase
   1,000,000 − 36,145 = 963,855
   EPS = $4,000,000/963,855 = $4.15

e. Price = P/E × EPS   20 × $4.15 = $83.00

f. No. With the cash dividend:

Market value per share	$80
Cash dividend per share	3
Total value	$83

With the repurchase of stock:

Total value per share	$83

g. The (potential) appreciation in value associated with a stock repurchase receives preferential capital gains tax treatment whereas a cash dividend is taxed at the investor's normal tax rate. The capital gains tax may also be deferred until the stock is sold.

h. The corporation may think its shares are underpriced in the market. The purchase may stave off further decline and perhaps even trigger a rally. Reacquired shares may also be used for employee stock options or as part of a tender offer in a merger or an acquisition. Firms may also reacquire part of their shares as a protective device against being taken over as a merger candidate.

18-20. The Hastings Sugar Corporation has the following pattern of net income each year, and associated capital expenditure projects. The firm can earn a higher return on the projects than the stockholders could earn if the funds were paid out in the form of dividends.

Year	Net Income	Profitable Capital Expenditure
1..........	$10 million	$ 7 million
2..........	15 million	11 million
3..........	9 million	6 million
4..........	12 million	7 million
5..........	14 million	8 million

The Hastings Corporation has 2 million shares outstanding (the following questions are separate from each other).

a. If the marginal principle of retained earnings is applied, how much in total cash dividends will be paid over the five years?

b. If the firm simply uses a payout ratio of 40 percent of new income, how much in total cash dividends will be paid?

c. If the firm pays a 10 percent stock dividend in years 2 through 5, and also pays a cash dividend of $2.40 per share for each of the five years, how much in total dividends will be paid?

d. Assume the payout ratio in each year is to be 30 percent of net income and the firm will pay a 20 percent stock dividend in years 2 through 5, how much will dividends per share for each year be?

Solution:

Hastings Sugar Corporation

a. Dividends represent what is left over after profitable capital expenditures are undertaken.

Year	Net Income	–	Profitable Capital Expenditures	Dividends
1	$10 mil.		$ 7 mil.	$ 3 mil.
2	15 mil.		11 mil.	4 mil.
3	9 mil.		6 mil.	3 mil.
4	12 mil.		7 mil.	5 mil.
5	14 mil.		8 mil.	6 mil.
			Total cash dividends	$21 mil.

b.

Year	Net Income	×	Payout ration	Dividends
1	$10 mil.		.40	$ 4.0 mil.
2	15 mil.		.40	6.0 mil.
3	9 mil.		.40	3.6 mil.
4	12 mil.		.40	4.8 mil.
5	14 mil.		.40	5.6 mil.
			Total cash dividends	$24.0 mil.

c.

Year	Shares outstanding		Dividends per share	Dividends
1	2,000,000	×	$2.40	$ 4,800,000
2	2,200,000	×	2.40	5,280,000
3	2,420,000	×	2.40	5,808,000
4	2,662,000	×	2.40	6,388,800
5	2,928,200	×	2.40	7,027,680
			Total cash dividends	$29,304,480

d.

Year	Net income	Payout ratio	Dividends	Shares (millions)	Dividends per share
1	$10 mil.	.30	$3.0 mil.	2.0	$1.50
2	15 mil.	.30	4.5 mil.	2.4	1.88
3	9 mil.	.30	2.7 mil.	2.88	.94
4	12 mil.	.30	3.6 mil.	3.456	1.04
5	14 mil.	.30	4.2 mil.	4.1472	1.01

Chapter 19

Discussion Questions

19-1.   What are the basic advantages to the corporation of issuing convertible securities?

The advantages to the corporation of a convertible security are:

a. The interest rate is lower than on a straight issue.
b. This type of security may be the only device for allowing a small firm access to the capital markets.
c. The convertible allows the firm to effectively sell stock at a higher price than that possible when the bond was initially issued (but perhaps at a lower price than future price potential might provide).

19-2.   Why are investors willing to pay a premium over the theoretical value (pure bond value or conversion value)?

Investors are willing to pay a premium over the theoretical value for a convertible bond issue because of the future prospects for the associated common stock. Thus, if there are many years remaining for the conversion privilege, the investor will be able to receive a reasonably high interest rate and still have the existing option of going to common stock if circumstances justify.

19-3.   Why is it said that convertible securities have a floor price?

The floor price of a convertible is based on the pure bond value associated with the interest payments on the bond as shown in Figure 19-1. Regardless of how low the associated common stock might go, the semiannual interest payments will set a floor price for the bond.

19-4. The price of Gordon Corporation 5 ½ 2018 convertible bonds is $1,390. For the Marshall Corporation, the 6 ⅜ 2017 convertible bonds are selling at $730.

   a. Explain what factors might cause their prices to be different from their par value of $1,000.
   b. What will happen to each bond's value if long-term interest rates decline?

   Convertible bond pricing

   a. Gordon bonds are well above par value because its common stock has probably increased substantially. In the case of Marshall, it is reasonable to assume that its common stock has declined. Also, its interest rate is probably well below the going market rate because of its low bond price.

   b. With the Gordon Corporation, there would be little or no impact. It is clearly controlled by its common stock value. With the Marshall Corporation, its potential value is somewhat associated with interest rates (rather than just conversion), so it is likely to go up somewhat in value.

19-5. How can a company force conversion of a convertible bond?

   A firm may force conversion of a bond issue through the use of the call privilege. If a bond has had a substantial gain in value due to an increase in price of the underlying common stock, the bondholder may prefer to convert to common stock rather than trade in the bond at some small premium over par as stipulated in a call agreement.

19-6. What is meant by a step-up in the conversion price?

   A "step-up" in conversion price will increase with the passage of time and likewise the conversion ratio will decline. Before each step-up, there is an inducement for bondholders to convert to common at the more desirable price.

19-7.   Explain the difference between basic earnings per share and diluted earnings per share.

Primary earnings per share consider some, but not all, of the potentially dilative effects of convertibles, warrants, and other securities that can generate new shares of common stock. Fully diluted earnings per share considers all dilative effects regardless of their origin. To be more specific, primary earnings per share include common stock and common stock equivalents—which are defined as warrants, options, and any convertible issues that pay less than two-thirds of the average Aa bond yield at time issue. Fully diluted earnings per share include the same categories plus all other convertibles regardless of the interest rate consideration.

19-8.   Explain how convertible bonds and warrants are similar and different.

Convertible bonds and warrants are similar in that they give the security holder a future option on the common stock of the corporation. They are dissimilar in that a convertible bond represents a debt obligation of the firm as well. When it is converted to common stock, corporate debt will actually be reduced and the capitalization of the firm will not increase. A warrant is different in that it is not a valuable instrument on its own merits, and also its exercise will increase the overall capitalization of the firm.

19-9.   Explain why warrants are issued. (Why are they used in corporate finance?)

Warrants may be used to sweeten a debt offering or as part of a merger offer or a bankruptcy proceeding.

19-10.   What are the reasons that warrants often sell above their intrinsic value?

Warrants may sell above their intrinsic value because the investor views the associated stock's prospects as being bright, or there is a reasonable amount of time to run before the warrant expires. Warrants also allow for the use of leveraged investing.

19-11.   What is the differences between a call option and a put option?

A call option is an option to buy, and a put option is an option to sell.

19-12.   Suggest two areas where the use of futures contracts are most common. What percent of the value of the underlying security is typical in a futures contract?

Futures contracts are most common for commodities and interest rate securities, especially government bonds.

19-13.   You buy a stock option with an exercise price of $50. The cost of the option is $3. If the stock ends up at $55, indicate whether you have a profit or loss with a call option? With a put option?

With a call option, you would have a profit. You bought the option for $3 and the market value is $5 over the exercise value. With a put option, you would have a loss. It is worthless to have the right to sell a stock for $50, when the cost of the stock is $55. You would lose your $3 investment.

Problems

19-1.   National Motors, Inc., has warrants outstanding that allow the holder to purchase 1.5 shares of stock per warrant at $28 per share (exercise price). Thus, each individual share can be purchased at $28 under the warrant.

The common stock is currently selling for $35. The warrant is selling for $14.

a. What is the intrinsic (minimum) value of this warrant?
b. What is the speculative premium on this warrant?
c. What should happen to the speculative premium as the expiration date approaches?

(Assume all bonds in the following problems have a par value of $1,000.)

Solution:

a.
$$I = (M - E) \times N$$

Where: I = Intrinsic value of a warrant
M = Market value of common stock
E = Exercise price of a warrant
N = Number of shares each warrant entitles the holder to purchase

I = ($35 − $28) × 1.5 = $10.50

b.
$$S = W - I$$

Where: S = Speculative premium
W = Warrant price
I = Intrinsic value

S = $14.00 − $10.50 = $3.50

c. The speculative premium should decrease and approach $0 as the expiration date nears.

19-2.   DNA Labs, Inc., has a $1,000 convertible bond outstanding that can be converted into 40 shares of common stock. The common stock is currently selling for $26.75 a share and the convertible bond is selling for $1,118.50.

   a.   What is the conversion value of the bond?
   b.   What is the conversion premium?
   c.   What is the conversion price?

Solution:

DNA Labs, Inc.

a. $26.75 stock price × 40 shares = $1,070 conversion value

b. $1,118.50 bond price – $1,070 conversion value = $48.50 conversion premium

c. $1,000 par value/40 conversion ratio = $25 conversion price

19-3. The bonds of Stein Co. have a conversion premium of $35. Their conversion price is $20. The common stock price is $18.50. What is the price of the convertible bonds?

Solution:

Stein Co.

First compute the conversion ratio

The conversion ratio is equal to the par value divided by the conversion price:

Par value/conversion price = conversion ratio
$1,000/$20 = 50 conversion ratio

Multiply the common stock price times the conversion ratio to get the conversion value:

Common stock price × conversion ratio = conversion value
$18.50 × 50 shares = $925 conversion value

Add the conversion premium to the conversion value to arrive at the convertible bond price:

Conversion Value + Conversion Premium = Convertible Bond Price
$925 + $35 = $960 convertible bond price

19-4.   Sherwood Forest Products has a convertible bond quoted on the NYSE bond market at 95. (Bond quotes represent percentage of par value. Thus, 70 represents $700, 80 represents $800, and so on.) It matures in 10 years and carries a coupon rate of 6 ½ percent. The conversion ratio is 25, and the common stock is currently selling for $35 per share on the NYSE.

a. Compute the conversion premium.
b. At what price does the common stock need to sell for the conversion value to be equal to the current bond price?

Solution:
Sherwood Forest Products

a. $35 common stock price × 25 shares =
   $875 conversion value
   $950 bond price – $875 = $75 conversion premium

b. $950 bond price/25 shares = $38

19-5. Pittsburgh Steel Company has a convertible bond outstanding, trading in the marketplace at $930. The par value is $1,000, the coupon rate is 8 percent, and the bond matures in 25 years. The conversion price is $50 and the company's common stock is selling for $44 per share. Interest is paid semiannually.

a. What is the conversion value?
b. If similar bonds, which are not convertible, are currently yielding 10 percent, what is the pure bond value of this convertible bond? (Use semiannual analysis as described in Chapter 10.)

Solution:
Pittsburgh Steel Company

a. Par value/conversion price = conversion ratio
   $1,000/$50 = 20
   20 shares × $44 common stock price =
   $880 conversion value

b. Pure bond value where n = 50, i = 5%
   Pure bond value = $40 semiannually × 18.256   = $730.24

   $1,000 principal value × .087 = __87.00__
   $817.24

19-6.   In problem 5, if the interest rate on similar bonds, which are not convertible, goes up from 10 percent to 12 percent, what will be the new pure bond value of the Pittsburgh Steel Company bonds? Assume the Pittsburgh Steel Company bonds have the same coupon rate of 8 percent as described in problem 5 and that 25 years remain to maturity. Use semiannual analysis.

Solution:
Pittsburgh Steel Company (Continued)

Pure bond value where n = 50, i = 6%

Pure bond value = $40 semiannually × 15.762   = $630.48

$1,000 principal value × .054 =   54.00

$684.48

19-7. The Olsen Mining Company has been very successful in the last five years. Its $1,000 par value convertible bonds have a conversion ratio of 32. The bonds have a quoted interest rate of 5 percent a year. The firm's common stock is currently selling for $39.50 per share. The current bond price has a conversion premium of $10 over the conversion value.

a. What is the current price of the bond?
b. What is the current yield on the bond (annual interest divided by the bond's market price)?
c. If the common stock price goes down to $21.50 and the conversion premium goes up to $100, what will be the new current yield on the bond?

Solution:

Olsen Mining Company

a. $39.50 stock price × 32 shares = $1,264 conversion value

$$\begin{array}{r} + \quad 10 \text{ conversion premium} \\ \hline \$1,274 \text{ Bond price} \end{array}$$

b. 5% × $1,000 = $50 Annual interest

$$\frac{\text{Annual interest}}{\text{Bond price}} = \frac{\$50}{\$1,274} = 3.92\%$$

c. $21.50 stock price × 32 shares = $688 conversion value

$$\begin{array}{r} +100 \quad \text{conversion premium} \\ \hline \$788 \quad \text{Bond price} \end{array}$$

$$\frac{\text{Annual interest}}{\text{Bond price}} = \frac{\$50}{\$788} = 6.35\%$$

19-8.   Standard Olive Company of California has a convertible bond outstanding with a coupon rate of 9 percent and a maturity date of 15 years. It is rated Aa, and competitive, nonconvertible bonds of the same risk class carry a 10 percent return. The conversion ratio is 25. Currently the common stock is selling for $30 per share on the New York Stock Exchange.

a. What is the conversion price?
b. What is the conversion value?
c. Compute the pure bond value. (Use semiannual analysis.)
d. Draw a graph that includes the pure bond value and the conversion value but not the convertible bond price. For the stock price on the horizontal axis, use 10, 20, 30, 40, 50, and 60.
e. Which will influence the bond price more—the pure bond value or the conversion value?

Solution:

Standard Olive Company of California

a. $1,000 par value/25 conversion ratio = 40 conversion price

b. $30 stock price × 25 conversion ratio = $750

c. Pure bond value where n = 30, i = 5%
   Pure bond value = $45 semiannually × 15.372   =$691.74

   $1,000 principal value × .231 = <u> 231.00</u>

   $922.74

d. Bond Values ($)

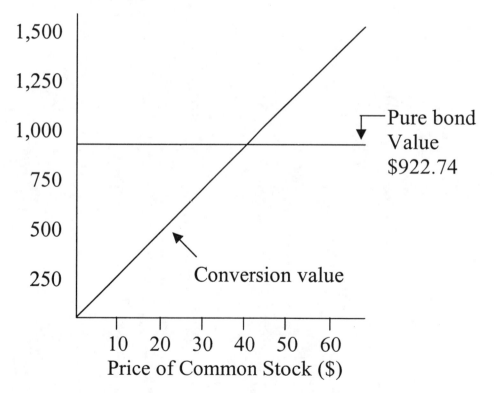

S-609

e. Most likely, the price of the bond will be influenced by the floor price and changing interest rates. The stock price needs to rise from $30 per share closer to $36.91 ($922.74/25) before the bond price will react directly to stock price changes.

19-9.   Swift Shoe Co. has convertible bonds outstanding that are callable at $1,080. The bonds are convertible into 22 shares of common stock. The stock is currently selling for $59.25 per share.

a.   If the firm announces it is going to call the bonds at $1,080, what action are bondholders likely to take, and why?

b.   Assume that instead of the call feature, the firm has the right to drop the conversion ratio from 22 down to 20 after 5 years and down to 18 after 10 years. If the bonds have been outstanding for 4 years and 11 months, what will the price of the bonds be if the stock price is $60? Assume the bonds carry no conversion premium.

c.   Further assume that you anticipate in two months that the common stock price will be up to $63.50. Considering the conversion feature, should you convert now or continue to hold the bond for at least two more months?

Solution:

Swift Shoe Company

a. They will probably convert the bonds to common stock. With a conversion ratio of 22 and a common stock price of $59.25, the value of the converted securities would be $1,303.50. This is substantially above the call value of $1,080. Thus, there is a strong inducement to convert.

b. Bond price = stock price × conversion ratio

$60 × 22 = $1,320

c. Bond price in two months = stock price × conversion ratio

$63.50 × 20 = $1,270

You should convert now rather than hold on to the bonds for two more months. The overall value will be $50 less at that point in time.

19-10. Vernon Glass Company has $20 million in 10 percent convertible bonds outstanding. The conversion ratio is 50, the stock price is $19, and the bond matures in 10 years. The bonds are currently selling at a conversion premium of $70 over their conversion value.

If the price of the common stock rises to $25 on this date next year, what would your rate of return be if you bought a convertible bond today and sold it in one year? Assume on this date next year, the conversion premium has shrunk from $70 to $15.

Solution:
Vernon Glass Company

First find the price of the convertible bond. The conversion value is $950 ($19 × 50). The value, $950, plus the premium, $70, equals $1,020, the current market price of the convertible bond.

Next, you find the price of the convertible bond on this day next year.

$25 stock price × 50 conversion ratio = $1,250 conversion value

$1,250 conversion value + $15 premium = $1,265 market value of the convertible bond.

Then determine the rate of return.
($1,265 − $1,020)/$1,020 = $245/$1,020 = 24.02%

19-11.   Assume you can buy a warrant for $5 that gives you the option to buy one share of common stock at $15 per share. The stock is currently selling at $18 per share.

    a.   What is the intrinsic value of the warrant?
    b.   What is the speculative premium on the warrant?
    c.   If the stock rises to $27 per share and the warrant sells at its theoretical value without a premium, what will be the percentage increase in the stock price and the warrant price if you bought the stock and the warrant at the prices stated above? Explain this relationship.

Solution:

a. ($18 stock price − $15 exercise price) × 1 share per warrant = $3 intrinsic value

b. $5 warrant price − $3 intrinsic value = $2 speculative premium

c. Percentage change if stock is purchased at $18

$$\frac{\$27 - \$18}{\$18} = \frac{\$9}{\$18} = 50\%$$

Percentage change if warrant is purchased at $5

New intrinsic value = ($27 − $15) × 1 = $12

$$\frac{\$12 - \$5}{\$5} = \frac{\$7}{\$5} = 140\%$$

The warrant is leveraged. A movement in the stock price will cause the warrant to rise on a smaller initial investment and, therefore, the percentage gain is larger for the warrant than for the stock.

19-12. The Gifford Investment Company bought 100 Cable Corporation warrants one year ago and would like to exercise them today. The warrants were purchase at $30 each, and they expire when trading ends today. (Assume there is no speculative premium left.) Cable Corp. common stock is selling today for $60 per share. The exercise price is $36, and each warrant entitles the holder to purchase two shares of stock, each at the exercise price.

a. If the warrants are exercised today, what would Gifford's *total* profit or loss be?

b. What is Gifford's percentage rate of return?

Solution:

Gifford Investment Company

a. Intrinsic value of a warrant = (Market value of common stock − exercise price of warrant) × No. of shares each warrant entitles holder to purchase.

($60 − $36) × 2	=	$48 intrinsic value
$48 × 100 warrants	=	$4,800 proceeds from sale
$30 × 100 warrants	=	$3,000 purchase price

Profit	=	Proceeds from sale − Purchase price
	=	$4,800 − $3,000
	=	$1,800

b. $1,800/$3,000 = 60% return

19-13.   Assume in problem 12 that Cable Corporation common stock was selling for
            $50 per share when Gifford Investment Company bought the warrants.

            a. What was the intrinsic value of a warrant at that time?
            b. What was the speculative premium per warrant when the warrants were
                purchased? The purchase price, as indicated above, was $30.
            c. What would Gifford's total dollar profit or loss have been had they invested
                the $3,000 directly in Cable Corporation's common stock one year ago at
                $50 per share? Recall the current value is $60 per share.
            d. What would the percentage rate of return be on this common stock
                investment? Compare this to the rate of return on the warrant computed in
                problem 12b.

Solution:
Gifford Investment Company (Continued)

a. ($50 stock price – $36 exercise price) × 2 shares = $28
    intrinsic value

b. $30 purchase price – $28 intrinsic value = $2 speculative
    premium per warrant.

c. $3,000 investment/$50 per share = 60 shares
    60 shares × ($60 – $50) = $600

d. $600/$3,000 = 20% return. There is clearly less than the
    60% return on the warrant.

19-14.   Mr. John Hailey has $1,000 to invest in the market. He is considering the purchase of 50 shares of Comet Airlines at $20 per share. His broker suggests that he may wish to consider purchasing warrants instead. The warrants are selling for $5, and each warrant allows him to purchase one share of Comet Airlines common stock at $18 per share.

    a. How many warrants can Mr. Hailey purchase for the same $1,000?
    b. If the price of the stock goes to $30, what would be his total dollar and percentage return on the stock?
    c. At the time the stock goes to $30, the speculative premium on the warrant goes to 0 (though the market value of the warrant goes up).

        What would be Mr. Hailey's total dollar and percentage return on the warrant?
    d. Assuming that the speculative premium remains $3.50 over the intrinsic value, how far would the price of the stock have to fall before the warrant has no value?

Solution:

Comet Airlines

a. $\dfrac{\$1,000}{\$5} = 200$ warrants

b. $ 30   new price
          – 20   old price
          $ 10   gain
          × 50   shares
          $500   total dollar gain

      $\dfrac{\$10}{\$20} = 50\%$ or $\dfrac{\$500}{\$1,000} = 50\%$

c.

$	30	stock price
–	18	exercise price
$	12	intrinsic value (0 speculative premium)

$	12	new price of warrant
–	5	old price of warrant
$	7	gain
×	200	warrants
$1,400		total dollar gain

$$\frac{\$7}{\$5} = 140\% \text{ or } \frac{\$1,400}{\$1,000} = 140\%$$

d. With an $18 exercise price, at a stock price of $14.50, the warrant would have a negative intrinsic value of $3.50. With a speculative premium of only $3.50, the warrant would be worthless. Under the problem as described, the warrant would be worthless at stock values of $14.50 or less.

19-15.   Online Network, Inc. has had a net income of $600,000 in the current fiscal year. There are 100,000 shares of common stock outstanding along with convertible bonds, which have a total face value of $1.4 million. The $1.4 million is represented by 1,400 different $1,000 bonds. Each $1,000 bond pays 5 percent interest. The conversion ratio is 20. The firm is in a 30 percent tax bracket.

a.   Calculate basic earnings per share.
b.   Calculate diluted earnings per share.

Solution:

Online Network, Inc.

a. Basic earnings per share

$$= \frac{Earnings}{Shares} = \frac{\$600,000}{100,000} = \$6.00$$

b. Diluted earnings per share

$$= \frac{Adjusted\ earnings\ after\ taxes}{Shares\ Outstanding + All\ convertible\ securities}$$

$$= \frac{\$600,000 + \$49,000*}{100,000 + 28,000**}$$

$$= \frac{\$649,000}{128,000} = \$5.07$$

*   interest savings × (1 − tax rate)
= $70,000 (1 − .30)
= $70,000 (.70) = $49,000
**= 28,000

1,400 convertible bonds × 20 conversion ratio

19-16.   Myers Drugs, Inc. has 2 million shares of stock outstanding. Earnings after taxes are $6 million. Myers also have warrants outstanding, which allow the holder to buy 100,000 shares of stock at $15 per share. The stock is currently selling for $50 per share.

a. Compute basic earnings per share.
b. Compute diluted earnings per share considering the possible impact of the warrants. Use the formula:

$$\frac{\text{Earnings after taxes}}{\text{Shares outstanding} + \text{Assumed net increase in shares from the warrants}}$$

Solution:

Myers Drugs, Inc.

a. Basic earnings per share

$$= \frac{\text{Earnings}}{\text{Shares}} = \frac{\$6,000,000}{2,000,000} = \$3.00$$

b. Diluted earnings per share

$$= \frac{\text{Earnings after taxes}}{\text{Shares outstanding} + \text{Assumed net increase in shares from the warrants}}$$

$$= \frac{\$6,000,000}{2,000,000 + 70,000 *}$$

$$= \frac{\$6,000,000}{2,070,000} = \$2.90$$

*1. New shares created   100,000

2. Reduction in shares from cash proceeds   30,000
    (computed below)

    Cash proceeds 100,000 @ $15 = $1,500,000
      Current price of stock $50

    Assumed reduction in shares
      Outstanding from cash

    Proceeds = $1,500,000/$50 = 30,000

3. Assumed net increase in shares from exercise _____
    of warrants   70,000

19-17.   Tulsa Drilling Company has $1 million in 11 percent convertible bonds
         outstanding. Each bond has a $1,000 par value. The conversion ratio is 40, the
         stock price is $32, and the bonds mature in 10 years. The bonds are currently
         selling at a conversion premium of $70 over the conversion value.

   a. If the price of Tulsa Drilling Company common stock rises to $42 on this
       date next year, what would your rate of return be if you bought a
       convertible bond today and sold it in one year? Assume that n this date next
       year, the conversion premium has shrunk from $70 to $20.
   b. Assume the yield on similar nonconvertible bonds has fallen to 8 percent at
       the time of sale. What would the pure bond value be at that point? (Use
       semiannual analysis.) Would the pure bond value have a significant effect
       on valuation then?

Solution:

Tulsa Drilling Company

a. First find the price of the convertible bond. The conversion value is $1,280 ($32 × 40). The conversion value, $1,280, plus the $70 premium, equals $1,350, the current market price of the convertible bond.

Next, you find the price of the convertible bond on this day next year.

$42 stock price × 40 conversion ratio = $1,680 conversion value $1,680 conversion value + $20 premium = $1,700 market price of the convertible bond ($1,700 − $1,350)/$1,350 = $350/$1,350 = 25.93% annual return.

b. Pure bond value after one year (nine years remaining).
   $n = 18$ and $i = 4\%$

   $55 semiannually × 12.659 (PV_{IFA}) = $ 696.24
   $1,000 principal value × .494 (PV_{IF})= 494.00
    $1,190.24

   Because the pure bond value of $1,190.24 is still well below the conversion value of $1,680 and the market value of $1,700, it would not have a significant effect on valuation.

Comprehensive Problems

CP 19-1.   Fondren Exploration, Ltd., has 1,000 convertible bonds ($1,000 par value) outstanding, each of which may be converted to 50 shares. The $1 million worth of bonds has 25 years to maturity. The current price of the stock is $26 per share. The firm's net income in the most recent fiscal year was $270,000. The bonds pay 12 percent interest. The corporation has 150,000 shares of common stock outstanding. Current market rates on long-term nonconvertible bonds of equal quality are 14 percent. A 35 percent tax rate is assumed.

a. Compute diluted earnings per share.
b. Assume the bonds currently sell at a 5 percent conversion premium over straight conversion value (based on a stock price of $26). However, as the price of the stock increases from $26 to $37 due to new events, there will be an increase in the bond price, but the conversion premium will be zero. Under these circumstances, determine the rate of return on a convertible bond investment that is part of this price change, based on the appreciation in value.
c. Now assume the stock price is $16 per share because a competitor introduced a new product. Would the straight conversion value be greater than the pure bond value, based on the interest rates stated above? (See Table 16-3 in Chapter 16 to get the bond value without having to go through the actual computation.)
d. Referring to part c, if the convertible traded at a 15 percent premium over the straight conversion value, would the convertible be priced above the pure bond value?
e. If long-term interest rates in the market go down to 10 percent while the stock price is at $23, with a 6 percent conversion premium, what would the difference be between the market price of the convertible bond and the pure bond value? Assume 25 years to maturity, and once again use Table 16-3 for part of your answer.
f. If Fondren were able to retire the convertibles and replace them with 50,000 shares of common stock selling at $26 per share and paying a 5 percent dividend yield (dividend to price ratio), would the aftertax cash outflow related to the original convertibles be greater or less than the cash outflow related to the stock?

CP Solution:

Rate of Return on Convertible Bond Investments

Fondren Exploration Limited

a. Diluted earnings per share

adjusted shares $= 150{,}000 + 50{,}000\ (1{,}000 \times 50) = 200{,}000$

adjusted earnings after taxes $= \$270{,}000$ actual earnings $+$ ($\$1{,}000{,}000 \times .12$ coupon rate) $\times (1 - .35$ tax rate)

adjusted earnings after tax $= \$270{,}000 + (\$120{,}000 \times .65) = \$270{,}000 + \$78{,}000 = \$348{,}000$

$\$348{,}000 / 200{,}000 = \$1.74$ diluted earnings per share

b. Current conversion value $= 50 \times \$26 = \quad \$1{,}300$

Premium $\underline{\times\ 1.05}$

Current value $\$1{,}365$

Future conversion value $= 50 \times \$37 = \$1{,}850$

Rate of Return $= \dfrac{\$1{,}850 - \$1{,}365}{\$1{,}365} = \dfrac{\$485}{\$1{,}365} = 35.53\%$

c. Straight conversion value = 50 × $16 = $800.00

Pure bond value (Table 16-3 for 12% interest rate and 14% market rate $862.06 for 25 years)

The straight conversion value is less than the pure bond value.

d. Conversion value × premium

$800 × 1.15 = $920

The convertible would be trading for greater than the pure bond value: ($920 > $862.06).

e.

Conversion value = 50 × $23 =	$1,150
Premium (6%)	1.06
Current value	$1,219
Pure bond value (10% market value) =	1,182.36
Differential	$ 36.64

f. Common stock

$26	price
× 50,000	shares
$1,300,000	total value
× 5%	dividend yield
$ 65,000	cash outflow

Convertibles

1,000	convertible bonds
× 1,000	par value
$1,000,000	total value
× 12%	coupon rate
$ 120,000	interest
× .65	(1 – T) aftertax cost
$ 78,000	cash outflow (aftertax)

The convertibles have greater aftertax cash outflow ($78,000) than the stock issue ($65,000). However, this does not consider the total return requirement on the stock (dividends + growth).

CP 19-2. United Technology Corporation (UTC) has $40 million of convertible bonds outstanding (40,000 bonds at $1,000 par value) with a coupon rate of 11 percent. Interest rates are currently 8 percent for bond of equal risk. The bonds have 15 years left to maturity. The bonds may be called at a 9 percent premium over par. They are convertible into 30 shares of common stock. The tax rate for the company is 25 percent.

The firm's common stock is currently selling for $41 and it pays a dividend of $3.50 per share. The expected income for the company is $38 million with 6 million shares outstanding.

Thoroughly analyze the bond and determine whether the firm should call the bond at the 9 percent call premium. In your analysis, consider the following:

a. The impact of the call on base and diluted earnings per share (assume the call forces conversion).
b. The consequences of your decision on financing flexibility.
c. The net change in cash outflows to the company as a result of the call and conversion.

CP Solution:
A Call Decision With Convertible Bonds

United Technology Corporation (UTC)

Interest expense 11% × $40 million = $4,400,000 million

Shares created from conversion = 30 × 40,000 bonds
= 1,200,000

Conversion value = 30 shares × $41 per share = $1,230

Call price = $1,000 × 1.09 = $1,090

a. If the bond is called, it will be converted because the conversion value is greater than the call price ($1,230 > $1,090).

The convertibles are not included in basic earnings per share.

We will compute basic EPS before and after the conversion.

Basic EPS before conversion = NI/shares outstanding
= $38 million/6 million shares
= $6.33

Basic EPS after conversion

$$= \frac{\text{Adjusted earnings after taxes}}{\text{Shares outstanding} + \text{New Shares issued}}$$

$$= \frac{\$38,000,000 + \$4,400,000\,(1-.25)}{6,000,000 + 1,200,000}$$

$$= \frac{\$38,000,000 + \$3,300,000}{7,200,000}$$

$$= \frac{\$41,300,000}{7,200,000} = \$5.74$$

There is a reduction in basic EPS from $6.33 to $5.74. Diluted EPS after conversion is the same as before conversion because the potential new shares and interest reduction were already accounted for in diluted EPS.

b. With the elimination of the convertible bond, UTC has reduced its debt and increased its equity financing. This provides more flexibility in the way of debt issues for the future. With the current interest rate at 8 percent, UTC could sell a new issue of straight debt and repurchase shares of common stock in the open market. This would serve the purpose of a partial refunding which would result in a lower outlay for interest and dividends. Flexibility is improved.

c. Aftertax dividend expense = 1,200,000 × \$3.50 = \$4,200,000
   Aftertax interest expense = \$4,400,000 (1 − .25) = \$3,300,000
   Aftertax net cash loss   \$ 900,000

Chapter 20

Discussion Questions

20-1.   What was the impetus behind the increased merger activity in the late 1990s and early 2000s?

The impetus could be found in low interest rates, changing stock prices, new regulations, intense competition, evolving technology, and many other factors. Companies were trying to position themselves for the 21st century.

20-2.   What is the difference between a merger and a consolidation?

In a merger two or more companies are combined, but only the identity of the acquiring firm is maintained. In a consolidation, an entirely new entity is formed from the combined companies.

20-3.   Why might the portfolio effect of a merger provide a higher valuation for the participating firms?

If two firms benefit from opposite phases of the business cycle, their variability in performance may be reduced. Risk-averse investors may then discount the future performance of the merged firms at a lower rate and thus assign a higher valuation than was assigned to the separate firms.

20-4.   What is the difference between horizontal integration and vertical integration? How does antitrust policy affect the nature of mergers?

Horizontal integration is the acquisition of competitors, and vertical integration is the acquisition of buys or sells of goods and services to the company.

Antitrust policy generally precludes the elimination of competition. For this reason, mergers are often with companies in allied but not directly related fields.

20-5. What is synergy? What might cause this result? Is there a tendency for management to *over-* or *underestimate* the potential synergistic benefits of a merger?

Synergy is said to occur when the whole is greater than the sum of the parts. This "2 + 2 = 5" effect may be the result of eliminating overlapping functions in production and marketing as well as meshing together various engineering capabilities. In terms of planning related to mergers, there is often a tendency to overestimate the possible synergistic benefits that might accrue.

20-6. If a firm wishes to achieve immediate appreciation in earnings per share as a result of a merger, how can this be best accomplished in terms of exchange variables? What is a possible drawback to this approach in terms of long-range considerations?

The firm can achieve this by acquiring a company at a lower P/E ratio than its own. The firm with lower P/E ratio may also have a lower growth rate. It is possible that the combined growth rate for the surviving firm may be reduced and long-term earnings growth diminished.

20-7. It is possible for the postmerger P/E ratio to move in a direction opposite to that of the immediate postmerger earnings per share. Explain why this could happen.

If earnings per share show an immediate appreciation, the acquiring firm may be buying a slower growth firm as reflected in relative P/E ratios. This immediate appreciation in earnings per share could be associated with a lower P/E ratio. The opposite effect could take place when there is an immediate dilution to earning per share. Obviously, a number of other factors will also come into play.

20-8. What is the essential difference between a pooling of interests and a purchase of assets accounting treatment of a merger?

Under "pooling of interest" the financial statements of the firms are combined subject to some minor adjustments and no goodwill is created. Under a "purchase of assets," the difference between purchase price and adjusted book value is established on the balance sheet as goodwill and must be written off over a maximum period of 40 years.

20-9.   Suggest some ways in which firms have tried to avoid being part of a target takeover.

An unfriendly takeover may be avoided by:

a. turning to a second possible acquiring company—a "White Knight."
b. moving corporate offices to states with tough pre-notification and protection provisions.
c. buying back outstanding corporate stock.
d. encouraging employees to buy stock.
e. staggering the election of directors.
f. increasing dividends to keep stockholders happy.
g. buying up other companies to increase size and reduce vulnerability.
h. reducing the cash position to avoid a leveraged takeover.

20-10.   What is a typical merger premium paid in a merger or acquisition? What effect does this premium have on the market value of the merger candidate and when is most of this movement likely to take place?

Typically a merger premium of 40-60 percent is paid over the Premerger price of the acquired company. The effect of the premium is to increase the price of the merger candidate and most of this movement is likely to take place before public announcement.

20-11.   Why do management and stockholders often have divergent viewpoints about the desirability of a takeover?

While management may wish to maintain their autonomy and perhaps keep their jobs, stockholders may wish to get the highest price possible for their holdings.

20-12.   What is the purpose(s) of the two-step buyout from the viewpoint of the acquiring company?

The two-step buy-out provides a strong inducement to target stockholders to quickly react to the acquiring company's initial offer. Also, it often allows the acquiring company to pay a lower total price than if a single offer is made.

Problems

20-1.   Boardwalk Corporation desires to expand. It is considering a cash purchase of Park Place Corporation for $2,400,000. Park Place has a $600,000 tax loss carry-forward that could be used immediately by Boardwalk, which is paying taxes at the rate of 35 percent. Park Place will provide $300,000 per year in cash flow (aftertax income plus depreciation) for the next 20 years. If Boardwalk Corporation has a cost of capital of 11 percent, should the merger be undertaken?

Solution:

Boardwalk Corporation

Cash outflow:

Purchase price	$2,400,000
Less tax shield benefit from tax	
loss carry-forward ($600,000 × 35%)	− 210,000
Net cash outflow	$2,190,000

Cash inflows:
$300,000, n = 20, i = 11% (Appendix D)

$300,000 × 7.963 =	$2,388,900

Cash inflows	$2,388,900
Cash outflow	2,190,000
Net present value	$ 198,900

The positive net present value indicates the merger should be undertaken.

20-2. Assume that Western Exploration Corp. is considering the acquisition of Ogden Drilling Company. The latter has a $400,000 tax loss-carry-forward. Projected earnings for the Western Exploration Corp. are as follows:

	1998	1999	2000	Total Values
Before-tax income	$160,000	$200,000	$320,000	$680,000
Taxes (40%)	64,000	80,000	128,000	272,000
Income available to stockholders	$ 96,000	$120,000	$192,000	$408,000

a. How much will the total taxes of Western Exploration Corp. be reduced as a result of the tax loss carry-forward?

b. How much will the total income available to stockholders be for the three years if the acquisition occurs? Use the same format as that in the text.

Solution:

Western Exploration Corp.

a. Reduction in taxes due to tax loss carry-forward = loss × tax rate

$400,000 × 40% = $160,000

b. Western Exploration Corp. (with merger and associated tax benefits)

	1998	1999	2000	Total Values
Before tax income	$160,000	$200,000	$320,000	$680,000
Tax loss carry-forward	160,000	200,000	40,000	400,000
Net taxable income	0	0	280,000	280,000
Taxes (40%)	0	0	112,000	112,000
Income available to stockholders (before tax income—taxes)	$160,000	$200,000	$208,000*	$568,000**

* Before-tax income—taxes ($320,000 – $112,000 = $208,000)
** Before-tax income—taxes ($680,000 – $112,000 = $568,000)

20-3.   J & J Enterprises is considering a cash acquisition of Patterson Steel Company for $4,000,000. Patterson will provide the following pattern of cash inflows and synergistic benefits for the next 20 years. There is no tax loss carry-forward.

	Years		
	1-5	6-15	16-20
Cash inflow (aftertax)	$440,000	$600,000	$800,000
Synergistic benefits (aftertax)	40,000	60,000	70,000

The cost of capital for the acquiring firm is 12 percent. Should the merger be undertaken? (If you have difficulty with delayed time value of money problems, consult Chapter 9.)

Solution:
J & J Enterprises

Cash outflow (Purchase price) $4,000,000

Cash inflows
PV factors for the analysis (12%) (Appendix D)

Years	(1-5)	(6-15)		(16-20)	
	3.605	1-15	6.811	1-20	7.469
		1-5	−3.605	−1-15	6.811
			3.206		.658

Year (1-5)
    Cash inflow $440,000
    Synergistic benefits   40,000
    Total cash inflow $480,000

    P.V. $480,000 × 3.605 = $1,730,400

Years (6-15)
    Cash inflow $600,000
    Synergistic benefits   60,000
    Total cash inflow $660,000
        P.V. $660,000 × 3.206 = $2,115,960

Years (16-20)
    Cash inflow $800,000
    Synergistic benefits   70,000
    Total cash inflow $870,000
        P.V. $870,000 × .658 = $ 572,460

    Total present value of inflows $4,418,820

    Cash inflows $4,418,820
    Cash outflow   4,000,000
    Net present value $ 418,820

The positive net present value indicates the merger should be undertaken.

20-4.   Worldwide Scientific Equipment is considering a cash acquisition of Medical Labs for $1.5 million. Medical Labs will provide the following pattern of cash inflows and synergistic benefits for the next 25 years. There is no tax loss carry-forward.

		Years	
	1-5	6-15	16-25
Cash inflow (aftertax)	$100,000	$120,000	$160,000
Synergistic benefits (aftertax)	15,000	25,000	45,000

The cost of capital for the acquiring firm is 9 percent. Should the merger be undertaken?

Solution:

Worldwide Scientific Equipment

Cash outflow (Purchase price) $1,500,000

Cash inflows
PV factors for the analysis (9%) (Appendix D)

Years	(1-5)		(6-15)		(16-25)
	3.890	1-15	8.061	1-25	9.823
		1-5	−3.890	1-15	8.061
			4.171		1.762

Year (1-5)
Cash inflow	$100,000	
Synergistic benefits	15,000	
Total cash inflow	$115,000	
P.V. $115,000 × 3.890 =		$447,350

Years (6-15)
Cash inflow	$120,000	
Synergistic benefits	25,000	
Total cash inflow	$145,000	
P.V. $145,000 × 4.171 =		$604,795

Years (16-20)
Cash inflow	$160,000	
Synergistic benefits	45,000	
Total cash inflow	$205,000	
P.V. $205,000 × 1.762 =		$361,210

Total present value of inflows $1,413,355

Cash inflows	$1,413,355
Cash outflow	1,500,000
Net present value	($ –86,645)

The negative net present value indicates the merger should not be taken.

20-5.   Assume the following financial data for Rembrandt Paint Co. and Picasso Art Supplies:

	Rembrandt Paint Co.	Picasso Art Supplies
Total earnings	$300,000	$900,000
Number of shares of stock outstanding	100,000	500,000
Earnings per share	$3.00	$1.80
Price-earnings ratio (P/E)	12×	20×
Market price per share	$36	$36

a. If all the shares of Rembrandt Paint Co. are exchanged for those of Picasso Art Supplies on a share-for-share basis, what will postmerger earnings per share be for Picasso Art Supplies? Use an approach similar to that in Table 20-3.

b. Explain why the earnings per share of Picasso Art Supplies changed.

c. Can we necessarily assume that Picasso Art Supplies is better off after the merger?

Solution:

Rembrandt Paint Co. and Picasso Art Supplies

(approach similar to Table 20-3)

a. Total earnings

Rembrandt	$	300,000
+ Picasso		900,000
		$1,200,000

Shares outstanding
In surviving corporation:

Old		500,000
+ New		100,000
		600,000

New earnings per share for Picasso Art Supplies

$$= \frac{\$1,200,000}{600,000} = \$2.00$$

b. Earnings per share of Picasso Art Supplies increased because it has a higher P/E ratio than Rembrandt Paint Co. (20x versus 12x). Any time a firm acquires another company at a lower P/E ratio than its own, there is an immediate increase in postmerger earnings per share.

c. Although earnings per share for Picasso Art Supplies went up, we can not automatically assume the firm is better off. We need to know whether the Rembrandt Paint Co. will increase or decrease the future growth in earnings per share for the Picasso Art Supplies and how it will influence its postmerger P/E ratio. The goal of financial management is not just immediate growth in earnings per share, but maximization of stockholder wealth over the long-term.

20-6. The Hollings Corporation is considering a two-step buyout of the Norton Corporation. The latter firm has 2 million shares outstanding and its stock price is currently $40 per share. In the two-step buyout, Hollings will offer to buy 51 percent of Norton's shares outstanding for $68 in cash, and the balance in a second offer of 980,000 convertible preferred stock shares. Each share of preferred stock would be valued at 45 percent over the current value of Norton's common stock. Mr. Green, a newcomer to the management team at Hollings, suggests that only one offer for all Norton's shares be made at $65.25 per share. Compare the total costs of the two alternatives. Which is preferred in terms of minimizing costs?

Solution:

Hollings Corporation

Two Step Offer

1. 51% × 2,000,000 shares = $1,020,000 shares

   1,020,000 shares × $68 cash = $ 69,360,000

2. 980,000 shares of convertible preferred stock X

   $40 (1.45) = 980,000 × $58 =   <u>$ 56,840,000</u>

   Cost of two-step offer $126,200,000

Single Offer

2,000,000 shares at $65.25 $130,500,000

The two-step offer is preferred because its cost is $4,300,000 less.

20-7.   Chicago Savings Corp. is planning to make an offer for Ernie's Bank & Trust. The stock of Ernie's Bank & Trust is currently selling for $40 a share.

a. If the tender offer is planned at a premium of 60 percent over market price, what will be the value offered per share for Ernie's Bank & Trust?
b. Suppose before the offer is actually announced, the stock price of Ernie's Bank & Trust goes to $56 because of strong merger rumors. If you buy the stock at that price and the merger goes through (at the price computed in part *a*), what will be your percentage gain?
c. Because there is always the possibility that the merger could be called off after it is announced, you also want to consider your percentage loss if that happens. Assume you buy the stock at $56 and it falls back to its original value after the merger cancellation, what will be your percentage loss?
d. If there is an 80 percent probability that the merger will go through when you buy the stock at $56 and only a 20 percent chance that it will be called off, does this appear to be a good investment? Compute the expected value of the return on the investment.

Solution:

Chicago Savings Corp.

a. Market price of Ernie's Bank & Trust $40
    + Premium of 60%   24
    Value offered per share $64

b. Value offered per share $64
    Purchase price   56
    Gain $ 8

    Percentage gain $\dfrac{\$\ 8}{\$56} = 14.29\%$

c. Value after cancellation (original value) $40
    Purchase price   56
    Loss $16

    Percentage loss $\dfrac{\$16}{\$56} = 28.57\%$

d.

Return	Probability	Expected Value
+14.29	.80	11.43%
−28.57	.20	−5.71%
Expected value of return		5.72%

It appears to be a good investment.

20-8. Gary Cole helped start Heat Engineering Company in 1956. At the time, he purchased 100,000 shares of stock at 10 cents per share. In 1997, he has the opportunity to sell his interest in the company to Elgin Technology for $60 a share in cash. His capital gains tax rate would be 20 percent.

a. If he sells out his interest, what will be the value for before-tax profit, taxes, and aftertax profit?
b. Assume, instead of cash, he accepts stock valued at $60 per share. He holds the stock for four years and then sells it for $98.80 (the stock pays no cash dividends). At the time of sale, what will be the value for before-tax profit, taxes, and aftertax profit? His tax at a 20 percent capital gains rate, will be based on the difference between his original purchase price and the selling price.
c. Using a 10 percent discount rate, compare the aftertax profit figure in part *b* to that in part *a*. (That is, discount back the answer in part *b* for four years and compare it to the answer in part *a*.) Which is the more desirable alternative?

Solution:
Heat Engineering Company

a. Sales amount   100,000 Shs. × $60 $6,000,000
   Purchase amount   100,000 Shs. × $.10   10,000
   Before-tax profit $5,990,000
   Taxes (20%)   1,198,000
   Aftertax profit $4,792,000

b. Sales amount   100,000 Shs. × $98.80 $9,880,000
   Purchase amount   100,000 Shs. × $.10   10,000
   Before-tax profit $9,870,000
   Taxes (20%)   1,974,000
   Aftertax profit $7,896,000

c. Discount back $7,896,000 for 4 years at 10 percent
   $7,896,000 n = 4, i = 10% (Appendix B)
   $7,896,000 × .683 = $5,392,968

   This value of $5,392,968 clearly exceeds the value in part a of $4,792,000. Deferring the sale (and the tax) appears to be the more desirable alternative.

20-9.   Assume the Shelton Corporation is considering the acquisition of Cook, Inc. The expected earnings per share for the Shelton Corporation will be $3.00 with or without the merger. However, the standard deviation of the earnings will go from $1.89 to $1.20 with the merger because the two firms are negatively correlated.

a. Compute the coefficient of variation for the Shelton Corporation before and after the merger. (Consult Chapter 13 to review statistical concepts if necessary.)
b. Comment on the possible impact on Shelton's postmerger P/E ratio, assuming investors are risk averse.

Solution:
Shelton Corporation

a.

$$V = \frac{\text{Standard deviation}}{\text{Mean or expected value}} \qquad \begin{matrix}\textbf{Premerger}\\ \dfrac{\$1.89}{\$3.00} = .63\end{matrix} \quad \begin{matrix}\textbf{Postmerger}\\ \dfrac{\$1.20}{\$3.00} = .40\end{matrix}$$

b. Risk averse investors are being offered less risk and may assign a higher P/E ratio to postmerger earnings.

20-10.   General Meters is considering two mergers. The first is with Firm A in its own volatile industry, the auto speedometer industry, whereas the second is a merger with Firm B in an industry that moves in the opposite direction (and will tend to level out performance due to negative correlation).

a. Compute the mean, standard deviation, and coefficient of variation for both investments.

General Meters Merger with Firm A		General Meters Merger with Firm B	
Possible Earnings ($ millions)	Probability	Possible Earnings ($ millions)	Probability
$40..............	.30	$10..................	.25
50..............	.40	50..................	.50
60..............	.30	90..................	.25

b. Assuming investors are risk averse, which alternative can be expected to bring the higher valuation?

Solution:

General Meters

a. Merger with A (answer in millions of dollars)

$$\overline{D} = \sum DP$$

D	P	DP
40	.30	12.0
50	.40	20.0
60	.30	18.0
		50.0 = $\overline{D}$

$$\sigma = \sqrt{\sum (D - \overline{D})^2 P}$$

D	$\overline{D}$	$(D - \overline{D})$	$(D - \overline{D})^2$	P	$(D - \overline{D})^2 P$
40	50	−10	100	.30	30
50	50	0	0	.40	0
60	50	+10	100	.30	30
					60

$$\sqrt{60} = 7.75 = \sigma$$

$$\text{Coefficient of variation} = \frac{\sigma}{\overline{D}} = \frac{7.75}{50} = .155$$

Merger with B (answer in millions of dollars)

$$\overline{D} = \sum DP$$

D	P	DP
10	.25	2.5
50	.50	25.0
90	.25	22.5
		50.0 = $\overline{D}$

$$\sigma = \sqrt{\sum(D-\overline{D})^2 P}$$

D	$\overline{D}$	$(D-\overline{D})$	$(D-\overline{D})^2$	P	$(D-\overline{D})^2 P$
10	50	−40	1,600	.25	400
50	50	0	0	.50	0
90	50	+40	1,600	.25	400
					800

$$\sqrt{800} = 28.28 = \sigma$$

$$\text{Coefficient of variation} = \frac{\sigma}{\overline{D}} = \frac{28.28}{50} = .566$$

b. Though both alternative have an expected value of $50 (million), the lower coefficient of variation, and thus lower risk in merger A should call for a higher valuation by risk averse investors.

20-11. The Wisconsin Corporation is considering the acquisition of the Badger Corporation. The book value of the Badger Corporation is $30 million, and the Wisconsin Corporation is willing to pay $80 million in cash and preferred stock. No upward adjustment of asset values is anticipated. The Wisconsin Corporation has 2 million shares outstanding. A purchase of assets financial recording will be used, with a 40-year write-off of goodwill.

a. How much will the annual amortization be?
b. How much will the annual amortization be on a per-share basis?
c. Under what circumstance would the annual write-off be tax deductible?

Solution:

General Meters

a.
Purchase price	$80,000,000
Book value	30,000,000
Goodwill	50,000,000

$$\frac{Goodwill}{40 \ years} = \frac{\$50,000,000}{40} = \$1,250,000 \ annual \ write\text{-}off$$

b. $$\frac{Annual \ write\text{-}off}{Shares} = \frac{\$1,250,000}{2,000,000} = \$.625 \ per \ share$$

c. If the merger is a taxable exchange for the shareholders.

Chapter 21

Discussion Questions

21-1.   What risks does a foreign affiliate of a multinational firm face in today's business world?

In addition to the normal risks that a domestic firm faces (such as the risk associated with maintaining sales and market share, the financial risk of too much leverage, etc.), the foreign affiliate of a multinational firm is exposed to foreign exchange risk and political risk.

21-2.   What allegations are sometimes made against foreign affiliates of multi-national firms and against the multinational firms themselves?

Some countries have charged that foreign affiliates subverted their governments and caused instability for their currencies in international money and foreign exchange markets. The less developed countries (LDC's) have, at times, alleged that foreign business firms exploit their labor with low wages. The multinational companies are also under constant criticism in their home countries. The home country's labor unions charge the MNC's with exporting jobs, capital, and technology to foreign nations, while avoiding their fair share of taxes. In spite of all these criticisms, the multinational companies have managed to survive and prosper.

21-3.   List the factors that affect the value of a currency in foreign exchange markets.

Factors affecting the value of a currency are: inflation, interest rates, balance of payments, and government policies. Other factors that have an influence include the stock market, gold prices, demand for oil, political turmoil, and labor strikes. All of the above factors will not affect each currency in the same way at any given point in time.

21-4.   Explain how exports and imports tend to influence the value of a currency.

When a country sells (exports) more goods and services to foreign countries than it purchases (imports), it will have a surplus in its balance of trade. Since foreigners are expected to pay their bills for the exporter's goods in the exporter's currency, the demand for that currency and its value will go up. On the other hand, continuous deficits in balance of payments are expected to depress the value of the currency of a country because such deficits would increase the supply of that currency relative to the demand. Of course, a number of other factors may also influence these patterns.

21-5.   Differentiate between the spot exchange rate and the forward exchange rate.

The spot rate for a currency is the exchange rate at which the currency is traded for immediate delivery. An exchange rate established for future delivery is a forward rate.

21-6.   What is meant by translation exposure in terms of foreign exchange risk?

The foreign-located assets and liabilities of a MNC, which are denominated in foreign currency exchange rates. This is called accounting or translation exposure. The amount of loss or gain resulting from this form of exposure and the treatment of it in the parent company's books, depends upon the accounting rules established by the parent company's government.

21-7.   What factors influence a U.S. business firm to go overseas?

Factors that influence a U.S. business firm to go overseas are: avoidance of tariffs; lower production and labor costs; usage of superior American technology abroad in such area as oil exploration, mining, and manufacturing; tax advantages such as postponement of U.S. taxes until foreign income is repatriated, lower foreign taxes, and special tax incentives; defensive measures to keep up with competitors going overseas; and the achievement of international diversification. There also is the potential for higher returns than on purely domestic investments.

21-8.   What procedure(s) would you recommend for a multinational company in studying exposure to political risk? What actual strategies can be used to guard against such risk?

In studying exposure to political risk, a company may hire outside consultants or form their own advisory committee consisting of top level managers from headquarters and foreign subsidiaries.

Strategic steps to guard against such risks include:

a. Establish a joint venture with a local entrepreneur.
b. Enter into a joint venture with firms from other countries.
c. Purchase insurance.

21-9.   What factors beyond the normal domestic analysis go into a financial feasibility study for a multinational firm?

An international financial feasibility study must go beyond domestic factors to also consider the treatment of foreign tax credits, foreign exchange risk, and remittance of cash flows.

21-10.   What is a letter of credit?

A letter of credit is normally issued by the importer's bank; in which the bank promises to pay money for the merchandise where delivered.

21-11.   Explain the functions of the following agencies:

Overseas Private Investment Corporation (OPIC).
Export-Import Bank (Eximbank).
Foreign Credit Insurance Association (FCIA).
International Finance Corporation (IFC).

Overseas Private Investment Corporation (OPIC)—A government agency that sells insurance policies to qualified firms. This agency insures against losses due to inconvertibility into dollars of amounts invested in a foreign country. Policies are also available from OPIC to insure against expropriation and against losses due to war or revolution.

Export-Import Bank (Eximbank)—An agency of the U.S. government that facilitates the financing of U.S. exports through its miscellaneous programs. In its direct loan program, the Eximbank lends money to foreign purchasers of

U.S. goods such as aircraft, electrical, equipment, heavy machinery, computers, and the like. The Eximbank also purchases medium-term obligations of foreign buyers of U.S. goods at a discount from face value. In this discount programs, private banks and other lenders are able to rediscount (sell at a lower-price) promissory notes and drafts acquired from foreign customers of U.S. firms.

Foreign Credit Insurance Association (FCIA)—An agency established by a group of 60 U.S. insurance companies. It sells credit export insurance to interested exporters. The FCIA promises to pay for the exported merchandises if the foreign importer defaults on payment.

International Finance Corporation (IFC)—An affiliate of the World Bank established with the sole purchase of providing partial seed capital for private ventures around the world. Whenever a multinational company has difficulty raising equity capital due to lack of adequate private capital, the firm may explore the opportunity of selling equity or debt (totaling up to 25 percent) to the International Finance Corporation.

21-12.   What are the differences between a parallel loan and a fronting loan?

In a parallel loan, the exchange rate markets are avoided entirely—that is, the funds do not enter the foreign exchange market at all. Also no financial institution is involved. In contrast, a fronting loan involves funds moving into foreign markets and the involvement of a financial institution to front for the loan.

21-13.   What is LIBOR? How does it compare to the U.S. prime rate?

LIBOR (London Interbank Offered Rate) is an interbank rate applicable for large deposits in the Eurodollar market. It is a bench mark rate just like the prime rate in the United States. Interest rates on Eurodollar loans are determined by adding premiums to this basic rate. Generally, Libor is lower than the U.S. prime rate.

21-14.   What is the danger or concern in floating a Eurobond issue?

When a multinational firm borrows money through the Eurobond market (foreign currency denominated debt), it creates transaction exposure, a kind of foreign exchange risk. If the foreign currency appreciates in value during the bond's life, the cost of servicing the debt could be quite high.

21-15.   What are ADRs?

ADRs (American Depository Receipts) represent the ownership interest in a foreign company's common stock. The shares of the foreign company are put in trust in a New York bank. The bank, in turn, issues its depository receipts to the American stockholders of the foreign firm.

21-16.   Comment on any dilemmas that multinational firms and their foreign affiliates may face in regard to debt ratio limits and dividend payouts.

Debt ratios in many countries are higher than those in the United States. A foreign affiliate faces a dilemma in its financing decision. Should it follow the parent firm's norm or that of the host country? Furthermore, should this be decided at corporate headquarters or by the foreign affiliate? Dividend policy may represent another difficult question. Should the parent company dictate the dividends that the foreign affiliate must distribute or should it be left to the discretion of the foreign affiliate?

Problems

21-1. Using the foreign exchange rates for October 19, 2000, in Table 21-2, determine the number of U.S. dollars required to buy the following amounts of foreign currencies.

  a. 10,000 guilders.
  b. 2,000 deutsche marks.
  c. 100,000 yen.
  d. 5,000 Swiss francs.
  e. 20,000 rupees.

Solution:

Dollars required to buy a given amount of these currencies

 a. 10,000   Guilders
   10,000 × .3826 = $3.826

 b. 2,000   Deutsche marks
   2,000 × .4311 = $8,622

 c. 100,000   Yen
   100,000 × .0092 = $920

 d. 5,000   Swiss francs
   5,000 × .5601 = $2,800.50

 e. 20,000   Rupees
   20,000 × .0216 = $432

21-2. *The Wall Street Journal* reported the following spot and forward rates for the euro ($/euro) as of October 26, 2000.

Spot..	$0.8280
30-day forward.......................	$0.8309
90-day forward.......................	$0.8339
180-day forward.....................	$0.8390

a. Was the euro selling at a discount or premium in the forward market on October 26, 2000?
b. What was the 30-day forward premium (or discount)?
c. What was the 90-day forward premium (or discount)?
d. Suppose you executed a 90-day forward contract to exchange 100,000 euros into U.S. dollars. How many dollars would you get 90 days hence?
e. Assume a Swiss bank entered into a 180-day forward contract with Citicorp to buy $100,000. How many euros will the Swiss bank deliver in six months to get the U.S. dollars?

Solution:

a. The euro was selling at a premium above the spot rate.

b. $$\text{Forward premium} = \frac{\text{Forward rate} - \text{Spot rate}}{\text{Spot rate}} \times \frac{12}{1} \times 100$$

$$= \frac{.8309 - .8280}{.8280} \times 12 \times 100$$

$$= \frac{.0029}{.8280} \times 12 \times 100$$

$$= .003502 \times 12 \times 100$$

$$= .042024 \times 100 = 4.2024\%$$

c. $\begin{array}{l} \text{Forward} \\ \text{premium} \end{array} = \dfrac{\text{Forward rate} - \text{Spot rate}}{\text{Spot rate}} \times \dfrac{12}{3} \times 100$

$$= \dfrac{.8339 - .8280}{.8280} \times 4 \times 100$$

$$= \dfrac{.0059}{.8280} \times 4 \times 100$$

$$= .007126 \times 4 \times 100$$

$$= .028504 \times 100 = 2.8504\%$$

d. 90-day forward rate = $.8339
   Dollar value of 100,000 euros
   $.8338 × 100,000 = $83,390

e. 180-day forward rate   = $.8390

$\begin{array}{l} \text{euro equivalent} \\ \text{of \$100,000} \end{array} = \dfrac{\$100,000}{\$.8390} = \text{Euro } \$119,189.51$

21-3.   Suppose an Austrian schilling is selling for $0.0613 and an Irish punt is selling for $1.0541. What is the exchange rate (cross rate) of the Austrian schilling to the Irish punt? That is, how many Austrian schilling are equal to an Irish punt?

Solution:

One dollar is worth 16.313 Austrian Schillings (1/.0613) and one Irish Punt is worth 1.0541 dollars. Thus: 16.313 Austrian Schillings per <u>dollar</u> times 1.0541 <u>dollar</u> per Irish Punt equals 17.20 Austrian Schillings per Irish Punt. The answer is 17.20.

21-4. Suppose a French franc is selling for $0.1286 and a Maltese lira is selling for $2.1372. What is the exchange rate (cross rate) of the French franc to the Maltese lira? That is, how many French francs are equal to a Maltese lira?

Solution:

One dollar is worth 7.776 French Francs (1/.1286) and one Maltan Lira is worth 2.1372 dollars. Thus: 7.776 French Francs per <u>dollar</u> times 2.1372 <u>dollars</u> per Maltan Lira equals 16.62 French Francs per Maltan Lira. The answer is 16.62.

21-5. From the base price level of 100 in 1974, German and U.S. price levels in 2001 stood at 200 and 370, respectively. If the 1974 $/DM exchange rate was $0.23/DM, what should the exchange rate be in 2001? Suggestion: Using the purchasing power parity, adjust the exchange rate to compensate for inflation. That is, determine the relative rate of inflation between the United States and Germany and multiply this times $/DM of .23.

Solution:

$/DM = $.23 in 1974

$$\text{Comparative rate of inflation} = \frac{\text{United States}}{\text{Germany}} = \frac{370}{200} = 1.85$$

The value of the deutsche mark to the dollar will rise in proportion to the rate of inflation in the United States compared to the rate of inflation in Germany.

$/DM (2001) = $.23/DM × 1.85 = .4255

21-6. In problem 5, if the United States had somehow managed no inflation since 1974, what should the exchange rate be in 2001, using the purchasing power theory?

Solution:

$$\text{Comparative rate of inflation} = \frac{\text{United States}}{\text{Germany}} = \frac{100}{200} = .5$$

$$\text{\$/DM (2001)} = \$.23/\text{DM} \times .5 = \$115$$

21-7. An investor in the United States bought a one-year Australian security valued at 200,000 Australian dollars. The U.S. dollar equivalent was $100,000. The Australian security earned 15 percent during the year, but the Australian dollar depreciated five cents against the U.S. dollar during the time period ($0.50/AD to $0.45/AD). After transferring the funds back to the United States, what was the investor's return on his $100,000? Determine the total ending value of the Australian investment in Australian dollars and then translate this value to U.S. dollars by multiplying by $0.45. Then compute the return on the $100,000 investment.

Solution:

Initial value × (1 + earnings)

200,000	× 1.15	=	230,000 Australian dollars
Australian dollars	× .45	=	U.S. dollars equivalent
230,000	× .45	=	103,500 U.S. dollars equivalent

$$\frac{\$103,500}{\$100,000} = 103.50 = 3.50\%$$

21-8.   A Peruvian investor buys 100 shares of Merck for $8,000 ($80 per share). Over the course of a year, the stock goes up by 12 dollars.

a. If there is a 10 percent gain in the value of the dollar versus the Peruvian rol, what will be the total percentage return to the Peruvian investor? First determine the new dollar value of the investment and multiply this figure by 1.10. Divide this answer by $8,000 and get a percentage value, and then subtract 100 percent to get the percentage return.
b. Now assume that the stock increases by 14 dollars, but that the dollar decreases by 10 percent versus the Peruvian rol. What will be the total percentage return to the Peruvian investor? Use 0.90 in place of 1.10 in this case.

Solution:

a. Initial investment $100 \times \$80$ $= \$8,000$

Value after one year $100 \times \$92$ $= \$9,200$

Equivalent value to the
Peruvian investor $\$9,200 \times 1.10$ $= 10,120$ rols

$$\frac{\$10,120}{\$8,000} = 126.50 = 26.50 \text{ percent}$$

b. Initial investment $100 \times \$80$ $= \$8,000$

Value after one year $100 \times \$94$ $= \$9,400$

Equivalent value to the
Peruvian investor $\$9,400 \times .90$ $= \$8,460$

$$\frac{\$8,460}{\$8,000} = 105.75\% = 5.75\%$$

21-9. You are the vice president of finance for Exploratory Resources, headquartered in Houston, Texas. In January 2001 your firm's Canadian subsidiary obtained a six-month loan of 100,000 Canadian dollars from a bank in Houston to finance the acquisition of a titanium mine in Quebec province. The loan will also be repaid in Canadian dollars. At the time of the loan, the spot exchange rate was U.S. $0.6580/Canadian dollar and the currency was selling at a discount in the forward market. The June 2001 contract (face value = $100,000 per contract) was quoted at U.S. $0.6520/Canadian dollar.

a. Explain how the Houston bank could lose on this transaction assuming no hedging.
b. If the bank does hedge with the forward contract, what is the maximum amount it can lose?

Solution:

a. The Houston bank has extended a loan denominated in Canadian dollars and will be repaid in Canadian dollars. If the Canadian dollar drops in the future (a possibility implied by the futures contract price), the Houston bank will be paid back in a currency that is worth less at the time it is repaid than it was at the time it was borrowed.

b. Basically the bank is buying Canadian dollars now for $.6580/CD and contracting to selling them in the future for $.6520/CD. The most it can lose if $.0060 on the $100,000 contract or $600.

Appendix

21A-1.   The Office Automation Corporation is considering a foreign investment. The initial cash outlay will be $10 million. The current foreign exchange rate is 2 francs = $1. Thus the investment in foreign currency will be 20 million francs. The assets have a useful life of five years and no expected salvage value. The firm uses a straight-line method of depreciation. Sales are expected to be 20 million francs and operating cash expenses 10 million francs every year for five years. The foreign income tax rate is 25 percent. The foreign subsidiary will repatriate all aftertax profits to Office Automation in the form of dividends. Furthermore, the depreciation cash flows (equal to each year's depreciation) will be repatriated during the same year they accrue to the foreign subsidiary. The application cost of capital that reflects the riskiness of the cash flows is 16 percent. The U.S. tax rate is 40 percent of foreign earnings before taxes.

a. Should the Office Automation Corporation undertake the investment if the foreign exchange rate is expected to remain constant during the five-year period?

b. Should Office Automation undertake the investment if the foreign exchange rate is expected to be as follows:

> Year 0 .... $1 = 2.0 francs
> Year 1 .... $1 = 2.2 francs
> Year 2 .... $1 = 2.4 francs
> Year 3 .... $1 = 2.7 francs
> Year 4 .... $1 = 2.9 francs
> Year 5 .... $1 = 3.2 francs

Solution:

The Office Automation Corporation
(values in millions of francs)

a.

	Year 1	Year 2	Year 3	Year 4	Year 5
Revenue	20.00	20.00	20.00	20.00	20.00
− Operating expense	10.00	10.00	10.00	10.00	10.00
− Depreciation (20 M/5)	4.00	4.00	4.00	4.00	4.00
= Earnings before foreign taxes	6.00	6.00	6.00	6.00	6.00
− Foreign income tax (25%)	1.50	1.50	1.50	1.50	1.50
= Earnings after foreign income taxes	4.50	4.50	4.50	4.50	4.50
Dividends repatriated*	4.50	4.50	4.50	4.50	4.50
Gross U.S. taxes (40% of earnings before foreign taxes)	2.40	2.40	2.40	2.40	2.40
− Foreign tax credit	1.50	1.50	1.50	1.50	1.50
= Net U.S. taxes payable	.90	.90	.90	.90	.90
Aftertax dividend received	3.60	3.60	3.60	3.60	3.60
Exchange rate (2 francs/$)	2.00	2.00	2.00	2.00	2.00
Aftertax dividend (U.S. $)	$1.80	$1.80	$1.80	$1.80	$1.80

PV_{IFA} (16% for 5 years)   3.274

PV of dividends equals	$1.80 × 3.274	= $5.893 million
Depreciation equals 4.00 per year	4.00/2 francs/$	=$2.00
PV of depreciation equals	$2.00 × 3.274	= $6.548 million

The PV of all the cash inflows equals $5.893 + $6.548	= $12.441 million
Cost of project	10.000 million
Net present value of the project	$ 2.441 million

Since NPV is positive, accept the project!

* Dividends repatriated assumes all earnings after foreign income taxes will be repatriated.

b. The change in foreign exchange values must be applied to both aftertax dividends received (in francs) and depreciation (in francs).

(in millions)

	Year 1	Year 2	Year 3	Year 4	Year 5
Aftertax dividend received	3.60	3.60	3.60	3.60	3.60
Depreciation	4.00	4.00	4.00	4.00	4.00
Total (in francs)	7.60	7.60	7.60	7.60	7.60
Exchange rate (F/$1)	2.2	2.4	2.7	2.9	3.2
Cash inflow (U.S. $)	3.45	3.17	2.81	2.62	2.38
PV_{IF} (16%)	.862	.743	.641	.552	.476
PV (U.S. $)	2.97	+2.36	+1.80	+1.45	+1.13

Total = 9.71

PV of all the inflows equals	$ 9.71	million
Cost of project	10.00	million
Net present value of the project	($ .29)	million

On a purely economic basis, the investment should now be rejected.